JA

INSIGHT GUIDE

ICELAND

APA PUBLICATIONS   L

Part of the Langenscheidt Publishing Group

INSIGHT GUIDE
Iceland

ABOUT THIS BOOK

Editorial

Project Editor
Jane Simmonds
Managing Editor
Tom Le Bas
Editorial Director
Brian Bell

Distribution

UK & Ireland
GeoCenter International Ltd
The Viables Centre, Harrow Way
Basingstoke, Hants RG22 4BJ
Fax: (44) 1256-817988

United States
Langenscheidt Publishers, Inc.
46–35 54th Road, Maspeth, NY 11378
Fax: (718) 784-0640

Canada
Thomas Allen & Son Ltd
390 Steelcase Road East
Markham, Ontario L3R 1G2
Fax: (1) 905 475 6747

Australia
Universal Press
1 Waterloo Road,
Macquarie Park, NSW 2113
Fax: (61) 2 9888 9074

New Zealand
Hema Maps New Zealand Ltd (HNZ)
Unit D, 24 Ra ORA Drive
East Tamaki, Auckland
Fax: (64) 9 273 6479

Worldwide
**Apa Publications GmbH & Co.
Verlag KG (Singapore branch)**
38 Joo Koon Road, Singapore 628990
Tel: (65) 865-1600. Fax: (65) 861-6438

Printing

Insight Print Services (Pte) Ltd
38 Joo Koon Road, Singapore 628990
Tel: (65) 865-1600. Fax: (65) 861-6438

©2002 Apa Publications GmbH & Co.
Verlag KG (Singapore branch)
All Rights Reserved
First Edition 1992
Fourth Edition 1999, updated 2002

CONTACTING THE EDITORS
We would appreciate it if readers
would alert us to errors or outdated
information by writing to:
**Insight Guides, P.O. Box 7910,
London SE1 1WE, England.
Fax: (44) 20 7403-0290.**
insight@apaguide.demon.co.uk

www.insightguides.com

This guidebook combines the interests and enthusiasms of two of the world's best-known information providers: Insight Guides, whose titles have set the standard for visual travel guides since 1970, and Discovery Channel, the world's premier source of nonfiction television programming.

The editors of Insight Guides provide both practical advice and general understanding about a destination's history, culture, institutions and people. Discovery Channel and its web site, www.discovery.com, help millions of viewers explore their world from the comfort of their own home and also encourage them to explore it first hand.

This new edition of *Insight: Iceland* is carefully structured to convey an understanding of Iceland and its culture as well as to guide readers through its sights and activities:

◆ The **Features** section, indicated by a yellow bar at the top of each page, covers the history and culture of the country in a series of informative essays.

◆ The main **Places** section, indicated by a blue bar, is a complete guide to all the sights and areas worth visiting. Places of special interest are coordinated by number with the maps.

◆ The **Travel Tips** listings section, with an orange bar, provides a handy point of reference for practical information on travel, hotels, shops, restaurants and more.

The contributors

This edition of *Insight: Iceland* was revised by

Map Legend

– – – –	County Boundary
– • – • –	National Park/Reserve
– – – –	Ferry Route
✈ ✈	Airport
🚌	Bus Station
🅿	Parking
❶	Tourist Information
✉	Post Office
✝ † ✝	Church / Ruins
†	Monastery
☪	Mosque
✡	Synagogue
🏰 🏚	Castle / Ruins
∴	Archaeological Site
∩	Cave
1	Statue/Monument
★	Place of Interest

The main places of interest in the Places section are coordinated by number with a full-colour map (e.g. ❶), and a symbol at the top of every right-hand page tells you where to find the map.

London-based editor **Jane Simmonds** and supervised by managing editor **Tom Le Bas** at Insight Guides. The book has been completely updated with the invaluable help of a number of people. The Features, the chapter on Reykjavík and the Travel Tips were all updated by **Alda Sigmundsdóttir**, a writer and translator living in Reykjavík. She also wrote the Embracing the Night essay and Insight on… Christmas and New Year. **Arthúr Bollason**, an Icelandic journalist and writer, updated the Places section, with the exception of Reykjavík, and contributed the Insight on… Saga Characters. **Doreen Taylor** wrote Insight on… Iceland's Sea Birds, and Natural Wonders, **Gary Gunning** contributed the essay on the Politics of Fishing, and **Baldvin Kristjánsson** had many good ideas for improving the book and helped to update the information in the Travel Tips.

The fourth edition builds on the excellent foundations of previous editions of the book. Of particular note is **Tony Perrottet**, editor of the original edition of *Insight: Iceland*, who also wrote the chapters on The Southwest, Vestmannaeyjar, The Southeast, Akureyri and Surroundings, Grímsey, Lake Mývatn, The Northeast, and The East Fjords, and contributed a wide selection of colour photographs.

Rowlinson Carter wrote on Iceland's history from the beginnings to the mid-20th century, while **Bernard Scudder** contributed the chapters on Modern History, Harvesting the Sea, Reykjavík, and Ram's Testicles and Rotten Shark.

Anna Yates wrote a number of natural history essays including Forged by Fire, Honed by Ice, Life on the Land, Nature's Bounty, Confronting Wild Iceland, A Birdwatcher's Paradise, Mammals in the Wild, the chapters on The Reykjanes Peninsula and Snæfellsnes and the West, and the essay on Flowers among the Lava.

Birna Helgadóttir wrote The Icelanders, Living with the Environment, The Sagas, The Power of Words and Icelandic Hauntings. The West Fjords was written by **Catherine Harlow**, and the chapters on Húnaflói and Skagafjörður and The Interior by **Julian Cremona**. **Jim Wesneski** contributed Why is Everything so Expensive? and Keflavík NATO Base. Thanks also to proofreader and indexer **Marian Broderick**.

The guide was fully updated in 2002 by **Mark Thompson** and edited in-house at Insight Guides by **Clare Peel**.

CONTENTS

*A map of the main bus
routes in Reykjavík is on the
inside back cover.*

The rooftops of Reykjavík
from Hallgrímskirkja belfry.
The snow peak of
Snæfellsjökull, over 100km
away, is visible in the distance

Insight on ...

Information panels

Travel Tips

Places

AN EXTRAORDINARY ISLAND

Iceland offers not only a wealth of natural wonders, from glaciers to geysers, but also a rich history and literature

The reason for hereness seems beyond conjecture,
There are no trees or trains or architecture,
Fruits and greens are insufficient for health
And culture is limited by lack of wealth.
The tourist sights have nothing like Stonehenge,
The literature is all about revenge.
And yet I like it if only because this nation
Enjoys a scarcity of population...
— W.H. Auden, *Letters from Iceland*

Iceland has come a long way since the English poet Auden penned these facetious lines in 1936. From an isolated agricultural society that many people thought had scarcely progressed beyond the Middle Ages there has emerged a high-tech welfare state with one of the highest standards of living in the world. Yet at least one thing hasn't changed since Auden's visit: with only 283,000 inhabitants – the same as an average English town or suburb in a US city – Iceland still has a scarcity of population that leaves it with some of the greatest wilderness areas in Europe.

In fact, Iceland may be the ultimate nature trip. It has virtually no pollution from industry (most people live, one way or another, from fishing) and all energy is either geothermal or hydro-electric. Drinking water comes from pure glaciers; fish, the staple food, is caught in unpolluted seas and rivers; even the lamb and cattle graze in fields untouched by fertiliser. The majority of Icelanders now live in and around the capital, Reykjavík, leaving huge swathes of the volcanically active island – one of the most recently formed on earth – quite deserted. Dotted by steaming lava fields, icecaps, glaciers, hot pools and geysers, the Icelandic landscape has an elemental rawness that nobody who sees it can easily forget.

Perhaps not surprisingly, the people who live on this extraordinary island are an eccentric breed. Speaking Europe's oldest language, little changed since the days of the Vikings, accustomed to the endless light of summer and Stygian gloom of the long winters, the Icelanders can be as extreme as their homeland. Rather shy, they will rarely be the first to talk to strangers. But once their traditional reserve is broken through, they can be among the most friendly and hospitable people in Europe.

Which may all help explain why Iceland exerts such a powerful hold over travellers – even those who have visited for only a few days – compelling them to return again and again. ❑

PRECEDING PAGES: Breiðamerkurjökull glacier; a snowy hillside near Akureyri; early morning at the remote farm of Húsey in the East Fjords; a fisherman and his boat in the northeast.
LEFT: Land Rover at Skógafoss waterfall.

FORGED BY FIRE, HONED BY ICE

Iceland is one of the youngest land masses in the world, geologically speaking.
As a result, its inhabitants are used to living with change and disruption

In geological terms, Iceland is a mere baby. No more than 20 million years have passed since volcanoes on the floor of the far northern Atlantic ocean began to spew lava, laying the foundations of what would become Iceland. Today it is still one of the most volcanically active spots on earth – giving geoscientists the chance of observing a land still in the making.

Movements of the earth's crust

According to the theory of plate tectonics, widely accepted as explaining the earth's development, the earth's surface comprises a number of rigid plates (six major and several minor plates), which "float" on the mass of magma beneath. Geographical features like the Andes and the Himalayas are evidence of massive collisions of tectonic plates, which have folded the earth's crust up to form great mountain ranges.

Plate junctions are invariably marked by narrow zones of volcanic and earthquake activity: at "destructive" junctions, the edge of one plate is forced underneath the other and part of the earth's surface is "lost", while at "constructive" junctions, two plates pull apart, allowing magma to rise from below, reaching the surface and forming new crust. This is what is still happening in Iceland.

Iceland straddles the Mid-Atlantic Ridge, where the African and American plates are being pulled apart. Thus the island is literally being torn in two, at a rate of 2 cm (nearly an inch) a year, with lava rising up from the earth's centre to more than fill the gap.

Volcanic belt

The Mid-Atlantic Ridge, running clear across Iceland from southwest to northeast, is marked by a belt of volcanic craters, hot springs, steam springs, *solfataras* (areas of high-temperature activity) and earthquakes. This belt extends to a width of about 40 km (25 miles) in the north,

and up to 60 km (40 miles) across in the south, and covers about a quarter of the country.

Not surprisingly, Iceland's rocks are almost all volcanic (predominantly basalt). The country's geological history falls into four periods, evidence of each being visible from region to region. The oldest rocks, from the Tertiary pre-

Ice Age period, are the plateau basalts of the East and West Fjords. Slightly inland are the younger grey basalts, from the interglacial periods. This is generally open moorland with less evidence of glaciation. Further in towards the present-day volcanic zone is the palagonite formation, from subglacial eruptions in the last part of the Ice Age. Typical of these belts are tuff ridges and table mountains, the soft rock often extensively eroded by wind and water. Iceland's youngest rocks are mainly in areas in and around the present-day volcanic zone.

The northwest and the east of Iceland are no longer volcanically active. Most of the rest of the island, however, conceals a seething mass

LEFT: the *solfatara,* or volcanic vent, of Hverarönd near Lake Mývatn.
RIGHT: on Vatnajökull, the largest icecap in Europe.

of volcanic and geothermal activity. About 25 of Iceland's volcanic systems have been active in post-glacial times (i.e. the past 10,000 years) – 18 on land and the rest offshore – and in the past few centuries Iceland has experienced an eruption every five years on average. Some are minor and short-lived, causing minimal damage, like the photogenic eruption of Mount Hekla in 1991. They are known as "tourist eruptions", as they are popular with sightseers.

In the shadow of disaster

Despite an apparently flippant attitude towards volcanoes, Icelanders do not forget the threat they live with. The catastrophic eruption of Lakagígar in the late 18th century poured out the largest lava flow ever produced by a single volcano in recorded history, with a volume of about 12 cubic km (3 cubic miles). As if that were not enough, it also emitted noxious gases which poisoned livestock and crops, blocked out the sun, and led to a disastrous famine. About one-third of the population died.

In 1973, the subterranean peril was brought home with a vengeance, when a new volcano flared up on Heimaey in the Vestmannaeyar. It buried one-third of the town under lava and ash (*see the panel on page 203*).

THE BIRTH OF SURTSEY

The ultimate "tourist eruption" was the formation of the island of Surtsey, which began on the ocean floor just southwest of the Vestmannaeyjar (Westmann Islands) in 1963. In addition to the familiar spectacle of lava and ash, the Surtsey eruption produced voluminous clouds of steam as cold seawater met hot lava and instantly boiled. Before the end of the eruption, the new island was 2.8 sq. km (1.1 sq. miles) in area – although erosion has now reduced this to about 1.57 sq. km (0.6 sq. mile). The new islet was a welcome gift to scientists, a natural laboratory which offered them a chance to observe how virgin land develops.

Evidence of subterranean unrest has been felt since the mid-1970s around Mount Krafla near Lake Mývatn, an area free of volcanic activity for over two centuries. A massive eruption in 1724–9 laid waste three farms, before the lava flow halted at Reykjahlíð church, where the congregation was praying for deliverance. Two centuries later, the earth began to move when construction started on the geothermal power station below Mount Krafla; many people concluded that man's interference with the forces of nature had set off a reaction within the earth. Mount Krafla has erupted several times since 1975, most recently in 1984, although the lava has never threatened Reykjahlíð.

It has been estimated that one-third of all the lava that has erupted on earth in recorded history has come from Iceland. As any visitor will soon discover, almost all of it is of the scoria type. Loose, sharp and difficult to cross, it also creates unusual and haunting formations. A small amount is smooth, hard "ropy" lava.

AMAZING ICECAP

Vatnajökull, up to 1 km (3,200 ft) thick and 8,300 sq. km (3,200 sq. miles) in area, is not only Europe's largest icecap, it is also bigger than all the rest put together.

Caps of ice

In spite of its subterranean heat, the island has largely been shaped by cold. Covered by glaciers in the Ice Age, Iceland has been sculpted by

the glaciers, with a few exceptions, have been gradually retreating. Ice now covers around 11 percent of the island's 103,000 sq. km (40,000 sq. miles).

Contrasts between heat and cold are nowhere so striking as in the glaciers that sit atop volcanoes. Some seem extinct: the volcanic crater on which the cone-shaped Snæfellsjökull glacier rests, for instance, has not erupted for 700 years. In Jules Verne's novel *Journey to the Centre of the Earth*, Snæfellsjökull is the entrance to the nether world.

moving ice. Glaciation has carved out its present form, gouging the plunging fjords which cut into the coastline on north, east and west, and honing mountain ridges to knife-edges.

Although Iceland emerged from its glacial pall about 10,000 years ago, it remains a land of glaciers and icecaps – curiously, they are believed to have been formed not in the Ice Age but during a cold spell around 500 BC, reaching their largest size during the "Little Ice Age" of AD 1500–1900. Over the last 80 years or so

Left: the 1973 eruption of Eldfell which threatened to engulf the town of Heimaey.
Above: the eruption of Grímsvötn in 1996.

Melting glaciers

Eruptions from subglacial volcanoes can cause more damage than those from open-air volcanoes. Hot lava melts the ice, triggering sudden floods – *hlaups* – with unpredictable results. Mount Katla, the volcano under the glacier Mýrdalsjökull, is Iceland's largest caldera, at 80 sq. km (30 sq. miles). When Katla erupts, the *hlaup* can be 200,000 cubic metres (7 million cubic ft) of water a second.

In 1996 a volcano in the Bárðarbunga-Grímsvötn fissure erupted beneath Vatnajökull, melting huge quantities of ice and scattering ash over a 100-km (60-mile) area. Meltwater from the eruption flowed into a sub-glacial caldera, which began to fill. On 5 November 1996, the water in the caldera spilled over the brim, resulting in a massive flood across the sand plain south of the glacier that swept away roads and bridges. It deposited icebergs the size of apartment blocks, which, as they melted, turned the sands into pits of quicksand.

Meltwater from the glaciers flows out into winding rivers, which swell whenever warm weather melts the glacial ice or when volcanic activity begins beneath the glacier. Unlike the crystal-clear rivers fed by rain or underground streams, glacial rivers carry silt from the glacier, so they are generally brownish and murky in colour. Unbridged rivers are one of the main dangers to travellers in the highlands, as the water can rise with alarming rapidity.

Iceland is no stranger to earthquakes. The stretching and straining of the earth's crust at the junction of tectonic plates inevitably produces sudden movements under pressure. Strict building regulations ensure that all man-made structures can withstand major earthquakes.

Using geothermal heat

Living on a "hot spot" implies coexistence with natural risks. Yet the heat in the earth has also brought its own inestimable benefits. In a cold

THE SOUTH ICELAND QUAKE

Every 100 years or so a major earthquake hits southern Iceland. In 1784 the South Iceland Quake, estimated at 7.5 on the Richter scale, destroyed houses, farms and a cathedral. In 1896, southern Iceland was convulsed by violent tremors and in 1912 a quake measuring 7 on the Richter scale shook South Iceland. A set of tremors in the summer of 1998, the largest measuring 5.3 on the Richter scale, precluded the earth's convulsions in June 2000, when three earthquakes, measuring 6.5, 5.5 and 6.6, struck over the course of three days. Experts warn that although a certain amount of tension on the earth's crust has been relieved, the "big one" is yet to come.

climate, what could be more valuable than endless natural hot water?

All spouting springs (geysers) in the world owe their name to the Great Geysir in Iceland's southwest, which spouts to a height of up to 60 metres (196 ft). These days Geysir has given up performing, except when artificially persuaded; soap is added to the water to reduce the surface tension, which means that the spring spouts with less pressure. These induced eruptions are only carried out very rarely, but nearby Strokkur ("churn") erupts every few minutes to a height of about 30 metres (100 ft), and several more spouting geysers can be seen around the country.

Natural hot water bubbling irrepressibly out of the earth has been prized by the Icelanders ever since they settled the country. The springs Ingólfur Arnarson saw when he named Reykjavík ("smoky bay") after clouds of steam he saw rising from today's Laugardalur valley, became the community's public laundry in later centuries. Housewives would trudge the 3 km (2 miles) from Reykjavík along Laugavegur ("hot spring road") carrying their washing to the springs. The laundry springs (now dry) can still be seen in Laugardalur, by the Botanical Gardens (*see page 166*). In 1930, geothermal energy was first piped from the springs to the

At Svartsengi in the southwest, superheated water (two-thirds of which is brine) from far beneath the earth's surface passes through a heat-exchange process to provide fresh water for heating, and generate electricity. A bonus is that the hot lake formed by the run-off water has developed into a popular spa, the Blue Lagoon (Bláa Lónið, *see page 176*). Rich in salt and other minerals, the waters of the lagoon are reputed to be beneficial for skin diseases.

Harnessing glacial rivers

Another, equally valuable resource is Iceland's glaciated mountains and rivers: the water that

town to heat a few dozen houses and a swimming pool. Developing technology has made it possible to look farther and drill deeper for hot water, and high-efficiency insulation means that water can be piped long distances.

Reykjavík's latest source of geothermal energy is at Nesjavellir, about 30 km (18 miles) from the city. Today 85 percent of Iceland's atmospheric heating is from geothermal sources, and almost every community has its own geothermally warmed open-air swimming pool.

LEFT: Krafla geothermal power plant near Lake Mývatn.
ABOVE: feeling the heat: one of the thousands of tourists who visit Mývatn every year.

comes tumbling over precipices and flowing down steep inclines means clean and constantly renewed hydroelectric power (HEP). The first small HEP plant opened in Iceland in 1904, and today giant hydropower stations supply almost all the Icelanders' own needs, and provide energy to power-intensive industries. About 15 percent of Iceland's exploitable HEP has so far been harnessed.

Whatever the changes their society is undergoing, the Icelanders still live very close to nature. They take for granted an untamed, unpolluted environment that is still growing, still changing, where eruptions and earthquakes are accepted as part of the tenor of life. ❑

ISLANDIA.

Privilegio Imp. et Belgica decennali A. Orten. excud. 1585.

Scala milliarium Islandicorum.

Septemtrio.

Grims ey.

A.

Rauda
gnupur.

Rolln haffn

Fulmungavig

Langanes prom.

Olafsfiord
Husley
Hualloturefiord
Rolsker
Flat ey.
Lundey.
Sumnugavig
Skauanar
Fogranes
Grimelsfiord

Surpat
dalur
Hualfiord
Eyafiord
Skaldfandsfiord
Rollss fiord
Dicbfiord.
Gumufiord
Miofiord
Finnafiord
Sandug
Digranes

era sedes
cuin
ca Dalur
Modur
uol ler
closter
Holgur
dalur
Hufeuay
Rydin
tordur
Strand
Hof
Q.

em tecto
cuenas
oues
NORDLEN
DINGAFIOR
DVNG.
Munke turre
closter
Bardur
dalur
Grenefholt
Muli
Balanes

Mokrufeld
Suart
notn
Reydar fiord

Sand
Iokul.
Fodina fulphurea
profluntiffima
Skiritu closter
Garavig
Bera fiord
Pap ey.

Arnafelds Iokul.

ul.
His notis distinguitur lines inter vtramqs diocefun
Floozdalir
Oriens.

bred.
Langedal
Ruina
Hepper
Aridal
AVSTLENDIN
GAFIORDVNG
Mofut
Horn foes
Horn

Blaskoger
heyd
SVNDLEN
DINGAFIOR
DVNG.
Fiske
notn
Hierfkeyd
Iokull
Str Crr
O

SKALHOLT sedes
episco palis, cui
adiun cta est schola
Hekla
Oddi
Mydals Iokul
Eyafialla
Iokul.
Solheyma
Iokul.
Breyd
Brolangs
eyer
P.

ormu
Equorum
tarita hic
velocitas, vt
continuo cur
su 20. milla
ria con
ficunt
Medalland.
Ingolt
hofdi
N.

Porlarks
haffn
Eyrarbach
Vucca marina
Corsu. et falcones albi
Aliuta volpe
culorum vna
tio, in pudu volu
crum inueftigando
atque deripendis
O.

fnanes
Iokul
K.

Eldor
M.

WESTMANNA
EIAR
L.

ies.

ILLVSTRISS. AC POTENTISS.
REGI FREDERICO II DANIAE,
NORVEGIAE, SLAVORVM, GO
THORVMQVE REGI, ETC. PRIN
CIPI SVO CLEMENTISSIMO,
ANDREAS VELLEIVS
DESCRIBEB. ET DEDICABAT.

Decisive Dates

4th century BC: Pytheas, a Greek explorer, reports sightings of an island which he called "Ultima Thule".
circa 6th or 7th century AD: Irish monks start to settle on "Thule", forming small communities.
mid-9th century: A Norwegian, Hrafna-Flóki, tries to settle in the West Fjords. Foiled by the harsh winter, he calls the land Ísland (Iceland).

VIKING SETTLEMENT

874: Ingólfur Arnarson (the "First Settler") and his brother Hjörleifur Hróðmarsson settle on Iceland on

the south coast and in the southwest respectively.
930: By 930 many Norwegian chieftains and their families have followed and the population stands at about 25,000. Creation of the Alþingi parliament, a central authority presided over by a Law-speaker.
10th century: Erik the Red settles on Greenland and persuades numerous Icelanders to follow.

CONVERSION AND FEUDING

984: Þorvaldur Koðránsson the Well-Travelled starts to convert Iceland to Christianity often using violent means. Later Olaf Tryggvason, King of Norway sends his chaplain Þangbrand to continue conversions.
1000: Christianity is adopted as Iceland's official religion at the annual meeting of the Alþingi.

1163: The "Stone-Throwing Summer" of violent clashes between different groups of Vikings.
1179: Birth of Snorri Sturluson, diplomat and saga writer.
1230–64: The Sturlung Age of feuds between private armies and political factions.
1241: Murder of Snorri Sturluson on the King of Norway's orders.
1262: The Alþingi agrees to allow King Haakon of Norway to collect taxes.

DISASTER AND DECLINE

1389: A huge eruption of Mount Hekla is followed by smallpox and other epidemics.
1397: Scandinavian union of Norway, Denmark and Sweden transfers the sovereignty of Iceland from Norway to Denmark. Denmark, following Norway's example, prohibits Iceland from trading with any other countries, and agrees to send supply ships in exchange for fish.
1469: England and Denmark go to war over England's illegal trading with Iceland.
1526: Feud between Lutheran Bishop Ögmund of Skálholt and Roman Catholic Bishop Jón at the Alþingi, leading to a duel.
1541: Denmark sends two warships to impose a new Church code through the Alþingi; Ögmund resists but dies on a ship bound for Denmark.
1548: Bishop Jón is summoned by the king to Copenhagen, but instead stays in Iceland and leads a rebellion against the Protestants.
1550: King Christian III of Denmark orders Jón's arrest; after being captured, he is beheaded along with his two sons.
1627: 3,000 pirates land on Heimaey in the Vestmannaeyjar (Westmann Islands), killing many of the inhabitants and taking others captive.
1662: Denmark divides Iceland into four commercial trading districts which are not permitted to trade with each other, only directly with Denmark. This is reinforced by a Danish naval blockade.
1783: Eruption of Laki volcano in southern Iceland destroys communities, livestock and, for many years, the fishing industry.
1800: Abolition of the Alþingi on the orders of the Danish king.

A REVIVAL OF FORTUNE

1801: Battle of Copenhagen, where the British fleet detroys the Danish Navy, and confiscates the entire Danish merchant fleet.
1809: "Revolution" led by Jorgen Jorgensen, a Danishman serving in the British Navy, who liberated

Iceland, declaring it independent. The revolution is quashed the same year by another member of the British Navy.

1811: Birth of Jón Sigurdsson who fought for Icelandic independence.

1830: Iceland allowed two seats among 70 on an advisory body to the Danish crown.

1840: King Christian VIII agrees to reinstate an Alþingi of 20 elected representatives and four or six chosen by the crown.

1854: Trade monopoly with Denmark ended.

1874: Denmark gives the Alþingi autonomy over domestic affairs, but retains a veto over all it does.

1879: Death of Jón Sigurdsson.

1881–1895: Benedikt Sveinsson, a campaigner for independence, calls for real self government every year at the Alþingi; attempts to pass the proposal are foiled by the royal veto.

THE 20TH CENTURY AND BEYOND

1904: Iceland is granted home rule.

1909: Introduction of prohibition.

1911: Founding of Reykjavík University.

1918: Denmark makes Iceland a sovereign state with its own flag, still with the king of Denmark as its head of state, and agrees to hold further negotiations on Iceland's status in 1940.

1940: With Iceland occupied by Britain and Denmark by Germany, there is no communication between them. The Alþingi announces that it has taken over the power of the king of Denmark with respect to governing Iceland.

1941: Iceland requests full independence from Denmark.

1944: Following a plebiscite at which the termination of the union with Denmark and a new constitution are approved, Iceland becomes a republic on 17 June.

1949: Iceland becomes a founding member of NATO, abandoning its "eternal neutrality".

1951: US military return to Iceland to set up an air base at Keflavík.

1952–76: Four Cod Wars (1952, 1958, 1972, 1975) with the UK over fishing rights. In 1976 an agreement is reached for a 200-mile fishing limit off Iceland.

1955: Icelandic writer Halldór Laxness wins the Nobel Prize for Literature.

1963: The island of Surtsey is created by an underwater volcanic eruption southwest of the Vestmannaeyjar (Westmann Islands).

PRECEDING PAGES: map of Iceland by Abraham Ortelius, Antwerp c. 1590. **LEFT:** statue of Ingólfur Arnarson, the First Settler. **RIGHT:** celebrations for the millennium of the Alþingi in 1930.

1973: Volcanic eruption on Heimaey island threatens to destroy it; an army of volunteers and new methods divert the lava flow, preventing complete disaster.

1980: Vigdís Finnbogadóttir, the world's first democratically elected female head of state, becomes President. She is thrice re-elected, holding office until 1996.

1986: Presidents Reagan and Gorbachev arrive in Reykjavík for a summit to start talks to end the Cold War.

1989: Beer Day on 1 March, in which Icelanders celebrate the abolition of a ban on strong beer.

1992: Iceland walks out of the International Whaling Commission after the country's request for a limited whaling quota is rejected. Iceland stops whaling, though does not declare itself a non-whaling country.

1994: Iceland enters the European Economic Area.

1996: The Grímsvötn volcano erupts under Vatnajökull, leading to a massive build-up of meltwater under the glacier, which floods out and sweeps away chunks of the ring-road and several bridges on the south coast.

2000: Iceland celebrates one thousand years of Christianity and Leifur Eriksson's discovery of North America in the year 1000; Reykjavik is voted a European City of Culture for the millennium. Mount Hekla erupts on 26 February, and new lava stretches 3–4 km (2–3 miles). Several earthquakes hit the south of the island in June.

2001: Iceland rejoins the International Whaling Commission. ❑

ULTIMA THULE

Irish monks were the first to live on Iceland but were soon outnumbered by Vikings who settled and started to farm the land

A recent visitor to Iceland overheard two farmers talking passionately in a field; they were lamenting the premature death of a young man whom they were sure would have been a great credit to the country. This sorely missed individual, it transpired, was a certain Skarphéðinn Njálsson, a character in one of the celebrated Icelandic sagas, and he had been dead for all of 1,000 years.

Various versions of this story are told by travellers to Iceland, all with the same kernel of truth: Icelanders are obsessed with their history, or at least a part of it. The period they prefer to remember is between the years 930 and 1030, with little after the 13th century on which they can reflect with pleasure. The country's current prosperity has occurred only since World War II. For the 600 or so years before, Iceland was a grim, depressing place, so much so that a 19th-century English visitor complained that he never once saw an Icelander smile.

This roller-coaster ride through history has tentative beginnings, with Irish monks looking for a quiet, isolated spot to meditate, and becomes substantive with the Norwegian Viking settlement, traditionally dated at 874. These same sword-wielding Vikings, who famously reduced hapless Europeans to prayers for the deliverance of their throats, then performed an astonishing volte-face. Within generations, they took up intellectual pursuits – without ever quite putting down their swords – and created a literary legend which scholars discuss in the same breath as Homer and the Golden Age of Greece.

These transformed Vikings not only wrote their own history as had been passed down to them, but also collected and saved the oral prehistory and religion of the whole Germanic race. They wrote in their own tongue rather than in the scholarly language of Latin, on manuscripts made of calf-skin, one of the few commodities in Iceland which, bar fish, was always plentiful. A great number of these manuscripts were lost or cut up and reused in a subsequent period of extreme hardship. Even so, those Icelandic sagas that have survived more than make up for an almost total absence of ancient monuments in the country.

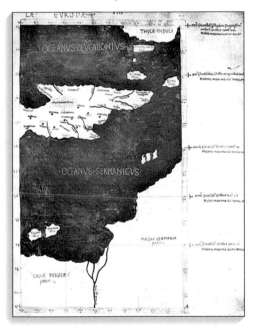

The uttermost end of the earth

The cherished history of Iceland is really quite short by European standards. As far as anyone can tell, no human had yet set foot in Iceland when, for example, the Parthenon in Athens was already some 800 years old and the capital of the disintegrating Roman Empire was being moved to Constantinople.

The classical Greeks and Romans were certainly interested in what existed at the northern fringe of the known world but were invariably misinformed. The most reliable information came from Pytheas, a Greek who lived in Marseilles. He explored the north personally and returned with an account of a country situated

LEFT: a Viking longship approaching the coast of Iceland. **RIGHT:** an early map showing the island of Thule at the world's northern edge

six days' sailing north of Britain and close to a frozen sea. At summer solstice, he said, the sun stayed above the horizon all through the night. The place was called, he said, "Thule".

"Iceland" only came into currency much later, apparently coined by a Norwegian named Hrafna-Flóki who attempted to settle in the West Fjords area but was defeated by the bitter winter. Earlier suggestions, which obviously did not catch on, were "Snowland" and even "Butterland", the latter by a Norwegian who was thereafter known as Þórolf "Butter". He said the grass was so rich that butter dripped from every blade.

booty or brought by chance visitors. Ireland was a redoubt of Graeco-Roman learning when the Western Roman Empire crumbled under barbarian pressure and Irish chroniclers, who were familiar with earlier writers and travellers including Pytheas, tended to embellish their work with borrowed, and sometimes counter-productive, erudition. Thus the story of St Brendan's discovery of "Thule" (*see below*) is on the one hand made quite plausible by a description of a volcanic eruption which could have been Mount Hekla; but on the other hand credibility suffers considerably when St Brendan discovers that "Thule" is inhabited.

Frozen gateway to hell

Nevertheless, it was not Scandinavians who first settled on Iceland but Irish monks driven by the desire to meditate undisturbed. They set out in coracles made of hides stretched over a framework of branches and twigs. With hardly any seafaring experience, they "sought with great labour... a desert in the ocean". The Shetlands, Faroe Islands and ultimately Iceland were just the ticket. The monks are unlikely to have arrived before St Patrick's celebrated missionary work in Ireland, which began in 432, so evidence of an even earlier presence, like a collection of Roman copper coins, recently found at an archaeological dig, were probably

ST BRENDAN IN ICELAND

St Brendan and crew were bobbing about offshore in their little boat when an inhabitant appeared: "he was all hairy and hideous, begrimed with fire and smoke". Sensing danger, St Brendan make a precautionary sign of the cross and urged the oarsmen to pull harder. "The savage man...rushed down to the shore, bearing in his hand a pair of tongs with a burning mass of slag of great size and intense heat, which he flung at once after the servants of Christ... 'Soldiers of Christ', said St Brendan, 'be strong in faith unfeigned and in the armour of the Spirit, for we are now on the confines of Hell'". He was not the last visitor to believe that eruptive Mount Hekla was the entrance to Hell.

Sound information about Irish activities in Iceland is contained in the works of Dicuil, author of *On Measuring the Earth*, and the Venerable Bede. Dicuil quoted priests who said that between February and August it was light enough at midnight to pick lice off one's shirt. It may be inferred from evidence – elsewhere, since there is none in Iceland – that the hermits lived in beehive huts arranged around a central well, church and garden. The monks came equipped with Latin devotional literature, bells used to summon the community to prayer and to exorcise evil spirits, and ceremonial regalia like the crozier, a cross denoting an abbot.

were unwilling to live among heathen. That may be putting it mildly. Nevertheless, the Vikings were usually very candid about their atrocities, and as there is no record of anyone boasting about burying an axe in a hermit's head, scare-mongering theories about the fate of the Irish do not necessarily hold water. The surest mementoes of the Irish occupation are the "papa" (i.e. priest) place-names.

Viking Exodus

According to Snorri Sturluson, the greatest of Icelandic saga-writers, the Norwegians who chased the Irish away were themselves fugi-

LEFT: episodes from St Brendan's journey from Ireland to Thule: meeting a whale, and encounter with a demon. **ABOVE:** the Norsemen arrive.

Since the communities were exclusively male, they would not have put down roots and multiplied in the usual way. The settlements were bound to wither, but was their decline in Iceland gradual? Peace of mind would not long have survived the arrival of the 9th-century Norwegians. Ari the Learned, a 13th-century Icelandic chronicler, tells the story from the Norwegian point of view. The disembarking Vikings encountered "some Christians" who shortly afterwards "went away" because they

tives, in their case from the tyranny of Harald Fairhair. He became the undisputed master and first king of Norway in 872 and immediately set about mopping up the opposition, seizing the property of defeated chieftains and so forth. Of the 400 names mentioned in the *Landnámabók (Book of Settlements)*, which lists the first settlers, 38 are known to have been previously powerful chieftains.

Some historians prefer the less dramatic impulse of poor economic conditions in Norway; others that the majority of settlers did not come from Norway at all but were the descendants of Norwegians who had already emigrated to older colonies, particularly in the

British Isles. "For the Icelanders," says one authority, "the islands west of Scotland are the cradle of their race in a much higher sense than even their motherland." This last school believes that the Norwegians may even have been outnumbered by the Irish slaves they took along, although only a small proportion of the names included in the *Landnámabók* is clearly of Irish origin.

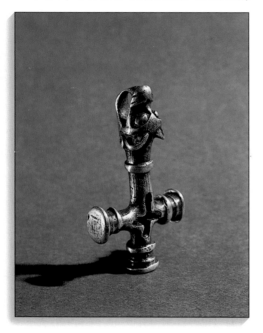

The best-known story about these early Norwegians concerns two foster-brothers, Ingólfur Arnarson (the official "First Settler" of Iceland) and Hjörleifur Hróðmarsson, who spent a winter in Iceland and were so impressed that they returned with two ships piled high with household goods. They were accompanied by family, friends and 10 slaves procured in Ireland. The two brothers parted company on reaching Iceland, Ingólfur going to the south coast (and later to the site of Reykjavík) and Hjörleifur to the west, near present-day Vík.

Hjörleifur was soon faced with a rebellion by his Irish slaves because they resented having to share plough-pulling duties with his only ox. Almost all the sagas carry disparaging remarks about the character of Irish slaves, and this lot were evidently no exception. They first killed

> ### EARLY SETTLERS
>
> By 930, the population of Iceland was about 25,000 – about as many as could be accommodated around the coastline.

the ox, blamed it on a bear and then laid an ambush to get Hjörleifur and his companions when they came looking for the bear. As the hunters fanned out, the slaves overwhelmed them one by one. They abducted the women, piled into a boat and decamped to an offshore island.

The discovery of the hunters' bodies shocked Ingólfur. Death at the hands of a slave was such a shameful fate that he could only think that his brother's Christian tendencies had caused him to neglect his pagan sacrifices. The rebels were tracked down to their island refuge and surprised in the middle of a meal of roast puffin. Those who escaped being killed there and then were probably mindful of the penalties meted out to slaves who rose against their masters. One Irish slave unwilling to forgive a master for castrating him (among other grievances), had tried to cut his own throat and consequently suffered the agony of a red-hot wash basin placed on his belly with gruesome results. Nevertheless, he survived – but only to be buried alive in a bog. The rebellious slaves fled to cliffs and threw themselves off. The island setting for this unpromising start to Icelandic history was Heimaey, one of the group known thereafter as the Vestmannaeyjar (Westmann or "Irish" Islands).

Dividing up the island

The Age of Settlement (874–930) followed these pioneering efforts and soon the coastline was more or less fully occupied by settlers. Iceland had not long been settled, however, when the whole cycle of emigration repeated itself and for the same reasons: either land hunger, adventurism or falling foul of authority. Erik the Red was a prime example of the last. Already banished from Norway for murder, he was banished from Iceland for more of the same. Having sailed off to the west and found somewhere else to settle, he then attempted to persuade others to join him. To succeed, he needed an attractive name for his new land, and in this he set a precedent for estate-agency hyperbole ever after. It was such a lush par-

LEFT: Thor's hammer amulet, a Viking artefact incorporating Christian and pagan symbolism.
RIGHT: Leifur Eiríksson sights the coast of America.

adise, he told prospective settlers, that only one name would do: Greenland. Enough people believed him to fill 25 ships, but only 14 ships survived the voyage to the promised land.

Vikings in America

Erik's son, Leifur, is credited with discoveries even farther afield. Old Erik would have been a partner in this enterprise, but en route to the ship leaving Greenland he was thrown from his horse and injured a foot. "It appears," he said, "that I am not destined to find any more lands than the one which we now inhabit." Leifur's first port of call was a place so dismally useless

that there was no point in stretching his imagination beyond "Helluland" ("Stoneland"). This seems to have been northern Labrador.

Conditions to the south improved, hence it was dubbed "Markland" or "Woodland". Further still, he came across a climate so mild that it seemed not to require winter fodder for cattle. It was clearly a worthy contender for settlement, the more so when Leifur's German foster-father returned from a sortie jabbering and "rolling his eyes in all directions and pulling faces". The fellow was understandably overcome by what he saw. The 10th-century Vikings were in the habit of consuming between 10 and 18 pints of

LAYING CLAIM TO LAND

The first Viking settlers laid claim to as much land as they thought they could manage, usually by throwing the pillars of the wooden high seats (a symbol of their authority) from their longboats and making their homes wherever they washed ashore. This tradition supposedly allowed the god Thor to choose the location.

The steady influx of new settlers meant rationing the remaining land by a process known as "carrying the fire". The owner of the ship bringing a group of immigrants was a chieftain or man of substance. The rest of the party would be families and attendant slaves or "thralls". The land they were entitled to was as much as could be encircled by a

ring of bonfires, with the proviso that they had to be lit with the same torch in one day and that, when burning, they were visible from one another. The criterion for women settlers – implying that some arrived independently – was the area that a two-year-old heifer could lap in a day.

The arable coastline was gradually settled in a similar pattern to that seen today – with most inhabitants on the coast, especially in the southwest. The interior – "nothing but ice and fire" – was out of bounds and remained so for all intents and purposes until the early 20th century. It still remains mostly uninhabited, with only a few farmers eeking out a living from the starkly beautiful but barrren land.

powerful mead per day – man, woman and child – along with the odd beaker of sour milk. Leifur and the rest of the company might have been primarily mead-men, but the German recognised grapes and knew what could be done with them. It was thus that they gave the name "Vínland" to the future America.

The explorations of Freydís

Leifur's observations inspired a surge of voyages to this wonderful place, including one by his dreadful half-sister Freydís in a joint venture with two Icelanders, Helgi and Finnbogi. Freydís seems to have inherited Old Erik's

had large eyes and broad cheekbones." Her crew retreated in bewilderment when attacked by these tribesmen armed with catapults, a weapon new to the Vikings. Freydís snatched the sword of a man killed by a stone and faced the attackers. Yanking out a breast, she gave it a resounding thump with the flat of her sword. The Indians were as alarmed by this as the Vikings had been by their catapults. They bolted to their boats and paddled off at speed.

The lure of the land of wine was strong, but repeated attempts to follow in Freydís's wake were similarly unsuccessful. "Although the land was excellent, they could never live there

worst characteristics – the sagas refer darkly to her "evil mind". She had married her husband Þorstein only for his money and despised him. Freydís fell out with Helgi and Finnbogi when they reached Vínland and, making the false accusation that they had insulted her, ordered Þorstein ("thou miserable wretch") to kill both of them and their party of 30 men and five women. Þorstein did as he was told but drew the line at killing the women. "Give me an axe," said the ghastly Freydís.

As Freydís was soon to discover, the greatest barrier to settlement in the New World was the hostility of the natives. "They were small and evil-looking, and their hair was coarse; they

in safety or freedom from fear because of the native inhabitants. So they made ready to leave the place and return home." Attempts continued at least until 1347, which has led to the theory that Christopher Columbus was inspired by Icelandic stories about this distant land. These stories were probably still being recounted in seafaring circles when in 1477, according to his son Fernando, Columbus called at Iceland as a crew member of an English ship.

The Icelandic commonwealth

Back in 10th-century Iceland, the displaced chieftains were determined never again to be relieved of their traditional authority by a single ruler. They entrenched themselves in their respective areas, or *þings*, and were called *goðar*, a word derived from "god". The commonwealth Alþingi, created in 930, was a parliament whose history is almost continuous to the present day. Presided over by a Speaker or Law-speaker, it was an acknowledgement that certain matters required a central authority. Lesser cases were dealt with by courts in the four "Quarters" of the land.

The Alþingi met for two weeks every year at the Þingvellir, a point roughly in the middle of the most densely populated part of Iceland and with a remarkable natural amphitheatre. The

to raise a military force or to exercise police authority. Moreover, the powers of the Law-speaker were deliberately circumscribed so that the office could not be used as a springboard to monarchy; when a chieftain turned up with as many as 1,500 men to support him in a feud, there was nothing the Law-speaker could do.

The Alþingi therefore had considerable difficulty living up to its ideals. In 1012, for example, a litigant who suspected that his case was slipping away on a legal technicality unleashed his private army. The plain of Þingvellir was strewn with corpses before proceedings could be resumed. Litigation abounded, but the law

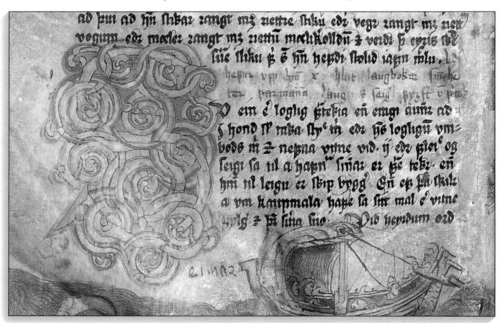

chieftains – 36 to begin with, later 39 – met in formal session, but every free man was entitled to attend and the occasion acted as a magnet for the whole population. These annual reunions were a great influence in promoting the development of a distinctive culture and help to explain, for example, why the language remained uniquely homogeneous without a trace of local dialects.

Although the Alþingi was the supreme spiritual and temporal authority, it was not allowed

LEFT: an image from the Icelandic film *In the Shadow of the Raven*, set in the harsh early years.
ABOVE: longship from a 14th-century manuscript.

was so complicated, and the society so riddled with vendettas, that the due process of the courts was forever on a knife-edge.

Life in the longhouses

Settlers tried to recreate the conditions of pre-monarchical Norway as far as local conditions permitted. In Norway, farmsteads were a collection of separate wooden buildings, one for sleeping, another for cooking and so on. Timber was plentiful there; in Iceland it was always in painfully short supply. The Icelandic farmstead was therefore a single unit, a row of rooms with common walls and a turf roof. Only the framework of the walls was timber; the rest was made up of stones and sod. While the Norwegian *stofa* or living-dining quarters were often large enough to accommodate several hundred guests, the Icelanders could not heat such a space. Their buildings became progressively smaller and the windows fewer.

Larger farmsteads able to afford the luxury of timber imported from Norway maintained the tradition of large festive halls, which also served as religious temples. In the winter a fire was lit in a hearth at the centre of the hall, the smoke being left to find its way out through shuttered apertures in the roof. The chieftain occupied a high seat at one end with the guests

lining benches on either side, their backs to the wall. "The flesh of the sacrificed animals, after being boiled in a large kettle over the fire," says an 18th-century study, "was served up to these rude banqueters, who frequently amused themselves by throwing the bones at one another, the manner in which they were placed on the opposite sides of the hall being very convenient for indulging in this elegant pastime."

Farmsteads were also equipped with an early version of the sauna, water being poured over a stone stove in the bath-house to produce vapour. The early settlers evidently made full use of the water from numerous hot springs to luxuriate in hot baths.

Early customs

Women of the period dressed extravagantly in gold-brocaded dresses, the men in brilliant mantles and ornamented helmets. Skarphéðinn, the ill-fated young man whom we met at the opening of this history, made his entrance at one Alþingi in a blue mantle, blue striped trousers with a silver belt, and high shoes. His hair was combed back behind his ears, and round his head was a gold embroidered silk ribbon. He carried a large shield but took most pride in the battle-axe which had just despatched a certain Práinn.

Skarphéðinn, like all young men, was addicted to what amounted to the national sports, horse-fighting and a kind of ball game called *knattleikur (see panel)*. Horse fights were theoretically a contest between animals, although owners and supporters could not restrain themselves. "I am tired of this noise," Skarphédinn declared at the height of a mêlée involving horses and onlookers, "it is much better that we fight with the sword."

Marriages were arranged by the male heads of families – young men could veto the decision, although brides had no say in the matter. Love had no part in the equation. On acceptance as a wife, the woman acquired considerable property rights and other privileges. These did not extend, however, to denying the husband his concubines. A wife could sue for divorce only if she was abused; the husband could obtain one for almost any reason that entered his head.   ❑

A VIOLENT PASTIME

Knattleikur was a ball-game described in the sagas, but it is hard to work out from commentaries on play what the rules were, if any. "Þorgrímur was unable to hold his own against Gísli, who threw him down and carried the ball away. Gísli sought again to take the ball, but Þorgrímur held it fast. Then Gísli threw him down so violently that he skinned his knees and knuckles, and blood was running from his nose... Gísli took the ball in one jump, threw it between the shoulders of Þorgrímur so that he fell forwards, and said: 'The ball on broad shoulders broke, which is not to be complained of'". At the end of the game, the two players part "not as good friends as before".

LEFT: a 19th-century artist's impression of Vikings at sea. **RIGHT:** Vikings on the warpath.

THE COMING OF CHRISTIANITY

Although Iceland's conversion to Christianity was at times turbulent,

it ushered in a period of relative stability and a literary golden age

On the rung of government below the Alþingi, the Icelandic chieftains fought tooth and nail to preserve their individual authority. The chieftainships were in reality more like political parties than regional entities. Dissatisfied "subjects" were at liberty to switch their allegiance – and divert their taxes – to some other chieftain, even one who lived at the opposite extremity of the land. These floating constituencies acted as a slight brake on the wilder excesses of ambitious chieftains; the rough and ready equilibrium, however, was severely tested by the advent of organised Christianity.

An Irish curse

The first settlement of Irish monks was at what is now known as Kirkjubæjarklaustur, or Church Farm Cloister. In going away rather than having anything to do with the Norwegian heathens, the monks left a curse on any pagan who occupied the site. The curse seems to have delivered the desired results at least in the case of pagan settler Hildir Eysteinsson; he dropped dead as soon as he laid eyes on his new home.

The Norwegian settlers arriving from the British islands must have encountered Christianity and some may even have practised it, but on reaching Iceland they reverted to paganism, or possibly paganism with a weak dash of Christianity. Icelandic paganism was a mixture of the old Norse deity, spirits who took on the likeness of men or beasts, and fetishes which made trees and waterfalls objects of veneration. Temples were built in holy places, ritual taking the form of animal sacrifices. Only in emergencies were human sacrifices offered. Temples might have specific house rules; on the holy mountain of Helgafell at Þórsnes, for example, those wishing to enter the temple had to wash their faces thoroughly.

One of the more concerted efforts to introduce orthodox Christianity was made by

Þorvaldur Koðránsson the Well-Travelled. His travels included Germany, and in 981 he was baptised there by a Bishop Frederick. With the bishop in tow, Þorvaldur returned to Iceland with the mission to convert his countrymen. The singing, ringing of bells, burning of incense and vestments involved in Christian

liturgy made a favourable impression, but the number of genuine converts was disappointing. Too many merely paid lip service to avoid paying the pagan temple tolls, which did not go down at all well with the chieftains for whom the tolls were a source of income.

Matters came to a head when Þorvaldur preached at the Alþingi of 984. Bishop Frederick never mastered the language and was therefore merely a consultant. Héðinn of Svalbarð, an arch-opponent of Christianity, engaged comedians to mimic and poke fun at the two of them. Forgetting himself, Þorvaldur leapt on two of the comedians and killed them. Bishop Frederick "bore all with patience" but was

LEFT: Þorgeir, the Law-speaker at the Alþingi of AD 1000, who decided in favour of Christianity.

RIGHT: a brawl between a Christian and a pagan.

outlawed from Iceland with Þorvaldur. They were preparing to sail when Þorvaldur spotted Héðinn of Svalbarð sawing some wood nearby. His parting shot was to kill him. "Because of this violent and unchristian act, Bishop Frederick parted from him and returned to his native country." Þorvaldur abandoned his mission to become a merchant and do yet more travelling.

Viking converts

Christianity made greater advances under the influence of Olaf Tryggvason, the future king of Norway. Saga-writer, Snorri Sturluson describes him as "the gladdest of all men and very play-

ful, blithe and forgiving, very heated in all things, generous and prominent amongst his fellows, bold before all in battle." His early life gave no clue to the future. He was a full-blooded Viking marauder at the age of 12, terrorising the English coast with his fleet of five longships. Resting in the Scilly Isles, off England's southwest coast, after months of strenuous atrocities, he made the acquaintance of an elderly sage who put him on the True Path.

Olaf's conversion was electric and he returned to England in a different frame of mind "for England was a Christian country and he was also a Christian". Olaf applied all his former Viking energies to the conversion of his

countrymen in Norway. They were, in short, given no choice. As a travelling missionary he went nowhere without a few severed heads.

News of Olaf's missionary zeal reached Iceland: "It was rumoured that the people of Norway had changed religion, that they had discarded the old faith, and that King Olaf had Christianised the western colonies; Shetland, the Orkneys and the Faroe Islands." Olaf was clearly heading their way as if Iceland were just another Norwegian colony, an offensive presumption to those who had developed a strong sense of separate identity and pointedly referred to themselves as "Icelanders".

It was one such proud Icelander, Kjartan Ólafsson, who was cajoled into entering a swimming gala while on a visit to Trondheim. He found himself racing a powerful swimmer who was not content merely to beat him but ducked him repeatedly until he was on the point of losing consciousness. The graceless victor introduced himself as Olaf Tryggvason and suggested baptism. Kjartan thought it prudent to agree, as did other Icelanders who happened to be in Trondheim at the time. "When they accepted baptism," however, "it was usually for some ulterior motive, or because they regarded it as an interesting adventure."

One of these cynical converts, the *skáld* (poet) Hallfreð, poked out the eye of a reluctant convert and ravished a certain Kolfinna to teach her hesitant husband a lesson. The saga's verdict on Hallfreð is unambiguous: "In all his conduct there is not a trace of Christian spirit."

Brutal methods

The personal history of Þangbrand, the chaplain to whom Olaf entrusted the conversion of Iceland, was not reassuring. "His knowledge of the Christian doctrine might have made him a valuable man had not his violent temper and vicious habits rendered him unfit for so sacred a calling. He not only squandered the income of his parish, but he organised piratical raids to replenish his depleted stores, an unchristian conduct for which the king finally called him to account. Due repentance saved him from banishment, but he was sent instead as a missionary to Iceland."

Relying on his patron's proven formula of exemplary terror, Þangbrand managed to win a few converts in the two years he spent in Iceland, but on returning to Norway in 999 he had to admit to Olaf that the mission had not been a total success. Olaf was furious and ordered the seizure and execution of all heathen Icelanders in Trondheim. The expatriate colony was then quite large and, freshly baptised, they were ordered to Iceland to spread the word. They timed their return to Iceland to coincide with the Alþingi of the year 1000.

Olaf was actually using Christianity as a cloak for his territorial ambitions on Iceland, and he first had to usurp the Christian party which had been developing in Iceland of its own accord. There had even been talk of the home-grown Christians setting up an alternative government, and the arrival of the Trondheim contingent in full battle array threatened to tip the country into civil war.

A crucial decision

Þorgeir, the current Law-speaker, asked for time to think. He spent a day and a night completely covered by the hide of an undefined species of animal, eventually to throw it off and make what has been described as "perhaps the most important oration ever delivered in Iceland": "It seems to be advisable that at this juncture…" he intoned, before coming down on the side of the Christians. Still, his oration was a masterpiece of compromise. His advice was that all parties back down and acknowledge that the law, and not any of them, was supreme. "It will prove true that when we sunder the law we end the peace."

The adoption of Christianity as the official religion in 1000 banned the worship of heathen gods in public, but not in private. Nor were the population required to give up their practices like exposing unwanted infants and eating horseflesh. Olaf's further plans for Iceland were never revealed because he died in battle at Svolder the same year. Olaf's Christian zealotry was his undoing. The war was the result of a grudge nursed by the wealthy Queen Sigrid of Sweden ever since Olaf first asked her to marry him and then withdrew the proposal when she declined his pre-condition: baptism as a

---

LEFT: saga hero Gunnar of Hlíðarendi.
RIGHT: opposing sides lined up for confrontation at the Alþingi of AD 1000.

> **ÞORGEIR'S LEGACY**
>
> Today, the phrase "að leggjast undir feld", loosely translated as "to lie down under a hide" is used when someone chooses isolation to think something through.

Christian. "Why should I wed thee, thou heathen bitch?" he shouted, giving her a slap in the face to reinforce the point. "That," she replied icily, "may well be thy death." And so it proved.

Olaf Haraldsson, the future patron saint who succeeded to the Norwegian throne in 1016, appealed to Iceland's Christian leadership to tighten the loopholes which allowed pagan practices to continue, and he was so pleased with the response that he sent not only timber and a bell for a church to be constructed at

Þingvellir but also an English bishop, Bernhard the Book-wise, whose aim was to speed up the conversion of the country.

One of the remaining obstacles to the establishment of orthodox Christianity was a shortage of priests. The chieftains regained a measure of authority by putting up themselves or equally unqualified nominees as candidates. As the choice of bishops had to be ratified by the Alþingi, the church was for a while fully integrated in the social system, and one chieftain at least "did everything in his power to strengthen Christianity". New bishoprics were set up at Hólar and Skálholt and these gradually became known as centres of learning.

The Golden Age

Iceland enjoyed almost a century of relative peace after 1030, as if the country were quietly digesting its stormy beginnings and putting them into a narrative sequence. Long hours of darkness indoors encouraged story-telling, and the people as a whole were remarkably adept at it. An unusually large proportion of the population could read; the introduction of the Latin alphabet instead of clumsy Runic encouraged them to write as well. The Dark Ages elsewhere in Europe were characterised by clerics copying religious tracts in Latin. In Iceland people wrote in their own language – and about themselves.

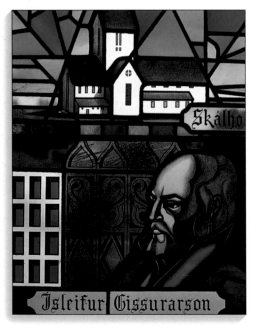

SNORRI STURLUSON

The violence of the Sturlung Age was chronicled by Snorri Sturluson, whose family gave the Age its name. They were descendants of the saga hero Egill Skalla-grímsson, and Snorri may well have written *Egils Saga*. Born in 1179, Snorri married an heiress and became a Law-speaker at the Alþingi twice. He was despatched to Norway as a diplomat, and when he returned to Iceland in 1241 against the King of Norway's wishes, he was murdered on his orders. Snorri's undisputed epitaph is the *Heimskringla*, a monumental history of the kings of Norway whose breathtaking scope is reflected in the first words: "The face of earth inhabited by man...".

Intellectual activity outstripped politics and law. The Alþingi of 1118 served as a reminder that government was still a hostage to the selfish machinations of chieftains. Proceedings against a notorious murderer named Mar degenerated into a bloody trial of strength between two chieftains which disrupted the Alþingi year after year. The general assembly passed numerous resolutions outlawing the culprits; they were laughed off.

The flaw in the legal system, as we have seen, was that the Alþingi could not initiate prosecutions nor force its decisions on spirited opposition. A complicated web of murder led in 1163 to violent clashes in what became known as the "Stone-Throwing Summer". The combatants were said to have been driven to such rage that they were hurling stones so heavy that normal men, when they tried to clean up the aftermath, could not lift them at all.

In the course of the 12th century, the country was divided between bishops aligned with the seat of Trondheim and half a dozen clans in a state of perpetual internecine warfare. At the same time economic conditions deteriorated and, as the Icelanders had no timber for shipbuilding, they were increasingly dependent on Norwegian suppliers and shippers. Matters came to a head in the so-called Sturlung Age (1230–64), with a combination of horrific violence and, ironically, an intellectual flowering, which has been called the Icelandic Renaissance.

The Alþingi's impotence in the face of feuds that were tearing apart the land's most powerful families underlined the fact that anarchy had taken over. The king of Norway was as ever ready and eager to step in and the papal legate approved saying, "it was unreasonable that (Icelanders) did not serve a king like every other country in the world."

In 1262 the Alþingi submitted to King Haakon by granting him the right to collect taxes. In practice, submission left the Icelandic chieftains in control of their own affairs as before except that they were forbidden to wage war on one another. The people won a respite from constant upheaval, but by the end of the 13th century it was apparent that Iceland had started an unstoppable decline. ❏

LEFT: stained-glass image of Ísleifur Gissurarson, the first bishop of Skálholt.
RIGHT: carved pulpit in Laufás church.

THE DARK AGES

A combination of absolute foreign rule, trade restrictions and a series of natural disasters led to the darkest period in Iceland's history

The terms of Iceland's submission to Norway were contained in the "Ancient Covenant" and every taxpayer was obliged to pay an annual royal tribute in the native wool. Royal officials replaced the *goðar*, and Snorri's murderer Gissur's reward was to be made the earl of Iceland. Even the weather served as a portent: it turned colder, and all over Scandinavia men dispensed with kilts and put on trousers. Temperatures continued to drop, necessitating underwear.

Gissur's "character and previous record", says Knut Gjerset, the eminent 20th-century Icelandic-American historian, "rendered him unfit to maintain peace and order, which was his principal official duty". In 1264, his enemies stormed his daughter's wedding, killing 25 guests while Gissur hid in a tub of whey. His revenge was to lay waste the Rangárvellir district and then invite his enemies to a peace conference. Their leader was executed, whereupon Gissur announced his retirement to a monastery. The Norwegian king decreed that Iceland would try to survive without any earls.

Imposing the law

Iceland clearly needed a new framework of government, starting with a new legal system. The "Code of Magnús Lagabøter" proved so efficient that it served with very few amendments until the 19th century. The crown, which was seen at the time as part of the divine order of things, was made the supreme legal authority, and lawbreakers were answerable to it, not to the injured party as previously. Murder, robbery, rape, counterfeiting, forgery and seduction became capital offences, but judges were supposed to administer the law dispassionately. "For we are to hate evil deeds," the judge's manual advised, "but love men by natural instinct as our fellow Christians, but most of all their souls."

LEFT: dried fish, a staple of the Icelandic diet and a key element in trade for centuries.
RIGHT: an early depiction of Mount Hekla erupting.

For the first time Iceland acquired a national army rather than dozens of private armies, although it was only 240 strong and the men were sent to Norway in defence of the realm against Danish and Hanseatic threats. The power of the Church was strengthened, but rested increasingly in the hands of foreign bishops. Church

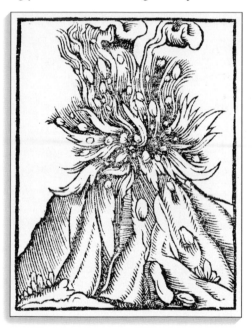

reforms required clerical celibacy; even subdeacons who had been married for years and had several children had to give up their wives.

Public dissatisfaction in a generally peaceful era was provoked by something that would haunt Iceland for centuries to come: the control of trade. Iceland had to trade to survive, and with no merchant fleet of its own the country was at the mercy of Norwegian merchants. The king was supposed to ensure that a certain number of ships called regularly to deliver essential supplies and take away the exports which paid for them. All too often the ships never came, particularly when they were most needed because of famine and natural disasters.

Even supplies of altar wine dried up and the celebration of mass had to be suspended.

Years of disaster

The 14th century presaged a run of calamities almost beyond belief. Hekla erupted repeatedly; each time a pall of darkness settled over southern Iceland for days on end and the following winter was unusually severe. Heavy snowfalls thawed to become devastating floods. Hekla's 1389 eruption could be felt and heard all over the island, according

to contemporary accounts: "Fire arose not only from the mountain but from the woods above Skarð, the eruption being so violent that two mountains were formed with a chasm between them. In the neighbourhood hot springs welled up, forming lakes of boiling water." Smallpox and other epidemics added to the misery.

The industrious Hanseatic merchants – by then well-established on Norway's west coast – undoubtedly could and would have traded with Iceland, but the Norwegian king set a precedent later to be slavishly followed by the Danes, declaring that trade with Iceland was a crown monopoly. Iceland thus went through the extremes of either being completely neglected

or facing demands for greater quantities of the prized codfish than the population could afford.

The Scandinavian union of Norway, Denmark and Sweden effected at Kalmar in 1397 transferred the sovereignty of Iceland from Norway to Denmark. The Danes were even more remote and less interested in Iceland than the Norwegians, and, in the country, conditions deteriorated accordingly: "Our laws provide that six ships should come hither from Norway every year, which has not happened for a long time," reads a plaintive message to the Danish king, "a cause from which Your Grace and our poor country has suffered most grievous harm. Therefore, trusting in God's grace and your help, we have traded with foreigners who have come hither peacefully on legitimate business, but we have punished those fishermen and owners of fishing-smacks who have robbed and caused disturbances."

Smugglers and pirates

The unauthorised foreign traders were mostly English and their activities would be Iceland's main access to the outside world for centuries to come. They provided essential commodities in exchange for fish, which would probably have been acceptable to the Icelanders had the English not decided that they were better equipped to catch the fish themselves. This fundamental conflict of interest would continue – all the way to the notorious "Cod Wars" between Iceland and England in the 1960s and 1970s.

The activities of the English traders were therefore a mixed blessing as far as the Icelanders were concerned, but to King Eric of Denmark, who held the trade monopoly with Iceland, they were an unmitigated outrage. Eric protested to King Henry V of England over the illegal trade, and his royal commissioners in Iceland did their best to stop it, but the mainland fleets had fallen into disrepair and there was no way of enforcing the prohibition.

Pirates among the English merchants – the distinction between them and merchants could not have been finer – were quick to recognise the opportunities presented by an undefended

---

LEFT: rough seas braved by traders around Iceland.
RIGHT: monsters were said to be an additional hazard.

coast, and their looting of Icelandic churches was an echo of what the Vikings had done in England. King Eric made attempts to stop the pirates but much of his strikeback was in vain. On one occasion, a couple of royal commissioners with orders to arrest the offenders were themselves bundled into a ship and sent off to the dungeons of England.

Eric's successor, King Christian I, also tried to defend his kingdom, sending out the chieftain Björn Þorleifsson to arrest the pirates. Just like the commissioners before him, Þorleifsson was captured and despatched to England, along with his wife Olaf. However, the determined chieftain managed to escape and make his return to Iceland. He tried his hand again at defeating the pirates, but this time he was killed and his son captured.

Olof paid a ransom to get her son back and then recruited an army to deal with the English. Some English were killed, and the affair escalated into a full-blown war between England and Denmark in 1469 although, ironically, the illegal traders and their customers on the spot seem to have continued their prickly but profitable dealings without even noticing.

The English traders did, however, run into stiff competition from the Hanseatic League, and the Danish kings at last found an effective weapon, which was to play off one against the other in what amounted to an auction for limited trading concessions.

WHALES, SERPENTS AND LOBSTERS

In addition to the hazards of rough seas, pirates and slave-traders, stories abounded of huge whales and other mysterious creatures to be found in the remote seas around Iceland. The country was so cut off at this time that there were few foreigners who were able to contradict the account of 16th-century writer Sebastian Münster, a mixture of fact and fantasy. "In the mountain of Hecla," he wrote, "there is a great abyss which cannot be sounded and here appear often people who have recently drowned as though they were alive. Their friends beg them to come home but they reply with great sighs that they must go into Hecla and then vanish forthwith." Münster went on to describe whales "as big as mountains... which capsize large ships and are not afraid of the sound of trumpets or of empty barrels thrown at them with which they gambol. It sometimes happens that seamen encounter a whale and if in distress cast anchor upon it thinking it to be an island... Many people in Iceland build their houses out of bones and skeletons of these whales". He also described sea serpents "200 or 300 feet long" which wound themselves around ships and "a fearful beast like unto a rhinoceros with a pointed nose and back (which) eats crabs called lobsters twelve feet long". These hefty lobsters, moreover, were said to be easily capable of seizing and strangling a man.

The long decline

The auctions lined royal pockets but did nothing for Iceland. The cumulative effect of natural disaster and stifled trade was simply too much. The most conclusive evidence of national lethargy was that literary activity ceased. The only creativity, which did not amount to much, was the lightweight ballad of wandering minstrels.

> **TRADING PRODUCTS**
>
> Cod was Iceland's main trading commodity; others included sulphur, tallow and sheepskin, as well as the pure white Icelandic falcon, by far the best for falconry.

The extent to which Iceland became dispirited and defenceless is revealed by an invasion in 1627 by 3,000 Barbary pirates commanded

by a "Rais Murad" who was actually a Dutchman named Jan Janezen. Having run wild through Grindavík, Faxaflói and the East Fjords, the pirates then descended on Heimaey, one of the Vestmannaeyjar (Westmann Islands) "and overran the whole island with loud yells, massacring the terror-stricken and helpless inhabitants". The youngest and strongest of the population were herded into their ships; the others into a warehouse which was then put to the torch. The local priest, a composer of hymns named Jón Þorsteinsson, was struck dead while kneeling in prayer; his wife and children and a second priest were taken to the ships, making a total of 242 captives bound for Africa.

The surviving priest was released the following spring to present the ransom demand to King Christian IV. He reported that many of the captives were already dead. The girls had been sold off to harems and the young men committed to lives as galley slaves. Some of the men had become pirates themselves. It took five years to raise funds to secure the release of 37 captives, but in the end only 13 got back.

Heimaey never recovered from the decimation of its population, and it was set even farther back by the colossal volcanic eruption in 1783 which poured so much poisonous lava into the ocean that the fishing industry was out of action for many years. A British traveller in the early 19th century told of a dwindling population of 200 whose children were dying because they ate nothing but the oily flesh of seabirds.

A dismal outpost

Iceland was almost oblivious of the Reformation in Europe. The people were contentedly, if forlornly, Roman Catholic, and the Reformation arrived not as an intellectual awakening or rebellion against the old order but as a series of dimly understood royal decrees from Copenhagen backed by military threats.

The Church in Iceland had slipped back into old habits. "Although priests were not allowed to marry," says one of the sagas, "holy and godfearing fathers would permit them (I know indeed not with what authority) to have concubines instead of wedded wives... It was easy for the priests to get women, so that they often got the daughters, sisters and relatives of chieftains for their helpmates. Proper and lawful agreement was entered into by both parties, so that nothing was lacking of real marriage but the name."

Feuding bishops

The old habits affected bishops too. Bishop Ögmund of Skálholt, whose sympathies were Lutheran, confronted the Roman Catholic Bishop Jón at the 1526 Alþingi with a force of 1,300 men against the latter's 900. Full-scale battle was averted by an agreement to let the issue be settled by a duel between champions. The duel was fought on an island in the Öxará. Ögmund's man was declared the winner, but the next day his cathedral at Skálholt was mysteriously destroyed by fire. This ironically softened his feelings towards Jón because he believed the latter could only have got away with arson with God at least slightly on his side.

In Denmark and Norway, the Reformation was primarily a dynastic struggle with many nobles waiting anxiously for a pretext to despoil the rich estates of the Roman Catholic Church. That ambition extended to Church possessions in Iceland too, and in 1541 two warships were despatched to Iceland with orders to use force if necessary to push a new Church code through the Alþingi.

tion to Jón's continuing defiance and in 1548 – two years after Luther's death – summoned him to Copenhagen. Jón chose instead to raise a rebellion. The geriatric bishop led 100 men down to the Protestant stronghold of Skálholt and ordered the defenders to surrender on pain of excommunication. The ultimatum brought jeers from within; Jón turned around and built himself what would be, if necessary, a last bastion at Hólar on Iceland's northern coast.

King Christian may have heard that Jón had sent a request for military assistance to Charles V, Holy Roman Emperor. In any event, he moved decisively against the stubborn bishop.

Bishop Ögmund, now 80 years old and blind, still mounted a spirited defence. He was dragged from his bed into a Danish ship. His captors offered to release him on payment of a ransom which amounted to his sister's money and deeds to all his property. Both were handed over but the ship sailed with Ögmund still in it. He is thought to have died on the voyage.

That left Bishop Jón, Ögmund's adversary and by now an old man himself. King Christian III, an arch Protestant king, took grave exception

LEFT: spartan living conditions from the Dark Ages.
ABOVE: an artist's impression of Iceland's turbulent fall into decay.

Another military force was sent to Iceland but he was not to be intimidated. On 27 June 1550 an exasperated Christian outlawed him and ordered his arrest.

Demise of the rebel

Bishop Jón's path of glory ended in his eventual incarceration. For several days his captors debated what to do with him. A priest suggested over breakfast one morning that he knew how the prisoner could most safely be kept. Asked to elaborate, he replied that an axe and the earth would do the trick. This suggestion was at first received as a joke, but on reflection the idea commended itself. On 7 November 1550 Bishop

Jón, and two sons captured with him, were beheaded at Skálholt, providing Scandinavian Catholicism with its first and last martyrs.

News of the executions aroused bitter resentment. Three masked men carrying coffins presented themselves at Skálholt and asked for the bodies. The request was granted, bells were attached to the coffins, and the cortège moved through the countryside to the chiming of church bells. The bishop was buried at Hólar and still remains something of a national hero.

The overthrow of the Catholic party soon followed Jón's death, and the king moved in quickly on its properties. He considered using

the income from the confiscated lands to build schools, but decided to keep the money himself. Thereafter, one quarter of the tithes payable to the Church were to be diverted to the royal purse, as were all fines imposed in law suits. Other reforms were progressively introduced. Adultery became punishable by death, although only on the third offence: men were hanged, women drowned. The eating of horseflesh was banned, and persistent absence from Lutheran services was punished by flogging.

The crux of the matter was that the confiscation of Church property, the imposition of new taxes, and alterations to the law were all carried out without reference to the Alþingi or with any regard for the existing Icelandic procedure. The country was, in short, feeling the draught of absolute monarchy in Denmark, and things were to get a lot worse.

Crushed by foreign rule

Trade was always Iceland's Achilles heel, and absolute rule in Denmark heralded a tyrannical monopoly from 1602 worse than anything that had preceded it. Iceland was obliged to buy everything it needed exclusively from court-appointed Danish trading companies at prices fixed by the company. It was a case of paying what the company demanded or doing without. With Iceland thus held to ransom, it was no surprise that the price of imports rose by 500 percent over a period in which the prices paid for home-grown products remained static. The purchase price of Icelandic fish was barely a fifth of what foreign buyers would readily have paid.

In 1662 matters were made worse by the division of the country into four commercial districts. These were prohibited from trading with one another; they could deal only with Danes and on the same Danish terms. Clandestine deals with foreign vessels were made more difficult by a Danish naval blockade and more dangerous by draconian penalties. A certain Páll Torfason took a couple of fishing lines from an English ship in return for some knitted goods which the Danish merchants had previously declined, and lost the entire contents of his house. Holmfast Gudmundsson was flogged for selling fish to a near neighbour who was technically in another district.

The colonial administrators were nothing if not an extension of the arrogant court officials in Denmark. If they needed a horse, the first peasant they asked had to provide one. If it was a question of crossing a fjord, the nearest farmer was required to drop everything and get his boat out. A grumble meant a sound flogging.

Unsurprisingly, the authority of the ancient Alþingi was undermined and in 1800, on royal orders, it was abolished. The new law court which took over its political functions and the surviving bishoprics were concentrated in Reykjavík, the population of which was a mere 300. The sense of separate identity was all but lost. "Up till 1800," says one of the annals, "the

---

LEFT: 18th-century tombstone kept at Skálholt.
RIGHT: en route to a funeral.

Icelanders, both men and women, dressed according to their national style, but after that they gradually adopted Danish styles."

Litany of wretchedness

The volcanic eruptions and earthquakes which had caused havoc in 1618, 1619, 1625, 1636, 1660 and 1693 continued practically unabated in 1727, 1732, 1755 and 1783. The last in the series, the eruption of Lakagígar (Laki), is still regarded as the worst in world history, scattering ash to every corner of the globe. The Icelanders' personal losses included 11,461 cattle, 190,448 sheep and 28,013 horses. Following the human casualties of the eruption there was famine due to the haze of smoke and ash, and a smallpox epidemic. Fully one-third of the population died as a result of the eruption and ensuing disasters.

Summing up the misery of the 18th century, the historian Magnús Stephensen says Iceland experienced "forty-three years of distress due to cold winters, ice-floes, failures of fisheries, shipwrecks, inundations, volcanic eruptions, earthquakes, epidemics and contagious diseases among men and animals, which often came separately, but often in connection with and as a result of one another". ❏

LIVING CONDITIONS IN THE DARK AGES

Impoverished following years of disaster, life was harsh for most Icelanders. Jón Jónsson brings conditions into focus: "The living room of the common peasant farmstead was usually not covered with boards on the inside. One could see between rafters to the grass-covered roof, which soon looked like ordinary sod, and from which mildew and cobwebs were hanging. The floor was uncovered, consisting only of earth trampled hard. But during heavy rains when the roof was leaking water dripped down, and it soon became a pool of mud through which people waded. The walls along which the bedsteads were nailed fast were covered with a grey coat of mildew, and green slime was constantly trickling down the walls, especially in the winter. Bed clothes were very few among the poor people. Old hay, seaweed or twigs did service as a mattress, and a few blankets constituted the covering." To make life even more wretched, there was a crippling shortage of firewood. In some houses the family slept on a platform with calves and lambs occupying the space underneath; this at least provided some heat which was conserved by keeping windows to a minimum both in size and numbers. A thin membrane – part of an animal's insides – served as glass, but it only allowed through a little light.

THE PUSH FOR INDEPENDENCE

*Upheavals throughout Europe put pressure on Denmark to loosen its
hold over Iceland; by 1944 Iceland had become a republic*

Iceland, like Scandinavia in general, sat out the impact of the American War of Independence and the French Revolution. Iceland did not even feel the whiff of liberalism which passed through Denmark towards the end of the 18th century under the auspices of Dr Johann Struensee.

Struensee was a German physician who was engaged to treat the malignantly half-witted King Christian VII and contrived to run Denmark personally. He introduced freedom of the press and personal liberties including the decriminalisation of adultery. His vested interest in this particular reform was the clandestine affair he was enjoying with the young Queen Caroline Matilda, sister of England's King George III, who was also mad. The affair was discovered, the law repealed, and Struensee's severed head was posted on a pole to advertise that the old absolutist order was back in charge.

Denmark's misfortune, broadly speaking, was to choose the losing side in the Napoleonic Wars. The British fleet destroyed the Royal Danish Navy at the Battle of Copenhagen in 1801 and then bombarded Copenhagen itself in 1807. The entire Danish merchant fleet (some 1,400 ships) was confiscated, which of course left poor Iceland more isolated than ever. British merchants were eager to take over Icelandic trade themselves, and this provided the backdrop to the most bizarre chapter in Iceland's history, the "revolution" of 1809.

An unlikely liberator

The central figure was Jorgen Jorgensen, born in Copenhagen in 1780, a son of the royal watchmaker. A brilliant but unruly student, he found himself serving in the British Navy almost by accident as "John Johnson". His early career was chequered, to say the least, and he was actually in prison in England for gambling debts when he was taken on as an

LEFT: travellers stopping at a village.
RIGHT: a portrait of Jorgen Jorgensen, leader of the 1809 "revolution".

interpreter for an opportunistic and unofficial English trade mission to Iceland.

After one abortive trip, the traders landed in Reykjavík to discover that the governor, anticipating their return, had plastered the town with notices prohibiting any trade with foreigners under pain of beheading. The governor, Count

Trampe, was not simply enforcing Copenhagen policy; he happened to own the one Danish ship still trading with Iceland. With a warship in the background, the English traders tried to reason with Trampe but he was adamant.

Jorgensen then came up with a bright idea: depose Trampe, reconvene the Alþingi (abolished nine years previously), declare Iceland's independence from Denmark, and make a treaty of alliance and trade with England. Some, but not all, of the English traders thought this an excellent idea. To cries of "Traitor, you'll hang for this", Trampe was marched out of his office and locked up in one of the English ships. Jorgensen could now properly begin.

Issuing proclamations under the self-appointed title of "His Excellency, the Protector of Iceland, Commander-in-Chief by Sea and Land", Jorgensen promised the Icelanders "peace and happiness little known in recent years" and their own national flag – three white codfish on a blue background. His Excellency was just 30 years old. Backed up by 12 armed sailors, Jorgensen "liberated" Iceland by seizing the property of Danish merchants. The Icelanders were not sure how to react. The fearsome Trampe was locked up in the ship's cabin but they could not be certain that he would remain there: the price of collaboration with

the English if ever he regained office did not bear thinking about.

The new regime had been in existence for a little more than a month when a second British warship, *HMS Talbot*, hove into view under the command of Captain the Hon. Alexander Jones, the younger son of an Irish peer and not sympathetic to revolutionary activity. Jones suspected that the British government might also have certain reservations.

The "revolution" squashed

The Hon. Alexander Jones's enquiries into what was going on – the flag was new to him, and he noticed that Jorgensen was building a fort at

Arnarhóll – brought Iceland's "independence" to an end as perfunctorily as it had been created. "All proclamations, laws and appointments made by Mr Jorgen Jorgensen, since his arrival in this country, are to be abolished and totally null and void…"

In his memoirs, Jorgensen described the manner of his departure. He stepped into a fishing-boat and was rowed out to the departing warship by a crew of Icelanders: "So I went on board quietly, many of the poor natives shedding tears at my departure. It is true, indeed, that I left the island with regret. I had established liberty and freedom there without a drop of blood being spilt, or a single person committed to prison. This revolution was brought about without mocking and insulting the Monarch, of whose saw it was deemed expedient to declare the island independent, and without inflaming the minds of the people against their former government. The thing spoke for itself; the oppressions were too great to be endured longer."

Jorgensen's subsequent career was equally colourful. He was jailed in a convict hulk on returning to England, released, imprisoned again for more gambling debts, did some sterling work for British Intelligence (at one point disguised as an Irish pilgrim), dashed off books on such weighty topics as the geography of Persia and Afghanistan, was sentenced to the gallows for selling the bedclothes off the bed he was using in his London lodgings, was instead transported to Australia – and there served with distinction in the police force. He died in Hobart, Tasmania in 1844.

A revival of spirit

The real price of Denmark's ultimately half-hearted alliance with Napoleon was paid at the postwar Vienna congress. Pressure from the victors forced Denmark to grant Norway its independence, albeit in a lopsided union with Sweden, and expectations rose in Iceland of a similar concession in the near future.

Visitors began to notice changes, and the foundations of Iceland's modern "cradle-to-grave" social security system particularly caught the attention of English reformers. "We have no hesitation in saying," they reported, "that in respect to the poor, an Icelandic parish was, to say the least, equally as well managed as an English one."

Care for the poor

The basic principle was that any person incapacitated by age, infirmity or "misfortune" should in the first instance be maintained by the next of kin according to their ability to pay, the criterion being the value of their property. If circumstances required a pecking order, priority was given to a distressed mother followed by the father, children, brothers and sisters. If supporting some or all of these demonstrably exceeded a person's resources, the parish authorities stepped in.

While parishes might keep a storehouse of emergency provisions for the destitute, the responsibility for actually looking after them was generally passed directly to the rate-payers, the number of paupers allocated to each depending on the value of the property owned. If the alimentor (i.e. he who paid alimony, before the term became bound up with unhappy marriage) failed to provide adequate support, the pauper could complain to the district Þing. The alimentor who left a parish to escape the burden was liable to the kind of house-arrest known as exclusion.

The English observers thought the Icelandic system clearly superior to the English in one respect. "The Icelanders... do not charge themselves with the support of the poor without taking especial care to keep the number of paupers within due limits; a care which we have grossly neglected, and are now enduring the fearful consequences of our want of foresight."

The number of paupers was controlled by, for example, not allowing a man to marry until he had the means to support a family. Nor was a slave to be freed unless the owner could provide him with an adequate plot of land. If a freed slave became destitute through the former owner's neglect, he retained his freedom but was entitled to alimony.

"Very stringent regulations were also passed to keep the poor within their respective parishes," the English observers also noted. "Clothes and shoes might be given to a pauper of another parish, but any parishioner who furnished such a pauper with victuals, except he was merely passing through the parish to go to his own, rendered himself liable to the punishment of exclusion. The Icelanders also took care to make able-bodied paupers work for their living. Begging was not tolerated, especially at the Alþingi. If a beggar entered a booth on the Þingvellir plain, the booth-man might forcibly eject him, and every one who furnished such a beggar with meat, was liable to be punished with exclusion. All persons who wandered about the country for fifteen days and upwards were to be regarded as vagabonds... and punished accordingly. Besides other punishments to which they were liable, any one who thought proper might mutilate them in the manner practised in the East to qualify a man for the service of the seraglio" – in other words, castration.

ROMANTICS VS RATIONALISTS

The 18th and 19th centuries saw a revival of intellectual activity in Iceland. The rationalists, under the forceful leadership of Magnús Stephensen, railed against the lack of foreign influence in the language, which was virtually pristine Old Norse, saying that it smacked of darkness and superstition. They advocated an intellectual *Aufklärung* which welcomed the best that the rest of the world could offer. The romantics, on the other hand, glorified Iceland's history and language. Their champion in the 19th century, Bjarni Thorarensen, wrote the hugely popular *Eldgamla Ísafold* to the tune of *God Save the King*, and his poems were mostly about heroic saga figures.

LEFT: turf houses at Laufás.
RIGHT: detail of the gable of a turf house.

Unsteady steps towards freedom

Some of these comments must have been out-of-date by the time they were written. Swift social progress was obviously being made, but Iceland still had to wait until 1830 before the ripples of Norway's 1814 independence reached its shores. Even then, the concession was merely two seats among 70 on an advisory body to the Danish crown. Prominent Icelanders such as the jurist Baldvin Einarsson protested that such feeble representation in a body based in Copenhagen and knowing next to nothing about Iceland was worthless. The romantics wanted the Alþingi restored. In 1840

the newly crowned King Christian VIII agreed to reinstate an Alþingi consisting of 20 representatives chosen by a qualified electorate and four or six royal nominees. The assemblies were not to be held at the old Þingvellir, as the romantics wished, but at Reykjavík, which would formally become the new capital.

As usual in such circumstances, radical elements felt that these gentle reforms did not go far enough. They insisted on holding the Alþingi at Þingvellir, on lower franchise qualifications and on the exclusive use of the Icelandic language in government. The nationalist cause was championed by the eclectic scholar Jón

Sigurðsson, whose statue stands in Austurvöllur, the old town square in Reykjavík, facing Parliament House. The nationalist movement demanded a totally independent national legislature and the ending of Denmark's final say over Icelandic judicial decisions.

Progress towards more substantial independence was delayed by Denmark's preoccupation with the Schleswig Holstein nightmare, a dispute with Prussia over the sovereignty of the frontier provinces, each with a divided population whose minorities refused to give in. Moreover, the Danish royal commissioner in Iceland was obstructive. The incumbent, still, was Jorgen Jorgensen's *bête noire*, Count

Trampe, and he was suspected of applying for a private army to exorcise what he considered unlawful, pseudo-patriotic nonsense. While Denmark continued to turn a deaf ear to the fundamental issue of Icelandic independence, the trade monopoly was ended in 1854.

The Icelandic exodus

With true independence still apparently unattainable, the newspaper *Norðanfari* suggested ironically in the 1870s that the only chance Icelanders had of tasting freedom was to emigrate en masse to Brazil or North America. As it was, Icelanders were soon leaving in such numbers

over everything the Alþingi did, but for the moment it was enough to celebrate, especially as the date coincided with the 1,000th anniversary of Iceland's settlement. King Christian IX attended the festivities and heard the first performance of *Iceland's Thousand Years* by Matthías Jochumsson, the present national anthem. Jón Sigurðsson was pointedly not invited, but it was said that in a private conversation afterwards the king asked him if Icelanders were satisfied with the new constitution. "As their chief wish had not been granted," he replied, "how could they be?" Sigurðsson recognised full independence or nothing.

1979

150

ÍSLAND

JÓN SIGURDSSON 1811-1879
INGIBJÖRG EINARSDÓTTIR 1804-1879

that the newspaper changed its tune. People were asked to postpone their departure for a year or so in case things changed, and at the same time a number of teetotal societies sprang up. The aim was not so much a campaign against alcohol as to deny Denmark the revenue from the tax on drinks.

Under this kind of pressure, the king apparently bowed to the inevitable in 1874 by giving the Alþingi autonomy over domestic affairs, including finance. It was not quite what it seemed because he retained an absolute veto

LEFT: Reykjavík in the early 19th century.
ABOVE: nationalist figures, still revered by Icelanders.

The first breakthrough

Full independence was a long time coming. Icelanders and Danes were generally talking at cross purposes. As far as the Danes were concerned, Iceland was inconceivable except as an integral part of the kingdom, although they were willing to tinker with semantics. One proposal would have made Christian IX "King of Denmark and Iceland" instead of just Denmark, with Iceland taken for granted. Iceland was in no mood for cosmetic compromise, and talk turned to secession, or what in the 20th century became known as a unilateral declaration of independence. After Sigurðsson's death, his successor, Benedikt Sveinsson, submitted to the

Alþingi a proposal calling for real self-government every year from 1881 to 1895. It was twice passed, in 1886 and 1894, only to encounter the impenetrable stumbling block of the royal veto. The breakthrough eventually came in Denmark with the election of a liberal government in 1901. On 1 February 1904 Iceland received home rule.

The saga-writers would have felt at home in the first years of Icelandic home rule as the country fragmented into a political free-for-all, various factions feuding with seemingly no

NEW UNIVERSITY

The university at Reykjavík was opened in 1911, a considerable achievement for a national population numbering only 90,000.

plebiscite with 12,040 votes in favour and only 897 against. This was agreed to be valid until 1940, when Iceland's status would again be open to negotiation.

"Occupation"

The end of 1940 was of course the worst imaginable time for Denmark and Iceland to enter into delicate constitutional negotiations. There was no contact whatever between them, Denmark having been occupied by Germany and Iceland by Britain. In the latter's case, strategic considerations had taken

greater purpose in mind than advancing self-interests. Prohibition was introduced in 1909, a move that was unpopular, especially in Spain, which had traditionally paid for Icelandic fish imports with surplus wine.

Icelanders could not agree on their relationship with Denmark, however, and the impasse continued until the whole question of national sovereignty in Europe was brought under microscopic scrutiny in the peace negotiations after World War I. The Danish government then took the initiative and on 1 December 1918 Iceland became a sovereign state with its own flag, linked to Denmark by virtue of having a common king. The arrangements were ratified by a

priority over the policy of "perpetual neutrality" which had been declared in 1915. Hitler's troops had marched into Norway and thus gained control of its immense, Atlantic-facing coastline and ports. Iceland was a logical next step, its mid-Atlantic position being of inestimable strategic value for submarine operations and for aircraft not yet able to cross the ocean in one hop. Iceland had no military defences of its own, so Britain stepped in and "occupied" the country to pre-empt any German moves in that direction, a role later taken over by the Americans.

The British and American forces, who at times amounted to one-third of the population, were not always popular, but resentment was softened by the unprecedented prosperity that the war years brought in Iceland. The national income shot up by 60 percent on the twin strengths of construction work on American airfields and free-spending US personnel. Fish exports fetched record prices and, since they were generally paid for in dollars, Iceland had the means to import large quantities of American goods.

Not being able to communicate with Denmark to negotiate on constitutional changes, the Alþingi took a decision to act unilaterally: "Seeing that the situation which has been cre-

its affairs." It added that Iceland would become a republic as soon as it was possible to terminate the union with Denmark formally.

The termination of the union and a new constitution were submitted to plebiscite in 1944 and both were approved by overwhelming majorities. The date chosen for the formal establishment of the republic at Þingvellir was, not by accident, the birthday of the great nationalist Jón Sigurðsson, 17 June.

Denmark was then still under German occupation, and many Danes felt that what amounted to a secession had been brought to fruition while they were hardly in a position to

ated makes it impossible for the king of Iceland to exercise the powers assigned to him by the constitution, the Alþingi announces that for the present it commits the exercise of these powers to the government of Iceland."

An Alþingi resolution made the following year went even further: "The Alþingi resolves to declare that it considers Iceland to have acquired the right to a complete breaking off of the union with Denmark, since it has now had to take into its own hands the conduct of all

do anything about it. King Christian X sent a telegram of good wishes – it was only received after a ceremony which attracted no less than 20,000 people to Þingvellir on a cold and blustery day. The first president of the new republic, who was elected to a four-year term, was Sveinn Björnsson.

Iceland's neutrality did not save 352 seamen from death as a result of German actions at sea, but it was adhered to on principle when Iceland turned down an offer to declare for the Allies in the final months of the war. One of the first actions of independent Iceland was, on the cessation of hostilities, to demand the immediate withdrawal of the American forces. ❑

LEFT: poet Grímur Thomsen reads to Danish King Christian IX at the 1874 National Festival.
ABOVE: a brass band greets the British troops.

MODERN ICELAND

Since World War II Iceland has come of age as a prosperous, hardworking, modern society enriched by a healthy respect for its past

Iceland today has all the trappings of an industrialised nation, with a sophisticated, consumer-orientated society, comprehensive welfare system and one of the highest standards of living in the world. It is almost impossible to imagine that, before World War II, many visitors thought Iceland to be barely out of the Middle Ages. The leap into the modern world has been fast and furious: greater changes have taken place in the past 50 years than in the more than 1,000 years of settlement beforehand.

Joining the modern world

The transformation occurred almost overnight. Even so, Icelandic society did not abandon its long past, but rather adapted it to the present, replanting an ancient heritage in modern soil where it has more or less flourished since. The Icelandic language has been the bridge of centuries: the history of the Old Republic had been written down in the Middle Ages using a language which modern Icelanders can and very often do read *(see pages 83–7 and 90–3)*.

The presence of first British and then American troops in Iceland during the war, although not exactly welcome, had its brighter sides. A frenzy of road-building and development created an economic infrastructure for the postwar period. Few Icelanders can deny that the prosperity brought by the war meant that national independence, declared in 1944, could be consolidated in peacetime.

More controversial was what to do after the war. Iceland's old stand of "eternal neutrality" was abandoned in 1949 when it became a founding member of NATO. The US military left Iceland but returned in 1951 with a vengeance to set up a permanent marine air base at Keflavík – a base that is still in use today. The fact that this made Iceland a major target in the event of nuclear war hardly endeared the US presence to the majority of Icelanders; nor did

Icelandic men appreciate rich American servicemen floating around the countryside. But the economic argument was powerful: Keflavík provided jobs. And strict controls on marines' movements, rarely allowing them out from behind a huge wire fence, meant that not too many ran off with Icelandic wives.

Even so, Iceland never established an army of its own and also managed to maintain good trade relations with the Eastern bloc during the chilliest spells of the Cold War. Anti-Keflavík feeling flared up from time to time during the Vietnam war and was a popular cause on the political Left – but by the late 1970s it had become a principle which was costing rather than winning votes.

As a non-nuclear base, Keflavík kept its nose clean during the arms race against Brezhnev, and its role largely involved escorting "stray" Soviet aircraft back out of Icelandic airspace – there were up to 200 violations some years – and monitoring submarine movements in the

LEFT: staircases reflected in the "Pearl", one of Reykjavík's most striking modern buildings.
RIGHT: US servicemen at Keflavík NATO base, 1951.

Politics of Fishing

Ever since Iceland gained full independence in 1944 the country's foreign policy has been moulded more by the international politics of fishing than by its role as a strategically crucial, albeit army-less, component of the NATO defence pact. Indeed, the level of dependence on seafood earnings runs to such an extent that Iceland's determination to repel any perceived encroachments on its fisheries resources has brought the country into a series of long-running conflicts with even its NATO allies.

The classic example of Iceland "getting tough" with an ally are the four Cod Wars with the UK between 1952 and 1976 (*see pages 109–10*), centering around the extension of the fishing zone around Iceland's coast. A more recent dispute has strained relations with Norway. At issue is the fishing by Icelandic vessels of the Barents Sea "loophole", international water bounded by Norway and Russia. Norway, claiming that the fishing damages cod stocks within its own waters, has on occasion seized Icelandic vessels and levied fines on Icelandic trawler owners. Iceland has also been in squabbles with Norway, Russia and the EU over catch quotas on migratory species such as redfish and herring.

The 1990s saw a gradual but fundamental shift in an area that marred a foreign policy otherwise perceived as a model of Nordic progressiveness -- whaling. When Iceland walked out of the International Whaling Commission in 1992 after the body rejected a request for a limited quota as "out of order", it seemed likely that the country's whalers would resume commercial whaling. But the Icelandic whaling fleet remained mothballed in Reykjavík harbour. Neither has Iceland resumed its controversial catch for research purposes, attacked by environmentalists as "commercial whaling in disguise".

Two factors influenced the decision to cease whaling. Firstly, Iceland was keen to restore an international image that had been tarnished in the global whaling debate. Secondly, the increasingly important tourist sector came to realise that there was more to be gained (both in terms of money and public relations) by attracting whale-watchers than exporting whalemeat to Japan. Although Iceland has not officially declared itself a non-whaling country, resumption now seems unlikely – especially with the high profile return of the killer whale Keiko, of *Free Willy* fame, to his native Icelandic waters.

Fisheries issues have also loomed large in Iceland's decision to remain outside the EU. Most leading politicians have ruled out joining, and of the mainstream political parties, only the Social Democrats have come out in favour of considering applying for membership. Opponents of membership cite Iceland's 1994 entry into the European Economic Area – a free-trade bloc between the EU and EFTA – as proof that Iceland doesn't need Brussels. In the opinion of Iceland's largest political camp, the centre-right Independence Party, the Economic Area treaty gives Iceland all the benefits of EU membership without any of the drawbacks.

There are however fears that Iceland is being left out in the cold. Even traditionally close ties to the other Nordic countries are coming under pressure; apart from the fisheries disputes with Norway, EU members Finland, Sweden and Denmark are becoming increasingly integrated into the New Europe.

With their survival as a nation still deeply dependent on seafood exports, Iceland's foreign policy seems destined to be shaped by the fishing industry. ❏

LEFT: washing down the boat after a fishing trip.

area. Always keeping a low profile, the US military effectively disappeared from view when a civilian passenger terminal was finally opened at Keflavík Airport in 1987. Until then, all visitors who arrived in the country by air had to land at the US military base before treading Icelandic soil (including Mikhail Gorbachev when he arrived for 1986 summit, *see page 63*).

> ### HARD WORK
> The average working week in Iceland – about 46–49 hours – is the longest in Europe.

Riches of the sea

After World War II, the Icelandic government – with economic foresight that has probably

During the 1950s and 1960s, import tariffs were thrown up to protect industry, but they gradually served to foster inefficiency and higher prices for everything from fruit to toothbrushes. It was not until the 1980s that Icelandic governments became committed, in the spirit of the day, to free market policies. The effects of loosening up the economy are still being felt – and, as travellers will attest, prices have hardly dropped from among the highest in Europe. The effect on Icelanders' lives may eventually be as great as the jump from the traditional to

never been matched since – channelled its wartime cash-in-hand into modernising the fishing fleet, laying the foundation for a powerful industry which has held firm right up to the present day. Soon Iceland would be producing more income per head from fishing than Saudi Arabians did from oil.

Rich on cod income, Iceland's government grew, building an impressive system of schools, public health and social security. At the same time, Iceland's regulation of the economy had few parallels in the developed Western world.

ABOVE: the Icelandic coastguard taking on the British Navy in the Cod Wars.

technological worlds since World War II. Throughout all of these policy changes, fishing was the mainstay of the economy (employing just a tenth of Icelanders, it provided three-quarters of the national income). Unfortunately, no amount of government regulation could sidestep its unpredictable nature, and fluctuations in both catches and market conditions have from time to time dealt severe blows to the virtually one-track economy.

Whenever fish catches or market prices deteriorated, the government's reaction was to devalue the Icelandic króna. This triggered an inflationary spiral in the 1970s. Wages were indexed to price rises, so that Icelanders joked that no news was better than a foreign disaster: for example a flood in Brazil which ruined the coffee-bean harvest could push up prices in Iceland which would result in wage rises all round.

Today, wage indexation has been outlawed, although pay deals commonly include an inflation "ceiling" which grants some compensation if prices rise above a certain level. Loans, however, are still indexed, which has put paid to one of the most popular national pastimes of the 1960s and '70s: owing money. Before indexing, it was possible to take

LOW UNEMPLOYMENT

Iceland's unemployment level – less than 4 percent – is one of the world's lowest.

countries on earth, a hangover from the high-inflation days when it paid to spend and cost a fortune to save. Icelanders are among the world's leading owners of consumer durables such as video players, cellular phones, cars, personal computers, foot massagers and, basically, any other piece of wizardry that promises high-tech comfort.

Icelandic society is one of the most literate in the world. Education levels are very high for both sexes: more than one-third of all 20-year-olds complete secondary grammar school, there

on huge debts and pray that inflation would go up enough to enable you to pay them back again. Generally it did, and whole generations bought or built the impressive apartment blocks and detached houses that decorate streets everywhere. Icelanders still live in the most spacious housing of all the Nordic countries – when they are at home and not out working to pay for it.

The affluent society

Today inflation has been brought under control and, with a fish-led recovery, Icelanders have a standard of living that few other countries enjoy. Despite gripes about the economy, it remains one of the most consumer-orientated

are around 5,500 students at the University of Iceland, and another 2,000 Icelanders at foreign universities (not bad for a total national population of only 283,000). More books are published and bought per head here than anywhere else in the world.

Icelanders also have one of the longest life expectancies in the world. Traditionally, Icelandic women have vied with the Japanese for first or second place, with an average life expectancy at birth of 81.3 years. Icelandic males are also high up in the world longevity stakes with a life expectancy of 76.4 years. Doctors say that the reasons include an unpolluted environment and the pure food that this offers; the outrageously fresh air of an Atlantic island on the rim of the Arctic Circle; a healthy fish-based diet; and exemplary public health care. Infant mortality in Iceland is, at 3.1 deaths per 1,000 children, among the lowest in the world, and certain aspects of preventitive medicine, such as early detection of female cancers, are unmatched.

Moments of glory

In recent years, Iceland has rarely hit world headlines, but some key dates stand out. In 1980, Icelanders chose Vigdís Finnbogadóttir as the world's first democratically elected woman head of state. Following a neck-and-neck race, the former theatre director, French teacher and tourist guide took the Presidency – an office outside party politics whose function is to provide a figure of national unity very similar to Western European monarchies and which does not include any involvement in day-to-day government. Vigdís was re-elected three times to the presidency, holding office until 1996 when she announced that she would not be running for a fifth term. In the early 1980s, Icelandic women produced the world's first purely feminist parliamentary party, The Women's Alliance.

On a different front, Iceland was invaded by foreign journalists in 1986 when it became host to the historic Reagan-Gorbachev summit. As the mid-point between Moscow and New York, Reykjavík seemed a reasonable symbolic meeting place for the leaders of the superpowers to discuss nuclear disarmament and begin the eventual ending of the Cold War. Over 2,000 foreign journalists, who had little hard news to cover for much of the time they were in Reykjavík, set about informing the rest of the world about the more eccentric aspects of this little-known fishing nation.

Lifting a ban

An event that brought almost as much attention to Iceland was "Beer Day" 1989, when a longstanding ban on strong beer was finally abolished. Total prohibition had gone into effect in 1915, but wine was legalised again in 1921. A national referendum of 1935 came out in

favour of legalising spirits too, but beer was not included in the vote, as a sop to the temperance lobby – which argued that because beer is cheaper than spirits, it would lead to more depravity. When the growth in international travel brought Icelanders back in touch with the forbidden drink, bills to legalise beer were regularly moved in parliament, but inevitably scuttled on technical grounds.

The absurdity of the beer ban came fully to light in 1985 when the teetotalling Minister of Justice prohibited pubs from pepping up legal non-alcoholic beer with legal spirits to make a potent imitation of strong beer. Finally beer

approached legalisation in parliament – the debate and knife-edge vote were televised live and watched by huge audiences.

Beer Day came on 1 March 1989, and was celebrated in style by crowds who thronged through −10°C (14°F) temperatures for their first taste of the true amber fluid. Contrary to predictions, the day passed without incident and now a beerless Iceland is unthinkable. This "corrupting foreign influence" has been swallowed and digested, like other banned luxuries assimilated overnight – including Thursday night TV, foreign investment, dog ownership in Reykjavík, bank accounts in foreign currencies, private broadcasting and many others.

LEFT: Vigdís Finnbogadóttir, president of Iceland betwen 1980 and 1996.
RIGHT: beer, finally legalised on 1 March 1989.

Keeping traditions alive

The concern at maintaining tradition does not always seem so frivolous. An ancient and homogenous culture of relatively few people is always at risk of being swallowed up whole-sale by the outside world.

Symbolic of the changes wrought in Iceland has been the growth of the capital, Reykjavík – with only 5,000 inhabitants in 1901, it now has about 175,000 in the greater Reykjavík area, or some 60 percent of all Icelanders. The shift from country to city has completely altered Ice-landic society: the generation of Reykjavík folk now around retirement age was largely born

and brought up in the countryside, on farms or in fishing villages. Their children, now middle-aged, were born and bred in the capital, but retained some links with the outside; and the generation now at or leaving school is thoroughbred urban, most of them brought up in the "concrete lava fields" of new residential suburbs such as Breiðholt and Árbær – whose populations alone outnumber those of the largest towns outside the capital area.

These are the first Icelanders to drift away from the "classical" colloquialisms of their ancient language, which is firmly rooted in the agricultural society of yesteryear. And they are the first to have no intimate, first-hand knowl-

edge of the mainstay industries of fishing, fish processing and agriculture – hands-on experi-ence which in the past had given Iceland's man-agers and technocrats a telling edge over their international competition. This lack of basic manual skills poses a threat to Iceland's few industries, a threat whose consequences few can guess.

Recognising that language is on the front line, Icelanders' defence of their ancient Norse tongue is fierce (*see the panel on page 91*). The same technological advances that the Icelanders welcome so warmly also pose the biggest threats. Satellite TV, for example, comes outside the jurisdiction of Iceland's legions of subtitlers, dubbers and professional and amateur word-coiners. Linguists say that the threats are becoming more subtle: borrowed words from foreign languages stand out instantly, but "hidden" foreignisms such as Anglo-Saxon syntax and thinking patterns are easier to slip into and more difficult to detect, yet undermine the very fabric of the language all the same.

And more remains of Iceland's past in today's materialistic world than the language that records it. Social scientists were astonished to discover in an opinion poll that a large majority of Icelanders still claim to believe in the existence of elves and spirits (*see* Icelandic Hauntings, *pages 266–7*). Almost all Icelanders still believe in God. Even though only a small fraction go to the Lutheran church they are all still registered at birth. At one stage during the 1960s, the Norse pagan religion was revived, although in truth it never really caught on again. Nowadays a congregation of some 280 peo-ple gathers to hear the archpriest read from ancient mythological poems on special cere-monial occasions.

But perhaps the real achievement of modern Iceland has been to remain essentially democ-ratic in a personal as well as a political sense. Iceland is at once a modern technological nation and a small village writ large – a place with little crime, few class distinctions and where everybody, thanks to the old Scandina-vian patronymic system still in use (*see panel on page 74*), addresses one another by their first name. ❏

LEFT AND RIGHT: children with Icelandic flags celebrating Independence Day – 17 June.

THE ICELANDERS

Today's Icelanders, a product of their landscape and history, are looking to the future with creativity and determination

Somewhere, in all these rocks and stones, is my home
— *Nationalist poet Pétur Gunnarsson*

Probably the first thought that occurs to many visitors as they drive through the desolate lava plain that separates Keflavík airport from the capital, is: "Very impressive – but why would anyone want to live here?"

The inhabitants of a country often tend to reflect their environment. The Danes, for example, live in a flat, fertile country, and are by and large an easy-going, laid-back bunch. Their Icelandic cousins, however, do not really know how to relax and enjoy life. The visitor may be puzzled at how they can be brash and completely uninhibited one minute, yet stubbornly taciturn the next, and may wonder how a nation so obsessed with the benefits of good honest labour can produce so many poets and writers.

But in these tendencies towards extremes, excess and unpredictablity, the Icelanders are only reflecting their homeland. Anyone would be a little crazy after centuries of long cold winters and a struggle for survival against a hostile environment – and managing to come out at the other end with one of the highest living standards in the world.

Icelanders have a reputation for being rather dour – but this quality does not go too deep. When the country enjoys one of its very rare long hot summers, the entire nation can be seen to undergo a metamorphosis. Out come the pavement tables outside the cafés, the bottles of red wine and barbecues. Some people even stop working overtime.

Medieval to modern

Icelanders have an extremely strong national identity, and a cultural heritage of which they are very proud. The constant suspicion that the

PRECEDING PAGES: playing soccer in the light of the midnight sun.
LEFT: an Icelander displaying a family picture.
RIGHT: downtown Reykjavík café.

outside world thinks them small and insignificant, coupled with having been isolated for so many years, sometimes makes them seem insular and absurdly patriotic. They are prone to harp on the nation's illustrious past, "cashing cheques on deeds committed 700 years ago," as writer and scholar Sigurður Norðal put it.

Yet no-one can deny that the Icelanders are a resilient bunch, having survived all sorts of calamities – both natural and induced – throughout the centuries. When the independence struggle began in the 19th century, Iceland was still deep in the Dark Ages. There were no roads and very few stone-built houses. But in a single generation, around the time Iceland gained self-government in 1918, the society moved, with no apparent difficulty, straight into the 20th century.

One of the most oft-cited reasons for the speed of this transition was the high standard of education in the country. While the people were poor, they were never ignorant. Nearly all of them could read and write, and quite a few could speak foreign languages.

Another is the strong sense of national identity and community. They have had to learn to stick together through necessity and overcome impossible odds. Thus, in the so-called Cod Wars with Britain in the 1960s and 1970s, this country without an army took on and defeated a world power that was threatening its interests and livelihood. A similar motivation lies behind the stubborn stand on whaling (*see page 60*). It is not so much the importance of the whale-hunt, but the questioning of Iceland's right to self-government that raises the national hackles.

Iceland's racial make-up was, and still is, mostly homogenously Nordic, with a dash of Celt. Today people are much more cosmopolitan, but before the 1960s a black person walking down the street in Reykjavík was invariably followed by a crowd of excited children. In the pre-war years Hitler and his Nazis assiduously courted the Icelanders as an example of a "pure Aryan colony"; to the country's credit few people took any notice of this dubious flattery.

In fact, Icelanders are generally free of racism. In 1989, when 5,000 foreign citizens were already resident in the country (making up 2 percent of the population) a survey showed that

Social changes

Their fierce patriotism can give Icelanders a rather inflated view of the country's importance on the world stage. They are very sensitive to slights to their national pride, and react strongly to any real or imagined threats to the community. This characteristic can sometimes manifest itself in an unpleasant way – such as the ban on black servicemen which the Icelandic government secretly insisted on imposing when the NATO military base was established at Keflavík during the 1950s. The ban is no longer in existence and the prejudice it displayed was based more on ignorance and fear than it was on malevolence.

a vast majority supported the idea of people of different races settling in Iceland. A large number of Icelandic couples adopted Vietnamese orphans during the Boat People crisis, and few of these children have experienced anything but a warm welcome into the community.

Recently an until-now-unexplored advantage of the homogenity of Iceland's population has been brought to the fore: unique opportunities for genetic research. In 1996, the first firm specialising in such research, DeCode Genetics, was founded. In its first two years DeCode grew exponentially, attracting foreign investors and generating considerable attention within the international medical community.

The genetic research discussion has been met with a mixture of awe and suspicion by the Icelanders. While DeCode's efforts and vision have been applauded, there has also been much controversy surrounding the company. This has mostly to do with questions such as whether a single company should have exclusive rights to medical information – though other companies are now being founded in addition to DeCode – and fears that the confidentiality of medical records might be violated.

A NEW DICTIONARY

The world's first Basque dictionary was written by a farmer in a desolate part of Northwest Iceland – he had learnt the language from Basque sailors who came to fish off the nearby coast.

when every self-respecting Viking started off his career by jorneying abroad, returning home laden with renown and gifts from European royalty. Modern-day young Vikings and Valkyries also have the community's blessing to quit the nation's shores and try their luck at seeking fame and fortune in foreign lands. They are said to be *að gera garðinn frægan*, "winning renown for the old homestead."

And certainly no-one has done that with as much panache as Björk Gudmundsdóttir. Björk

Looking to foreign shores

It is one of the many paradoxes typical of Icelanders that they are, at the same time as being insular, insatiably curious about the outside world, even to the most obscure detail. The only epic poem that has ever been written in honour of the medieval Balkan hero Skanderbeg was composed by an otherwise unknown Icelandic clergyman in 1861.

Icelanders lay great store by being cosmopolitan and well-travelled – "sailed", as they put it. This dates back to the days of the sagas

LEFT: dressing up on Heimaey.
ABOVE: young girls in the Northeast.

became a household name in Iceland at age 11, when she released her first solo record. During her teens and early twenties she sang with a handful of bands before becoming a founding member of The Sugarcubes. The Cubes were catapulted to stardom all over the world in 1988 with their quirky song *Birthday* – largely on the strength of Björk's inimitable vocal style. Björk launched her international solo career in the UK 1993 and has since won the widespread acclaim and respect of fans and critics alike for her unique sound and experimental style. Along the way she has done more to promote her home country than any amount of advertising ever could. In May 2000 Björk added another string to her bow and heaped yet more honour on Iceland, when she won the award for Best Actress at the Cannes Film Festival. The newcomer to acting won the award for her role as Selma in director Lars von Trier's *Dancer in the Dark*, which stars Catherine Deneuve and also took the award for Best Film.

Björk's success in the international arena has flung open the doors for other Icelandic musicians to become better known internationally. Talent scouts from every corner of the globe have made their way to this tiny north-Atlantic island to see what other talent might be hiding among the ice and lava. Evidently, their efforts

boasts a schedule packed with singing engagements in the world's top opera houses, two to three years into the future.

Another heavyweight figure on the Icelandic cultural scene is filmmaker Friðrik Þór Friðriksson. His film *Children of Nature*, written in collaboration with Iceland's literary golden boy Einar Már Guðmundsson, was nominated for an Academy Award in the Best Foreign Film category, in 1992. Although it did not win, it helped pave the way for Friðriksson abroad. His subsequent films have been met with overwhelmingly favourable reviews and have won awards at numerous festivals throughout the

have paid off, for a number of musicians and bands, notably Indie band Sigur Rós, have since landed deals with foreign recording companies.

In the classical sector, Icelanders have also excelled. The Iceland Symphony Orchestra has been winning great critical acclaim in the recent past, not least for their recordings of the works of the composer Jón Leifs. Leifs, who died in 1968 and whose unconventional – but decidedly Icelandic – sound was shunned by the establishment for decades, has recently been "discovered" by Icelanders and foreigners alike. Meanwhile, the opera singer Kristján Jóhannsson – a former Akureyri native and ex-motor mechanic – today resides in Italy and

world. Friðriksson has been named one of the most influential filmmakers in Europe and his Reykjavík-based production company is a major player in Icelandic film production, in conjunction with filmmakers both in Iceland and abroad.

Icelanders are also terribly proud of their two Miss Worlds. As if to give credit to the common notion that Icelandic women are among the most beautiful in the world, two Icelandic women were awarded the Miss World title within three years of each other: Hólmfríður Gísladóttir in 1985 and Linda Pétursdóttir in 1988. Other Icelandic women have received other more minor titles on the beauty circuit.

Sports and business

Two Icelanders have taken the title "Strongest Man in the World" four times each: Magnús Ver Magnússon and Jón Páll Sigmarsson, who died in 1993. Hjalti Ursus Árnason, won top prize at the World Strongmen Championships in Montreal in 1988 and Árnason and Magnússon, working together as a team, won the Scottish Pure Strength Championships in 1989.

A few other Icelanders have made the transition into the international sphere, most notably footballers and Ágúst Sigurvinnson, who recently retired in Iceland after a successful career with clubs in Belgium and Germany. It was cause

A handful of Icelandic companies have been excelling in the international business arena in the recent past. As well as DeCode Genetics (*see page 70*), the brainchild of ex-Harvard professor Kári Stefánsson, there is Össur, which has been carving out a name for itself as a leading researcher and producer of prosthetics. Another is Marel, a top developer and producer of high-technology scales and software for the fishing industry. Oz, a producer of internet software and applications, sprung from nowhere in the early 1990s, led by a couple of twentysomething computer geniuses; the company now has its headquarters in San Francisco.

for public lament in the German press that he refused to give up his Icelandic citizenship in order to become a naturalised German and play with the German national team.

In the UK, Iceland have an unlikely stronghold in the Staffordshire town of Stoke-on-Trent. In 1999 a consortium of Icelanders, spearheaded by fruit-and-vegetable distributor, Thor Gislason, took over Stoke City Football Club. The former Icelandic national coach, Gudjon Thordarsson was appointed as manager, and the team now boasts several Icelandic football stars.

LEFT: the Iceland Symphony Orchestra.
ABOVE: street art in a Reykjavík suburb.

Whenever an Icelander "makes it" on the international level the entire Icelandic nation basks in his or her success. These people often achieve larger-than-life status in their home country; never mind that they may be queueing in front of you at the supermarket. President Ólafur Ragnar Grímsson, for instance, won office in 1996 partly on the strength of his previous experience in the international arena. The ex-parliamentarian is a former chairman and president of the organization Parliamentarians for Global Action, with which he worked actively towards disarmament and peace. Prior to his election he had done a great deal to open doors for Icelandic businesses in

Asia and America and had been granted numerous international awards for his work.

My people and your people

Icelanders often claim theirs is a classless society. This claim has some basis: there is certainly a lot of class mobility. But there exist, like everywhere else, disparities of income, and some families are considered older and more "aristocratic" than others. Icelanders are obsessed with their genealogy and most can trace their ancestry back at least six or seven generations. Some even have family tables that go back beyond the age of Iceland's settlement into the realm of legend – perhaps with a Norse god or two sitting proudly at the top of the family tree. The common enquiry "who are his people?" is not just snobbery, however. It is a relevant question in a society where everyone is related to everyone else in the tenth generation.

The national inferiority complex also comes into play – and it has obviously been around for some considerable time. The author of the 12th-century *Landnámabók* (*Book of Settlements*), which charted the progress of the first pioneers who came to Iceland, stated his purpose in writing as follows: "so we would better be able to answer foreigners who upbraid us

for our descent from slaves or scoundrels if we knew our true origins for certain."

Small-scale society

Despite remnants of old snobberies, modern-day Iceland is on the whole an informal, egalitarian and familiar society. Everyone from the President down is addressed by their first names. Jón the doorman greets Jón the eminent politician with a cheery hello – they come from the same fishing village and are probably second cousins. As you shower after an early-morning dip in the local swimming baths there might be a famous pop-star getting changed in the cubicle next to you.

ICELANDIC NAMES

The general use of the patronymic, in accordance with ancient Scandinavian custom, makes the genealogists' jobs easier. Icelandic surnames are made up from the father's first name with "son" or "daughter" tacked on; thus Björk Gudmundsdóttir is Björk, daughter of Gudmundur. Her brother would be Gudmundsson. Some families do have family names, but they are often of foreign origin: Zoega, Schram, Richter and Petersen. In the past it was possible for family names to be bought for cash by up-and-coming parvenus who considered them smarter and more aristocratic; now it is not permitted to take a new family name.

Icelanders do not identify easily with the idea of fame, with its paraphernalia of bodyguards and exclusiveness. They are used to everyone being accessible. The President grants interviews to any member of the public who wishes to see him. Top sportsmen and pop-stars usually have to keep their day-jobs, as few can afford to go professional.

And it is very easy to be famous yourself. Anyone with application and talent can stand for parliament, present a television programme, set up an art exhibition or play in a football team. Anyone can be a published author – and usually is. One in 10 Icelanders publishes something in the course of their life and writing a book is considered almost a form of National Service. If you fail to hit the headlines in your lifetime you will at least do so after your death. Even the most obscure person can be sure of at least one long obituary, with a photo, in the newspapers on the day of their funeral. Pillars of the community may run to several pages over many days.

The concept of being a participating member of society is very strong. As a Japanese academic who settled in the country noticed: "Everyone is equal, so everyone is important. Everyone is a participant in society, it isn't possible to opt out, to deny your responsibility." Just as being a member of the community is an honour, being excluded from it is the worst possible dishonour. In the Saga Age, criminals were not killed or imprisoned, but outlawed – made outcasts from society.

Every individual matters and in return is obliged to participate. Iceland supports three daily newspapers, six TV channels, a national theatre and opera plus dozens of orchestras, art galleries, theatre companies, radio stations and museums. None of these could hope to survive unless individuals made sure they visited the theatre at least once a year, took two newspapers, went to concerts and so on.

Spending power

Surveys have shown that in many areas Icelanders are closer to the US in their attitudes

MAD ABOUT BOOKS

More books are written, published and sold in Iceland per capita than anywhere else in the world. 400–500 new titles are released yearly – the equivalent of 1,200 books per *day* in the United States.

than to Europe. Icelanders are firm believers in market forces. In their personal tastes, they have a slight tendency towards ostentation, glamour and display of wealth. But this materialism is partly a matter of economic survival. Importers and retailers would go out of business unless every household found it an absolute necessity to purchase a television, a video recorder and a compact disc player.

The spend, spend, spend mentality has been encouraged by an economy plagued through

the years by soaring inflation. Today, high interest rates and inflation at last brought down to single figures may dampen the spirits of some shopaholics, but most seem to carry on in their spendthrift ways regardless. Icelanders tend to be compulsive in their spending habits and are renowned for scooping up the latest gadgets. Moreover, "keeping up with the Joneses" is a national pastime and one must, of course, keep earning accordingly.

The "shopping trips" organised by Icelandair to the Scottish city of Glasgow became legendary amongst the retailers of that city, and when similar trips were organised to Newcastle in the north of England they made headline

LEFT: going for a walk in a residential area of Hafnarfjörður near Reykjavík.
RIGHT: enjoying a pipe on a sunny afternoon.

news locally. No wonder – a small but determined army of 50,000 Icelandic tourists manages to spend £23 million (US$37 million) each year in Britain.

As the late Nobel-prize winning author Halldór Laxness once declared, "it is, in general, expensive to be an Icelander." And to finance the expense, the nation is gripped by a collective compulsion to work all the hours that God sends. Icelanders are fierce devotees of the Protestant work ethic – no doubt a throwback to the days when a person's worth was measured in the number of hours of hard labour they could deliver per day.

Moonlighting is extremely common, and many people manage to hold down two or even three jobs at the same time. (As a result, they are always doing things at the last minute and are late for everything. Unpunctuality is one of the country's vices.)

Since the late 20th century there has been a budding awareness that this absolute devotion to the work ethic is turning into a national malaise. The accepted standard in the majority of companies is that employees – particularly men – must be on hand whenever required. Consequently, the strain on family life is very great and, ironically, the bottom line is that the number of hours put in does not necessarily

deliver higher productivity – in fact often the reverse is true. Some companies have recognised the problem and taken steps to counter it; others lag further behind.

Working hard

It often puzzles foreigners why Icelanders devote so much time, money and effort to building palatial houses equipped with state-of-the-art furnishings when they are always at work and therefore never at home to appreciate them. However, work is not just a way of getting money, it is seen as an end in itself, a means of gaining self-respect. Although the Icelandic welfare state is not as highly evolved as those of some of its Scandinavian neighbours, it is still fairly comprehensive. Nevertheless, few people would ever dream of claiming money off the state. "The comprehensive ability to work is the hallmark of the Icelander, whether a desk-bound intellectual, a farmer or a fisherman," comments anthropologist Finnur Magnússon.

This extreme devotion to the Protestant work ethic was demonstrated during the World War II. "British work" – employment that was offered by the English military forces occupying the country – was despised by the Icelanders as fit only for layabouts and degenerates. The reason seems to have been because it was too easy and well-paid.

But at the same time many Icelanders have a secret fascination for a more bohemian lifestyle. Hard-nosed yuppies will occasionally take the time to hang out philosophising with the regulars in one of Reykjavík's innumerable coffee-bars, and even publish a book of poems on the quiet.

Prime Minister Davíð Oddsson is a prime example of one who devotes himself to writing in his spare time: a collection of short stories written by him was, impressively, at the top of the best-seller lists in the 1997 Christmas book season.

In Iceland, poets and artists command begrudging respect and seem to have a special dispensation to lead a ramshackle, layabout lifestyle. As Laxness put it ironically, "since time immemorial, the Icelandic nation has had to battle with men who call themselves poets and refuse to work for a living."

However, it must be admitted that in most cases the old Protestant work ethic tends to win out. Back in the 1960s, Icelandic hippies, although they were quite adept at tuning in and turning on, never really got the hang of dropping out. The real diehards had to head over to Copenhagen if they wanted to bum around in style – back home in Reykjavík they would have been too embarrassed not to have a job.

Playing harder

Icelanders may take their work seriously but they are equally single-minded about their play. An inability to do anything in moderation is in fact one of the most characteristic national traits, as is demonstrated by a trip to downtown Reykjavík on a Friday or Saturday night (*see* Embracing the Night, *page 160*). This excess, however, is also partly explained by the high price of alcohol – it is too expensive to indulge in every day so many people prefer to save up for one almighty binge at the weekend.

Most Icelanders are also very quick to latch onto new trends, which can sweep across the entire nation with lightning speed. Video recorders had only been in the country for a couple of months before there were film-rental shops established on every street corner. It has been the same story with aerobics, sunbeds and new-age crystals. Aerobics teacher Sóley Jóhannsdóttir began her career in Denmark, where people would come for once-a-week dancing sessions. When she opened up a studio in Reykjavík it was a different story. She recounts: "Icelanders never do anything by halves – it's four times a week for most of my regulars with additional circuit-training lessons as well."

Non-violent society

The Icelanders are intrinsically a gentle people, and, despite having a fair share of the prevailing late-20th century social plagues – including drugs, porn, latch-key kids and so on – society is essentially non-violent, and Reykjavík is one of the safest capitals in the world. Even boxing is banned – Icelanders prefer the far more elegant ancient sport of *glíma* (which resembles sumo wrestling).

LEFT: a baby joining in on a Lutheran service.
RIGHT: praying to Thor.

The lack of serious crime means that society can be rather at a loss as to how to treat its more anti-social and violent elements. Even the most vicious of criminals rarely gets sentences of more than seven years, and the lenient sentencing in sexual abuse and incest cases – in which the perpetrator often escapes any sort of rehabilitation – has been criticised in recent years. Progressive and forward-looking as it may be, Iceland still seems to prefer to turn a blind eye to some of the more "sensitive" issues.

The other side of the coin is that, in general, Icelanders are broad-minded and tolerant about most things. Single mothers, for example, are admired rather than frowned upon. Besides, everyone loves children and is happy to welcome them into the world whether they have two resident parents or one. Although a few moralists have predicted imminent destruction of the social fabric from such a lax set-up, marriage, which for many years was seen as irrelevant, is coming back into fashion – even though many bridal couples have their own offspring acting as bridesmaids and pageboys.

Above all, Icelanders also have a greater respect for family ties than most other societies.

They take care of each other – there are few neglected grannies and grandpas left to fend for themselves in high-rise blocks. A recent survey showed that Icelanders put family as their top priority – above friends, free time and even their beloved work.

Iceland's Valkyries

In recent times the Icelandic woman has become somewhat of an archetype, combining Nordic beauty with physical and spiritual strength. While probably a variety of factors

contribute to the popularity of this image at this particular time, it undoubtedly received a boost through the two Miss World titles and the election, in 1980, of Vigdís Finnbogadóttir to the office of President. At the time of her election Vigdís was a single mother with an adopted daughter and, as such, represented a new era. She was also a survivor, having triumphed over breast cancer. In short, she combined femininity with strength, and common sense with strongly held personal views, albeit ones that she was not permitted to voice publicly by virtue of her office.

But the election of Vigdís was only the beginning: in 1983, Iceland became the first country to

> **FEMALE FIGUREHEAD**
>
> The nation's symbolic figurehead is the Woman of the Mountains, a quasi-supernatural persona who plays a similar role in the national psyche to Marianne in France and John Bull in England.

elect a women-only party to parliament. The Women's Alliance (WA), a grass-roots radical movement with no leaders and an economic model based on the concept of "the thrifty housewife," had three of its members elected only a couple of months after the party was formed – and doubled its support at the following election. Support for the WA went down in the 1990s, however, mostly due to internal disagreements and the party formally disbanded before the 1999 elections; its remaining members joined the movement that became The Alliance.

The feminist movement in Iceland also suffered a backlash in the 1995 federal elections, when just one of the ten cabinet ministries was assigned to a woman. Subsequently the ruling Independence Party, which had specifically tailored its campaign to appeal to women voters, was harshly criticised, both by the general public and by women from within its ranks. Bowing to public opinion, the Independent-Progressive coalition assigned four cabinet ministries to women in the following term.

Despite these problems, the women of Iceland are veterans of mould-breaking feminist activity. They first hit the international headlines in 1975, when they marked the beginning of the United Nations Women's Decade by going on a one-day mass strike to remind their menfolk of the essential role they played in society. Secretaries downed note-pads, bank-clerks and teachers stayed at home, mothers handed babies over to bewildered fathers – and the country was brought to a standstill.

When the Women's Decade drew to a close in 1985, they staged another walk-out. Then-President Vígdis joined the protest, causing a constitutional crisis by refusing to sign a decree that would force striking air stewardesses back to work. Male government ministers eventually forced her to sign, but her stand was much appreciated by her female compatriots.

In fact, women have always played a forceful role in Icelandic society. The sagas and old tales are full of strong, matriarchal figures – from Aud the Deep-Minded, one of the greatest of the pioneers, to the irascible Bergþora, Njáll's wife – while ancient lawbooks indicate that the medieval Icelandic woman enjoyed a great deal more emancipation than the majority of her European counterparts. She had equal rights in marriage, could own property and even hold a *goðorð,* or chieftainship.

Feminist advances

Iceland was one of the first countries in the world to introduce female suffrage: women were given the right to vote in municipal elections in 1908 and general enfranchisement in 1915. The Women's Alliance party also has a historical precedent. Between 1908 and 1922 a number of women-only panels of candidates were put forward for municipal and parliamentary elections, with considerable success.

surnames when they marry. But the factor that all eminent women in Iceland mention when asked about their emancipation is – the sea. "Icelandic women are strong because the wives of seafarers have to be," says former President Vigdís Finnbogadóttir.

Indeed, this tradition of holding the fort stretches right back to the Viking era, when women would be left in control of the farms while the men went pillaging and raiding. Today, women play a more vital role than ever in the economy – as they have demonstrated through their national strikes. Over 70 percent of women work outside the home in either full

What has made this remote island in the North Atlantic such a hot-bed of feminist activity? Dr. Guðrún Agnarsdóttir, a founding member of the WA, says the low population is highly relevant. "A small community expects a lot from each individual, and each individual's contributions are also more likely to be noticed and appreciated." Supreme Court judge Guðrún Erlendsdóttir considers very important the fact that women in Iceland have always kept the old Norse tradition of retaining their natal

LEFT: Icelandic women have always played a key role in their society. **ABOVE:** young women enjoying a pavement picnic in Reykjavík.

or part-time employment. One of their main grievances is that their salaries are still on average 40 percent lower than that of men, and that like their sisters elsewhere in the world, they are still having to do most of the work in the home as well as outside it.

Svanur Kristjánsson, Social Sciences professor at the University of Iceland, concurs with the view that Icelandic women need still further emancipation. "Foreigners who hear about Vigdís and the Women's Alliance assume we must live in a matriarchy, but this is not so. The very existence of the Women's Alliance is symptomatic of the weak political position women have." ❑

alsu ē ac lagde hvarni þa v̄ ha
ui ⁊ skipadi ⁊ sett skript v̓ h hefr
upp sogu ol ks haralldz sun̄

ÞA ER LANGT VAR

þca hegar liuird ucgr
hrra ihu xpi nuu hundrat
nuuta ag ⁊ þiriu tu ē þē
olaꝼi hr hinſ hauꝑ ok
xv ar. en a þyckia ꝼore ꝑ
vægiligr hīt olaꝼr tr s.
þcedde alla gudbrande
dott sueī barn þeg ecpt
et hue haꝑde v̄ ha lagt
bollatc. ꝑ vchi v̄ sumur sa
suerm uar nepndr olaꝼr
ē h uar uarlic aulin hiu
aerguligr sue at hr. kgl ok.

THE SAGAS

The medieval Icelandic sagas tell of the early settlers, their lives, families and struggles. These exciting stories, accessibly written, remain as popular as ever

The Icelandic saga is one of the world's most astonishing literary achievements. The anonymous 13th-century saga authors, who lived in a desolate northerly island in the midst of a raging civil war, were the first Europeans to write prose in their own language rather than in Latin. Why the sagas were written, whether they are history or fiction, who composed them, no-one knows. But the greatest of them – the romantic *Laxdæla Saga*; the thrilling adventures of the two outlaws Gísli Súrsson and Grettir; the tale of the rogue warrior-poet Egill Skallagrímsson; and above all the magnificent epic *Njáls Saga* – can hold up their heads proudly in the midst of any literary company from Homer to Shakespeare.

Classified under the term "saga" – which in Icelandic simply means "story" – are countless historical chronicles, romances, legends, and lives of kings and holy men. But what most people have in mind are the family sagas – 40 or so chronicles about the lives of various Icelandic families in the years following the land's settlement. The events they describe therefore occur around 200 to 300 years before the sagas were written, but until the 20th century they were taken as undisputed historical fact, passed down the generations orally until being finally recorded on manuscript. More recent scholarship, however, holds that they are basically works of fiction. The identity of the authors remains a mystery, although the chieftain Snorri Sturluson (*see panel on page 40*), author of *Heimskringla*, the history of the Norwegian kings, is generally acknowledged to have written the saga of Egill Skallagrímsson.

Bloody chronicles

To summarise a saga story-line is almost impossible. They are great epic sprawls, which span many generations with dozens of characters and sub-plots. One 18th-century Icelandic

PRECEDING PAGES: detail of a vellum manuscript of one of the sagas. **LEFT AND RIGHT:** saga manuscripts on display at the Árni Magnússon Institute.

scholar summed them up with the sardonic epigram "farmers at fisticuffs". He has a point – much of the action centres around blood-feuds, killings and conflict. But there is, of course, much more to them than that. They were written at a time of social chaos, when Iceland, North Europe's first republic, was being brought back under the rule of foreign monarchs because of internal power struggles and conflicts. They contain a retrospective warning to the authors' contemporaries. As Njáll, the sage-prophet hero of *Njáls Saga*, says: "with laws we shall build our land, but with lawlessness it shall be laid waste." At the same time, there is a certain nostalgia for a heroic golden age where men fought, to be sure, but for honour rather than power and politics.

Bearing in mind that Iceland was being subjugated to the Norwegian king, there is a rather wistful recurring theme of Icelanders being feted and honoured at foreign courts, and being showered with gifts by, or getting the better of, various European monarchs. In the short saga of Halldór Snorrason, for example, the eponymous hero actually forces the Norwegian king Harald Hardrada at swordpoint to hand over his rightful bounty.

Morality and fate

The narrator of the sagas makes few moral judgements, but the sagas themselves are not much preoccupied with good and evil in the modern sense. Most of the characters are mixed, and unmitigated villains are rare – the cunning lawyer in *Njáls Saga*, Mörður Valgarðsson, is one of the few that spring to mind.

dying Viking's words, as he has a spear thrust into his gut, were "I see the broad spears are now in fashion."

The story of Egill

An archetypal dark hero (*see also pages 88–9*) is Egill Skallagrímsson. Historically, Egill was one of the greatest of the early Icelandic *skálds* (poets), but unfortunately, as his saga records, also a phenomenal drinker and a murderous psychopath. The grandchild of a werewolf and a most precocious youth, he was forbidden to go to a feast when he was three years old because, as his father said, "you are difficult

Despite being composed in a Christian society, the sagas portray the old pagan Viking morality. Oathbreaking, meanness and cowardice are the worst sins; open-handedness, courage and honour the greatest virtues. "Better to die honourably than to live on in shame," as *Flóamanna Saga* puts it.

Fate plays the strongest role in determining men's actions. Tragedy is usually the result of *ógæfa* – a near-untranslatable word, meaning more or less "ill luck."

The sagas are written in a highly distinctive terse and economic style. The dry, laconic viewpoint, both of the narrative and the characters, sometimes borders on parody. One

enough to cope with when you are sober." The toddler made his way alone across country to the feast regardless, sat at high table and composed a boastful rhyme in honour of his exploit. He committed his first killing when he was eight, and went on to cause trouble wherever he went. Never the most placid of men, he once took such umbrage at a drinking feast that he vomited vast quantities of sour milk-curds into the mouth of his host, and, waking next morning with a raging hangover, continued to act

---

ABOVE: illustrated saga manuscript dating from the 13th century.
RIGHT: a display from the Árni Magnússon Institute.

the perfect guest by storming into his host's bedchamber and gouging out his eye.

Egill was, it would seem, a poet almost by necessity – he composed his greatest poem, *Sonatorrek*, to stop himself committing suicide after the death of his two sons. Another of his most celebrated poems, *Höfuðlausn* (Head-ransom), was to save his head after having foolishly upset King Eric Bloodaxe at York. He was to be executed in the morning, but, on reciting to the king the poem he had composed in his dungeon overnight, he was pardoned.

Inexplicably, Egill lived to a ripe and cantankerous old age. His final act, when he was aged around 80, was to hide his treasure so others could not enjoy it, and then to kill the unfortunate slaves that had helped him to do the deed.

The early settlers were mostly inter-related – not surprisingly in such a small community – and many of the characters pop up in more than one saga. Thus, the fearsome Egill turns up again in *Laxdæla Saga*, rather uncharacteristically, as a kindly and considerate father who refuses to marry his daughter Þorgerður to Ólafur the Peacock without her consent. This Þorgerður is certainly her father's daughter: when her son Kjartan is slain, she presses her

A LIFE'S WORK

Árni Magnússon was an Icelandic scholar who devoted his life to tracking down, saving and collating the vast number of vellum saga manuscripts that were taken away to Denmark during the days of colonial rule. Educated in Denmark, Árni returned to Iceland in 1702 to conduct a census and spent the next decade obtaining every medieval document that could be bought and laboriously copying out the rest.

Árni's almost supernatural knack of sniffing out manuscripts has become legendary: on one occasion he discovered a vellum that had been made into a template from which to cut out waistcoats! Árni took back with him no fewer than 55 cases full of manuscripts. As one of the leading scholars in Scandinavia, he was able to continue the task from his post as Secretary of the Royal Archives in the University of Copenhagen, using his considerable influence to amass the world's best collection of Old Icelandic documents.

Tragically, fire swept through Copenhagen in 1728 and although Árni pulled most of his manuscripts from the flames, many were lost. Modern historians believe that the best parts of the collection were probably saved, but the trauma may have been too much for the ageing scholar, who died 15 months later.

menfolk to avenge him, and then accompanies them to the slaughter, afraid that their blood-lust might falter unless she was present to egg them on.

The long journey home

The sagas themselves play a key role in the national psyche – they are symbolic not only of the nation's heroic past and of its literary achievements, but also of its survival. Thus it was a matter of intense national importance to have the original manuscripts returned to Iceland after centuries of "exile" overseas. Many had been taken to Denmark, the ruling colonial

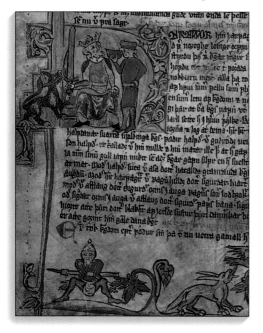

power, by researchers who combed Iceland during the 17th and 18th centuries. The most famous and indefatigable of these researchers was Árni Magnússon (*see page 85*).

The Icelandic manuscripts that Árni Magnússon amassed remained at the University of Copenhagen – the undisputed centre of learning for Denmark, Norway and Iceland – for more than two and a half centuries. But as Iceland began to claim self-rule from Denmark in the late 1800s, so too did nationalists press for the return of its literary heritage. When the country became independent in 1944, the fate of the manuscripts was contested. After years of wrangling and legal cases, Denmark finally agreed

to return the bulk of the Icelandic manuscripts in 1961, hanging onto those relating to other Scandinavian countries. But it was not until a decade later that the first two books – the precious *Codex Regius* (containing the Poetic Eddas) and *Flateyjarbók* (the most important collection of sagas) – crossed the Atlantic in a Danish naval frigate. On 21 April 1971, thousands of spectators flocked to Reykjavík harbour to watch the manuscripts' arrival, carried ashore by naval officers in a solemn ceremony.

Since that day, 1,800 manuscripts have been returned by successive Danish governments. The Icelandic Manuscript Institute, founded in 1961 to take on the responsibility of caring for the books, was renamed the Árni Magnússon Institute (*see page 163*) in 1972 after the great Icelandic researcher.

Sagas in modern Iceland

Numerous phrases from the old sagas spring readily to the lips of many modern Icelanders. For example, "*Fögur er hlíðin*" (how fair the slopes are), the first line of Gunnar of Hlíðarendi's lyrical speech, when he decides not to go into foreign exile but instead to stay in his beloved homeland and face his doom, has been a patriotic catchphrase since the days of the independence struggle in the 19th century. One of Njáll's famous sayings, "*með lögum skal land byggja*" (with laws shall we build our land) was a punning slogan of one of the leading Icelandic record companies – "*lögum*" can also mean tunes.

Heroes and villains of the sagas live on in the language. A large boulder is known as a *Grettistak* after the saga strongman's ability to lift such things, and a liar is known as a *lygamörður* after the nefarious scoundrel of *Njáls Saga,* Mörður Valgarðsson.

Visible remains of the sagas

Although the sagas are a complex mix of fact and fiction, most of their events can be located at actual places in Iceland. In many cases there are no remains of any buildings or features mentioned, but there are a few exceptions. Many saga readers find it fascinating to visit these valleys, hills and occasionally buildings that still resonate with the historical events portrayed. Perhaps the most well-known and best preserved saga site is Snorri's pool at Reykholt in the West of Iceland (*see page 227*).

Also in the West are the remains of Erik the Red's farmstead. Erik married Þjóðhildur, a local farmer's daughter in Haukadalur valley, and built a farm there called Eiríksstaðir. His son Leifur, who later travelled to America, was born near there. Erik went on to be exiled from Haukadalur for killing some of his enemies, and made his way to Brokey island in Breiðafjörður, from where he was also exiled. Excavations on a site thought to be Eiríksstaðir in 1997 proved that the ruins dated from between 890 and 980.

A LIVING LANGUAGE

The Icelandic language is almost unchanged since the Middle Ages, making the medieval sagas readily understandable to the modern Icelandic reader.

Keeping the sagas alive

Unlike most ancient literature elsewhere, which was both composed and enjoyed by a small and privileged elite, the sagas have, since the time of their conception, been the property of the common people. Also uniquely, they remain accessible to the ordinary people of Iceland in their original language.

The sagas are still a living literature – numerous films and plays have been made based on the saga stories, and nearly every Icelander is familiar with the characters

They revealed that Erik lived in a hall with a central fireplace and a ledge for seating set into the walls. The walls themselves, made of turf on a rock foundation were about 1.5 metres (5 ft) thick. The design is fairly basic, suggesting that the farm was only occupied for a few years.

The Rangárvallasýsla in the Southwest is the location of many of the events in *Njáls Saga*, and a Saga Centre has been opened there which offers jeep tours to many of the sites (*see pages 193 and 196–7*).

LEFT: a 13th-century saga manuscript.
ABOVE: Snorri's pool at Reykholt, where the great chieftain used to bathe.

and plots of the major works. Nevertheless, there is some concern that the sagas are developing into rarefied literary relics – with the advent of television, video and paperback bestsellers, young people are no longer reading the sagas as before.

Some critics feel that in all the fuss and discussion over their historical, national and academic importance, the fact that they are, above all, excellent stories has been forgotten. As Jón Böðvarsson, who runs saga study groups for the general public, says: "We should treat them like ordinary novels. That way people can carry on reading them for enjoyment – the way they were originally intended." ❏

HEROES AND HEROINES OF THE SAGAS

The sagas are populated with memorable and vividly drawn characters that are very human in their desires, actions and frailties.

One of the recurring themes of the Icelandic sagas is the difference between the fortunate "light" heroes and the unlucky "dark" heroes. The romantic Kjartan Ólafsson of *Laxdæla Saga* is an archetypal light hero – handsome, accomplished and brave. In a similar mould is Gunnar of Hlíðarendi in *Njáls Saga*: "He was a handsome man...extremely well-bred, fearless, generous and even-tempered... It has been said that there has never been his equal."

The peerless Gunnar contrasts sharply with Skarphéðinn, son of Njáll, who was "quick to speak and scathing in his words... He had a crooked nose and prominent teeth, which made him ugly round the mouth. He looked every inch a warrior." Dark heroes such as Skarphéðinn are often ugly, awkward men, at odds with society – the conventional romantic hero pales into insignificance compared with these enigmatic, tormented figures.

The saga women were no less formidable than their male counterparts. *Njáls Saga* contain two bloodthirsty and ruthless women – Hildigunnur and Hallgerður Long-Legs. But queen of these indomitable women is Guðrún Ósvífursdóttir, heroine of *Laxdæla Saga*, who marries four times in the course of her stormy career, and ends her days as Iceland's first nun.

▽ **NJÁLL THE WISE**
One of the main "light" heroes, and the main protagonist of *Njáls Saga*, a wise man, a pacifist and a true friend.

▽ **GRETTIR THE STRONG**
The "dark" hero of *Grettis Saga*: an outlaw, strong and courageous, but quarrelsome and extremely unfortunate.

△ ASSEMBLY PLAINS

For centuries, the Alþingi, the national assembly of the Icelanders, took place on the plains at Þingvellir, the scene of many of the events recounted in the sagas.

HISTORY AND FICTION

In the Middle Ages the Icelanders were the historians of the North. The surviving saga manuscripts by anonymous authors preserve most of our present knowledge of North European history and learning during this period. At the same time they sketch the outlines of Nordic identity. In a sense, they are frontier literature, in which the descendants of the settlers reflect on their origins, legends and myths, while dealing with some difficult aspects of their own contemporary reality, like the 13th century civil war. They looked back upon the settlement period as a golden age, with a well-functioning commonwealth of free chieftains.

The sagas were intended not only as a record of events but also as entertainment. Their authors therefore added a generous pinch of fiction to these tales of families and feuds. This mixture is probably what has given them their enduring appeal. Passed down through generations of Icelanders retelling saga tales on a winter's night, they are still a central part of the national consciousness.

△ HALLGERÐUR LONG-LEGS
One of the most remarkable female saga-heroes: wicked, beautiful and partly responsible for her husband Gunnar of Hlíðarendi's death.

▷ AMULET OF THOR
During the course of the sagas, the heroes changed from worship of Odin and Thor to belief in Christianity – a cause of many disputes.

THE POWER OF WORDS

Modern Icelanders are avid readers – in this they are carrying on
a passion for language and literature that has existed for centuries

To the Icelander, the mother tongue is far more than just a method of communication – it is the essence of culture, and its nurture and preservation is inextricably tied up with the survival of national identity and pride. Icelanders know in their heart of hearts that the Icelandic language is, as the poet Einar

Preserving an ancient language

What would be regarded in other countries as normal linguistic developments are seen as national disasters in Iceland. There is, for example, "dative sickness" – a terrible and contagious disease which causes sufferers to put nouns which should be in the nominative or

Benediktsson said, "more noble than that of any other nation."

Icelandic is one of the North Germanic family of languages, its nearest relatives still in use being Norwegian and Faroese. Thanks to centuries of comparative isolation, it is still very similar to old Norse, the language that was spoken by most of Northern Europe during the 7th to 11th centuries, and is the only language to still use the old runic symbols of ð (ed) and þ (thorn). Although no longer isolated, the language continues in its unaltered state – for Icelanders will fight to the death against any influences which might corrupt or change their beloved mother tongue.

accusative case into the dative. Like most ancient languages, Icelandic is a complex minefield of case endings, subjunctives and inflections which can catch out many native speakers, let alone foreign students. Nevertheless, any grammatical slip-ups are considered social solecisms of the worst order, and if committed by a guardian of public linguistic morals, such as a radio-show host, a grave offence.

Icelandic is known as Latin of the North not only because the language itself has remained unchanged – it has also preserved, in its litera-

ABOVE: reading on a long winter's night.
RIGHT: an enormous choice in a Reykjavík bookshop.

ture, the ancient Norse culture. The golden age of Icelandic literature, beginning around 1100 with the historical chronicle *Landnámabók* (*Book of Settlements*), was one of the richest and most diverse in medieval Europe (*see* The Sagas, *pages 83–7*). Even more invaluable, for providing a feeling of the way of life, thoughts and priorities of these people, is the poetry they have left behind them. Icelanders were, from the start, poets. Between the 9th and 13th centuries there were 100 Icelandic poets working around the courts of Europe; after the end of the 10th century the position of court poet in Scandinavia was held only by Icelanders.

A PATRIOTIC POET

The poet Snorri Hjartason wrote: "Land, nation and language – the only true trinity."

The role of the poet

The poet or *skáld* had an elevated, even mystical status. He was entrusted with preserving the tribe's deeds in his poems, and raising morale with heroic verse. The Icelandic *skálds* have always been important members of society. Many, for example, took an active part in the independence struggle – and poetic talent has always been regarded as the sign of a noble personality.

KEEPING THE LANGUAGE PURE

In the spirit of individuality typical of Iceland, foreign influences on the Icelandic language are kept strictly in check, and great care is taken to prevent the language becoming diluted. Icelanders have no truck with such international loan-words as "radio", "telephone" or "computer", which have infiltrated many other languages. Academic committees are set up to find proper, Icelandic words for these various new-fangled phenomena. Thus, the computer was christened *tölva* – a mixture of the word *tala* ("number") and *völva* ("prophetess"). The telephone became *sími*, from an ancient word meaning "thread". A helicopter is a *þyrla* or "whirler"; a jet aircraft is a *þota* or

"zoomer". Even scientific language is kept as firmly non-Latin as possible. The general public joins in the fun of "word-building", and a raging debate almost always seems to ensue.

Some of these neologisms are wittily creative. Even such an eminently post-Freudian figure as the voyeur is cut down to size in Icelandic as a *gluggagægir*, the name of one of the 13 traditional harbingers of Christmas, who used to spy in through farm windows. And the tiny "beepers" or breast-pocket pagers used to call busy businessmen to the nearest phone have been dubbed *Friðþjófur*, a man's name meaning literally "thief of the peace".

The Eddic poems, like those by the *skálds*, were composed in accordance with strict rules of internal rhyme and alliteration, but are much more accessible. These works, which deal with heroic or mythological subjects, were written down at the same time as the sagas, but most of them were probably composed much earlier. Poems such as *Hávamál* give a vivid insight into the Viking mind, revealing a people preoccupied with honour, who were sociable, generous but highly pragmatic: "Cattle die, kindred die, we ourselves also die," runs one oft-quoted line, "but the fair fame never dies, of him who well deserves it". Thus another: "A man should

be a friend to his friend, and repay gift with gift. Men should meet smiles with smiles and lies with treachery".

Then there is *Völuspá*, or Sybil's prophecy, a poem composed by an unknown Icelander in the 11th century, and the best information we have today about the old pagan mythology. It tells the history of the world, its destruction at Ragnarök (the Wagnerian *Götterdämmerung* or Twilight of the Gods) and its eventual rebirth.

In the Dark Ages, Iceland's loss of independence dampened literary creativity, although some original literature was produced, such as the Passion Psalms of 17th-century clergyman Hallgrímur Pétursson. The old language and literature were treasured through the years of poverty, dirt, death and disease. Since medieval times, Icelanders have always been able to read and write – children could not be confirmed until they were literate – and learning has been held in high esteem. Foreign travellers wrote of being addressed in Latin and ancient Greek by filthy half-starved natives, and taken into huts to look at priceless manuscripts.

Poetry and politics

In the 19th century, with improving social conditions and a growing independence movement, the *skáld* came back into his own. The poet Jónas Hallgrímsson, born in 1807, was the poet who reached the hearts of his people as no-one else has before or since. Known as "the nation's beloved son," he was the first Icelander to have a statue raised to his memory by his countrymen. A Romantic in the high tradition, Jónas was at the forefront of the struggle for Icelandic independence from Danish rule, and his poetry is full of love for his native land: its language, heritage, countryside and golden-haired girls.

He was a poetic radical – like Wordsworth, he wrote in the common tongue rather than high-flown poetic simile. He was also a highly qualified botanist, and travelled round the highlands each summer, collecting material for a comprehensive account of Iceland's natural history – a huge task he was never to complete.

Jónas, from rural North Iceland, spent much of his adult life in Copenhagen where he wrote some of his best work, including *Ísland*, a testimony to former glories and call for a better future that every Icelander knows by heart:

Iceland, happy homeland,
fortunate frost-white mother,
where is your ancient honour,
your freedom and deeds of renown...

Jónas suffered a great deal of hardship and exposure during his botanical explorations, and these, coupled with poverty and drink, took a heavy toll on his health. He put the seal on his reputation by dying a true poet's death – young, poverty-stricken and alone.

By the early 20th century, the Icelandic *skáld* was taking his first tentative steps into the modern world. Einar Benediktsson (1864–1940) wrote beautiful, eminently quotable poetry. An

LEFT: the 19th-century poet Jónas Hallgrímsson.
RIGHT: the late Halldór Laxness.

exceptionally urbane and cosmopolitan man, he was also somewhat eccentric and gained notoriety after allegedly trying to sell the Gullfoss waterfall and the northern lights abroad.

Contemporary voices

Pétur Gunnarsson, one of the first "urban novelists", innovated the use of colloquial, humorous first person narrative. Þór Vilhjálmsson makes use of fragmented language and cultural reference to come to terms with modern life, while Guðbergur Bergsson criticises the nouveau riche American-worshipping culture of the postwar period through absurd humour.

Writer Einar Már Guðmundsson was awarded the Nordic Council's Literature Award in 1995. Among women writers Svava Jakobsdóttir has developed a unique brand of surreal feminism, while the lyrical narrative method of Vigdís Grímsdóttir is much admired.

There have also been great innovations in poetry. The *atomskálds* of the 1950s caused a storm of controversy when they broke all the rigid, old poetic rules and began to write in free verse. But modern or traditional, the latter-day *skálds* of Iceland still take their responsibilities seriously. They are above all guardians of the holy trinity: language, land and nation. ❏

HALLDÓR LAXNESS

By far the most important modern literary figure is Halldór Kiljan Laxness, winner of the 1955 Nobel Prize for Literature, who died in 1998. Laxness broke away from the idealisation of peasant life prevalent in Icelandic writing, portraying the dark underside of rural life, which caused resentment amongst those who felt he was presenting Iceland in a bad light. But, in his own way, Laxness was as fervent a patriot as any. His novel *Bell of Iceland*, set in the 18th century, contains references to the contemporary independence struggle: "A fat and sleek servant is not a great man," Laxness wrote. "A beaten slave is a great man, for freedom lives in his breast". The postwar *Atom Station*, from the time of the NATO airbase controversy, contains pointed criticism of the politicians who were ready to sign away their country's independence out of greed. His best-known creation is Bjartur of Summerhouses, the peasant crofter hero of *Independent People*. Stubborn, infuriating but "the most independent man in the country", Bjartur has come to represent the archetypal Icelander. His best work, *World Light*, is a trilogy dealing with the poet's role in society. He showed other writers what could be done with the language – he played around with it, changed spellings, used street language and made up or even borrowed words.

LIVING WITH THE ENVIRONMENT

Iceland is a place of extremes, from long nights in winter and even longer days in summer, to heavy snow, to the threat of volcanic eruptions

The English traveller John Stanley, who visited Iceland in 1789, commented: "I pitied the poor Icelanders who could not like swallows gather themselves together for a flight to a climate less hostile to the comforts of human existence. What the Icelanders can enjoy deserving the name of happiness during the long winter I cannot imagine."

There is not so much reason to pity the poor Icelanders these days. Warm, centrally heated houses have taken the place of damp turf huts, electric light does much to compensate for the long hours of darkness, and powerful snow-ploughs mean that only the most isolated settlements are cut off during the winter months.

In fact, during winter, the inhabited areas around Iceland's coast do not experience the bitter extremes of cold that the country's name would suggest. Iceland is washed by the warm waters of the Gulf Stream and moderate south-westerly Atlantic winds, ensuring that – although summers are definitely chilly by most people's standards – the Icelandic winters are actually milder than in more southerly places such as New York or Moscow. Temperatures below -10°C (14°F) in Reykjavík are unusual.

The dreaded wind and rain

Even so, as any visitor to Iceland will quickly find out, living with the climate here is still no picnic. Iceland's real plague is wind and rain. The same Gulf Stream and mild winds that bring moderate weather run up against the Icelandic mountains and the icy polar air to create some wretched weather. Although there are the occasional freak summers, Reykjavík normally enjoys only one completely clear day every July. In January, the average goes up to three.

The combination of gales and rain renders umbrellas completely useless, and a local joke is that Iceland is the only place where the rain falls from all directions – including horizontal.

PRECEDING PAGES: riding the stocky Icelandic horse.
LEFT: dressing up against extreme conditions at sea.
RIGHT: another rainy day in Reykjavík.

Even so, it is not uncommon to see Icelanders wandering around without any protection during quite heavy downpours. Ask them why and they might shrug: "It's rained here since I was a child. I don't even notice it any more."

The weather is worst around the southwest, improving markedly around Akureyri, the north

and east. But luckily for travellers and Icelanders alike, the true norm for Icelandic weather is its sheer unpredictability, shifting rapidly from clear to miserably wet, then back again, several times in the course of a single day.

The polar night

Despite the blessings that the Gulf Stream brings, the Icelandic winter can still be a cold, long and miserable affair. At this high latitude, it is also particularly dark. Iceland is almost completely outside the Arctic Circle (only part of the northern island of Grímsey is within its bounds), so it avoids the true extremes of months of darkness that are associated with northern Greenland and the Arctic icecap. Even so, things here are quite bad enough. During the months of December and January there are no more than five hours of daylight a day anywhere in the country.

That's when Icelanders begin to suffer from *skammdegis-þunglyndi*, "short day depression". As some sort of compensation, winter is the best time to see the ghostly aurora borealis (northern lights) – shimmering green and mauve waves of astral electricity flickering in the starry sky.

CELEBRATING THE LIGHT

Many villages in the West Fjords are dark all winter as mountains block out all the sunlight. At the first sighting of the sun in February or March, inhabitants celebrate with "sunshine coffee".

This can be seen on the island of Grímsey, from the mountains close to Ólafsfjörður or from the northeast coastline near Raufarhöfn (where the northernmost point of the mainland lies just 2.5km south of the Arctic Circle). However, even without the true midnight sun, for the rest of Iceland real night never falls during the months of June and July, with the sun only just skimming below the horizon at midnight: an extended dusk is the only sign of the passing of the day, and the stars do not come out until August.

Waiting for the sunshine

Across the country, Icelanders wait impatiently each year for the first signs of spring. The first sightings of migrating birds, particularly the golden plover *(lóa)* – the "harbinger of spring" – are reported extensively in the local press. By the middle of May the grass is turning green and wild flowers are appearing. When summer truly arrives in June, the long winter wait seems almost worth it. Although temperatures are hardly tropical, between 12–15°C (54–60°F), the sun shines almost all night.

Strictly speaking, it is only above the Arctic Circle that the true "midnight sun" occurs, whereby the sun never dips below the horizon.

Summer fever

Foreign visitors have often commented that Icelanders remind them of hibernating animals, sleeping in winter and letting rip in summer. June and July – and, to a lesser extent, August – are the times when Iceland's national parks are filled to overflowing on weekends and when the country's interior is criss-crossed with frantic drivers speeding around in their huge-wheeled vehicles. The *joie de vivre* is contagious and normal rules go by the board, with even very small children playing out in the street until midnight. Foreign visitors often find these endless days as difficult to cope with as the long winter nights: it's not easy to sleep when the sun is glistening through the window. However, there are advantages for the visitor. Photographers will find the golden light of the early mornings and late nights in Iceland at this time of year particularly beautiful.

At any time of year, Iceland's unpolluted arctic air makes visibility almost supernaturally clear. Far away objects often seem deceptively close: on a fine day in Reykjavík, for example, the distant icecap of Snæfellsnes looks as if it is only a few miles across a small bay.

FATA MORGANA

A curious form of mirage, the Fata Morgana, can occur on Iceland's sandy glacial deserts *(sandur)*, whereby islands or rock formations appear on the horizon.

work entirely on a voluntary basis, will monitor travellers and organise search-parties if they do not return to base on schedule. They do get rather annoyed, however, at having to risk life and limb rescuing people who have got into trouble through sheer foolhardiness, so it is best to use your commonsense and ensure that you take sensible precautions, such as not venturing onto a glacier alone, and not attempting to climb unknown mountains or in unfamiliar areas except with an experienced guide.

The dangers of nature

Icelandic weather is notoriously unpredictable, and a raging storm can appear out of a clear blue sky in minutes. Temperatures can plummet to -30°C (-22°F), with wind chill factor, in the deserted highlands of the interior.

Stranded trippers and mountaineers need not despair completely, however – as long as they had the presence of mind to notify the National Association of Rescue Groups of their journey before they set off. This fine body of men, who

The treacherous sea

Against some natural forces even the most careful precautions are to all intents and purposes useless. The ocean is the source of Iceland's livelihood, but it can also be a killer. Despite enormous improvements in safety aboard fishing vessels, the life of the fisherman remains a dangerous one, and there are many Icelandic women who have been widowed by the treacherous seas.

Nor is one safe on Icelandic dry land, either. Scientists at National Civil Defence monitor each tiny seismological tremor with concern. In the absence of an army, the NCD is also responsible for conducting rescue operations in

LEFT: lounging by a natural jacuzzi at Hveravellir.
ABOVE: snatching the opportunity to soak up some of those rare summer rays.

the event of other natural disasters; storms, avalanches, floods and volcanic eruptions are all major threats.

On average, there is a volcanic eruption somewhere in Iceland every five years. During the 20th century there were more than 20 eruptions, many of which occurred unseen, deep beneath the mighty glacier Vatnajökull. No-one, however failed to notice the two most celebrated eruptions – the one off the south coast in 1963, which formed a completely new island, Surt-

> **AVALANCHE DANGER**
>
> Perhaps surprisingly, avalanches are the most dangerous of all the natural hazards that plague Iceland: 63 people have died in them since 1974.

sey, and 10 years later, the eruption on the Vestmannaeyjar (Westmann Islands). Suddenly, in the middle of the night, what was believed to be an extinct volcano on the inhabited island of Heimaey began to erupt. Fortunately, the fishing fleet was moored in the harbour that night, and every one of the 5,300 inhabitants of the island was successfully evacuated to the mainland (*see panel on page 203*).

A more devastating eruption was that of Lakagígar in 1783, especially as the country's inhabitants could not then call upon modern technology to aid them. The lava flow, produced by some 100 craters in a volcanic fissure more than 25 km (15 miles) long, was the great-

est ever recorded in human world history, and it eventually covered an area of 565 sq. km (218 sq. miles). It was Iceland's most cataclysmic natural disaster, and the eruption, and the Haze Famine that came in its aftermath, caused the deaths of thousands of people.

This episode, terrible though it was, is just one of many in the long saga of the Icelanders' battle with their environment. Nor are these the only environmental problems.

Another old enemy is erosion. Iceland was once, according to the old chronicles, heavily forested, but now there is a startling absence of trees, and most natural vegetation is scrubby tundra. Not only is this a shame aesthetically, but the lack of trees means there is little to bind the soil, which is bad news on a such a windswept island.

Exploiting the volcanic landscape

A natural force can occasionally be tamed and made to earn its keep. Iceland's homes have been provided with cheap and environmentally friendly hot water and heating for the past 60 years by geothermal energy – water heated naturally under the earth's crust. This water is also used to heat the 150,000 sq. metres (37 acres) of greenhouse, used for growing fruit and vegetables, in the town of Hveragerði – the country's market-garden under glass.

And geothermal energy is also the reason that Icelanders can enjoy an open-air swim on the most bitterly cold and snowy morning – and soak afterwards in a 45°C (113°F) hot pool. Swimming in Iceland is not so much a hobby as a way of life, and the geothermal pools have a total attendance of around 1.5 million people a year. Swimming baths are one of the main focuses of social life, and many of the country's most important decisions are made in lunch-time hot pool sessions.

Icelanders have been used to regarding their geothermal water as a bottomless pit – one swimming pool, for example, uses up 1.3 million tons of water a day – but there are indications that the reserves in Reykjavík may be drying up because of overuse.

One natural resource that is in no current danger of overexploitation is hydroelectricity. With so much surplus energy, it seems logical to try to export some of it abroad. Now, with the development of ultra-low resistance wires, this scheme may soon become technologically and economically feasible, and there are already plans afoot to lay underwater cables across the ocean to Britain, and even to Germany.

Tourism is very much on the increase in Iceland, and is one of the island's most important industries, bringing in 12–15 percent of the total foreign currency earnings. However, the environment, which is seemingly so rugged and powerful, is extremely fragile – and the authorities are as a result not keen to see it grow out of control. "Iceland isn't open safari country," says Þíroddur Þóroddsen of the National Conservation Council. "We want tourists who are sensitive to the environment."

ROAD NETWORK

Iceland has more than 13,000 km (8,000 miles) of roads, and approximately 8,000 km (5,000 miles) of them are classified as major roads.

Keeping the roads open

Although Iceland does not fully merit its chilly name, winters are prolonged and snow can be heavy, but this does not discourage the Icelanders from travelling as much as possible all year round. A few decades ago, the sea was the most important route for travel between Iceland's dispersed coastal communities. Roads hardly existed, and the coastal boats transported passengers and goods alike. Today, however, the motor vehicle is king, and overland travel has become the norm.

A vastly improved road system means that land travel is possible throughout the year, if a little difficult at times. If the road network seems, to the outsider, to be a series of primitive unsurfaced tracks with the occasional stretch of tarmac, the outsider should bear in mind that it is a huge, and vastly expensive, transport network for such a small population in such a large country. The quality of the roads has advanced by leaps and bounds since the 1960s, and will undoubtedly continue to do so.

Policy laid down by the Ministry of Communications aims to keep all major roads passable, as far as possible, throughout the winter months: the first priority is given to keeping open routes between centres of population

LEFT: a geothermally heated pool in Reykjavík.
RIGHT: keeping roads open during the winter is a major task.

within each region. These are generally cleared every working day, and even more frequently in the event of unusually heavy snow. Roads out of Reykjavík, north to Borgarfjörður and east to Hvolsvöllur, for instance, are very rarely closed to traffic for more than a few hours at a time.

The second-highest priority is placed upon keeping clear roads linking one region to the next, such as the South to the East Fjords, or the route from Akureyri to Reykjavík. These roads are cleared two or three times weekly on

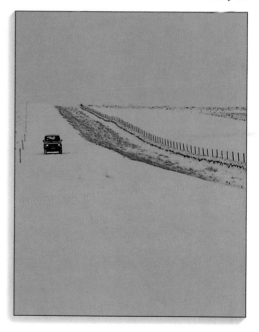

average, ensuring that traffic will get through at least on those days.

Minor roads, however, are cleared less frequently, if at all. Mountain tracks across the interior, such as Kjölur and Sprengisandur, are summer-only roads and are normally closed by snow by the end of October. Although mountain roads are largely free of snow again by May, meltwater from the same snow turns them into impassable seas of mud, and they are only reopened once they are dry enough to sustain traffic, usually in late June or early July.

The Public Roads Administration assesses the state of the highland roads, decides when to open them for traffic, and closely monitors traffic on the highlands. Unauthorised travel on the muddy roads in early spring can cause havoc to the road surface, and offenders are subject to heavy fines.

Although all efforts are made to keep the road network functioning, even in severe winters, the possibilities of wintertime travelling in an ordinary family car are severely limited, not least due to the unpredictable climate. The traveller may set off from home on a fine clear winter day, only to find a blinding snowstorm just over the next mountain. Ordinary saloon cars (especially without four-wheel-drive) are not happy with this kind of test. Icelanders,

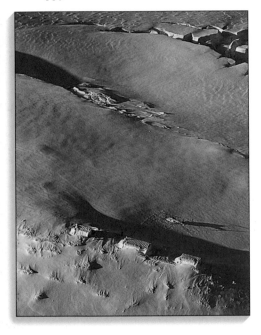

however, have taken enthusiastically to big four-wheel-drive vehicles which can operate in almost any road conditions, and wintertime travel has become a popular hobby.

Alternative routes

Some major routes over highland passes – such as those into the mountainous West Fjords – are subject to such heavy snowfalls that they cannot necessarily be kept open through the winter, and they may be closed for weeks or months. Alternative routes at lower altitudes remain open, and in some regions the sea route provides the main winter link between communities. In the West Fjords in particular, travel

by sea still remains almost as important as in the past.

Air travel is of unusual importance in Iceland, and even more so in winter. It takes about five hours to drive the 389 km (243 miles) to Akureyri from Reykjavík, in good conditions. By air, you can get there in 45 minutes. In winter, with uncertain road conditions, the comparison becomes even more favourable. Flights are relatively rarely cancelled, although there can be delays, and Icelandic pilots attain great expertise in taking off, flying and landing in difficult, icy conditions.

The air route is also, of course, the emergency route into and out of most communities during the winter months. Scheduled flights operate frequently to major centres such as Akureyri, Ísafjörður, Höfn and Egilsstaðir, and they run less often – although still regularly – to a host of small centres around the country, where there may be no more than a landing strip and a windsock to indicate the "airport". For convenience and security, all airport roads are cleared regularly, and invariably in connection with scheduled flights.

Icy conditions

Snow is not the only hindrance to winter travel, though. Roads are often dangerously icy, mainly because of a tendency for Icelandic temperatures to hover around freezing point for much of the winter. The temperature may be 2–3°C (35–38°F) when snow falls, then warm up to reduce the snow to the consistency of a smooth mush. The thermometer might then plummet to -10°C (14°F), and the mush freezes, smooth as a skating rink.

Winter tyres are essential from October to May, even in towns, where all roads are cleared regularly in snow, and salted to reduce ice. Many Icelanders opt for nailed tyres, which give a better grip on icy road surfaces, although braking remains a problem on slippery roads. Heavy-tread snow tyres offer better braking, but may not provide enough grip for driving up slippery slopes. If you want to learn how to handle a car in a skid, Iceland is the place. With roads this slippery, you learn fast. ❑

LEFT: air access to remote huts near Grímsvötn on Vatnajökull icecap.
RIGHT: maximizing the growing season in one of Iceland's many greenhouses.

HARVESTING THE SEA

Fishing has provided food, employment and wealth for Iceland for centuries;
the challenge now is to avoid overexploiting the limited resources of the sea

"Life is saltfish," wrote Iceland's Nobel Laureate, the late Halldór Laxness in the 1930s. At the beginning of the 21st century, with the country's economy dependent on the sea more than ever before, life is still saltfish, but it's also canned fish, smoked salmon, frozen shrimps and caviar.

Fish has been an important export item from Iceland ever since the stockfish trade to Britain commenced in the Middle Ages. But fishing only began to outpace agriculture in economic status with the advent of motorised fishing vessels around the start of the 20th century. And while improvements in vessel technology soon made fisheries into Iceland's mainstay national industry, at the same time they intensified the threat of overfishing by foreign deep-sea fleets, which escalated until the famous Cod Wars with Britain.

The first 30 years of the 20th century were a time of intense, fisheries-led economic growth. Iceland was gradually escaping from Danish colonial rule, and economic independence was an obvious prerequisite for true political independence. Iceland's fishing industry has been coloured by fierce nationalism ever since.

Salted whitefish – mainly cod, sold to Spain – and iced whitefish and herring, sold to the UK and northern Europe, were the mainstays of Icelandic fisheries right up until World War II. Dependence on those few markets had its limitations: for example, Spanish wine producers threatening to ban imports of saltfish were able to "twist Iceland's arm" into lifting a six-year alcohol prohibition in 1921. Later, the collapse of the fish market in the Great Depression devastated Iceland's economy.

The fish boom begins

Unemployment ran high right up until World War II, when Iceland suddenly became the only large fish-producer in the whole of northern Europe. Icing their catches, Icelandic fishing vessels sailed directly to Britain, often suffering fatalities from U-boat attacks. Meanwhile, superior freezing technology was developed. This would become the key to the postwar fisheries boom which was targeted at both the UK and American markets.

PRECEDING PAGES: the morning catch.
LEFT: fishing boat entering Heimaey harbour.
RIGHT: a fisherman at Þórshöfn in 1908.

RICHES FROM THE SEA

Situated where warm Gulf Stream waters merge with the cold currents travelling down from the Arctic, Iceland's fishing grounds offer choice growth conditions for an enormous variety of species. These include demersal or bottom-feeding fish, led by cod, haddock, redfish (ocean perch), saithe (pollack), ocean catfish and flatfish such as Greenland halibut and plaice. There are also shellfish such as shrimp, scallops and Norway lobster (nephrops or scampi tails). Finally there are river-migrating fish, such as wild salmon, trout and Arctic charr, as well as pelagic (topwater) fish including herring and capelin.

Iceland made good money during the war and allocated funds for the modernisation of the trawler fleet, and an era of larger catches and more diverse markets began. Frozen block and fillets went to both sides of the Atlantic. During the Cold War, Iceland kept good trading relations with Eastern Europe, and the Soviet Union became a major buyer of products such as salted herring. Meanwhile, the diversification began which remains the key to Iceland's survival as a specialist fish-producing nation.

Of increasing importance in this environmentally conscious age is the cleanness of Iceland's fish. The fishing grounds are far enough land-based food processing. Unstable as its economy has been, Iceland has buffered itself against some heavy market shocks by shrewdly spreading its coverage and its product range.

The US was Iceland's main buyer of frozen fish from the 1970s to the mid-1980s, until a sliding dollar made Europe a more attractive proposition. Today, the two main European markets for both frozen and fresh (unprocessed) fish are the UK and Germany. Yet the two countries rarely compete, since the UK buys cod and haddock while the Germans prefer redfish and saithe. A north-south split in European buying trends also exists, with Portugal, Spain

from the industrial centres of Europe and North America to remain very pure, while the small local population and absence of large-scale manufacturing industries keep "home-grown" pollution to a bare minimum. And Iceland has even begun exporting the technology for catching and handling fish: in some specialist areas, such as the electronic weighing of fish at sea using scales that automatically compensate for the roll of the boat, Iceland is a world leader.

Surviving in a high-risk industry

Seafood is, however, a notoriously shaky business – size of catches can never be taken for granted and prices fluctuate far more than in and Italy (which all rank among Iceland's top 10 market countries) buying almost entirely saltfish and virtually no frozen or fresh.

Japan, the world's largest seafood market, became important for Iceland in the 1980s, yet hardly competed with established lines sold elsewhere. The oriental taste is for flatfish, whole-frozen redfish (Europeans and Americans prefer fillets), shell-on shrimp (the British and Danes prefer peeled), and previously unexploited delicacies such as capelin roe, whole-frozen female herring, cod milt (sperm) and sea urchins. France has also shot up the market table recently, with a more catholic appetite than most other buyers.

In terms of demand, the future looks promising. Awareness of the healthiness of a protein-rich, low-cholesterol seafood diet, backed by the clean image of the waters where Iceland catches its fish, look set to keep demand buoyant well into the 21st century. An agreement negotiated in 1991 with the EC removes most remaining tariff barriers for fish from Iceland in the 19-nation European "super-market." The onset of Creuztfeldt-Jacob and Foot and Mouth diseases has also led to an added demand for fish in important markets.

> **SUCCESSFUL INDUSTRY**
>
> Although only about 10 percent of the Icelandic population is employed in the fishing industry, it makes up 90 percent of the GNP.

the maximum level of safe harvesting, and with a fleet powerful enough to vacuum-clean the ocean floor in a couple of weeks, the industry is being forced to scale down its operations. This is not a new problem. Over-fishing by foreign fleets was a strong fear in Iceland in the early postwar period. The traditional 3-mile (5-km) exclusive fishing zone around Iceland's coast was extended to 4 miles (6.5 km) in 1952, and even though this seems like a drop in the ocean now, it sparked massive protests and a temporary ban on fish imports

Fisheries contribute three quarters of Iceland's exports, and a seafood-led boom in 1987–88 saw the country's economy clock up one of the highest annual growth rates in Gross Domestic Product in European history, at over 8 percent. All this, although only 4.4 percent of Iceland's population is employed on fishing vessels and 5.6 percent in land-based processing plants.

The Cod Wars

The big problem since the start of the 1990s has been supply. Major stocks are at or beyond

---

LEFT: fish-processing indoors.
ABOVE: testing another popular product, cod-liver oil.

from Iceland in the UK. The first real "Cod War" began in 1959 when Iceland upped its territorial waters to 12 miles (20 km) and Royal Navy frigates were sent in to protect, unsuccessfully, British trawlers from being evicted or arrested by Iceland's tiny coastguard force.

Eventually the dispute was resolved, only to be followed by successive extensions to 50 miles (80 km) in 1972 and 200 miles (330 km) in 1975. This renewed more ferocious clashes, although no fatalities ever occurred. While the British gunboats rammed coastguard vessels and fired shots over their bows, the ultimate deterrent in the Icelandic arsenal was the dreaded "clippers" – rather like garden shears –

which were used to cut trawls from British vessels, removing both their nets and their catches. Some of these clippers are now proudly, if rather mock-heroically, on display in the National Museum in Reykjavík.

On one occasion, the world's press almost outnumbered the naval ratings when a British frigate and Icelandic gunboat had a confrontation on the high seas. Fortunately, the opposing captains had a keen sense of occasion and the ensuing exchange was not of shots but of Biblical quotations which were delivered broadside by loud-hailer. Initially taken aback, journalists managed to salvage just enough

Scripture knowledge to award the result to the Icelandic team. More formal arguments gradually swung international opinion over to Iceland's point of view and a "truce" was agreed in 1976 – by which time the UK itself had announced its own 200-mile limit. The territorial waters limit that Iceland established has since become a standard for international marine legislation.

Protecting the sea's bounty

In the wake of the Cod Wars, Iceland upgraded its fishing fleet. Part of the philosophy behind extending the fishing zone was not just to prevent foreign fishing as such, but also to be able

to control how much was caught. After several years of bumper harvests, with the cod take nearing 508,000 tonnes (460,000 US tons) in 1982, the time came for holding back the nation's own fleet. Even as the Cod Wars were going on, Iceland had learned that it could overfish all by itself: the so-called "herring boom" in the Northeast collapsed in the late 1960s when the fish virtually disappeared from one season to the next.

A complex vessel quota system came into effect in 1984. In its present form, the system grants individual vessels tonnage quotas for individual species of fish based on recent catches, and the owners are free to swap or trade their quotas among themselves to maximize efficiency – and to make money.

Originally aimed at the all-important cod, the quota system has tended to increase diversification among fishing vessels of catches towards other species, most of which are also close to becoming overfished themselves now. Many skippers claim they have been transformed overnight from old-style heroic hunters into accountants, armed no longer with nets and maps but with chequebooks and spreadsheets. Unfortunately, years of poor spawning have forced the government to cut quotas regularly. Tradeable quotas have become a claim on a scarce resource and "paper fish" – the cod swimming unsuspectingly with a quota on its head – have grown in value at a rate that would draw looks of disbelief even from people who habitually play the money markets.

While the fleet's total quota for cod has been cut back by some 40 percent in recent years, the cost of buying the rights to catch cod has jumped alarmingly. Small-boat operators claim that they are being priced out of business. Meanwhile, fish processors are finding that they can hardly make a profit on the highly priced raw fish: European processing companies are ready to pay more for unprocessed fish than domestic processors could get after salting or freezing it themselves.

Optimists say that these are just teething troubles – and that the quota system should leave Iceland's main industry leaner, meaner and more able than ever to keep Iceland one of the wealthiest nations in the world. ❏

LEFT: unloading crates of fish packed in ice.
RIGHT: a fisherman checking his net.

LIFE ON THE LAND

*With a short growing season and land of variable fertility, the Icelanders
have come up with inventive and successful ways of farming*

For first-time visitors, who often expect eternal winter, Iceland is a pleasant surprise. This is, in fact, a remarkably green country in high summer: the lowlands are verdant with pasture land, while mosses and shrubs give the uplands their colour. Yet the climate is cool (averaging 11°C/52°F in June, around freezing in January) and sometimes harsh, summers are short and cultivable soil is restricted to narrow coastal plains. This all adds up to a pattern of agriculture quite unlike that of countries more abundant in the riches of the earth.

Traditionally, farming in Iceland meant sheep, sheep and more sheep. Lamb was the staple diet, eaten fresh, salted and smoked, and every part of the animal was put to use. Even today, traditional fare such as blood sausage, liver sausage, pickled rams' testicles and sheep heads count among national delicacies. Nothing edible was thrown away.

While farming has diversified in the past 50 years and the rural world changed rapidly, the memory of when all Icelanders lived on the land still grips the national imagination.

Iceland's rural myth

The simple life of the traditional farming family – surrounded by nature and animals, yet keenly interested in literature and history – is the background of every Icelander. It is celebrated in a thousand folktales and novels, engraved on the Icelandic consciousness. When an Icelander dons a hand-knitted *lopi* (Icelandic wool) sweater in natural colours, or has a feast of *hangikjöt* (smoked lamb) at Christmas, he is affirming his identity as a true Icelander.

This is a rather rose-tinted version of reality. For, in fact, the traditional life of the farmer in those days was usually one of unceasing toil and hardship. Many farming families scraped a bare living with the help of their sheep, which provided food, clothing, even shoes (of a kind).

PRECEDING PAGES: at work near Akureyri.
LEFT: the annual sheep round-up, a tradition since the Middle Ages. **RIGHT:** the hardy Icelandic sheep.

In his classic novel *Independent People*, Halldór Laxness depicted the farmer Bjartur and his family, whose small turf house is little more than a dark, fetid, disease-riddled hovel. When his young wife Rósa, who has been a servant on a wealthy farm, says she longs for meat to eat and milk to drink, Bjartur concludes

that she must be seriously ill. Such luxuries are only for the rich! "We eat good salted catfish, and until recently we had Danish potatoes to go with it. We've got rye bread in plenty, and loads of sugar," he says. Even less likely to supplement this dismal diet were fresh fruit and vegetables: Bjartur's children are baffled by the Biblical tale of Adam and Eve because they cannot imagine what an apple looks like.

Bjartur's family, "independent" though they may be, have no coats to wear, nor even woollen sweaters, "because in these hard times you can't go weaving or knitting wool except for essential underwear." When the coatless and sweaterless children have worked a 16-hour day at haymaking in the pouring rain (the adults worked longer), Bjartur comments: "It's a feeble kind of person who cares whether he's wet or dry. I've been damp more than half my life, and I've never had a day's illness."

In the early 20th century, Iceland's farmers lived much as their forebears had done for 1,000 years: they kept their sheep, grazed them in summer on the highlands, cut the hay in summer, rounded up the sheep in autumn. After the autumn slaughter, some of the livestock were foddered on hay through the winter, while the meat was salted, smoked and otherwise preserved. During the winter, wool was knitted and

sold, and renege on agreements. When the farmers launched their own cooperatives in competition with the Danish merchants, they cut out the middle-men and took control. The cooperative accepted products from the farmers, and with the credit they accumulated they could buy necessities (and even luxuries).

The cooperative movement developed into a massive business empire, involved in every sector of the Icelandic economy. The many tentacles of the Federation of Iceland Cooperative Societies (Samband Íslenskra Samvinnufélaga – SÍS) included a bank, an insurance company, retail shops, agricultural suppliers, a shipping

woven into clothes (or thermal underwear) for the household. The horse, man's helpmate since the settlement, was still crucial to all farming tasks, and provided the main form of transport (*see page 295*).

Escape from the Middle Ages

The foundation of Iceland's first cooperative society, in 1882 in the north, heralded new times for the farming community. Farmers were tired of being dependent on the whims of a few (mostly Danish) merchants, to whom they sold their products in exchange for various supplies. The merchants could (and often did) undervalue what they bought, over-price what they

line, fish processing and exports, and more. But SÍS ran into financial disaster during the 1980s: some of its divisions lost money, bleeding the profitable sectors dry. After mergers of some of the ailing divisions, SÍS was split in 1991 into its component parts, individual limited companies which must make it on their own.

As a result of all this, the countryside has been transformed. Young people have left the land in droves to seek education and a better life. Some of the most rugged and hostile regions, where farming was a constant struggle, have become totally depopulated in a matter of decades: Hornstrandir, for instance, in the West Fjords, was simply abandoned.

Mechanisation has altered all the work of the farm, making it less labour-intensive. Roads have been pushed through and communications revolutionised, making isolation a thing of the past. The subsistence farmer has practically ceased to exist; today's farmers, essentially, produce meat, milk and crops for the market, and they themselves consume purchased products like the rest of the population – though some, of course, take a certain pleasure in self-sufficiency, and grow their own vegetables.

Iceland is too far north to grow cereal crops comfortably, as the climate is too cool and the growing season too short. A number of farmers by the impact of 1,000 years of settlement. Icelandic soils are light, lacking clay materials to bind them, with a large proportion of volatile volcanic-based loams. Nonetheless, before herbivores arrived to threaten the fragile ecology of the island, about two-thirds of Iceland's 103,000 sq. km (39,000 sq. miles) were covered by trees, shrubs and other vegetation.

The *Landnámabók (Book of Settlements)* says that Iceland was covered with trees "from the mountains to the sea" when the settlers arrived. But not for long. The settlers used the wood indiscriminately for fuel, while their livestock ate their way through the vegetation. As

have started to grow the hardier cereals, like rye and barley, with the help of fertilisers. These grains are used in animal fodder, replacing expensive imported cereals, and barley is also being grown for human consumption.

Gone with the wind

Soil erosion is probably the single most important environmental problem facing the Icelandic farmer today. The vegetation of the country, in delicate equilibrium before man's arrival in the 9th century, has been devastated

LETTING THE GRASS GROW

Growing enough grass has always been one of the farmer's main concerns. By the end of the summer, he or she must have sufficient hay to fodder the livestock through the winter. Today's farmers are less dependent on the weather than their forebears; with modern technology they can dry hay artificially, and in a poor year, buy fodder. Most now store their hay, not in traditional bales but wound up in airtight white plastic wrapping. A good hay harvest, however, is still vital. Along the south coast, forward-looking farmers have planted grass on the barren volcanic sands, adding to their grassland and fighting soil erosion.

LEFT: man against horse.
ABOVE: taking cattle for milking in Skagafjörður.

the protective layer of vegetation disappeared, topsoil was blown away in the wind and washed away by rivers, leading to massive desertification. Only about 1 percent of the country's original woods remain; 30–40,000 sq. km (11–15,000 sq. miles) have been stripped bare since the land was first settled.

It became clear that something was wrong when sand drift from desert areas laid waste many farms in the 19th century. In 1907 organised efforts to combat desertification began. The Soil Conservation Service works to control soil erosion, reclaim waste land and improve and protect existing vegetation.

Spreading roots

Undoing the work of centuries of destruction and neglect is a slow task, but over 90 years of effort have produced cheering results. Hardy lymegrass has been widely sown to stabilise drifting sands, while the Alaskan lupin has been highly successful in binding loose and volatile soil, preparing the way for more vegetation.

Campaigns for reafforestation of the once-wooded country have received enthusiastic public support over the past few decades, and the Icelanders have taken to tree-planting with a will. Former President Vigdís Finnbogadóttir was an unflagging champion of the cause of

AN AIRBORNE OFFENSIVE

Since 1958, the Soil Conservation Service has attacked erosion from the air, spreading grass seed and fertiliser over thousands of hectares of barren land each summer. In 1990, 1,400 tons of grass seed and fertiliser were spread in this way, over 4,500 hectares of land. The SCS has its own plane, an old DC-3 donated in 1973 by Icelandair after its retirement from active service. As well as flying over the highlands, which are inaccessible for other means of seeding, the SCS has also seeded volcanic regions in the south and southwest, as well as lending a hand in the recultivation of the Vestmannaeyjar after the devastating 1973 eruption.

afforestation during her time in office, and her support certainly boosted public interest. There is no reason why trees should not flourish once again all over Iceland.

Experiments have shown that reafforestation and land reclamation can work together. Seedling trees will take hold, even in barren country, if they are protected from browsing sheep and other livestock. This has led to a new development in land reclamation – planting little trees rather than grass or lupins.

Farmers are being encouraged to turn over suitable land to forestry, and there has even been a suggestion that Iceland could have its own commercially utilisable forests within a few decades. Remote though this prospect may seem at present, it is no more absurd than visions of changing the face of Iceland – now implemented – must have seemed at the beginning of the 20th century. Land is now probably being reclaimed a little faster than it is being lost. With redoubled efforts, the Icelanders may yet redress the balance, and revive the green and pleasant land of their forebears.

Challenge to the almighty sheep

The rapid urbanisation of Icelandic society has been far from painless. The past few decades have turned all traditional notions of farming upside down. For a start, the sheep (mainstay and saviour of Iceland since the settlement) has lost its supremacy. The Icelandic sheep is unique, the direct descendant of the animals brought to Iceland by the settlers in the 9th century. This sturdy, self-reliant creature will graze on almost anything. Sheep have always been herded into mountain pastures for the summer months, so the typical Icelandic sheep grows strong and muscular, and the herbs and grasses it grazes on give its meat a delicate flavour.

But today's Icelanders no longer want to live exclusively on lamb (whether fresh, salted or smoked). The Icelanders have developed cosmopolitan tastes and the modern consumer demands beef, poultry and pork. Production of these meats has been growing fast, although lamb is still Iceland's most-eaten meat.

Dairy farming grew fast during the 20th century, and the Icelanders are phenomenal consumers of dairy products, eating and drinking the equivalent of about 395 litres (103 gallons) per head each year. Any visitor to an Icelandic supermarket will be baffled by the range of milk (whole, semi-skimmed, skimmed and soured), cream, cheese, butter, yoghurt and the unique Icelandic milk-curd, *skyr*.

Growing demand for fresh fruits and vegetables (almost unheard-of in Iceland until the past 30 years) has also led to large-scale development of market gardening. In a good year, Iceland's potato farmers produce enough to see the nation through to the following year's harvest. While Iceland's climate is too cool for growing many vegetables in the open air, inexpensive geo-thermal energy provides the resources to cultivate plenty of exotic crops in greenhouses.

Market gardeners, in geothermal areas, produce tomatoes, cucumbers, carrots, capsicums, lettuce and other salad crops, plus various kinds of cabbage, in the summer months. Hothouse cultivators can even grow bananas and grapes, but not usually on a commercial scale. The bananas, grapes, apples and citrus fruits sold in Iceland are always imported.

An uncertain future

There are still some 3,800 working farms in Iceland. But what is the shape of things to

come? Farming in Iceland moved directly from the Middle Ages to the 20th century without pausing for breath, and now farmers are plagued with problems, from desertification to over-production. While farmers proved that they were willing to adapt to new methods and new markets, they have not responded fast enough. Over-production of lamb and milk has led to a quota system, whereby each farmer may only produce up to a certain maximum. As one set of agricultural cuts follows another, quotas have been reduced to the point where some farms have ceased to be viable.

The 21st century is certain to bring greater competition. Protectionist legislation and heavy

LEFT: grasses and lupins planted to stabilise the black sands by the south coast.
RIGHT: processing *skyr*, Icelandic milk curd.

government subsidies have hitherto helped farmers survive, but these are likely to be threatened in future by Iceland's participation in the European Economic Area formed by EFTA (the European Free Trade Association) and the European Union.

Radical action is clearly necessary, but opinions are mixed on what it should be. Some extremists say that farming should simply be abandoned; instead of paying massive subsidies, the country could import the agricultural products it needs. Few would go this far, but there is a general consensus that the number of farms should be reduced. Incentives are being

tile industry, however, are not encouraging. Icelandic sheep fleece is made up of two layers. The inner layer of short, fine fibres *(thel)* was used for knitting delicate laces, while the coarser, longer outer fibres *(tog)* made warm, water-resistant winter garments. Today, soft half-spun *lopi* wool is used in traditionally patterned hand-knitted sweaters, which are some of the most popular souvenirs of Iceland.

While hand-knitting and weaving never died out, large-scale industrialised woollen production developed to produce fashionwear, blankets, carpets, and so on. The recent trend towards lighter man-made yarns and cotton

offered to farmers who wish to leave their farms and "cash in" their quota, and the possibility has been discussed of totally abolishing sheep farming in some areas where the vegetation is particularly sensitive to grazing.

On top of all its other problems, the sheep turns out to be the main culprit in Iceland's problem with soil erosion; it may have kept the Icelanders alive, but it did so at the cost of destroying the vegetation of the uplands.

Lopi wool, one of the country's most important exports in the Middle Ages (along with the dried fish known as stockfish), rose again to become the basis of a valuable export industry in the 20th century. Recent events in the tex-

knits spelled disaster for wool producers. Woollens exports have declined steadily, and in 1991 Iceland's major textiles company, Álafoss, went broke after a long struggle. Two new small companies, Folda and Ístex, are re-launching on a more modest scale.

Round-up ritual

The annual autumn round-up is a ritual which holds a significant place in the national psyche. In early September, before the first snows fall on the uplands, farmers don their warm woollen sweaters and waterproofs and saddle up their horses, loading up a sleeping bag, a saddlebag of food and an indispensable hip flask. With their dogs, they set off into the uplands. The Icelandic dog, a thick-furred, curly-tailed breed with upright ears, is a favourite with Icelandic farmers, although other types of dog also do service as sheep-dogs. Directly descended from the animals brought to Iceland by Viking settlers, the dog also has a certain following abroad among breeders.

A LARGE FLOCK

Although the sheep is not as central to Icelandic life as it used to be, there are still twice as many sheep as people.

Working in teams, horsemen and dogs systematically search the highland pastures for sheep. The searchers stay overnight in mountain huts, where they pen in the sheep they have gathered so far, then hang up their damp clothes, uncork their hip flasks and swap stories and songs. After two or three days all the sheep are accounted for, and the fat and frisky lambs, ewes and rams are herded down to the lowlands and into a corral, where they are identified by their ear-marks and sorted into the correct pens.

All the local people gather to take part, and a dance is often held once the work is over. As evening falls, the farmers share a drink or two in the sheep-filled corral, and lift their voices in part-songs, just as their forefathers have done for hundreds of years.

This part of the process is known in Icelandic as *réttir*. *Réttir* take place in various places throughout the country, and there are even some quite close to Reykjavík. It is not uncommon for parents to take their children to give them a glimpse into what life was like in times past. Also, the annual round-up has attracted an increasing number of tourists in recent years.

Fish, fur and "tourist farming"

When it became clear, in the early 1980s, that old farming ways were out of sync with today's market, some revolutionary ideas came up to redirect farmers into new, profitable businesses.

One of these was salmon farming. This exists in various forms, from "ocean ranching" to fish farming in offshore sea pens, or in tanks on dry land, using geothermal resources. There is concern, however, at the effect of "farmed" salmon on the wild stock. In "ocean ranching", young salmon are released into the sea to forage for themselves, and some return full-grown, to the place of release where they can be harvested. Others wander into rivers where they do not belong, to mix with the wild salmon which are following their homing instincts back to their breeding ground. Specialists fear that adding alien salmon may debase the existing stock, and ultimately confuse the homing instinct.

Due to such concerns, as well as other difficulties, most salmon farms have gone out of business.

Fur farming (fox and mink) was another idea for diversification which looked promising on

paper. Commercially farmed skins fetch high prices at auction, and Iceland's cool climate produced luxuriant pelts. Fur breeders did not attempt to farm the native fox, but imported commercial species from abroad. However, it proved hard to master fur farming, and international prices have also dropped, as few people now agree with wearing fur. Most fur farms have gone the same way as the fish farms.

Another new venture proved more successful. Angora rabbits were imported to be farmed for their hair. This small-scale farming sideline now supplies a factory producing 100 percent angora garments, which are popular with Icelanders and tourists alike.

LEFT: the annual sheep round-up. **RIGHT:** hard at work on a salmon estuary on the Hvítá river.

As farmers make a painful adjustment to changing times, the biggest success story of all has nothing to do with farming. In Iceland they call it, jokingly, "tourist farming" – offering farm holidays as an alternative to hotels or camping. Farming families started offering bed and breakfast in their own homes, self-catering accommodation, summerhouses, and the like. Usually, existing accommodation can be adapted for this purpose without major investment. Visitors can go riding, angle for trout, or even lend a hand at – on their land. If a farmer's waters or rivers are thick with salmon, for instance, it can be a real money-spinner. Iceland's salmon rivers, reputed to be some of the best in the world, attract anglers from every corner of the globe, who spend as much as US$1,300 a day for the best rivers (all-inclusive rates with full board). The most popular have to be booked many months in advance. A total ban on salmon fishing at sea helps to ensure that Iceland's salmon find their way back to their home waters.

FARM HOLIDAYS

The Farm Holiday Service has grown and grown. Today around 130 farms all over the country offer accommodation and services of various kinds.

bringing in the hay. The idea has been a great success. For the farmers, too, tourist farming made good financial sense. While quota restrictions limit what a farmer may produce, no quota has been imposed on tourists (yet!), and tourism offers a steadily growing market for these services.

Traditional boons

In centuries past, the peripheral resources attached to a farm or community were a vital source of income and often spelled the difference between utter poverty and relative prosperity. Today farmers still have exclusive rights to exploit the *hlunnindi* – peripheral resources

One of the most important of the traditional rights of farmers was the right to gather and use driftwood: whole trees can sometimes be washed ashore, carried on ocean streams from as far away as Siberia. In this near-treeless country, driftwood provided the main source of building timber for many centuries, and so was a highly valuable commodity. Even today, any driftwood that can be gathered does not go to waste: most of it goes to make fenceposts for Iceland's farms.

ABOVE: the remote farmstead at Húsey.
RIGHT: sealskins drying in the sun.
FAR RIGHT: a puffin-catcher on the cliffs of Heimaey.

Seals, whales and puffins

In the past, the Icelanders hunted seals for their meat and skins. Although they are no longer caught commercially today, seals are still hunted on a small scale in a few places around the country.

In former ages, a beached whale was a welcome source of food, and even today, the Icelandic word for a "windfall" is *hvalreki* (whale beaching). Whales have been hunted through the centuries as sources of food and oil, until 1992 when whaling was suspended.

The island's steep sea-cliffs, clustered with millions of sea birds, were once known as Iceland's "pantries". Icelanders would often have gone hungry had they not had the nourishment of these natural food stores. In all the areas where sea-bird colonies are found, men would rappel on ropes down the vertical cliff-faces, gathering eggs from the nests. Today sea-birds' eggs are still gathered in some quantity. *Sprang,* the art of swinging nimbly down a cliff-face on a long rope, is still a much-practised skill in the Vestmannaeyjar (Westmann Islands).

Regarded as a great delicacy by many Icelanders, sea-birds' eggs are commonly eaten in coastal villages in season, and are sold in supermarkets in urban areas. The eggs of the guille-

EIDER FARMING

The eider duck is a peaceful bird, returning year after year to certain nesting colonies. Man and the eider have learned to live together for their mutual benefit: farmers with eider colonies on their land provide welcoming nesting places, and protect the birds, their eggs and their young from predators. In return, farmers gather the down left behind in the nests once eiders and chicks have left. Each nest yields only a few wisps; picked clean of all twigs, dirt and scraps of eggshell, the down is washed before being sold at over US$600 per kilogramme (a kilo will fill an average-sized quilt and last a lifetime with proper care).

mot are those most often commercially sold: larger than hens' eggs, they are a mottled blue. Designed by nature for narrow cliff-ledge nesting sites, they taper sharply to one end. If accidentally nudged, they will simply spin around rather than plunging off the cliff.

Some sea-bird species were also hunted for food, and still are today, notably puffins and guillemots. Other than sea birds, the goose and ptarmigan are practically the only birds hunted for human consumption. Hunters, who must hold gun licences, can shoot goose all winter, while ptarmigan are hunted from September until just before Christmas, when they make a favourite festive dinner in many homes. ❏

CONFRONTING WILD ICELAND

The vast open spaces and wild landscapes of Iceland offer a wealth
of opportunities for all who love the great outdoors

Mountains, glaciers, lakes and thundering waterfalls are the very stuff of Icelandic tourism. With its wilderness areas and clear air, Iceland makes an exotic and intoxicating change, and more and more visitors want to get out and experience all that wild nature for themselves.

A world of ice

One of the fastest-growing sectors in the tourism industry has grown up around the glaciers, which have a slightly mystical appeal. Lofty, almost unearthly, they seem strangely inaccessible, yet they can be approached in various ways. It is generally possible, for instance, to walk to the summit of Snæfellsjökull – though this should not be attempted without a guide. On Mýrdalsjökull icecap, you can go skiing in the middle of summer.

Walking on the vast, crevassed expanse of Vatnajökull, however, is only for experienced alpinists – and even they may find it more than they bargained for. The icecap is a wild place. The weather is harsh and unpredictable, and fog and snow can strike at any time. Mountain rescue teams are regularly called out to look for walkers who have gone astray on glacial expeditions, and lives have been lost. While full-scale glacier expeditions are beyond the stamina of most travellers, Vatnajökull icecap is now accessible to those who still want to experience 8,000 sq. km (3,000 sq. miles) of ice.

Day-trippers are transported from the south-eastern town of Höfn up onto the icecap by snowcat and/or jeep, to be shown some of the strange and spectacular sights. For those with less time to spend, it is possible to fly directly up onto the icecap by helicopter, with the incidental advantage of breathtaking views.

The icecap, far from being simply an expanse of snow and ice, has its own landscape (or icescape): barren, rocky peaks project up

through the ice; narrow crevices extend down for hundreds of metres; and at Grímsvötn, geothermal springs bubble under the age-old ice. After sightseeing, visitors can have a go at skimming over the vast glacial expanse on nippy snow scooters. As a finishing touch, superb banquets can be served up on the ice-

cap, at a table carved from the ice. The ice in the drinks is, of course, pure glacier.

Winter expeditions

Glaciers are probably best left alone in winter – the very time when Iceland opens up to a whole new form of travel. Rough-country vehicles with four-wheel drive have become a craze in Iceland in recent years, and in Reykjavík and other towns these huge-tyred customised machines tower over ordinary traffic. The fanatics of the 4x4 have developed great expertise. While off-road driving is strictly banned in summer in order to protect the delicate upland vegetation, in winter it is possible to travel

---

PRECEDING PAGES: hikers leaving Þórsmörk for Skógar. **LEFT:** beneath Svartifoss in Skaftafell National Park. **RIGHT:** the Ásbyrgi canyon in Jökulsárgljúfur.

almost anywhere on a blanket of snow without damaging what lies underneath. With tyre pressure drastically reduced, the 4x4 simply "floats" across the snow. Loran navigational equipment and radio contact help to ensure safety, even in the worst of conditions. The 4x4 travellers always proceed in groups, ready to help each other in case of problems. The worst that can happen is having to lie low in the vehicles for a few hours if a snowstorm blows up.

Guided 4x4 trips into the interior are now a regular feature of winter tourism in Iceland, giving a chance to see places which are normally inaccessible outside the summer season –

such as the hot-spring oasis of Landmannalaugar in the southern highlands, where you can strip off on a snow-covered riverbank to take a dip in a natural hot river. For the active wintersport enthusiast, there is also cross-country skiing into the interior (only for the very fit).

Lakes and rivers

One of the easiest Icelandic adventures is a visit to Jökulsárlón, at the southern edge of Vatnajökull icecap, where an icy blue-green lagoon has formed at the base of a wall of ice. Great ice floes separate from the advancing outlet glacier to float eerily on the lagoon. A cruise among the

SNOW SPORTS IN ICELAND

Skiing, both downhill and cross-country, and, increasingly, snowboarding, are hugely popular winter pastimes in Iceland, and many families wait with bated breath for the first proper snow of the season. Excellent slopes can be found in the north and around the West Fjords, where good snow cover is usually guaranteed. In and around Akureyri, an area with relatively cold winters due to its situation away from the Gulf Stream, coverage is fairly regular.

Farther south, however, skiing is subject to the vagaries of the weather. In a good winter (in skier's terms), the Bláfjöll ski area just outside Reykjavík is swarming with skiers every weekend, yet a warm and rainy winter season

will have skiers tearing their hair out in frustration, cursing the bare slopes. This explains the apparent paradox of Icelanders who take their skiing holidays in mainland Europe. In Iceland, the main skiing season does not generally begin until after Christmas, and usually lasts until about Easter. For true skiing fanatics who want to pursue the sport all year round, Kerlingarfjöll in the central uplands operates as a summertime ski centre.

While all the major ski areas have ski lifts, they generally offer little else in the way of services, and nothing like the superstructure of an alpine ski resort. Iceland's only ski hotel is at Akureyri.

ice floes, beneath the towering bulk of Europe's largest icecap, is like nothing on earth. Don't miss it. This bizarre place did not exist 50 years ago: the lagoon has formed as the icecap has shrunk. And within another few years the lagoon may open out into the sea, adding one more fjord to Iceland's jagged southern coastline.

More excitement, again courtesy of the glaciers, can be had by white-water rafting down the Hvítá river. Very few of Iceland's rivers are navigable: fast-flowing, they are dotted with waterfalls and rapids. The Hvítá, fed by glacial meltwater, is the river which thunders over Gullfoss falls, commonly regarded as Iceland's most beautiful cascade. Those who want a more intimate experience of the Hvítá river can shoot the rapids upstream of the falls with full equipment and experienced guides.

Thrills and spills are not all that Iceland has to offer in the way of adventure. One of the many amenities of a rugged, sparsely populated country (about two people per sq. km) is that you can really get away from it all. If you want peace and solitude, this is where you can be sure of finding it.

Backpacking holidays are the classic way to experience faraway and roadless regions. The interior is the classic wilderness area, but there are also places like Hornstrandir in Iceland's far northwest, reclaimed by nature after its last human residents left in the early 1960s. You can travel to Hornstrandir by sea or by road, but then you are on your own.

By foot, bike or horse

Touring clubs such as Útivist and Ferðafélag Íslands offer a year-round schedule of guided walking tours, from a few hours up to a week or two in the wilderness. Since the Icelandic interior is emphatically not a place for amateurs to blunder about in, these guided tours are excellent for walkers not familiar with the country.

For those who like to walk, but not to excess, tour companies have come up with tours where your luggage is transported, so you only have to carry a small pack with your lunch and some extra clothes. A highly popular innovation has been the walking/biking bus tour, where you can sit on the bus if it rains, or ride a bike or walk when the spirit moves you.

LEFT: a lone cyclist can find it hard going.
RIGHT: snowcatting on Vatnajökull icecap.

Cycling in Iceland has become increasingly popular in recent years. To most Icelanders, this development is all but incomprehensible. A large proportion of Iceland's roads are still gravel-surfaced, and some of them are bumpy, stony, and downright hazardous. The country is mountainous, and often very windy. If it rains, cyclists get plastered with sludge. If it is dry, they choke on clouds of dust. Cycling around Iceland is strictly for masochists.

A better way to travel, especially to places where no vehicle (even a 4x4) can easily take you, is on horseback. This has the incidental advantage of giving invaluable insight into

the Icelanders' age-old relationship with the horse. Well into the 20th century, the horse was the only form of land transport, the faithful friend without whom life would not have been liveable.

Horse farms all over the country can organise treks. Near Eyjafjörður in the north, horse treks can be made into an uninhabited region, Fjörður. Riding all day among deserted valleys and mountains, fording rivers, leading your second mount which carries supplies and bedroll, you will gain real insight into the way Icelanders used to live. These longer treks are, needless to say, demanding, and suitable for experienced riders only. ❏

A BIRDWATCHER'S PARADISE

Iceland is home to, or a stopping off point for, a wide variety of birdlife. This is most spectacular on the sea-cliffs where huge numbers gather in the breeding season

Any traveller to Iceland with even a vague interest in birdlife should bring along a pair of binoculars and a good ornithological guide. Around 70 species of birds breed annually in every corner of Iceland (including year-round residents and those which migrate to Iceland each spring), while a total of over 300 different species have been seen in the country at one time or another.

Some species regularly winter in Iceland before flying further north to breed in summer. Others are birds of passage "stopping over" on a long migratory journey. Many are accidentals – individual birds which have drifted across the ocean on prevailing winds; those of North American origin are of great interest to European birdwatchers – the majority of sightings of these birds are in the south during the autumn months.

Seventy breeding species is not a great deal, although the actual bird population is numerically large: some of the commonest species, like the puffin, are present in millions. The Icelandic environment is particularly favourable to sea birds, which make up 23 of the country's breeding species (*see also pages 246–7*), while it is less welcoming for passerines (perching birds). With trees in short supply, these birds have difficulty in finding places to perch, and their favoured food, insects, is not plentiful. While about 60 percent of the world's birds are passerines, they make up only one seventh of Iceland's avian population.

Most of Iceland's birds are also found in Scandinavia and Northern Europe. Three species, however, are American: the Barrow's goldeneye, the great northern diver or common loon, and the harlequin duck, which breed practically nowhere else outside North America.

Heralds of spring

Both the arctic tern and the golden plover are migratory birds commonly regarded as harbingers of spring. The golden plover, which

generally arrives in early April, is a particular favourite with Icelandic poets:

> *Lóan er komin að kveða burt snjóinn,*
> *kveða burt leiðindin, það getur hún.*
> *Hún hefur sagt mér að senn komi spóinn,*
> *sólskin í heiði og blómstur í tún.*

"The plover has come and she'll sing away

winter / Drive off all sorrow as only she can / She says that the whimbrel soon will be coming / Sun on the valley and hayfields in bloom."

The arctic tern, which usually appears in early May, is one of the wonders of the ornithological world. It migrates each spring from Antarctica, 17,000 km (10,500 miles) away. The arctic tern is a graceful flyer, often seen hovering over water. It also makes unnerving "dive-bombing" attacks on humans who enter its nesting colonies in June and July, screeching "*kría!*" (also the bird's name in Icelandic).

The puffin is Iceland's commonest bird, with a population of 8–10 million. The comically dignified stance of this decorative bird has earned it the nickname of *Prófastur* (The Dean). Around 20 May each year, puffins start flying ashore for the breeding season, after spending the winter out on the North Atlantic. Their main breeding grounds are on sea-cliffs (particularly in the Vestmannaeyjar/Westmann Islands and the West Fjords), and also on low-lying offshore islands such as Grímsey.

These unusual birds do not simply build a nest – they dig a burrow, up to 1.5 metres (5 ft) deep, where a single egg is laid. On the sea cliff, puffins are usually found nesting at the top, where a little soil and vegetation provides the space to dig. Puffin pairs will return year after year to the same burrow. After the Vestmannaeyjar on Heimaey eruption in 1973, many returned to find their burrows buried under a thick layer of lava. Rather than nest elsewhere, they tried to burrow to their old nesting places; some died in the attempt.

Rare birds

One of the most famous of the island's bird species is, sadly, extinct. The great auk (*Pinguinus impennis*) was a big, awkward, flightless sea bird, about 70 cm (27 in) high, and very tasty, according to the fishermen who hunted it for food. The last two great auks were clubbed

STORIES AND POEMS ABOUT RAVENS

Special importance has been attributed to the raven, known by the affectionate nickname "Krummi", ever since pre-Christian days. This was the chosen bird of Odin, the one-eyed High God of Norse mythology, and as such has always enjoyed respect. In more recent times, Icelanders believed that ravens could prophesise the future: a raven cawing at the window presages a death, while if the bird jumps around in an agitated manner, limps, ruffles its feathers and caws into the air, it is a portent of danger at sea.

Most Icelandic farms have a resident pair of ravens, which may even be fed with scraps of food. The bird's popularity is such that *Hrafn* (Raven) is a common personal name. The raven features in many verses and rhymes, some of which are sinister, and some humorous:

> *Krummi krunkar úti,*
> *kallar á nafna sinn.*
> *Ég fann höfuð af hrúti,*
> *hrygg og gæruskinn.*
> *Komdu nú og kroppað u með mér,*
> *krummi nafni minn.*

"The Raven caws outside / Calls to his namesake / I found a ram's head / With bones and fleece / Come and have a snack with me / Krummi, my namesake!"

to death on Eldey in 1844 (*see also* Iceland's Sea Birds *on pages 246–7*). The Natural History Museum in Reykjavík has on display a stuffed great auk, originally part of the taxidermic collection of a Danish nobleman, which was bought at auction in London in 1971.

Today all rare and endangered species are protected by law. An endangered species native to Iceland is the gyrfalcon, the largest of all falcons at 51–60 cm (20–23 in) long. About 200 pairs are estimated to breed each year. The gyrfalcon has a colourful history as one of Iceland's most prestigious and valuable exports. Due to their skill and manoeuvrability in the

and chicks and smuggle them out of the country. The smugglers (including, on one occasion, a German "tourist" with two chicks hidden in his luggage) have been apprehended and heavily fined. Iceland's gyrfalcons enjoy special protection: their nesting places are kept secret, and carefully monitored. No-one may approach the nests, or photograph them, except by permission of the Ministry of Culture.

The gyrfalcon lives in close community with its preferred prey, the ptarmigan, although it also hunts down other birds when ptarmigans are unavailable. Humans share the falcon's taste for ptarmigan (*Lagopus mutus*), a species of grouse.

air, gyrfalcons were prized as hunting birds and made gifts fit for kings and princes. In medieval times, up to 200 trained birds were exported each year, and in the 16th century the king of Denmark (who also ruled over Iceland) claimed a monopoly on the trade, which made a significant contribution to the royal coffers.

Although falconry largely died out in Europe by the 18th century, it continues in other parts of the world. Even today, an illicit trade in hunting falcons exists, and isolated attempts have been made in recent years to steal falcon eggs

Considerably smaller at 35 cm (13 in) than its European relatives, the red and black grouse and the capercaillie, the ptarmigan adopts protective white colouring in winter. This does not stop hunters going out to shoot it in large numbers throughout the winter hunting season.

The gyrfalcon may be spotted in most parts of the country, but Iceland's most numerous bird of prey is the merlin. Smaller than the gyrfalcon at 27–32 cm (10–12 in) long, the Icelandic merlin is a unique subspecies, *Falco columbarius subaesalon*. It lives mostly on passerines such as redwings, wheatears and meadow pipits.

LEFT: Barrow's goldeneyes, one of three American species to breed in Iceland. **ABOVE:** a gyrfalcon.

Lord of the skies

The largest of Iceland's birds of prey is the white-tailed eagle, up to 90 cm (3 ft) long, with a wingspan of up to 2.5 metres (8 ft). This is a close relative of the bald eagle, the US national bird. It is a rare sight today, following determined extermination. During the early 19th century, there were 200–300 breeding pairs in Iceland. The bird was accused, however, of carrying off lambs, and it certainly disturbed eider colonies by taking both eggs and chicks. A

CITY BIRDS

The lake (Tjörn) in Reykjavík is a natural habitat for wild birds. As well as a variety of ducks, geese and swans, it also has a breeding colony of arctic terns and the occasional red-necked phalarope.

bounty was offered for eagles. They were shot and poisoned by farmers and eider breeders until, in 1920, only 10 pairs remained. Since 1913 the eagle has been protected by law, and is making a slow recovery. Today breeding pairs number 35 to 40, so prospects for the future seem promising.

By the sea

Iceland's coasts and offshore islands provide marvellous opportunities to see sea birds at close quarters. The islands of Breiðafjörður, for instance, teem with shag and cormorant, and the occasional white-tailed eagle may be seen. The grey phalarope (which is much rarer than

its red-necked cousin) also breeds on the islands. On sightseeing cruises from Stykkishólmur, birdwatchers can sail in close to see the birds.

Bird-cliffs are found in many places around the country, although the mixture of species nesting on the cliffs varies from region to region. The common guillemot, for instance, prefers the north, while the Brunnich's guillemot is found most commonly in the south. Sea-cliffs provide ledges and hollows not only for the ubiquitous puffin, but also for fulmars, kittiwakes, guillemots and razorbills.

Látrabjarg, at Iceland's westernmost point, is one of the world's great bird-cliffs. Sixteen km (10 miles) long, the cliffs soar 500 metres (1,600 ft) up from the sea. The cliffs that fringe Hælavíkurbjarg and Hornbjarg, in the far northwest, are less accessible, but certainly no less spectacular. Other bird-cliffs can be seen on the Vestmannaeyjar (accessible by sightseeing cruises from the main island, Heimaey), plus Krísuvíkurbjarg on the southwestern peninsula, Reykjanes. The Snæfellsnes peninsula is also an excellent area for viewing cliff birds and other seabird species.

Grímsey island, 40 km (25 miles) off the north coast, is a must for birdwatchers, with dramatic bird-cliffs. It is also the only Icelandic habitat of the very rare little auk, which is so well protected by law that you need to obtain a permit simply to approach the nesting area. About 16,000 pairs of gannets nest on Eldey island off the Reykjanes peninsula, the fourth-largest gannet colony in the world. Casual birdwatchers, however, are not welcome as Eldey is a closely protected bird sanctuary.

Bogs, marshes and wetlands also provide important habitats for many species of birds, including the whooper swan, the greylag goose, and waders like the whimbrel and golden plover. In Þjórsárver, in the depths of the highlands, Iceland boasts one of the largest breeding sites of the pink-footed goose. About 10,000 pairs of pink-footed geese, winter residents in England and Scotland, breed here each year.

The southern coast of Iceland is a particular favourite with birdwatchers who are on the

LEFT: a white-tailed eagle moves in for the kill.
RIGHT: the great skua.

lookout for exotic "accidentals", lost birds that have flown from North America and mainland Europe. At Skaftafell National Park, an excellent location for birdwatching, the wren is particularly common. Though the smallest of all the Icelandic birds at 12–13 cm (5 in), it is larger than wrens in nearby countries, and is defined as a special subspecies, *Troglodytes troglodytes islandicus*.

One Icelandic bird you cannot expect to see is the water rail. This extremely shy bird is so wary and elusive that it has hardly ever been photographed, although its call may be heard in its typical habitat, reedbanks edging marshy lowlands. Wholesale draining of marshland has slowly but surely been destroying the water rail's habitat, and it is also an easy prey for the fast-moving and bloodthirsty mink, so its call may not be heard in the marshes of Iceland for very much longer.

From common-or-garden sparrows, starlings (Icelandic residents only since 1912) and red-wings to the rarely glimpsed white-tailed eagle or little auk, Iceland promises the birdwatcher endless pleasure. Even those who cannot tell a hawk from a handsaw may find themselves flicking through ornithological guides in search of identifying features. ❏

BIRDLIFE AT LAKE MÝVATN

Lake Mývatn, in the north, is a unique natural phenomenon; a large lake, 37 sq. km (14 sq. miles) in area, yet with a depth of only 1–4 metres (3–13 ft). It is also fed by underground hot streams from the adjacent active geothermal and volcanic area, which raise the temperature higher than one would expect both at this northerly latitude and at its altitude of 277 metres (908 ft) above sea level. Even in severe winters, the lake never freezes completely, thanks to this input of warm water. Mývatn is a paradise for ducks, providing lavish feeding whether for divers or dabblers, and all of Iceland's duck species save the eider (which prefers life at sea) are found breeding here. Most common is the tufted duck (3,000 pairs), then the scaup (1,700 pairs) and Barrow's goldeneye (700 pairs). Other common species include the common scoter, red-breasted merganser, long-tailed duck, gadwall and teal, while the mallard and pintail are less common. The goosander, shoveller and pochard are rare. The harlequin, which likes fast-flowing waters, is found on the adjacent Laxá river.

Many other bird species are also found in the area: the slavonian grebe nests at Mývatn, and the short-eared owl on nearby marshes, along with snipe and red-necked phalarope. Merlins and gyrfalcons nest in the nearby mountainous areas.

MAMMALS IN THE WILD

Although Iceland has only one indigenous land mammal, the arctic fox, there are a number of introduced species. Its seas are rich in marine mammals

Because Iceland was never connected to any of the ancient land masses, it's hardly surprising that it has few native animals – although a variety of marine mammals have been established on its coasts for millennia.

The only land-based Icelandic mammal which pre-dates the settlement in the 9th century is the arctic fox (*Alopex lagopus*), a small breed found throughout the Arctic region. Two variants exist: the "blue", relatively rare in other Arctic areas, comprises about two-thirds of Iceland's fox population; it is dark brown in summer, and turns a lighter brown in winter, with a bluish sheen. The "white" variety only lives up to its name when in winter camouflage; its summer coat is greyish-brown with a grey or white belly. Exceptionally well insulated, the arctic fox grows a thick and furry winter coat, including fur on the soles of its paws.

Icelandic farmers have always believed that foxes killed lambs, and retaliated by trying to exterminate them, simply going out with their shotguns, shooting to kill. Research has, however, shown that Iceland's foxes pose little threat to livestock, and today, it is no longer regarded as an unmitigated pest – fox-hunting aims only to control numbers. In recent years, a few commercial species of fox have been imported to farm for their fur. Some have, however, escaped to the wild and mated with native arctic foxes, producing hybrids.

Rodent residents

Iceland has several naturalised mammals introduced, deliberately or not, over the years. Four rodent species have settled here, arriving as stowaways on ships. These are the long-tailed field mouse or wood mouse (*Apodemus sylvaticus*), house mouse (*Mus musculus*), brown rat (*Rattus norvegicus*) and black rat (*Rattus rattus*). The house mouse, brown rat and black rat are only found in and around urban areas; of them only the brown rat is common.

LEFT: a baby seal in the East Fjords.
RIGHT: a young arctic fox with its brown summer coat.

The long-tailed field mouse (a uniquely Icelandic sub-species, *Apodemus sylvaticus grandiculus*) certainly deserves its name, with a tail as long as its body (8–10 cm/3–4 inches). It is found all over the country, near human habitation and in remote areas. The mouse lives mostly off the land, eating plants, berries and

fungi, as well as small insects. It does not hibernate, and sometimes takes shelter in houses and outbuildings in cold weather.

Both the house mouse and long-tailed mouse are long-established residents in Iceland, probably dating back to the original settlement. Some zoologists believe that the long-tailed mouse must, like the fox, pre-date human habitation, as 1,000 years would not account for the development of this sub-species' differences from its mainland cousins. The brown rat is believed to have arrived in 1840, and spread rapidly to every region. The black rat has been sighted from time to time since 1919, but is not firmly established.

Another addition to Icelandic fauna was accidentally introduced into the wild. The American mink (*Mustela vison*) was brought to Iceland in the 1930s for the first attempts at fur farming, but a number of animals escaped. Within 35 years, the species had spread all over the country except for the central highlands, a localised area of the southeast and some islands. These blood-thirsty predators cause havoc among nesting birds such as puffins, guillemots, ducks and eiders by taking eggs and chicks. They also feed on fish, small birds and mammals. They are hunted by farmers, although their numbers remain high.

By 1817, reindeer were widely distributed in many areas, and their growing numbers gave rise to fears that they were overgrazing the upland pastures, traditionally sacrosanct to the sheep. A royal charter of 1817 permitted unlimited hunting of the animals, except for juveniles under a year old. Half a century of indiscriminate slaughter left the reindeer stocks in a poor state by 1882, when hunting was restricted.

Thanks to a total hunting ban from 1901 to 1940, the herds made an excellent recovery, and the population is now about 3,000. The reindeer is protected, but in most years a limited cull is allowed to control the population.

Imports from Lapland

Another of Iceland's wild mammals is a reminder of a well-meaning but misguided attempt to alter the Icelandic way of life. Several dozen reindeer (*Rangifer tarandus*) were introduced from northern Scandinavia in the 1771–87, when the Icelanders lived in penury, on the verge of starvation. The beasts were imported on the grounds that some Icelanders could adopt the nomadic herders' existence of the Sami people, also known as Lapps, in northern Norway, Sweden and Finland. The experiment did not work and the reindeer reverted to the wild, to add an exotic touch to the uplands, and some meat to hunters' tables.

Herds of deer are now found only in the mountains and valleys in the east of Iceland. They graze on mosses, fungi, lichens and grasses, but will also nibble shoots of shrubs and young trees. The shy creatures can rarely be spotted in summer, but in the depths of winter they sometimes descend to lowland farms and villages in search of adequate grazing.

Attempts have been made to introduce the musk ox (*Ovibos moschatus*) and the snowshoe or mountain hare (*Lepus timidus*) into Iceland, but with no success.

Above: Icelandic horses run wild in the countryside.
Right: a successful whale-watching trip.

Examples of Iceland's wild mammals, which are at times hard to spot in the wild, can be viewed at Reykjavík's zoo: fox, mink and reindeer in semi-wild open-air pens (*see page 166*).

Mammals of the sea

A range of marine mammals have been long established around Iceland's rugged coast. Seals are most likely to be spotted. Breeding in Iceland are two species, the common or harbour seal and the grey seal – Iceland boasts about half the world population of harbour seals, which often can be seen sunning themselves on the black sands of remote fjords. Five other species breed on Greenland and the polar ice floes but make occasional visits to northern Iceland: they include the ringed, bearded, harp and hooded seals, and the Atlantic walrus. The walrus is probably the least frequent visitor.

Iceland was famous in the Middle Ages for the whales off its coast and these days whale-watching tours do a booming business. The most common by far is the killer whale, or orca, which hunts in shallow waters. Of the larger whale species, the sperm, fin, humpback and minke whales are probably the most common. Off the south coast, dolphins are frequently seen, especially in late spring and summer. ❑

A VISITOR FROM GREENLAND

The polar bear is just an occasional visitor to Iceland. Bears sometimes drift across the ocean from Greenland on ice floes, or even walk the 400 km (250 miles) across the Arctic pack-ice when it temporarily bridges the gap between the two countries. Most sightings occur in the North and Northwest, the regions nearest to Greenland.

Folklore abounds with colourful beliefs about these powerful carnivores. The polar bear was thought to be a human under a spell, and tales assert that the bear gives birth to human young, which are then transformed into cubs. A quality much envied by humans was the bear's resistance to cold – "bear-warmth". Icelanders believed that if a child were born on a polar-bear skin, he or she would gain this quality. Polar bears were at their most popular in the Middle Ages, when they became a priceless status symbol to the kings and princes of Europe. The difficulty of capturing such a fierce beast alive in distant Greenland or Iceland, then transporting it across the ocean, ensured its novelty value. Probably far more polar bears reached Iceland then, when the climate was cooler and the pack-ice reached farther south. This would explain their influence in folklore. Today any bears that arrive tend to be ravenously hungry and dangerous after their long journey, so they are always shot on sight.

PLACES

A detailed guide to every region of Iceland, with principal sites clearly cross-referenced by number to the maps

Iceland is one of the world's most expensive countries, and this basic fact helps shape every Icelandic itinerary. Renting a car gives the most freedom in a visit, but can cost an arm and a leg (and five minutes on most Icelandic roads, which can seem little more than rutted dirt tracks, will explain why). Luckily, a range of bus and air tours operates to all major destinations throughout the summer season, early June to mid-August – which is also the only time that many museums and hotels are open, and when the vast majority of people come to Iceland.

Most visitors first arrive at Keflavík airport and stay in the capital, Reykjavík – a city that is almost painfully quiet except on Friday and Saturday nights, when Icelanders let loose in the bars and discos in true Viking fashion. But few people come to Iceland for its urban life. The real star is nature, and you don't have to go far to find it.

Each region has its own attractions. A few hours' drive from Reykjavík in the Southwest is the so-called "Golden Circle", which includes some of Iceland's best-known natural spectacles, such as the waterfall Gullfoss, the eponymous Geysir and Iceland's historical centre, Þingvellir. Just off the south coast are the Vestmannaeyjar (Westmann Islands), still scarred by the effects of a 1973 volcanic eruption. The Southeast offers Iceland's most accessible glaciers and Skaftafell National Park, a favourite hiking spot among Icelanders.

North of Reykjavík is the historic Snæfellsnes Peninsula, setting for many Icelandic sagas and Jules Verne's *Journey to the Centre of the Earth*. Beyond Snæfellsnes, the remote, windswept West Fjords region offers some of the wildest (and wettest) landscapes in Iceland. Akureyri, arguably Iceland's most pleasant town, is the jumping-off point for exploring the North. Nearby Lake Mývatn is Iceland's most popular tourist spot outside the "Golden Circle", where dramatic volcanic activity can be seen at close range. In the Northeast is Jökulsárgljúfur National Park, an awe-inspiring series of canyons leading to Dettifoss, Europe's most powerful waterfall. The East Fjords region is the warmest in Iceland, where quiet fishing villages are surrounded by rugged scenery.

Finally, there is the interior – an area quite different from the rest of Iceland. Almost all coastal roads, including the "Ring Road" that circles the country, are passable in two-wheel drive cars; the various routes through the interior demand four-wheel drive or a specially designed touring bus. The coast has hundreds of villages and farms offering accommodation; in the interior, camping is the only option. Weather by the coast is relatively warm, if often wet; temperatures in the interior can plunge to dangerous levels without warning.   ❑

PRECEDING PAGES: Jökulsarlón in the Southeast; a farmer rounding up horses; bold sculptures from the Ásmundur Sveinsson Sculpture Gallery in Reykjavík.
LEFT: hiking to the sea in the West Fjords.

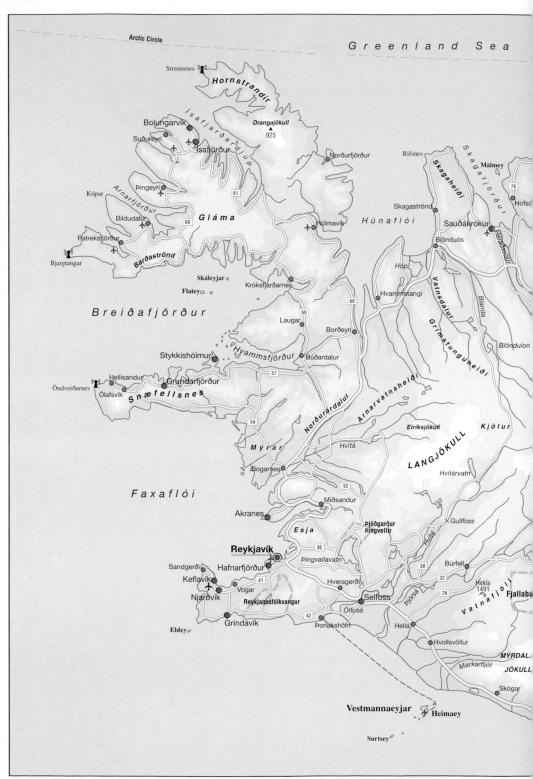

Arctic Circle

Greenland Sea

Straumnes
Hornstrandir
Bolungarvík
Suðureyri
Ísafjörður
Drangajökull
925
Norðurfjörður
Rifsnes
Málmey
Skagaheiði
Skagafjörður
76
Hofsó
Pingeyri
Kópur
Arnarfjörður
Bíldudalur
Gláma
61
60
Hólmavík
Skagaströnd
Sauðárkrókur
Húnaflói
Patreksfjörður
Bjargtangar
Barðaströnd
Blönduós
Hóp
Vatnsdalur
Blanda
Skáleyjar
Flatey
Króksfjarðarnes
Hvammstangi
Grímstunguheiði
Blöndulón
Breiðafjörður
60
68
Laugar
Borðeyri
Stykkishólmur
Hvammsfjörður
Búðardalur
57
Hellisandur
Grundarfjörður
Öndverðarnes
Ólafsvík
Snæfellsnes
Norðurárdalur
Arnarvatnsheiði
Eiríksjökull
Kjölur
LANGJÖKULL
Mýrar
Hvítá
Hvítárvatn
Bogarnes
54
Faxaflói
52
Miðsandur
Akranes
Esja
Gullfoss
Pjóðgarður
Pingvellir
Hvítá
Reykjavík
36
Pingvallavatn
30
Búrfell
Sandgerði
Hafnarfjörður
Keflavík
41
Hveragerði
32
Hekla
1491
Fjallaba
Vogar
26
Njarðvík
Reykjanesfólkvangur
Selfoss
Pjórsá
Vatnafjöll
Eldey
Grindavík
42
Ólfusá
Porlákshöfn
Hella
Hvolsvöllur
MÝRDAL
Markarfljót
JÖKULL
Skógar
Vestmannaeyjar
Heimaey
Surtsey

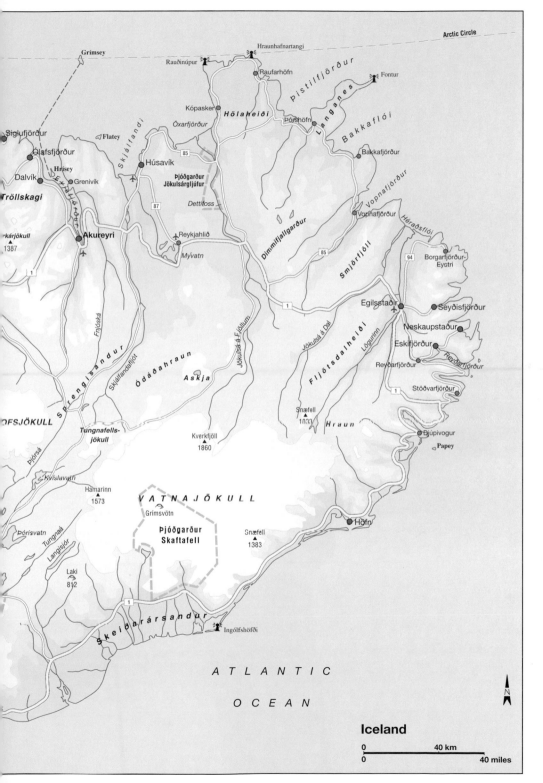

Iceland

0		40 km
0		40 miles

REYKJAVÍK

The world's northernmost capital is a bright, colourful city. Rich in cultural attractions and with a vibrant nightlife, Reykjavík also has parks and wildlife areas surprisingly close to its centre

Map on pages 154–5

Visitors are often unsure whether Reykjavík is a scaled-down city or scaled-up village. Probably it is both. Housing nearly two-fifths of Iceland's population, it is the undisputed political, business, cultural and intellectual centre of the country. Yet it retains a certain slow pace and almost rustic charm that makes it unique amongst the world's capitals.

It was here that the "official" settlement of Iceland began, after a few false starts, in the late 9th century AD. For centuries there was little to distinguish it from any other cluster of farms elsewhere in the country, although the strands of its noble fate had already been woven: while the practical details of settlement and development were entrusted to man, the site itself was originally chosen by the pagan gods. Ingólfur Arnarson, who has been given the title First Settler of Iceland, brought with him from Norway not only his family and cattle but also the high seat that was the symbol of the homestead. Following established Viking custom, Ingólfur dutifully tossed overboard the pillars on which the high seat was mounted – wherever they washed ashore, that was where the gods willed him to live.

It took over three years for Ingólfur's slaves to find the pillars, while the Viking himself stayed temporarily in the south, but eventually they turned up on the shores of what is now Iceland's capital. One of the slaves, less than impressed with the gods' choice, snapped that "to no avail we have crossed fine districts to live on this outlying wilderness", and ran off with one of Ingólfur's maidservants. But the other slave, Vífill, was given his freedom; he lived at Vífilsstaðir, now the site of a sanatorium, between Reykjavík and neighbouring Garðabær, just to the south of the city. Ingólfur himself submitted to the gods' judgement and probably built his house in the old city centre, with a view of the duck-filled Tjörn – literally, the lake.

In the shadow of steam

The First Settler, Ingólfur, named his new home Reykjavík (Smoky Bay), after clouds he saw rising from the ground, probably in what is now the Laugardalur area. The "smoke" was steam from geothermal springs – ironically, the same "smoke" that today makes Reykjavík an almost completely pollution-free city. The first pipes bringing hot water to the city were laid in 1930. Today all the city's houses are heated from natural geothermal sources, removing the need for fossil fuels.

As for Ingólfur, he still has a presence in the shape of one of the statues so characteristic of the capital (by Einar Jónsson, 1874–1954). The First Settler is now perched atop **Arnarhóll** ("eagle hill"), at the

PRECEDING PAGES:
Leifur Eiríksson looks down on Reykjavík by the Hallgrímskirkja.
LEFT: aerial view of the city.
BELOW:
a traditional touch.

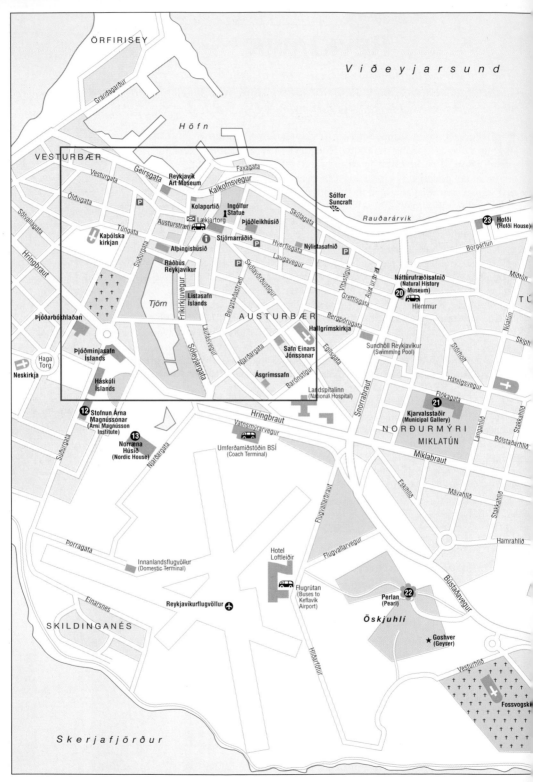

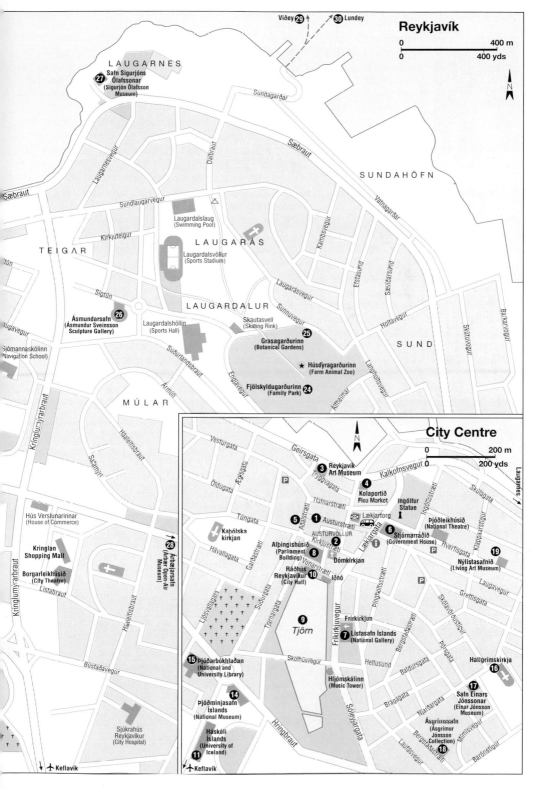

Reykjavík

Viðey 29   30 Lundey

0   400 m
0   400 yds

N

LAUGARNES

Safn Sigurjóns
Ólafssonar
(Sigurjón Ólafsson
Museum) 27

Sundagarðar

Sæbraut

SUNDAHÖFN

Dalbraut

Sæbraut

Laugarnesvegur

Sundlaugarvegur

Kirkjuteigur

Laugardalslaug
(Swimming Pool)

LAUGARÁS

TEIGAR

Laugardalsvöllur
(Sports Stadium)

Sigtún

Laugarásvegur

LAUGARDALUR

Ásmundarsafn
(Ásmundur Sveinsson
Sculpture Gallery) 26

Laugardalshöllin
(Sports Hall)

Skautasvell
(Skating Rink)

Sunnuvegur

Grasagarðurinn
(Botanical Gardens) 25

SUND

Sjómannaskólinn
(Navigation School)

Suðurlandsbraut

Ármúli

Húsdýragarðurinn
(Farm Animal Zoo) ★

Engjavegur

Fjölskyldugarðurinn
(Family Park) 24

MÚLAR

Háaleitisbraut

Kringlumýrarbraut

Sæmýri

City Centre

0   200 m
0   200 yds

N

Vesturgata

Geirsgata

Reykjavik
Art Museum 3

Kolaportið
Flea Market 4

Kalkofnsvegur

Ægisgata

Öldugata

Túngata

Hafnarstræti

Tryggvagata

Ingólfur
Statue

5 1 Austurstræti
Lækjartorg

Þjóðleikhúsið
(National Theatre)

Kaþólska
kirkjan

Aðalstræti

AUSTURVÖLLUR

6 Stjórnarráðið
(Government House)

Hverfisgata

19

Hávallagata

Garðastræti

Alþingishúsið
(Parliament
Building) 8

Kirkjustræti

2

Vonarstræti

Dómkirkjan

Nylistasafnið
(Living Art Museum)

Ráðhús
Reykjavíkur
(City Hall) 10

Iðnó

Þingholtsstræti

Laugavegur

Grettisgata

9

Tjörn

Frikirkjuvegur

Frikirkjan

7 Listasafn Íslands
(National Gallery)

Bergstaðastræti

Skólavörðustígur

Þórsgata

Hús Verslunarinnar
(House of Commerce)

Kringlan
Shopping Mall

Borgarleikhúsið
(City Theatre)

Listabraut

Árbæjarsafn
(Árbær Open-Air
Museum) 28

Suðurgata

Tjarnargata

Skothúsvegur

Hljómskálinn
(Music Tower)

Hellusund

Baldursgata

Hallgrímskirkja

16

Bústaðavegur

15 Þjóðarbókhlaðan
(National and
University Library)

Bræðraborgarstígur

Laufásvegur

17 Safn Einars
Jónssonar
(Einar Jónsson
Museum)

Sjúkrahús
Reykjavikur
(City Hospital)

14 Þjóðminjasafn
Íslands
(National Museum)

Háskóli
Íslands
(University of
Iceland) 11

Hringbraut

Sóleyjargata

Njarðargata

Ásgrímssafn
(Ásgrímur
Jónsson
Collection)

18

Mímisvegur

Bergstaðastræti

Laufásvegur

Barónsstígur

✈ Keflavík

✈ Keflavík

Reykjavík gets plenty of snow between November and March.

BELOW: summer-time in Austurvöllur town plaza.

virtual central point of the city: next to Government House, his back turned upon the Judicial Building and the Culture House (open daily 11am–5pm; entrance fee), with the Central Bank and several government ministries to his right, Ingólfur gazes across the harbour to where the glacial cap of Snæfell-sjökull twinkles mystically on the horizon on clear days, almost 100 km (60 miles) away to the north.

For centuries after settlement, Reykjavík remained little more than a few farmhouses. In a census taken in 1801 its population was a mere 301 souls, mainly spread between the lake and the Old Harbour where the shops and offices of the old city centre now lie. The population was presumably even less in 1786, when Reykjavík was first granted a municipal charter as an official trading post. In 1901, Reykjavík still only had 5,000 inhabitants. The sudden leap to today's 112,000 has occurred mostly since World War II.

Reykjavík today

For a visitor, the old city centre is definitely the most charming part of the capital. Well-to-do residential streets, with their brightly coloured corrugated-metal-clad houses and mossy lawns enclosed by picket fences, run alongside the shops, cafés and galleries of the main commercial thoroughfares. In contrast to the compact centre, Reykjavík's sprawling suburbs extend eastwards for mile after mile, all drab apartment blocks and busy roads.

The city as a whole has been undergoing a transformation of character in the recent past. Whereas visitors to Iceland once considered Reykjavík little more than a stop-over en route to the country's undisputed main attraction – the landscape – the city has now earned its stripes as a destination in its own right.

Its energetic and distinctive cultural scene is a constant source of fascination. After all, what other city with a population of a little over 100,000 has an internationally acclaimed symphony orchestra, two major professional theatre companies, numerous independent theatre groups, an opera company, a national ballet and both a national and municipal art gallery? On top of this, dozens of smaller independent galleries and venues offer continuous exhibitions, recitals and performances throughout the year, and a biannual arts festival attracts renowned artists of international standing.

Reykjavík nightlife has also recently been "discovered" by visitors from around the world eager for something different and vibrant. The city's reputation as a "happening" place has largely grown out of the success of pop diva Björk and the roster of international stars that have since taken to visiting the country. The international press has taken note, and reporters are routinely sent over to document the merriment.

Unlikely as it may sound, Reykjavík has also become increasingly popular as an attractive option for the cosmopolitan shopping enthusiast. Those wishing to attract shoppers emphasise that, as a result of low overhead costs and mark-up, retail prices for designer wares are much lower in Reykjavík than in the world's metropolises. The city also has a wide range of shops, from ultra-trendy to conservative, all within a relatively small geographical area.

Exploring the old city

The old city centre is bordered roughly by Suðurgata to the west, Hafnarstræti to the north, Lækjargata and Fríkirkjuvegur to the east and Hringbraut to the south. Street names give some hint of the way Reykjavík looked in the 19th

Map on pages 154–5

LEFT: view of the city centre from the spire of Hallgrímskirkja.
BELOW: Tjörn lake in the city centre.

century and before. The traffic artery of Lækjargata ("brook street"), for example, followed a stream between the shore and the lake; eels were caught here once, but it is now buried beneath asphalt and flagstones. Today's main shopping street of Laugavegur ("pools road") points the way that women followed on foot or horseback to the Laugardalur hot springs to do their washing.

Austurstræti ❶ was until recently the city's most easterly point – the street's maidens were immortalised, like distant cousins of Heine's *Daughters of the Rhine*, by Tómas Gudmundsson (1901–83), Iceland's first urban poet. The town plaza **Austurvöllur ❷** ("eastern field") is today a small park laid out around a statue of the nationalist hero Jón Sigurðsson. It is said that Ingólfur Arnarson actually grew his hay here.

Parallel to Austurstræti, Hafnarstræti ("harbour street") is no longer on the harbourfront – it was superseded by Tryggvagata, built during World War I on gravel and sand dumped to extend the waterfront, then by the modern Geirsgata which is now on the harbourfront. Hafnarstræti houses the customs office, tax office and a couple of pubs, but the houses on the southern side of Hafnarstræti date back to the 19th century. At Tryggvagata 17 is the **Reykjavík Art Museum ❸** (Listasafn Reykjavíkur Hafnarhús; open daily 11am–6pm, until 7pm on Thurs; entrance fee), situated in the stylishly renovated former warehouse of the Port.

Kolaportið Flea Market ❹ (open Sat and Sun 11am–5pm), situated on Geirsgata, across from the harbour, is a cheerful occasion selling clothes, books and other assorted odds and ends. The food section is a must for anyone who is curious about traditional Icelandic fare; here are featured the tasty *harðfiskur* (dried fish), *hákarl* (cured shark), *síld* (pickled herring) and the infamous pickled rams' testicles, as well as a host of other culinary delights.

Houses clad in corrugated metal are a common sight in Reykjavík – a tradition dating back to when all houses were made of timber. Corrugated metal is a great shield against wind and rain, and allows the timber to breathe, so it is still used to cover timber houses today.

BELOW: browsing in the flea market.

Aðalstræti

Reykjavík's oldest buildings are on **Aðalstræti ❺** ("main street"). In the 18th century, Aðalstræti was earmarked by High Sheriff Skúli Magnússon (nicknamed "the Father of Reykjavík") for a crafts and trades development project. An unusual effort to catch up with the outside world, it was a scheme for creating cottage industries – wool-dyeing, knitting, weaving, etc. Although it folded, the project left not only inspiration, ambition and skills, but also the capital's earliest surviving architecture. Parts of the workshops have been renovated.

Aðalstræti 10 is the oldest surviving building in the city, built in 1764 to replace a 1752 weaver's shop that had burnt down. Its history is dotted with larger-than-life characters, including one-time owner Bishop Geir Vídalín (1761–1823). A cleric famed for his hospitality, Bishop Vídalín left an immortal dedication to the city's nightlife: "There are two places where the fires never die down – Hell and my house." Burning a hole through his wallet in the process, Vídalín won the dubious honour of becoming the only bishop in ecclesiastical history to be declared bankrupt. The bar/bistro that currently occupies the building is named in his honour. On show across the road, beneath a thick layer of clear plastic, is one of the old wells that used to provide Reykjavík's residents with drinking water. Relics dating back to the Settlement have been found to the right of the well, at the corner of Aðalstræti and Túngata.

Although the old centre has diminished in importance by day as the newer areas have developed and come to life, once night falls it regains something of its former character. A plethora of pubs and restaurants lends a boisterous atmosphere to downtown Reykjavík by night, creating a beehive of activity more in

Map on pages 154–5

Aðalstræti 10 housed the first shop to import fruit to Iceland. It sported the country's first advertising slogan in its window, a quote from St Matthew: "By their fruits ye shall know them".

BELOW: the city from the banks of the Tjörn.

Embracing the Night

Something curious has happened to Reykjavík nightlife since the early 1990s – it has become very hip, especially with foreigners with money, such as young, well-to-do Europeans. One example is the British pop star who was so taken with the scene that he returned again and again before finally purchasing a share in his favourite pub – and a flat nearby.

Clearly, Reykjavík nightlife is something to write home about. International media send their people over to chronicle the festivities and wind up with exposés as colourful as a Reykjavík sunset in summer. Quite a change from the old days when tourists wearing hiking boots and cameras around their necks barely awarded the capital a second glance.

And what is so appealing? Perhaps it is the rip-roaring, spine-tingling Viking intensity with which the Icelanders approach their

merriment. Or all those Beautiful People, packed like sardines into the small trendy cafés. Or lined up in queues outside those hot night spots, shivering in the latest Parisian fashions: never mind that it is a mere 5°C outside – that slip dress and those strap sandals will stay on!

Inside, there is pulsating action and bartenders have their work cut out. A steady stream of alcoholic beverages leaves the bar, cocktail waiters and waitresses moving with amazing agility through the crowd. The loudness of the music makes regular conversation impossible. Bodies bop up and down and should there be a shortage of space the tabletops will do just fine, thank you. Actors and actresses rub shoulders with upstart politicians who rub shoulders with inebriated bohemians who claim to have solved the riddle of life.

At closing time, typically 5, 6 or 7am, the lights go on and everyone has to leave, but the action continues out in the street. Everyone heads on down to Lækjartorg square; if it is summer and the weather is good there will most certainly be a 5,000-strong crowd there. It will be only slightly smaller if it is winter and there is a blizzard.

Navigate your way through the throng and behold anything from ecstasy to wretched misery, all within a single city block. For all this celebration is not without cost. There exists a dark side, in the form of drunken minors passed out in doorways or whacked out on illicit substances. Although the city's law-enforcement officers are doing a commendable job, Reykjavík nightlife is neither as simple nor as benign as it used to be. Now, for instance, there are many more acts of random violence which may or may not cost someone their life. And while one of the main hazards used to be traffic – the motorised kind – now there is trafficking – the highly organised kind. This, too, is a part of Reykjavík nightlife.

But for the most part, capital revellers can enjoy the absence of serious crimes and misdemeanours: it is still relatively safe to embrace the night. And this, too, may be something to write home about. ❑

LEFT: revellers congregating late at night on the streets of Reykjavík.

Map on pages 154–5

keeping with a city many times the size. Nightlife begins late and lasts until early morning. Bar prices are high and most nightlifers "warm up" with a few drinks at home before taking the plunge. The "in" spots tend to change regularly; what was hip today may be passé tomorrow. Queues are quick to form when the action gets underway.

Humble beginnings

Iceland's **Government House** ❻ (Stjórnarráðið) stands on a small grassy bank overlooking Lækjartorg square, a stone's throw downhill from the First Settler, Ingólfur's statue on Arnarhóll. Built between 1765 and 1770, which makes it one of Reykjavík's oldest buildings, this unassuming whitewashed structure now houses the offices of the Prime Minister, yet it began its days less gloriously, as a prison workhouse. This building also housed the offices of the President of the Republic until 1996, when they were moved to premises at Sóleyjargata 1.

Further along Lækjargata, on the same side as Government House, stands a row of houses built in the mid-19th century. These narrowly escaped demolition some years ago and have been renovated to house two restaurants and the Iceland Tourist Board. Here is also where the well-equipped **Tourist Information Centre** is located (there is another information centre in the City Hall). Further still, shortly before Tjörn lake, the stately **Reykjavík Secondary Grammar School** (Menntaskólinn í Reykjavík) presides over the streetscape. This was the first school of its kind in the country and among its alumni are two Nobel Laureates: Halldór Laxness (literature, 1955) and Níels Finsen (medicine, 1903).

BELOW: Government House.

*The entrance to the
National Gallery.*

The **National Gallery** ❼ (Listasafn Íslands), overlooking the lake and next door to the grey and green Fríkirkjan (Free Church), is yet another historical building which has had its ups and downs (Fríkirkjuvegur 7; open Tues–Sun 11–5pm; entrance fee). It was originally built as a cold store in which to keep ice cut from the lake which was then used for preserving fish. Later it served as a fish-freezing plant and a hot dance spot – so hot, in fact, that it once caught fire. Now renovated in a light-filled modern style, the small gallery has a fine permanent collection of work by Icelandic artists that is supplemented by changing exhibitions. There is a café on the first floor with internet access.

The grey basalt **Parliament Building** (Alþingishúsið) ❽ on Austurvöllur square was custom-built in 1880–81 to house the ancient assembly. After more or less continuous operation in nearby Þingvellir *(see pages 184–9)* since the year 930 (albeit mostly as a court, because Iceland lost its independence in 1262), the Alþingi moved to Reykjavík in 1798. The building visible today was built to house it during the tide of the 19th-century nationalist awakening.

Around the Tjörn

On a clear day, it is worth taking some time to have a stroll around the **Tjörn** ❾ ("lake") itself. Extraordinarily, this is still a natural breeding habitat for over 40 species of birds – most noticeably ducks. There are seats and a pleasant walkway along its eastern side (below Fríkirkjuvegur), giving views of a splendid row of houses on the opposite bank.

BELOW: swans on the Tjörn in front of the City Hall.

A controversial new **City Hall** ❿ (Ráðhús Reykjavíkur) was built on the edge of the lake in the 1980s – an impressive postmodern edifice in its own right, but attacked by many Reykjavík residents for clashing with its serene environs.

There is a huge relief map of Iceland in the entrance hall which is well worth a look, and at times this is the venue for free concerts and exhibitions. There is also a pleasant coffee-shop with a lovely view of the lake.

On the north bank of the Tjörn, at the end of the City Hall walking bridge, is a corrugated-metal clad structure, which is fondly known as **Iðnó**. It was originally constructed to house a craftsmen's guild but is best-known for being the home of the Reykjavík Municipal Theatre Company from 1897 to 1987. Iðnó has recently been reopened after painstaking renovation which has transformed it into one of Reykjavík's historical gems; it now serves as a venue for cultural performances and also houses a quaint little coffee bar and a fine restaurant. Iðnó is the setting for one of Reykjavík's most popular tourist shows, **Light Nights**; the drama is based on the sagas and Viking tales and is performed every Sunday and Monday in summer at 8.30pm. Also popular with tourists is **The Volcano Show** on Hellusund, a series of documentaries and talks on Iceland's geology, presented by noted film-maker Vilhjálmur Knudsen.

South of the Tjörn

A bridge across the Tjörn leads to some grassy park areas with a series of public sculptures, followed by the **University of Iceland** ⓫ (Háskóli Íslands), which was founded in 1911 – although its ponderous Third Reich-style main building dates from the 1930s.

Located on the University campus is the **Árni Magnússon Institute** ⓬ (Stofnun Árna Magnússonar), an unassuming building that is home to some of Iceland's most treasured medieval manuscripts containing the famous sagas and the Poetic Eddas (Suðurgata; open summer: Mon–Sat 11am–4pm; winter: Tues–Fri 2–4pm; entrance fee). The libraries and permanent displays here have become pilgrimage sites for anyone who is interested in the literary traditions of Northern Europe. The Institute looks after everything from restoring manuscripts, controlling the humidity of their storage rooms and transcribing sagas for new editions to publishing cultural treatises on Icelandic folklore.

Situated just east of the Institute is the **Nordic House** ⓭ (Norræna Húsið), designed by the highly respected Finnish architect Alvar Aalto (Sturlugata; open daily). Its purpose is to cultivate and strengthen ties between the Nordic countries. To that end, it has a coffee shop complete with current Scandinavian newspapers, a library and an ongoing programme of Scandinavian cultural events – many of which are free of charge.

On the outskirts of the university is the **National Museum** ⓮ (Þjóðminjasafn Íslands), which is essential viewing for anyone interested in Icelandic history (Suðurgata 41; open Tues–Sun 11am–5pm; entrance fee; closed for major renovations until December 2002). Most of the archaeological finds around Iceland in the past few hundred years have ended up in its halls – including the wooden church door from Valþjófsstaður in the east, carved in the 13th century with the story of a knight who slays a dragon. This is the main place in Iceland to see Viking relics.

Map on pages 154–5

BELOW: American culture in the Icelandic capital.

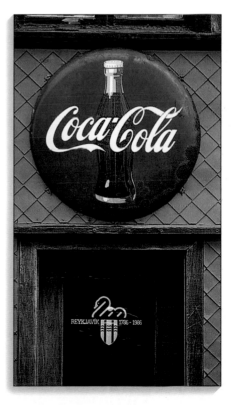

Across from the National Museum, on the other side of Suðurgata, is the **National and University Library** ⑮ (Þjóðarbókhlaðan) an airy, modern structure which opened in 1994 after some two decades of construction (Arngríms-gata 3; open summer: Mon–Fri 9am–5pm, Sat 10am–2pm; winter: Mon–Thur 8.15am–10pm, Fri 8.15am–7pm, Sat 9am–5pm, Sun 11am–5pm). The library houses a manuscript collection and there are excellent research facilities for scholars, students and the public in general.

Completed in 1974, Hallgrímskirkja is designed to resemble columns of Iceland's basaltic lava.

Hallgrímskirkja and around

East from the lake, all roads climb to the imposing **Hallgrímskirkja church** ⑯, a modern basalt structure that many visitors find profoundly ugly. You can, however, climb the tower – or take the lift (open daily: summer 9am–6pm, winter 9am–5pm; entrance fee) – for the best views of Reykjavík and the deceptively close Snæfellsnes peninsula. On a clear day, as they say, you can see forever. In front of the church is a huge and impressive statue of Leifur Eiríksson, "Discoverer of America", a gift from the US on the 1,000th anniversary of the founding of the Alþingi in 1930.

Next to Hallgrímskirkja is the studio home of Einar Jónsson, now the **Einar Jónsson Museum** ⑰ (Safn Einars Jónssonar), which houses a collection of works by one of Iceland's great sculptors (Njarðargata; open summer: Tues–Sun 2–5pm; winter: Sat, Sun 2–5pm; closed Dec–Jan; entrance fee). Jónsson was a master of symbolism and epic, and many of his works combine a classical human form with symbols drawn from Norse, Greek and Oriental mythology.

BELOW: the airy interior of Hallgrímskirkja.

A short walk to the south of Hallgrímskirkja, you might like to stop off at the **Ásgrímur Jónsson Collection** ⑱ (Ásgrímssafn; Bergstaðastræti 74; open summer: Tues–Sun 1.30–4pm; winter: by arrangement; closed Dec–Jan; entrance fee). Jónsson was Iceland's first professional painter and one of the nation's foremost landscape artists. The Ásgrímur Jónsson Collection is his donation to the Icelandic nation and is now a department within the National Gallery.

If you head north from Hallgrímskirkja, you will come to the **Living Art Museum** ⑲ (Nýlistasafnið), another must-see for art connoisseurs (Vatnsstígur 3b; open Tues–Sun 2–6pm; entrance fee). It was originally founded as a cooperative in the 1970s by a group of artists who opposed what they saw as the National Gallery's shunning of experimental art. The museum stages ongoing exhibitions by artists both Icelandic and foreign and has become a permanent fixture on the artistic landscape.

Conveniently located at one of the main bus terminals is the **Natural History Museum** ⑳ (Náttúru-fræðisafnið; Hlemmur 3–5; open Tues, Thur, Sat, Sun: summer 1–5pm; winter 1.30–4.30pm; entrance fee). This is a great place to learn about Iceland's geology and there are exhibits dedicated to Icelandic flora and fauna, including a specimen of the now-extinct Great Auk (*see page 247*).

Southeast from the Natural History Museum is the **Kjarvalsstaðir Municipal Gallery** ㉑ in Miklatún park, dedicated to Iceland's most famous modern artist, Jóhannes Kjarval (Flókagata; open daily:

10am–5pm, until 7pm on Wed; entrance fee). Born in 1885, Kjarval worked on a fishing trawler until his artistically minded fellow workers ran a lottery to raise money for him to study in Copenhagen. The collection of his landscapes here is well worth seeing.

Map on pages 154–5

Landmark buildings

Building in Reykjavík is still taking place on a grand scale. The literally outstanding feature of the Reykjavík skyline these days is the glass-domed **"Pearl"** ㉒ (Perlan) – a revolving restaurant that sits on top of the glistening silver hot-water tanks on **Öskjuhlíð** hill, offering a breathtaking view of the city on clear days. The tanks can take 24 million litres (more than 5 million gallons) of hot water and cater for almost half of Reykjavík's water consumption. An impressive man-made **geyser** spewing water at five-minute intervals has been constructed near the "Pearl", and efforts over the past two decades to turn Öskjuhlíð into a nature sanctuary have delivered impressive results.

Located back down near the shoreline is what is probably Reykjavík's best-known building internationally, the **Höfði House** ㉓ (tel: 563-2000 for information on guided tours). This is the municipal reception hall behind whose clapboard exterior former presidents Ronald Reagan and Mikhail Gorbachev met in October 1986 to take their first bows before the *pas-de-deux* towards global disarmament. Now it is used for official city social functions. At the time of its completion in 1909 to house the French consulate, Höfði was on the outskirts of the capital, and became the exclusive residence of poet and businessman Einar Benediktsson (1864–1940). This famous figure brought to the house not only his family but also a ghost. Reportedly, the ghost stayed on

The Höfði House, location of the 1986 summit between Reagan and Gorbachev.

BELOW: the "Pearl" hot water tanks topped by a revolving restaurant.

Modern sculpture at the Ásmundur Sveinsson Sculpture Gallery.

rent-free when the poet's family sold it to the British consulate, which grew in turn so tired of being haunted that the building was eventually sold to the city.

Nature and high art

For all Reykjavík's modern expansion, the city's natural treasures remain as precious as ever. The **Laugardalur** area, a green belt situated slightly to the northeast of the old city centre by the side of one of the main roads through town, has been largely preserved from development and until recently still had sheep and horses on it. It serves as the capital's main sports area with a large open-air, geothermally heated swimming pool, soccer stadium, sports hall and artificially frozen ice-skating rink. There is also the Viking theme park rides of the **Family Park** (Fjölskyldugaðurinn) and adjoining **Farm Animal Zoo** ㉔ (Húsdyragarðurinn) (both open summer: daily 10am–6pm; winter: Thurs–Tues 10am–5pm; entrance fee) with domestic animals as well as animals that are native to Iceland. The nearby **Botanical Gardens** ㉕ (Grasagarðurinn) have an impressive collection of 5,000 plants and nearly the entire Icelandic flora (open Apr–Sept: daily 10am–10pm; Oct–Mar: Mon–Fri 8am–3pm, Sat and Sun 10am–5pm).

Over the road from the soccer stadium is the **Ásmundur Sveinsson Sculpture Gallery** ㉖ (Ásmundarsafn; Sigtún; open daily: summer 10am–4 pm; winter 1–4pm; entrance fee). Sveinsson (1893–1982) drew inspiration from saga events, folklore and everyday life. His works are set in and around his bizarre dome and pyramid studio/home. The outdoor sculpture garden is impressive, and open at all hours – many tourists pass it regularly, as several new hotels, including the Grand Hotel Reykjavík and Hotel Ísland, are situated nearby.

BELOW: the geo-thermally heated swimming pool in Laugardalur.

Not far away on the shoreline is the **Sigurjón Ólafsson Museum** (Safn Sigurjóns Ólafssonar), dedicated to an Icelandic painter who lived from 1908 to 1982 (Laugarnestangi 70; open summer: Tues–Sun 2–5pm; winter: Sat, Sun 2–5pm). In addition to the art collection there is a small family-run café with a lovely sea view and weekly music recitals in the summer.

The New Reykjavík

Since World War II the capital has been expanding to the east, leaving its past behind. In the 1980s, as it approached a six-digit population, more modern and grandiose architecture appeared on its skyline. A new city centre was built entirely from scratch, including not only the large indoor shopping mall, **Kringlan**, but also a complex to house the Municipal Theatre company, after it moved from Iðno in the old centre in 1987.

As new residential suburbs sprang up – tasteless "concrete lava fields" like Breiðholt and Árbær, each many times more populous than the largest of rural Icelandic towns – so this new part of Reykjavík has become the geographical as well as the business and commercial centre. This expansion is perhaps the most instantly visible result of Iceland's rapid shift from a traditional, rural country to a modern technological society.

Located on the edge of the Árbær suburb is the **Árbær Open-Air Museum** (Árbæjarsafn), a living history museum that in the summer offers a schedule of events at weekends (open summer: Mon 11am–4pm, Tues–Fri 9am–5pm, Sat, Sun 10am–6pm; guided tours in winter Mon, Wed and Fri 1pm; entrance fee). A number of historical houses have been moved here from various locations in Reykjavík and around Iceland, and the past is re-created as accurately as possible.

BELOW: a splash of colour in Reykjavík's Botanical Gardens.

Map
on pages
154–5

*Before the Reforma-
tion, Viðey island
housed the richest
monastery in Iceland,
which owned a good
part of Reykjavík and
the land beyond,
until it was torn
down by Lutheran
zealots.*

BELOW:
boats at anchor in
the harbour.

Household items and furnishings used throughout the centuries are on permanent display, and there is also an old turf church which is a popular spot for wedding services. The atmosphere is compromised by the busy road that runs next to it.

Between the suburbs of Breiðholt and Árbær, and well within the city limits, runs the idyllic **Elliðaár** river, which pays handsome tribute to the lack of pollution in Reykjavík as one of the best salmon rivers in Iceland, with annual catches of around 1,600 fish. By tradition the city's burgomaster opens the fishing season on 1 May every year . Angling permits, being carefully shared out, are difficult for visitors to come by, but there is no problem in buying permits during the summer season for nearby **Lake Elliðavatn**, where there is good local trout in wonderfully calm and picturesque surroundings.

Elliðavatn borders the capital's **Heiðmörk** nature reserve to the south of the city, a popular spot for picnics and strolls, where wild patches merge harmoniously with areas reclaimed from wind erosion by the planting of trees.

Boat excursions

The island of **Viðey** ❷, five minutes by motorboat off the north shore from the new Sundahöfn harbour, was given to the Reykjavík authorities as a birthday present in 1987 when the capital celebrated the 200th anniversary of its municipal charter (boat trips leave from Sundahöfn–Klettavör harbour Mon–Fri: 1, 2 and 3pm; Sat, Sun: on the hour from 1 to 5pm; evening trips: Thur–Sun at 7, 7.30 and 8pm; call 581-1010 for further information). Today the island provides a haven for Reykjavík's inhabitants to "get away from it all".

High Sheriff Skúli Magnússon moved to Viðey in 1751 and had a residence built there, which was completed in 1755. It has recently been restored and now houses a splendid, if somewhat pricey, restaurant. The church on the island dates from 1794 and is also one of the oldest in the country. An ambitious scheme for a fisheries operation was launched in the early 20th century but eventually went bankrupt; remains of the "ghost town" can be visited on a pleasant walk around the eastern part of the island, which takes about an hour.

Another short boat trip (daily at 4.45pm; fee), organised by Viðeyjarferjan, leaves from the Sundahöfn docks to **Lundey** ❸ (known as "puffin island"). It is popular with travellers who aren't travelling far into Iceland but who want to catch a glimpse of puffins (tel: 892 0099 for information and bookings).

Reykjavík and the towns surrounding it have been growing so fast that they now form an almost continuous conurbation, known as the **Greater Reykjavík Area** and home to some 175,000 people – around three-fifths of Iceland's total population. Most of these towns are new and quite colourless, including Kópavogur, which has swollen in recent years to accommodate 23,000 people and is thus the second-largest community in Iceland. One of Kópavogur's claims to fame is that it is home to the country's biggest shopping mall, Smáralind, opened in October 2001. Sightseeing tours from Reykjavík take in some of the more interesting and historic places, such as Bessastaðir and Hafnarfjörður *(see pages 174–5).* ❑

Why is Everything So Expensive?

Visitors to Iceland are often shocked by the high price of everything. It's not at all uncommon to discover that one has just paid two, three, or four times as much as one would expect to part with back home for the same item of comparable quality.

Why is everything so expensive? For starters, Iceland's geographical isolation and harsh climate make it virtually 100 percent dependent on imports for everything except meat, potatoes, fish and dairy products. As a result, a web of importers, wholesalers and other middlemen has developed, supplying every corner of the land. While virtually every conceivable item is available, import tariffs and multiple layers of price markup can, and do, drive retail prices sky-high.

Imports of agricultural products are, with few exceptions, banned; at the same time, an overproducing farming sector is propped up by government subsidies which allow lamb, beef, milk, potatoes and other products to be produced at a huge loss in this highly inefficient sector. Although these subsidies should help to keep prices down, due to the lack of economies of scale to fall back on, supermarkets and other food retailers must count on huge markups to make up for the lack of volume. Throw in a 24.5 percent value-added tax on farm supplies, equipment and fuel that are already expensive – plus the VAT at the supermarket checkout – and you have a recipe for some of the highest priced victuals money can buy.

How can Icelanders afford to live here? The answer is relatively simple: almost everyone who is able to, works. Nearly eighty percent of those between the ages of 15 and 74 are employed outside the home, including seven out of 10 women; unemployment is less than 4 percent. Generally, low wages are compensated for by working weeks of 50, 60 or even 80 hours. In many instances, even this isn't enough to make ends meet. Thousands of families are heavily in debt and struggle to pay off their mortgage, car, and appliance loans, a situation compounded by Icelanders' expensive tastes.

The dilemma is not limited to domestic households. Since around the 1960s, government borrowing abroad has helped create a highly developed and costly system of social services. Iceland now has one of the world's highest levels of foreign debt per capita in the world, with repayment obligations consuming one-fifth of the country's export revenues annually.

Of course, with nearly everyone working, taxes shouldn't really need to be so high. However, approximately one-quarter of the population are civil servants and as such do not contribute to the national wealth in the same way as, say, fish exporters do. The eleven Icelandic embassies in Europe, Scandinavia, Russia, China and North America – a lot for a nation barely the size of an American suburb – are also costly to run.

It all adds up. A tiny, isolated population with one of the highest living standards in the world is an expensive proposition. ❑

RIGHT: the high price of alcohol in Iceland would drive anyone to drink.

CHRISTMAS AND NEW YEAR: SEASON OF LIGHT

Christmas in Iceland is a festive affair. The Yule spirit permeates everything and is for most a much-needed antidote to the winter blues.

Preparations for this festival of light usually begin on the first Sunday in advent with the lighting of the first candle on the advent wreath. From then on things take off: the hustle and bustle of Christmas shopping, the baking of cookies and cakes, and a multitude of other seasonal happenings.

Iceland has its own traditional version of Santa Claus in the form of the *jólasveinar*, or "Yule Lads". These are a group of 13 pranksters, each with their own definite character, who live with their parents in the mountains. They come to town on the 13 days before Christmas, one each day until Christmas Eve. In the old days they created mischief and were a huge nuisance; these days they are kinder, gentler and leave little presents behind for children in shoes strategically placed by an open bedroom window.

The official celebration begins at 6pm on December 24. Many people then head off to mass before going home to a festive dinner, followed by the opening of presents and dancing around the Christmas tree. The immediate family tends to be together on Christmas Eve, while Christmas Day is typically reserved for the extended family.

The next few days are usually filled with more visits and parties, leading up to another big event: New Year's Eve. Typically families dine together and then head off to a *brenna* – a huge bonfire lit to symbolise the burning of the old. By 10.30pm there is hardly a soul about, however, as the natives gather around their television sets for the annual year-end comedy show, where the nation's top comedians parody the year's main events. This ends just in time to allow people to take to the streets and fire into the sky millions of króna's worth of cascading, sparkling colour.

△ **GLUGGAGÆGIR**
"Window Peeper" is the tenth Yule Lad. He peeped through windows and then later returned to steal what he coveted.

▽ **SKYRGÁMUR**
"Curd Glutton" is the eighth Yule Lad in line. He crept into the pantry, found some curds and then gorged himself insensible.

◁ **FAMILY PHOTO**
Some of the Yule Lads with their parents, Grýla the ogre and Leppalúði the horrid, who both, it is said, eat naughty children.

THE FINAL CELEBRATIONS

In Iceland the *þrettándinn* celebrations on 6 January provide an official sense of closure to the holidays. Once again bonfires are lit throughout the country, though generally they are on a smaller scale than the New Year's *brennur*. These are called *álfabrennur* – elf bonfires – and in some places the elf king and queen make an appearance, sometimes even riding a white steed.

Different parts of the country have their own traditions for this night; in the Vestmannaeyjar (above) the 13 Yule Lads appear on a cliff ledge above the town then file down and lead torchbearers through the streets, ending at a merry bonfire.

In the past 6 January was the main holiday evening for playing cards, with friends gathering to "play out the holidays". Old folktales also hold that cows gained the gift of speech for one night on *þrettándinn*, though none have been heard in recent times. These days 6 January is usually a time for dismantling the Christmas tree.

△ **NEW YEAR'S EVE**
The celebrations consist of huge bonfires and an explosion of fireworks at midnight. The central Reykjavík pyrotechnics are spectacular.

◁ **LUMINOUS GIFT**
The Norwegian city of Oslo has sent Reykjavík a large Christmas tree every year since 1951. The tree, swathed in lights, is placed in Austurvöllur square.

▷ **DECK THE WALLS**
Coloured lights are a joy to behold in the mid-winter darkness. Quite a number of houses, such as this one in Reykjavík, put up their own Christmas lights to create festive decorations, outside as well as in.

THE REYKJANES PENINSULA

Situated just south of the capital, the Reykjanes peninsula is a compact area to visit. Its highlights include excellent birdwatching, several nature reserves and the stunning Blue Lagoon

Map on page 174

The Reykjanes peninsula is easy to ignore – a smallish promontory south of Reykjavík **❶**, it is undeniably overshadowed by the capital's greater pulling power. Yet most people's first glimpse of Iceland is actually of Reykjanes – Keflavík international airport is situated right in its heart.

Almost all arriving tourists simply jump aboard a bus or hire a car, and head for the mountains or the city without a backward glance. But one really should give the region a little time: the principal sights can be seen on a day tour, but hikers, whale-watchers, birdwatchers and devotees of the Blue Lagoon may find it hard to tear themselves away.

Lashed by the Atlantic

Reykjanes is a wind-blown area, lying open to the violent North Atlantic ocean – which supplies a large proportion of the population with their livelihood. Small, nondescript fishing villages dot the peninsula's coastline.

Much of this low-lying promontory consists of lava fields, some of which flowed as recently as the 14th century. In fact the peninsula is a continuation of the Mid-Atlantic Ridge which pushes apart two immense plates of the earth's crust at the rate of 2 cm (¾ inch) each year. Pillow lava and tufa formations from Ice-Age eruptions give some indication of what the submarine ridge looks like. While the broad expanses of volcanic rock may seem grey and barren at first glance, in fact they have donned a coat of Iceland's typical grey-green moss, soft and springy underfoot. The tenacious moss has paved the way for higher plants, which thrive in the more sheltered areas. Two hundred species of grasses, mosses and flowering plants have been identified, with the occasional birch or other tree.

A trail, called "Reykjavegur", will take you through this exciting and fire-scarred region. Marked with blue signs, this is one of Iceland's longest signposted trails, at more than 130 km (80 miles) long. It stretches from one geothermal region to another, starting from the Reykjanes lighthouse at the southeastern tip of the peninsula, and ending at Nesjavellir power plant east of Reykjavík, and is divided into seven stages. It is possible to reach most of the trail's stage points by car, and walk from one stage to the next in a day. This unique trail is one of the few places on earth where you can observe the phenomenon of continental drift from marked out and accessible areas. The trail is clearly mapped in a map-booklet available from major tourist information centres.

The gateway to Reykjanes, only 15 minutes journey by bus south of central Reykjavík, is the old town of

LEFT: the warm waters of the Blue Lagoon.
BELOW: vivid spring colours.

The corrugated-metal-clad church in Hafnarfjörður.

Hafnarfjörður ❷. This was one of Iceland's most important ports long before Reykjavík had even grown into a village: in the 15th century it was run by English traders and in the 16th century by Germans, before the Danes imposed their trade monopoly of 1602.

Picturesquely situated in the craggy Búrfell lava field which covers most of the peninsula, Hafnarfjörður has a population of 18,000. It is a part of the Greater Reykjavik Area but is by no means a satellite town of the capital, with its own thriving port and fishing industry, and a broadly based local economy. A pleasant public park, **Hellisgerði**, is situated in the middle of the town, in among the lava. The **Hafnarborg Arts Centre** by the harbourside offers art shows and musical events, as well as a cosy coffee-shop. The Hafnarfjörður **Maritime Museum** (open summer: daily 1–5pm; winter: Sat, Sun 1–5pm) is considered one of the best in the country, and many Reykjavík dwellers make the short trip here to visit the several upmarket restaurants on the waterfront.

But Hafnarfjörður is also well known for its "hidden population". For as long as can be remembered, people have believed that elves, dwarfs and other harmless urchins live in the lava cliffs of Hafnarfjörður in peaceful coexistence with other town residents. There is even a map available at the local tourist information centre, showing hidden sites where these mysterious beings live (*see also* Icelandic Hauntings, *pages 266–7*).

In addition, Hafnarfjörður has become the "Viking centre" of Iceland. The nation's only Viking restaurant, Fjörukráin, is located at the harbour, where traditional food is served in a Vikingfest atmosphere, with lively song and celebration. And every other summer hundreds of foreign and local "Vikings" participate in an international Viking Festival.

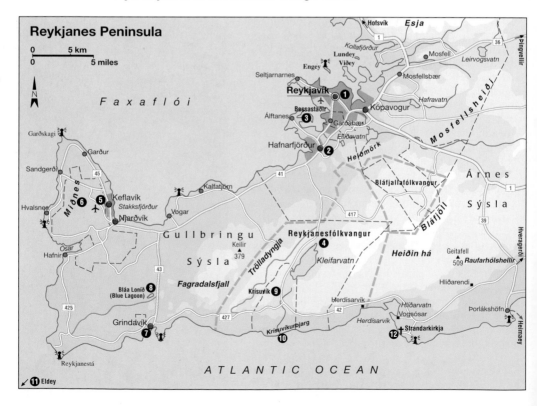

Reykjanes Peninsula

Map on page 174

At **Bessastaðir** ❸, north of Hafnarfjörður, is the presidential residence. Bessastaðir is first mentioned in the *Íslendiga Saga (Saga of the Icelanders)* by Sturla Þórðarson. The place then belonged to the famous Edda-author Snorri Sturluson *(see page 40)*. Later it became the first royal estate in Iceland, a possession of the king of Norway until the late 18th century. From 1805 Bessastaðir was the site of the highest educational institution in Iceland, the Lærði skólinn, for some 40 years. Since 1941 it has been the presidential residence. The present-day building dates from the colonial period, and was originally constructed as a governor's residence in 1763. The residence has been renovated, giving the opportunity for archaeological excavations on the site which have yielded a range of artefacts dating back to the Middle Ages. The adjacent church was built in 1780–1823. Considerable repairs were carried out in 1946–48: the original stone floor disappeared under concrete, but can still be seen in the vestibule and tower. The windows illustrate themes from Icelandic ecclesiastical history. The altarpiece, by the Icelandic artist Muggur, is a triptych, painted in 1921.

Treasures owned by Bessastaðir church include silverware made by Sigurður Þorsteinsson, such as a pyx from 1774. The original is in the National Museum, and a replica can be seen in the church.

Wilderness area

A large sector of the 300-sq. km (115-sq. mile) Reykjanes peninsula is a nature reserve, **Reykjanesfólkvangur** ❹. Stretching from Hafnarfjörður to the south coast, the area is criss-crossed with pleasant walking routes and bridle paths. The Reykjanes nature reserve is contiguous with two others, the **Bláfjöll** (blue mountains) area (popular for skiing in winter) and **Heiðmörk**, a stretch of hilly birch-and-vegetation-covered lava country running from Reykjavík to Hafnarfjörður.

Route 41 along the north coast of Reykjanes leads to the twin towns of **Njarðvík** (population 2,500) and **Keflavík** ❺ (population 7,300). Both trading

BELOW: fishing boats in Hafnar-fjörður harbour.

The creeping thistle (Cirsium arvense), otherwise rare in Iceland, grows in Grindavík. Local tradition claims that it grew up on the spot where both Christian and heathen blood was spilt.

centres since the Middle Ages, they have virtually joined together in recent years. Fishing and other commercial enterprises are strong here, but the big employer of local labour is the nearby Keflavík naval and air base.

Beyond Keflavík is the outcrop known as **Miðnes ❻**, with the tiny fishing outposts of **Garður** and **Sandgerði**. Just south of Sandgerði is the small **Hvalsnes** church, built in 1887. The church's most treasured posession is a gravestone handcut by the poet Reverend Hallgrímur Pétursson in 1649. The stone came to light during excavations in 1964. The ruins of the village **Bátsendar** are nearby, destroyed by a freak tide at the end of the 18th century.

The dirt road Route 425 follows the coast to the peninsula's southeastern tip. There is a lighthouse and view out to a 50-metre (165-ft) rock pinnacle Karl ("man"), while pillars of steam spray from the lava fields on the horizon.

Grindavík ❼, now a typical fishing community of about 2,000 people, can look back on a long and eventful history. It was a major trading centre during the Middle Ages, and in 1532 a business rivalry between English and Hanseatic merchants led to the murder of an Englishman, John "the Broad". Barbary pirates raided Grindavík in 1627, capturing a number of Danes and Icelanders, plus two merchant ships. Today Grindavík is a quiet and unassuming town, with a statue to the families of local fishermen lost at sea.

Surreal spa

BELOW: moss-covered rocks, abundant in the Reykjanes-folksvangur.

Just outside Grindavík, and a handy 15 km (10 miles) from the airport is the **Blue Lagoon** (Bláa Lonið) **❽** (open summer: daily 9am–9pm; winter: Mon–Thurs 11am–7pm, Fri–Sun 10am–7pm; entrance fee). The evocative name notwithstanding, this is not a natural phenomenon, but a recent by-product of geothermal energy usage. The Svartsengi power plant pumps mineral-laden water from up to 2 km (1¼ miles) beneath the earth's surface, at a temperature of 240°C (470°F). The superheated water passes through a dual process, on the one hand to generate electricity, and on the other to heat fresh water. The run-off water, rich in silica, salt and other elements, flows out at a lower temperature to collect in the Blue Lagoon. Psoriasis and eczema sufferers noticed some years ago that bathing in the lagoon seemed to ease their symptoms, and, once the word was out, the place started developing a reputation as a health spa.

The lagoon has become so popular, in fact, that major refurbishment was deemed necessary. The lagoon itself was moved a few hundred metres from its original site in 1999. State-of-the-art facilities, carefully designed to complement the surrounding landscape, were then built, notably a cave-like sauna carved into the lava. There are conference facilities, a restaurant, snack bar, shop and, should you care to spend the night, a guesthouse just a stone's throw away. One thing that is slightly below standard, however, is the size of the changing rooms: on sunny days, particularly at weekends, they get very crowded and it may be worth getting up early to beat the crowds. If you're impressed by the lagoon's waters, note that their beneficial properties can now be enjoyed at home – a range of skin and bathing products are on sale across the island.

Map on page 174

Hot spot

Geothermal power in a more natural setting can be seen east of Grindavík at **Krísuvík** ❾, within the Reykjanesfólksvangur. Here *solfataras* and boiling mud springs surround the world's largest blowing steam vent. While the intention has always been to harness the geothermal energy at Krísuvík for heating purposes, nothing has yet come of this. The whole area seethes with subterranean heat, so tread carefully and keep to the paths to avoid being scalded.

Near Krísuvík is the dramatic and somewhat spooky **Lake Kleifarvatn**, reputed to be the home of an aquatic monster. If you are not put off by this, you can also fish for trout here. Permits are available in Reykjavík, Hafnarfjörður and Keflavík. On the coast beyond Krísuvík is **Krísuvíkurbjarg** ❿, one of Iceland's best-known bird-cliffs: most numerous are kittiwakes, while fulmar, razorbill, common guillemot and Brunnich's guillemot are also plentiful. Puffin, shag, herring gull and black guillemot, though less common, can be observed at Krísuvíkurbjarg, and seals can often be seen basking on the shore. Farther offshore, one may occasionally glimpse groups of whales.

About 14 km (9 miles) off the Reykjanes shore lies the island of **Eldey** ⓫, a high rocky pillar standing 77 metres (250 ft) out of the sea. Eldey is home to the world's largest gannet colony – around 70,000 birds nest on the island each year. The island is a nature reserve, and a permit is needed to visit. Here the last of the great auks was clubbed to death in 1844 (*see page 247*).

Church of miracles

The little **Strandarkirkja** ⓬ church on the south coast between Krísuvík and Þorlákshöfn has a bizarre history. Tradition says that a ship on its way to Iceland

At the Innri-Stapi cliff near Lake Kleifarvatn, there is a bronze plate beside the road commemorating an Icelandic guide who was so fond of the area that his ashes were scattered over the lake at his own request.

BELOW: in the Blue Lagoon.

Map
on page
174

The peninsula is dotted with lighthouses on rocky headlands.

BELOW: Atlantic storms regularly batter the peninsula.

ran into a storm; the crew prayed for deliverance, and promised to build a church if they were saved. An angel appeared on the shore and guided them to safety; they landed at the spot where Strandarkirkja stands today. A tradition arose that the church could work miracles: through the centuries seamen in peril have prayed and promised donations to Strandarkirkja, and they still do so today. As a result, this little church, which no longer has any parish to serve, is reputed to be one of the wealthiest in Iceland.

Near Strandarkirkja, at the small lake Hlíðarvatn, is the farm **Vogsósar**. Formerly a parsonage, the farm is well known as the home of the clergyman-magician Eiríkur (1638–1716), who is mentioned in many folktales. One such story shows that Eiríkur was not a person to fool around with. Once travellers came to Vogsós in winter and some of them went without leave to the pastor's haystack and helped themselves to hay for their horses. The next morning they continued on their way, but when they reached the estuary, their horses began to drink, and went on drinking, however hard they tried to urge them on. Hearing that the travellers were stuck at the river, Reverend Eiríkur went down to find out what was happening, and when he came there he said, "It's thirsty, the hay of Vogsós. You should not give it to your horses again." With this they parted, each going his own way.

A little further to the west is the abandoned farm **Herdísarvík**. Above the farm is a big crag from which impressive lava streams have flowed. This was the home of the great Icelandic poet Einar Benediktsson, who died here in 1940. Herdísarvík bay may have inspired some of Benediktsson's lines from *Surf*: "I hear in thy short-lived waves weeringly rolled / The footfall of time that e'er onward must hold / And my blood surges on with the bruit of the main....". ❑

Keflavík NATO Base

The midnight sun bounces off myriad shiny surfaces on the barren earth. A scene on nocturnal Mars? Not quite, but to many of the 4,000 Americans stationed at the Naval Air Station in Keflavík, southwest Iceland, it's just about the closest thing to it.

Surrounded by a vast lava field, military personnel at the base are famous for taping aluminium foil on windows during summer months in an attempt to keep out the all-night, sleep-robbing light.

Foil and celestial bodies aside, the United States military personnel haven't always been able to sleep easy in Keflavík. This Naval Air Station – comprised mostly of Navy and Air Force personnel together with family members, plus a small contingent of Marines assigned to guard the US embassy in Reykjavík – has been the centre of controversy in Iceland ever since it was established in 1951. The prospect of hosting a foreign army on home soil – Iceland has never fielded an army in its 1,100-year history – disturbed a population that had ended its centuries-long status as a colony of Denmark only in 1944.

Following independence, a strong left-wing movement amongst Icelandic workers pushed for the country to remain neutral. When the government voted to join NATO in 1949, the issue even provoked a riot outside the Alþingi in Reykjavík – Iceland's only civil disturbance to date. Regular marches against the base have taken place virtually ever since.

Without a doubt, opposition to the present *kanar* (short for *Amerikanar*, or Americans) was also due to Icelanders' experience with Allied soldiers during World War II. Fear of a German invasion brought a flood of first British and later American soldiers. Although engagement with enemy forces was virtually zero, Icelandic males lost many a battle for love to uniformed Brits and Americans, and were forced to watch as hundreds of war brides departed for foreign shores.

But back to the present day. With the Cold War having thawed, anti-base sentiment has fizzled out (mostly) and has given way to a pragmatic viewpoint, with the Keflavík installation seen more as a source of revenue than anything else. Marches are still held every few years in protest at the foreign presence, but xenophobic zeal has dwindled since the National Economic Institute revealed that the base has provided 10 percent of Iceland's annual net export revenue since 1951.

About 850 Icelanders are employed directly by the US forces, that's about 1 percent of the total labour force, and close to 2,000 families in the southwest derive their income entirely from the *útlendingar* (foreigners). Troops remain isolated from Icelandic life. Strict rules imposed by both the US and Iceland authorities govern behaviour and limit mobility for off-duty troops.

For many years Keflavík Naval Air Station was the country's only international airport. However, the completion of the nearby passenger terminal in 1987 has given the country a surprisingly modern facility without the drawbacks of big-city bustle. The base now has an exclusively military role. ❑

RIGHT: a protest march against the US military presence.

THE SOUTHWEST

*This area is full of historical sites from the time of the Sagas,
plus a wealth of natural wonders, all within comparatively
easy reach of the coastal Ring Road*

Map
on page
188

The rich farming land of the Southwest has made it one of the most densely populated parts of Iceland since the Saga Age. Today it is also the most heavily visited: some of Iceland's most famous attractions are within striking distance of Reykjavík, tied together under the label of "the Golden Circle".

Every day, hundreds of travellers are bussed from one natural marvel to another, with scarcely enough time to draw breath between snapshots. This may be fine for anyone on a short stopover in Iceland and is probably an unfortunate necessity for those without their own transport. But others will prefer to take a more leisurely pace around the region, stopping in the more obscure valleys and farmhouses to appreciate Iceland's mellow rural atmosphere.

Christian lava field

The Ring Road east of Reykjavík quickly ascends to a volcanically scarred mountain pass. The moss-covered scoria lava field here, known as **Kristnitökuhraun**, was spewed up from the earth around AD 1000. The **Hellisheiði** area is a good walking destination en route from Reykjavík, with a well signposted trail network and detailed maps available.

There are panoramic views as the road descends towards the southwestern plain, with steaming crevasses and yellow sulphur markings on the slopes above **Hveragerði ❶**, a town of 1,500 people that has made a living from harnessing geothermal activity. Greenhouses provide the bulk of Iceland's home-grown produce, including bananas and tropical fruit. Although an unashamed tourist trap, the **Eden** greenhouse is among several that are open to visitors (open summer: daily 8.30am–11pm; winter: daily 9am–7pm), while the Naturopathic Health Association of Iceland operates a clinic here for spa and mud cures. Lying just to the north of town are the hot springs of **Grýla**, named after a hungry local she-troll with a penchant for devouring small children.

While Hveragerði itself is unlikely to hold travellers' attention for more than a couple of hours, it can be a base for hikes into the surrounding countryside – the nearby mountain **Selfjall** to the north of the town and the lava tube **Raufarhólshellir** to the southwest are popular destinations.

The next town along the Ring Road is **Selfoss ❷** (population 4,000), the centre of Iceland's thriving dairy industry and a major road intersection. On the highway just before town, **Hjarðarból** offers farmhouse accommodation. To the south of Selfoss lie a trio of fishing towns, including **Stokkseyri ❸**, where a **Maritime Museum** (open daily) has been set up in the house of Þuríður Einarsdóttir, a 19th-century woman who captained a local fishing boat. More

PRECEDING PAGES:
Gullfoss waterfall.
LEFT: Strokkur
exploding at Geysir.
BELOW: growing
roses under glass
at Hveragerði.

Eyrarbakki's oldest building, dating from 1754, houses the folk museum.

RIGHT: the Lögberg from which the Law-speaker addressed the Alþingi at Þingvellir.

atmospheric is **Eyrarbakki** ❹, set by the shores of a driftwood-strewn black sand beach. This was one of Iceland's main fishing ports from the 12th to the 19th centuries, and has several 18th-century buildings still intact – the oldest of which houses the **Söfnin Folk Museum** (open summer: daily 10am–6pm; Apr, May, Sept and Oct: Sat & Sun 2–5pm). The **Maritime Museum** is in an adjacent building. Across the wide Ölfusa estuary, a prime location for birdwatching, lies **Þorlákshöfn** ❺, the departure point for the twice-daily ferry to the Vestmannaeyjar (Westmann Islands), a journey that can be very pleasant in mild weather but wretched in rough seas.

Nature and history meet

Route 35 turns off north of Selfoss at the hillock of **Ingólfsfjall**, where the First Settler, Ingólfur Arnarson, is held to be buried. Among a group of smaller craters is the 55-metre (180-ft) deep Kerið, blasted out 3,000 years ago and now containing a small lake. Continuing north it is possible to reach **Þingvellir National Park** ❻ (also accessible directly from Reykjavík). When Iceland's unruly early settlers decided to form a commonwealth in AD 930 the site they chose for their new national assembly, the Alþingi, was the natural amphitheatre of Þingvellir ("parliament plains"). It was a grand experiment in republicanism at a time when the rest of Europe wallowed in rigid feudal monarchies, and it lasted, despite the odd lapses into chaos, for over three centuries.

Today Þingvellir is still regarded with reverence by Icelanders, its historical weight reinforced by a serene natural beauty. Declared part of a national park in 1928, the historical section is set along the north of Þingvallavatn – at 84 sq. km (30 sq. miles), Iceland's largest lake – and by the banks of the **River Öxará**

("axe river"). On the horizon in every direction lie low, snow-capped mountains: to the north lies the volcano of Skjaldbreiður ("broad-shield") whose lavas created Þingvellir, flanked by the mountains Botnssúlur, Hrafnabjörg and Ármannsfell (home, it's said, to Ármann, a spirit who is the guardian of Þingvellir). To the south lies the geothermally active Hengill.

The lava plain of Þingvellir itself is covered with wildflowers in summer and sumptuous shades of red in the autumn. This is also a spot where the two halves of Iceland – the European and American tectonic plates – are tearing apart. Aerial photographs show that the great crack of **Almannagjá** ("everyman's chasm"), on whose flanks the Alþingi was held, is just one fissure in a huge series running northeast like an ancient wound through the plains. Occasional earthquakes have reshaped the site: a quake in 1789 caused the plain to drop about 1 metre (3 ft).

Maps on pages 184/188

Journey into the past

Þingvellir's historical district can be reached from two separate parking areas. The path through the Almannagjá fissure crosses a bridge over to the west side of the Öxará. Below the bridge is **Drekkingarhylur**, the famed "drowning pool" that came into use in the 16th century. Men condemned to death were beheaded, but women who committed adultery, infanticide or perjury were tied up in a sack and flung into the pool – deeper and more turbulent than it is today.

The path continues over the Almannagjá fissure to what was the focal point of every Viking Alþingi: **Lögberg Ⓐ**, the "Law Rock", today marked by a stone and a flapping Icelandic flag. On the smoother ground below, the Lögrétta (Legislature) took place, attended by the 36 (later increased to 39) *goðar* or chieftains who would debate new laws. All free men were welcome to listen or

Þingvellir is the only place in Iceland which has been declared by law to be a "sacred place".

BELOW: the interior of Þingvallakirkja, dating from 1859.

A KEY PLACE IN HISTORY

Almost every important moment in Icelandic history has taken place at Þingvellir. When the Alþingi was first held here, this was the fringe of the farm Reykjavík, which was owned by the descendents of the First Settler, Ingólfur Arnarson. It was, and remains, in the centre of of the densely populated farming areas of the land. Here the decision was made for Iceland to convert to Christianity in AD 1000. This was the place for Byzantine legal cases to be argued and voted on, although they were often finally resolved by the Viking recourse to arms and the field of Þingvellir would be soaked in blood. In time, this violence would grow out of control, and it was at Þingvellir in 1271 that Icelanders voted away their independence. The Alþingi at Þingvellir kept operating as a court until the 1760s, although with less and less relevance as first Norway and then Denmark asserted colonial control. Even so, Icelanders kept a special affection for Þingvellir, as a place where, no matter how imperfectly, the country had managed its own affairs. Poets and agitators would appeal to the saga past when they pushed for independence and, when Iceland finally did declare its nationhood again in 1944, the field of Þingvellir was the obvious place for the ceremony.

Laying Down the Law

By their own admission, Icelanders have always been rather quarrelsome, and it is true that much of their history concerns aggrieved characters choosing between taking up the sword and going to court. The annual Alþingi set up in 930 gave the best of both worlds: legal proceedings with an adjournment while the litigants fought pitched battles. They could then apologise to the court, sit down and allow the proceedings to continue.

"Icelanders", wrote an 18th-century English commentator, "have surpassed all other nations in legal chicanery. Jurisprudence was the favourite study of the rich. A wealthy Icelander was always ambitious to plead a cause before the Alþingi, and the greater skill he showed in the art of prolonging... the greater was his celebrity. A man gained as much reputation for defeating his adversary in a lawsuit as for killing him in a duel."

Law covered every contingency imaginable. Thus: "If a man holds his weapons in a peaceable manner, as a person ordinarily does when he is not going to use them, and when they are in this position another man runs against them and wounds himself, he who held the weapons is liable to the punishment of banishment if competent witnesses can prove that he held them in this apparently quiet manner, in order that the other might run against them and be wounded thereby."

This law – and a hundred like it – reflected the fine calculation that made punishment fit the crime. The case of a man who seduced a girl and was then wounded by the girl's father was considered all square. Punishment, when required, fell into three categories: death and two types of "banishment", exile or house arrest. The last normally carried the option of a fine, which was just as well because it was almost impossible not to break laws and most people would have spent a large part of their lives indoors.

Witchcraft and theft commonly carried the death penalty, murder or manslaughter rarely so. Thieves were beheaded; those convicted of witchcraft, usually men, were burnt or drowned to reduce the risk of trouble with their ghosts. Killing was shameful only if it was done in an underhand manner, like killing someone asleep. In other circumstances, which drew no distinction between self-defence and mindless butchery, it could be sorted out by the payment of a fixed penalty determined by the victim's social status.

In retaliation for effrontery or insult, killing was absolutely honourable, merely requiring a public announcement of the deed, which had to be made on the same day. After the event, care had to be taken not to conceal the body beyond a covering to protect it from scavengers. If insults were not immediately dealt with by the offended party, offenders were liable to exile. Indictable insults included throwing sand at someone, a punch, and attempting to throw a man into a mire "though he may actually not fall therein". Exile lasted 20 years and in practice was not far short of the death penalty. An exile had a price on his head and could be killed with impunity. ❑

LEFT: Vikings in discussion.

comment, but only the *goðar* could vote. It was also the site of the Quarter Courts, one for each section of the country. The proceedings were considered so important that farmer-warriors rode in from every corner of Iceland, some taking as long as 17 days to arrive from the East Fjords.

The whole business was run by the Law-speaker, who was elected from among the chieftans. His was a difficult job: apart from keeping the proceedings orderly, he had to recite from memory all of the Icelandic laws, one third every year, from the Lögberg. The acoustics here are still excellent.

Scattered amongst the grass and lava on either side of the Lögberg are the few remains of various **búðir** , or booths – although, frustratingly, none are sign-posted. Every chieftain set up his own personal booth for the two weeks that the Alþingi lasted (usually from the Thursday after 18 June each year), a canvas-covered place to sleep, eat, drink and meet. The stones that can be seen today all probably belong to booths from the 18th century. The **Hotel Valhöll** ⓒ, built in 1898, is on the site of Snorri Sturluson's booth, Valhöll.

Bells and burials

On the east bank of the river is the glistening white **Þingvallabær farmhouse** ⓓ and **Þingvallakirkja church** ⓔ. A church at Þingvellir was the first in Iceland to be consecrated, probably soon after the conversion of 1000, although not at this location. The present version dates from 1859. To enter, ask at the farmhouse – the older part, built in 1930, is occupied by the park warden, who also happens to be the priest; the newer section, dating from 1974, is the summer residence of the Prime Minister. Visitors are loaned the huge, gilded church key, almost more impressive than the church itself.

The Lögrétta was part parliament, part carnival. Great issues were debated among a babble of food vendors, sword-smiths, beer drinkers and hangers-on, while saga heroes forged their new allegiances and met their future brides.

BELOW: the rich colours of autumn in Þingvellir National Park.

Four-wheel drives with huge tyres are virtually the only way to venture off the beaten track, summer or winter.

Inside, there is a pulpit from 1683 and a treasured altarpiece, painted by Ófcigur Jónsson of Heiðarbær in 1834, that had been taken from Iceland and wound up in a church on the Isle of Wight. It was rediscovered only in 1974, and returned to Iceland in time for the 1,100th anniversary of the settlement, which was celebrated at Þingvellir. There are three bells in the church steeple: one dating from the Middle Ages, one from 1698, and the third called Íslandsklukkan – "Iceland's bell" – moulded to ring out for Iceland's independence in 1944.

There are two cemeteries at the church, the higher one a circular plot of ground with only two graves in it: both of poets, the illustrious nationalists Jónas Halgrímsson (1807–45) and Einar Benediktsson (1864–1940). Just to the north of the church is **Biskupabúð**, the "Bishops' booth", which is the largest ruined booth in Þingvellir and one that dates back to its earliest Viking times.

It is possible to walk back to the parking areas from here, with a short detour to a strip of land, **Spöngin** ❻, caught between two fissures. Some historians believe that the Lögrétta was initially held on the flat land near here, but had to

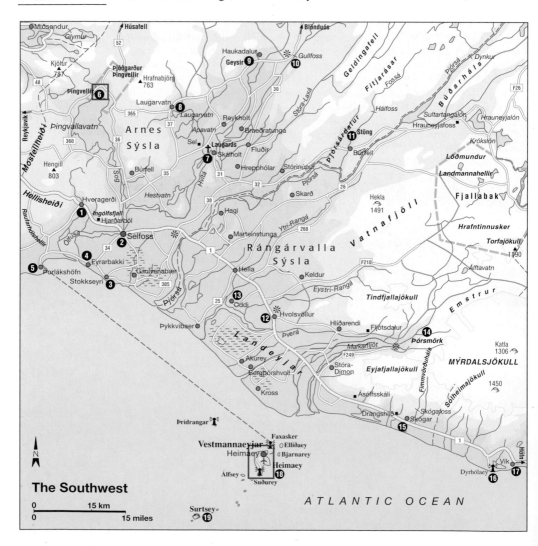

The Southwest

0   15 km
0   15 miles

ATLANTIC OCEAN

be moved closer to the Lögberg when the River Öxará was diverted. On the opposite side of the bridge here is **Peningagjá G** ("coin rift"), a natural wishing well. Toss in a coin and ask a yes-no question: if you can follow the coin with your eyes right to the bottom, the answer is Yes; if not, it's No.

Maps on pages 184/188

Around Þingvellir

It is possible to take day hikes into the surrounding countryside. Almost all paths lead to the old sheep farm of **Skógarhot**, abandoned in 1936, to the west of Þingvellir. About a kilometre south is **Skógarkotshellir**, a long cave that has never been fully explored. The less energetic can enjoy a drive around Lake Þingvallavatn on the narrow dirt roads – although this can get a little hectic on summer weekends and might best be avoided. Luxurious summer houses line the whole lakeside, retreats for Reykjavík inhabitants.

From Þingvallavatn, roads cut off in every direction – west to Reykjavík, north to the deserts, east to Geysir and south to Selfoss – following the ancient routes that were once ridden by Viking farmers, every June, to their unique, quixotic assembly. The road north is the **Kaldidalur** route between Þingvellir and Húsafell. This rocky track usually opens during July when the snows melt around the Langjökull icecap, and will give a small taste of the interior. Shield volcanoes dominate the skyline, the most impressive being the evenly shaped Skjaldbreiður (1,060 metres/3,500 ft), while, on the ground, colourful tundra flowers stud ancient lava flows. River crossings are straightforward and the track runs very close to the hanging glaciers of the icecap.

A Christian centre

Returning to Route 35, heading northwards, the road now enters an area that is known as Biskupstungur ("fields between rivers"), between the rivers Brúará and Hvítá. The main attraction is **Skálholt ⑦**, Iceland's first Christian bishopric and for over 700 years its theological powerhouse. Skálholt's power was built by an influential dynasty of chieftain-priests. First it was the farm of Gissur the White, the browbeating holy man who had led the pro-Christian faction at the AD 1000 Alþingi. His talented son, Ísleifur, was educated in Germany to become the first properly trained Icelandic priest and, in 1056, Iceland's first bishop. Finally, Ísleifur's eldest son, Gissur, took up where his father had left off, making Skálholt the undisputed Church centre of Iceland, its many schools financed by the first tithe to be imposed in northern Europe.

Skálholt maintained its position of power even through the Reformation, but in 1797 the holy see was moved to Reykjavík and Skálholt all but disappeared. In 1953 – precisely 900 years after the ordination of Bishop Ísleifur – the foundations were laid for the new church that now stands on the site. In the process, archaeologists found the remains of one of Skálholt's many cathedrals that had burned down in 1309. At 50 metres (165 ft) in length, it was the largest wooden church in Iceland at the time of building.

Even more oddly, excavators found the carved stone coffin of Páll Jónsson, another of the learned, tough

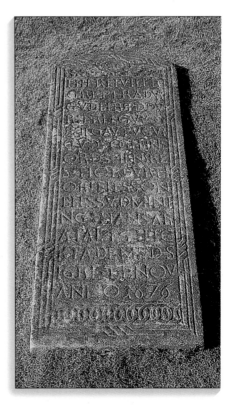

BELOW: a 17th-century grave in Þingvellir cemetery.

Tractor travel on a lonely stretch of road in the Southwest.

early bishops. According to *Páls Saga*, the bishop's death in 1211 was greeted by an earth tremor and deluge. When excavators opened the coffin in 1953 – revealing the skeleton and walrus-bone bishop's crook – there was one of the biggest downpours that Skálholt had seen in years. Today Páll's coffin is in the church's crypt. The best exit from the crypt is out of the wooden door, through an underground passage that was part of the medieval cathedral.

The land of boiling waters

Within sight of Skálholt, 3 km (2 miles) away, the idyllic working farm of **Sel** offers accommodation among sheep-filled fields. Just further on is the village of **Reykholt**, which has a geyser that erupts several times an hour and a pleasant, thermally heated swimming pool. Lying south of Skálholt is **Laugarás**, a verdant, geothermally active area with a camping ground. The paved Route 37 turns off directly north of Route 35 to the spa village of **Laugarvatn ❽** by the shores of the lake of the same name. Summer brings hundreds from Reykjavík to enjoy its pleasures, including the hot spring **Vígðalaug**, used as an all-weather baptism spot by the first bishops of Skálholt.

Both Routes 35 and 37 finally lead to **Geysir ❾**, which has given its name to all such water spouts around the world. Sadly, the Great Geysir, which started erupting in 1294, hasn't performed well for decades: in the 20th century, eager tourists poured gravel into its mouth to lower the water level and force an explosion, but the process seems to have only made it more and more difficult. Nowadays soap is used to break the surface tension, but only on special occasions such as Independence Day. Even then, there are no guarantees that the geyser will perform. If it does, the spume can hit 60 metres (200 ft).

BELOW: the mouth of the Great Geysir.

In the light of this, many people were stunned when Geysir suddenly erupted in June 2001, seemingly quite out of the blue. Water spouted up to 40 metres (130 ft) into the air, and the activity continued periodically over several weeks. However, this extraordinary occurence had a perfectly rational explanation: earthquakes in Southern Iceland caused subterranean pressure that gave the great Geysir renewed vitality.

For the rest of the time, visitors will have to be content with the smaller but more reliable geyser, **Strokkur** ("the churn"), which spits up its column of water every five minutes or so to a height of around 20 metres (66 ft). Meanwhile, the whole Geysir area is geothermically active, with walking trails marked out among steaming vents and glistening, multi-coloured mud formations. Never stand too near to Strokkur – an average of seven tourists are scalded every week in summer, mostly from putting their hands in water pools to test their temperatures.

The greatest waterfall

Nine km (6 miles) further along Route 35 is the big attraction of the Golden Circle tour and perhaps Iceland's best-known natural wonder: the waterfall **Gullfoss ❿** ("golden falls"). A path from the parking area leads alongside the deafening double falls, where the River Hvítá tumbles 32 metres (105 ft) into a 2.5-km (1½-mile) ravine. Trails climb past the waterfall's northern face, allowing you to get within an arm's length of the awesome flow. Wear a raincoat, or the clouds of spray that create photogenic rainbows on sunny days will douse you from head to foot.

A stone plaque near the parking area remembers Sigriður Tómasdóttir, a farmer's daughter who lived on the nearby farm Brattholt. Private plans had been drawn up to dam the Hvítá river at Gullfoss for a hydroelectric project, but Sigriður walked to Reykjavík to protest to the government and even announced that she would fling herself into the waterfalls if construction went ahead. The government instead bought the falls and made them a national monument.

Another path leaving from the parking area climbs to the top of the surrounding cliffs for a panoramic view of the falls. From Gullfoss, the road stretches ahead into the uninhabited deserts of central Iceland, and on a clear day you can see the icecap **Langjökull** ("long glacier").

Viking relics

For anyone even vaguely interested in Saga Age history, it is worth making the tortuous trip to the excavated Viking longhouse of **Stöng** ⓫ and its re-created twin, **Þjóðveldisbær** ("the Commonwealth farm").

Both lie in **Þjórsárdalur** ("bull river valley"), off Route 32, formed 8,000 years ago by the biggest lava outpouring since the Ice Age. The valley is overshadowed by the snow-capped form of **Mount Hekla**. Instead of a classic volcano cone, Hekla is part of a rather squat series of ridges, becoming progressively squatter with each eruption; however, even this is usually hidden behind the thick bank of clouds that earned Hekla its menacing name, which means "hooded." The seafaring Irish monk St Brendan might have been the

The English poet W.H. Auden noted in the 1930s that Icelanders were already using liquid Sunlight soap to encourage Geysir to explode. The soap had to be imported, since the thinner local type did not work.

BELOW: Mount Hekla dominating the Þjórsárdalur valley.

first to see Hekla's volcanic pyrotechnics as he sailed past Iceland in the 8th century, and soon after settlement Hekla showed that it was a presence to be feared. The volcano's notoriety grew such that, in medieval Europe, Hekla was widely known to be one of the twin mouths of hell. It has remained active, with the last eruption in February 2000.

The interior details of Þjódveldisbær were provided by artists and historians using information from archaeological digs in Iceland and Greenland, and descriptions of living conditions in the sagas.

Stöng was the farm of the warrior-farmer Gaukur Trándilsson, whose saga, sadly, has been lost. He moved there at the end of the 11th century, but in 1104 Mount Hekla erupted without warning, soon covering the once-lush valley with a thick layer of white ash. Stöng and 20 other nearby farms had to be abandoned, and Þjórsárdalur was never resettled. In 1939, archaeologists uncovered Gaukur's house: it was in the form of two long rooms built end to end, with two annexes for the dairy and lavatory. As Iceland's best example of an early medieval home, it became the model for the nearby reconstruction of Þjóðveldisbær, begun in 1974 to mark the 1,100th anniversary of Iceland's settlement.

It's worth visiting the turf-covered reconstruction first, designed by architect Hörður Ágústsson using the Stöng floorplan and built by traditional methods (note the irregular-shaped planks of wood for the roof, fitted together so as not to waste an inch of precious wood, and the marks of axes used to plane them).

BELOW: the serene farmland of the Southwest.

The original Stöng is hidden away several kilometres further along a very poor dirt road. A large wooden shed has been built over the ruins to protect them from the elements, but it is never locked. Although only the stone foundations remain, this damp, slightly overgrown set of stones is the best place in Iceland to get the historical imagination working. On a fine day, those with spare time might want to take the two-hour walk beyond Stöng to Iceland's second-highest waterfall, **Háifoss**.

Following the south coast

Back on the Ring Road, the unassuming towns of **Hella** and **Hvolsvöllur** ⓬, both with around 500 inhabitants, mark the beginning of the countryside where perhaps the most famous of the Icelandic Sagas, *Njáls Saga*, took place. The new **Saga Centre** (open summer: daily 9am–6pm) in Hvolsvöllur, has a very accessible exhibition showing life in Iceland in the Viking Age and telling the story of *Njáls Saga* in an easy yet comprehensive way. The Centre is signposted from the main road.

Between the two towns, Route 266 heads south to **Oddi** ⓭ which quickly became home to Iceland's most learned saga writers, including Snorri Sturluson. Oddi's first inhabitant, Sæmundur the Learned, was well known to be a wizard: the man had no shadow, since it had been stolen by the devil while he was studying at the "Black School" for satanists in Paris. Sæmundur offered his soul if Satan could take him back to Iceland without getting him wet. In the shape of a giant seal, the devil swam the North Atlantic with Sæmundur on his back, but as soon as they got near the coast, Sæmundur whacked him on the head with a prayer book. The wily wizard swam the rest of the way and, since he was soaked, kept his soul.

The church at Oddi today was built in the 1920s, but has a number of curious artefacts on display, including a silver chalice dating from the 14th century.

Thunder god's forest

East of the Ring Road along Route 249 is the valley of **Þórsmörk** ⓮ – literally, "Thor's forest", one of Iceland's most spectacular but inaccessible wilderness areas. Sealed off by three glaciers, two deep rivers and a string of mountains,

Map on page 188

Legend has it that Oddi's first church was built on the strength of a vision: a giant spear flew from the heavens and landed here.

BELOW: a glacier burrows into Þórsmörk.

Map
on page
188

*Þórður Tómasson,
the curator of Skógar
Museum.*

BELOW: ruins of turf
houses by the
Drangshlíð farm.
RIGHT: the black
sand beach at Vík.

Þórsmörk has received added protection since the 1920s as a nature reserve operated by the Icelandic Forestry Commission. The single dirt road into the park is impassable to everything but the specially designed high-carriage buses – some of the oversized Icelandic four-wheel drives can make it in when the glacial rivers are low, which is usually in the early morning.

Despite the difficulties, Þórsmörk often attracts well over 1,000 Icelandic campers every summer weekend and a growing number of foreigners on day trips (there are no hotels or guesthouses here, but there are two tourist huts). Visitors are rewarded with spectacular glacier views, fields of wildflowers, pure glacial streams and forests of birch and willow full of birds – particularly blackbirds, ravens and wagtails.

The Ring Road continues south along a narrow plain of farmland between the black sand coast and rugged cliffs that lead to the icecap **Eyjafjallajökull**, riddled with caves and marked by thin waterfalls. Ruins of indeterminate age crop up at intervals here, giving the area considerable atmosphere. Beside the driveway to the farm **Drangshlíð** are some collapsed turf houses built into caves.

Three km (2 miles) further east, **Skógar ⑮** is home to a meticulously managed **Folk Museum** (open summer: daily 9am–7pm), the most visited of its kind in Iceland, run since 1959 by a local character Þórður Tómasson. Apart from a 6,000-piece collection, the museum has examples of different types of Icelandic housing down through the ages. There is a summer Edda Hotel at Skógar, as well as the splendid waterfall **Skógafoss**, whose sheer fall offers one of south Iceland's best photo opportunities. The trek from here to Þórsmörk, passing between the icecaps of Eyjafjallajökull and Mýrdalsjökull over the **Fimmvörðuháls** pass, is popular with the hardy between June and September, so much so that it becomes quite crowded, particularly in July. There are two huts between the icecaps, one an emergency shelter, the other bookable ahead.

Six km (4 miles) east of Skógar, **Fúlilækur** ("foul river") announces itself with the overpowering rotten-egg stench of sulphur. The river emerges from beneath the **Sólheimajökull** glacier, which can be seen from the road, and originates near the volcano Katla, whose subterranean activities beneath the Mýrdalsjökull icecap have often sent glacial tides to devastate this area. Further on, Route 218 cuts south to **Dyrhólaey ⑯**, a protected nature area with a steep cliff and a much-photographed natural rock arch out to sea; this is one of the best places to photograph puffins in south Iceland. Saga hero Njáll's son-in-law Kári had his farm here.

Vík ⑰ (sometimes referred to as Vík i Myrdal to distinguish it from other Víks), is a small town of around 400 people set along a dramatic stretch of coastline: here the dark North Atlantic hits the land with surprising violence, its waves crashing dramatically on a long beach of black sand. At the end of the beach are the **Reynisdrangur**, towering fingers of black rock standing out to sea and inhabited by colonies of arctic terns. The relentless, battering wind adds to the Gothic scene – helping to make this the only non-tropical beach to be rated by *Islands*, a US magazine, as one of the world's top 10 beaches. ❑

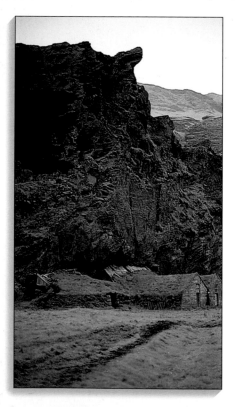

In Pursuit of Njáll

The action of *Njáls Saga* – considered the greatest of the sagas and the most widely read today – takes place in a small stretch of the southwestern coastal plains between the rivers Rangá and Markarfljót. Written by an unknown scholar in the 13th century, *Njáls Saga* is the rip-roaring tale of a 50-year blood feud.

Njáls Saga is divided into three parts. The title character, Njáll Þorgeirsson, is the most skilled lawyer in Iceland, blessed with second sight and universally respected for his fairness and integrity. A farmer who never raises his sword in anger, he is bound by the strict codes of family loyalty and honour. Oddly, Njáll plays a small role in much of the saga, reacting to rather than shaping events.

The first part of the saga concerns Njáll's friendship with the greatest champion of the land, Gunnar. So, the best place to start a saga tour is at Gunnar's farm, Hlíðarendi. Set above the marshy Rangá plains on Route 261

(turning south from the Ring Road east of Hvolsvöllur), the farm now consists of a few white buildings and pretty church among some trees in a mellow, peaceful landscape.

Gunnar could fight so skilfully that "he seemed to be brandishing three swords at once,". He was a fair-minded fellow, slow to anger and keen to avoid trouble. His problems began when he married the beautiful, manipulative Hallgerður Long-legs, who had arranged the demise of two previous husbands for slapping her face.

Hallgerður started up a feud with Njáll's equally shrewish wife, Bergþóra. Each of the women ordered the murder of the other's slaves in an escalating feud that the friends Njáll and Gunnar refused to be drawn into. Relatives of the victims became involved, until Gunnar was prosecuted at the Alþingi for butchering some assailants in self-defence. Sentenced to outlawry for three years, he was riding away from Híldarenði when his horse stumbled and he looked back. "How lovely these slopes are," he said, "more lovely than they ever seemed to me before, golden corn-

41. Skarphéðinn á Markarfljóti.

fields and new-mown hay. I am going back home, and I will not go away."

The decision was fatal. Gunnar's enemies soon surrounded the farm, although he kept them at bay with his bow and arrow until his string broke. Gunnar asked his wife for two locks of her hair to plait a new bowstring, but the treacherous Hallgerður – who had once been slapped by Gunnar – refused. Gunnar's reply to this death-sentence is one of the sagas' most famous lines: "To each his own way of earning fame... You will not be asked again." Although Gunnar took many of his enemies with him, he was finally slaughtered.

The bloodshed was far from over. Njáll's three sons – Helgi, Grímur and the eldest, Skarphéðinn – helped take vengeance on the killers of Gunnar. But they also wanted to kill Þráinn Sigfússon, a vain relative of Gunnar's who had been present at an earlier ambush. Directly south of Hildarenði, half way between Gunnar's home and Njáll's on the rough but passable Route 250 is a rounded hill in the middle of the plain. Today called Stóra-Dímon, it was in Njáll's time called Rauðaskriður, or "Red Skree" and is where the three Njálssons lay in wait one winter's morning in 995 for Þráinn Sigfússon and his friends.

The ambush was spotted, and it looked as if Þráinn would get away, but Skarphéðinn leapt onto the glassy ice of the Markarfljót, skidded downstream and sliced Þráinn over the head with his axe. The gymnastic Skarphéðinn had swooped off to safety before anyone knew what had happened.

Njáll was horrified when he heard of the killing, but organised a settlement at the Alþingi. To smooth things over, Njáll even adopted Þráinn's orphaned son, the cherubic Höskuldur. Höskuldur grew up to take over the farm Ossabær, which is now a ruined site on Route 252 heading south, but the Njálssons grew jealous of him. One day the three sprung upon him without warning in a corn field and cut him down.

Putting the Njálssons up to this butchery was the diabolical Mörður Valgarðsson who loathed Gunnar and plotted to destroy Njáll's family. His chance came when arrangements for a money settlement over Höskuldur's murder fell through at the Alþingi. Höskuldur's kinsman, Flosi Þórðarson from the Skaftafell area, was about to accept a deal from Njáll when Skarphéðinn insulted him, suggesting that he was regularly sodomised by a troll.

Follow route 252 to the site of Njáll's farm, Bergþórshvoll. The modern farmhouse is uninspiring, but you can still see the three hills of the saga. On a clear day, the snow-covered mountains on the horizon make a spectacular sight. Having stuck by his blood-thirsty sons, Njáll spotted Flosi with 100 men bearing down on the farm. Instead of fighting, he ordered them all to retire into the house – effectively committing suicide, since Flosi promptly set the place on fire. Njáll and his wife refused an offer of mercy, preferring to die with their three sons. Only Kári Sólmundarson escaped.

Interestingly, archaeological digs undertaken at Bergþórshvoll in the 1920s and '50s have found evidence of a Saga Age burning (the accepted date is 1011), suggesting that the dramatic story may be true. ❑

LEFT: Skarphéðinn slides away on a frozen river after killing Þráinn Sigfússon. **RIGHT:** Stóra-Dímon across the plains of the Markarfljót river.

VESTMANNAEYJAR (THE WESTMANN ISLANDS)

Maps
on pages
188/202

The comparatively recent volcanic origins of this small and scattered group of islands off the southwest coast are clearly visible in their rugged appearance

In the earliest years of Iceland's settlement, five Irish slaves ambushed and butchered their master Hjörleifur Hrodmarsson, brother of the first successful settler, Ingólfur Arnarson. Dragging along a handful of slave women, they commandeered a rowing boat and – according to the ancient *Landnámabók (Book of Settlements)* – escaped from their farm near Vík to one of the small green islands visible from the country's south coast.

Not surprisingly, the slaves' new-found freedom was short-lived. Two weeks later, the other Viking settlers tracked them down, stormed their camp and mercilessly put the escapees to death. Even so, the whole archipelago has since been known in the slaves' honour as the Vestmannaeyjar – the Westmanns, or islands of the western men.

Today the Vestmannaeyjar (pronounced, roughly, *vestman-air*) have become one of Iceland's most popular destinations. Comprising 13 small islands and some 30 rocks or skerries, they combine a seductive serenity with raw natural beauty: the archipelago is among the world's newest volcanic creations, and one of its islands, Surtsey, only emerged from the ocean in 1963.

Even Heimaey – the largest of the Westmanns and the only one with a permanent human population – is scarred black with fresh volcanic flow from the 1973 eruption that nearly caused it to be permanently abandoned *(see panel on page 203)*. The eruption changed the shape of the island forever, adding 15 percent to its area and introducing a new volcanic peak, Eldfell, which now dominates the main town. In parts of Heimaey the ground still steams and is warm to the touch, and one can easily imagine that this is how the earth looked at the time of its formation.

Violent birth

Although this area off Iceland's southern coast had been the scene of underwater volcanic activity for hundreds of thousands of years, scientists estimate that the first land did not emerge from the sea here until 10,000 years ago, and most islands were not formed until 5,000 years ago – the blink of an eye, in geological terms.

As a result, most of the Westmanns are tiny, rugged and inhospitable. Each is ringed by sheer cliffs, topped with lush vegetation and crowded with sea birds: more species gather here than anywhere else in Iceland. Most are populated only by seasonal puffin-catchers, whose huts can be seen from the sea.

For the vast majority of visitors, the point of arrival will be **Heimaey** ⑱ (pronounced *hay-may*). The

PRECEDING PAGES: fishermen off Heimaey. **LEFT:** Heimaey from the flanks of Elfell volcano, created in the 1973 eruption. **BELOW:** a boat tour around Heimaey.

*The 1973 eruption
left one-third of the
town under lava and
the harbour entrance
a fraction of its for-
mer size. However,
the new harbour is
completely protected
from the wind, and
thus a great improve-
ment on the old.*

name of both the largest island and its township, Heimaey can be reached by a 25-minute flight from Reykjavík or a three-and-a-quarter-hour ferry trip from Þorlákshöfn on the coast (a glorious journey when it is sunny, but when the sea is rough, one of Iceland's most dismal). Many visitors make only a day-trip to the island, although it is worth staying overnight.

Heimaey's 5,300 inhabitants are a hardy and independent breed, steeled by generations of isolation, brutal living conditions and an extensive history of disasters. After the Irish slaves' abortive attempt to hide out here, the island was first occupied by a certain Herjólfur Barðursson, a reclusive farmer who had become tired of the constant strife on the mainland. Life was relatively peaceful – if not particularly easy – on the island for several centuries, until it became a target for pirate raids.

As if to repay the islanders for the depredations of their Viking ancestors, a series of cut-throats descended on the Westmanns: British pirates ruled the islands for almost a century, and then, in 1627, the Turks arrived. Well into the 20th century, island children were terrified by the tale of the bloodthirsty heathens who put 34 men and women to the sword and carried off more than 200 as slaves. Those who tried to hide in the cliffs were shot down like birds.

Epidemics wracked Heimaey for the next couple of centuries, while the 1783 eruption of Laki on the mainland killed off all the fish around the islands, reducing its inhabitants to living on sea birds and an edible root called *hvönn* (with plenty falling to their deaths from cliffs in pursuit of both).

BELOW: Heimaey harbour

Later, fishing accidents would take a dreadful toll: twice, when the island's population was less than 350, storms would send more than 50 men to the bottom of the sea on a single day. In the 19th century, some 100 fishermen drowned

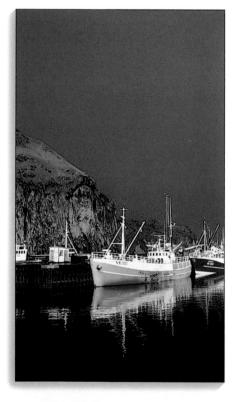

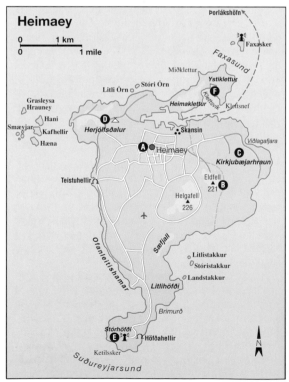

Heimaey

from Heimaey, a fact of life which may have accounted for the population's famous sangfroid in the face of the 1973 volcanic eruption.

Fishing capital

Today Heimaey is the most important fishing centre in the whole of Iceland – with only 2 percent of the country's population, it supplies some 12 percent of its exports. A large part of the catch is processed on the island, giving locals a healthy slice of Iceland's modern prosperity.

Heimaey town ❹ itself is spread out around the harbour, where over 100 colourful trawlers can dock in the natural windbreak of the lava wall created by the 1973 eruption. The setting is spectacular, with rugged brown bluffs on one side and the two volcanic peaks, Eldfell and Helgafell on the other. Keep an eye out for the colourful mural painted by school children on the side of a building near the harbour, depicting the fateful morning of the eruption.

Walking away from the harbour into town along **Kirkjuvegar** (to the left of the harbour, with the water at your back), the streets run along the base of the lava wall where it was stopped in 1973 – literally, in some people's backyards. The ruins of one house still haven't been removed, as a reminder of the destruction. Steps have been built up onto the convoluted lava fields, here covered with a thin film of green moss, through which the wind whistles eerily.

With few cars in Heimaey, the streets are empty and peaceful – in fact, their utter desolation on Sundays gives them the haunting feel of a Bergman film. Points of interest include the picturesque white **church**, with a statue commemorating the island's fishermen lost at sea, and the **Folk Museum** (open summer: daily 2–5pm; winter: Tues–Sat 2–5pm) above the library, which has a

Map on page 202

A mural in Heimaey depicting different aspects of the fishing industry.

BELOW: evacuating Heimaey in 1973.

CRISIS ON HEIMAEY

Early on 23 January 1973, a mile-long fissure cracked open without warning on the eastern side of Heimaey, and a wall of molten lava poured out towards the town. Islanders were told to abandon their houses. By great good fortune, the entire Heimaey fishing fleet was in dock that night: some 5,300 people left the island on trawlers. Not a life was lost. Over the next five months, some 33 million tons of lava spewed from the fissure, threatening to devastate the island. Hundreds of tonnes of tephra (volcanic debris) hailed down on the town, smashing windows and igniting houses. By early February the greatest danger was from the 165-metre (500-ft) wall of lava moving towards the harbour – the lifeline of the local community. After initial successful experiments, the physicist Þorbjörn Sigurgeirsson insigated the use of jets of water to cool the lava. Two commercial dredging ships with water cannons pumped over 43 million litres (11½ million gallons) of water a day. Heimaey was covered in a blanket of steam, and the lava flow was stopped before it blocked the harbour entrance. More pumps worked around the clock for the next three months to help cool over 5 million cubic metres of lava. Scientists pronounced the eruption over in July, and the residents began returning home.

well-organised set of relics, model ships and photographs. Well worth a visit to see its extraordinary live collection of Icelandic fish is the **Aquarium and Natural History Museum** (open summer: daily 11am–5pm; winter: Sat, Sun 3–5pm). Particularly odd are the Icelandic cod, which appear to be made of white plastic, and the horrifying Icelandic catfish, a fish that boasts piranha teeth and a bad-tempered, strangely human expression.

Exploring the island

Unless you have brought a car over by ferry from the mainland, or have the time and energy to walk, the easiest way to visit Heimaey's attractions is on one of the twice-daily bus tours run by Páll Helgason (the ubiquitous islander who owns hotels, boats and a good deal more on Heimaey). The tour meets most flights at the airport, or you can arrange to be picked up at your hotel.

A rough dirt road has been cut to **Eldfell ❸**, the 221-metre (725-ft) high peak formed during the 1973 eruption. The spectacular view from the base clearly shows how a sixth of the island is now fresh lava flow. The vista stretches across the brightly painted corrugated iron roofs of Heimaey to the harbour and, on a clear day, to the mainland. A short walk up leads to barren, steaming tephra fields. If the ground seems warm to the touch, dig a few inches down – it's hot enough to bake bread, and Heimaey housewives, in their more whimsical moments, still use the earth for that purpose. Roads have also been cut into **Kirkjubæjarhraun ❻**, the 3-sq. km (7.4-acre) lava field spat up in 1973. Apart from a pillar marking where the oldest settlement on the island once was (now 300 metres/980 ft below ground), little disturbs the dark lava's contorted expanse besides geothermal units, heating the town's water and houses.

BELOW: Heimaey church and the memorial to lost fishermen, with Eldfell in the background.

Map on page 202

On the other side of the town, a road leads past a surreal monument in the shape of giant football, to the lush natural amphitheatre of **Herjólfsðalur ⓓ**. Archaeologists found the ruins of a Saga Age home here, assumed to be that of the island's first settler, Herjólfur Barðursson. These days, however, it is more famous as the camping ground where thousands of Icelanders gather around a giant bonfire for three days to celebrate the Þjódhátíð festival in early August. The prodigious feats of drinking make this long weekend a must for many Icelanders, but most foreigners find it a good time to avoid the island.

Puffin cliffs

A path across the golf course near here leads to a splendid view of several block-shaped islands including **Hæna**, **Kafhellir** and **Hani**. The cliffs here house the island's most accessible puffin colony. Although the islanders hunt puffins (*see panel on page 206*), their attitude towards these ungainly birds is not always entirely mercenary. Late in August every year, thousands of baby puffins waddle into the township of Heimaey – lured by the bright lights in their search of food, since their parents cease feeding them in late summer. To save the puffins from a grisly end from cats, dogs and cars, Heimaey's children flock to the streets and collect them in cardboard boxes. Next day, the baby puffins are taken to the coast and ritualistically flung out to sea – and, hopefully, a successful puffin career. At least they will not end up on island dinner tables until they reach adulthood, since an unwritten law holds that the young puffins should not be eaten.

From Herjólfsðalur, precarious trails requiring mountain equipment can be taken along the cliffs to the northern promontory of **Ystiklettur**, above the har-

A somewhat crass Westmann Islands saying declares: "Wine, women and puffins – the older they get, the better they taste".

BELOW: the three-day Þjódhátíð party in early August.

*Fishing floats
tangled in a net.*

BELOW: a puffin.

bour. An easier trail also follows the road south to **Stórhöfði** ❺, where a lighthouse looks out over the island's most exposed coastline. Winds of 250 kph (150 mph) and waves of 23 metres (75 ft) have been recorded here in storms.

Boat cruises

A visit to Heimaey would not be complete without an excursion on the waves. Regular departures in small boats leave from the harbour docks, weaving out past the salmon farm (the huge salmon can actually be seen leaping from the water) and around the island. The trip gives views of Heimaey's steep cliffs crowded with sea birds (gannets, five species of auk, storm petrels, guillemots and puffins) and usually several sure-footed sheep perched on what appear to be almost vertical green fields.

If you're lucky, orcas (killer whales) can be spotted among the smaller islands, their glistening black and white flanks clearly visible as they leap from the waves. Boats also pull in to several of the natural caves on the coast.

In Klettsvík, near the harbour, the waves are so calm and acoustics so good that the captain usually climbs out on the bow and gives a short flute concert. **Klettsvík bay** ❻ has become the new home of Keiko, the world-famous killer whale, star of the film *Free Willy*. Captured off the coast of Iceland 1979, Keiko spent three years in an Icelandic aquarium. Then the whale was airlifted to Marineland in Niagara Falls, Ontario, where it was trained to perform. After spending some 10 years in an amusement park in Mexico City, Keiko had become sick and was flown to Oregon Coast Aquarium, where it was nursed back to health. And in September 1998 the 6.5-metre (21-ft) long animal, weighing about 4,500 kg (10,000 lb), was airlifted to a protected cove in

HUNTING FOR PUFFINS

The charming, stubby-winged puffin is regarded as a particularly mouthwatering morsel in Iceland, especially in the Vestmannaeyjar. The islanders' affection for the puffin as Iceland's national emblem does not discourage them from seeing it as a source of food – and one which has helped them to survive hard times.

Today's puffin-catchers swing nets with 3-metre (10-ft) long handles to catch the birds on the wing – puffins are slightly clumsy in the air. On Heimaey the puffin-catchers can most frequently be seen at work on windy days on top of the cliffs by the golf course in the west of the island. Some 16,000 puffins are caught on the island every summer to make up Iceland's national dinner. The catchers are careful to avoid catching immature birds so that the colony's numbers are not endangered. The record for a single puffin-catcher is 1,202 in one day. Puffin and guillemot, usually under the generic name of *svartifugi* (the Alcidae family of birds), appear on the menus of some of the more adventurous restaurants in Reykjavík. The dark, gamey meat, with a slightly fishy taste, is sometimes served fried or boiled, often with a curry sauce, or alternatively it may be smoked. It is a great favourite with Icelandic gourmets.

Klettsvík bay, where it lives in a 145 million-litre (3.2 million-gallon) pen, the largest of its kind in the world.

The final summer attraction in Heimaey is the local **Volcano Show** (which is different from the show of the same name in Reykjavík) – including a documented story that has become emblematic of the Westmann islanders' constant battle with Nature.

Half man, half seal

One night in March 1983, a fishing vessel capsized 5 km (3 miles) off Heimaey's coast. All of the crew quickly perished in the freezing winter seas, except for a fisherman named Guðlaugur Friðfljófsson. He staved off the confusion of hypothermia by talking to hovering sea birds, and set off swimming for shore. It took him six hours – about five hours longer than anyone else has ever survived in water that temperature.

As if that wasn't enough, Guðlaugur swam ashore onto some of the sharpest lava on the island, cutting his feet to ribbons and losing considerable blood as he stumbled to the town. Doctors could not find his pulse, but the fisherman survived. Later, when the London Hospital Medical College performed tests, Guðlaugur's body fat proved to closely resemble that of a seal. It's a story that islanders recount fondly, as if to steel themselves for the next skirmish with the sea, the winds or the volcanic peaks that threaten them every day.

The birth of an island

The youngest of the Westmann islands, **Surtsey ⓳**, burst from the North Atlantic in a dramatic eruption in 1963. Captured on film by airborne camera crews, high-

Maps on pages 188/202

BELOW: Heimaey harbour entrance seen from the wall of lava that threatened it in 1973.

Map on page 188

lights of its fiery, four-year-long birth were seen around the world, providing a unique glimpse of how Iceland was formed and still giving scientists unique and invaluable data on how virgin habitats are colonised by plant and animal life.

The eruption began below the waves in the Mid-Atlantic Ridge, the submarine mountain chain that runs into the south coast of Iceland. Island fishermen were the first to notice smoke rising from the sea in November 1963. Molten lava spewing onto the sea floor was cooling on contact with the icy waters, but soon a pile of volcanic debris had risen the 130 metres (430 ft) to the surface to create a burning mass above sea level. A pillar of black ash, intertwined with a stream of steam, was sent 10 km (6 miles) into the air – looking menacing from nearby Heimaey and visible from as far away as Reykjavík. The first flights over the site confirmed that the Westmanns now had a 16th island, and that eruption was continuing: fluid lava was piling up over the mound of tephra and solidifying, turning it from a giant volcanic refuse heap into a permanent presence.

A scientific laboratory

The new island was named after the fiery Norse giant Surtur, who sets the world alight at Ragnarök, the end of the world. For the next four years, until June 1967, Surtsey provided the world's scientific community with the spectacle of its ongoing formation, before finally settling down to an area of 1.57 sq. km (½ sq. mile) and 155 metres (510 ft) in height. During the same period, two smaller islands emerged from the eruption but have since eroded away and disappeared below the waves.

Fascinating as Surtsey's formation had been, its greatest scientific value started after the eruption had ended. Its 1,000°C (1,830°F) surface temperatures during the eruption had left it completely free of any living organism: the island became a sort of natural laboratory approximating how Iceland itself must have been when its first segments emerged from the sea some 20 million years ago.

BELOW: some of the smaller Westmann Islands.
RIGHT: scientists recording the development of plants on Surtsey.

Seeds arrived on the island in its first summer, carried by the wind, sea and passing sea birds. The first sprouting plants were noticed during the following year, 1965, even before the island's eruption had completely finished. By the end of 1967, no less than four species of plants had established themselves around the coastline.

Midges and flies were the first animals to settle the island, with seals making an appearance after the surrounding seas became restocked with fish. In 1970, black-backed gulls became the first birds to nest on Surtsey. Since that time, scientists have observed 60 bird species on the island – some are just stopping off on their migration to other shores, while others are making this their new home.

Surtsey is still a scientific station and is off-limits to casual visitors. Any uncontrolled intrusion might upset the island's natural development, either by damaging fragile plant life or accidentally bringing in new presences (a seed caught on a visitor's shoe, for example, might sprout into a plant). Fly-overs in light aircraft, taking about two hours, however, can be organised in Reykjavík. ❏

Map
on page
214

THE SOUTHEAST

*In this region overshadowed by the vast Vatnajökull icecap
and precariously situated on expanses of glacial debris,
the highlight is the rugged and popular Skaftafell National Park*

Icelanders often say that their country was unfairly named, since it is, after all, strikingly green for much of the year. But anyone paying a visit to the Southeast will have ice on their minds, no matter what the season. The whole area is dominated by Europe's largest icecap, Vatnajökull, whose enormous glaciers creep down through every crack in the coastal mountains like oozing blue putty.

Volcanoes regularly erupt beneath it, devastating farmland with flows of melted ice and debris as large in volume as the Amazon river. Little wonder then if the Viking explorers – including the First Settler, Ingólfur Arnarson, who spent three years in the Southeast – thought the name "Iceland" appropriate.

The damage caused by Vatnajökull's glacial flows (called *hlaups*) made much of the coast next to impassable for centuries. Until the Ring Road was finally driven through in 1974, parts of the Southeast were among the remotest in Iceland. To reach Skaftafell or Höfn by land, for example, one had to drive the entire 1,100 km (680 miles) around the north of the country.

Today the highway from Reykjavík to the Southeast is fully paved, and the glacier-riddled Skaftafell National Park has become the most popular wilderness area in the country. (In fact, on June and July weekends, it becomes so crowded that it is probably best avoided by travellers.) Meanwhile, the drive along the coast passes a luxuriant, haunting landscape dotted with tiny farms and historic settlements.

PRECEDING PAGES:
Hiking near Höfn.
LEFT: Skaftafells-
jökull reflected in a
lake in Skaftafell
National Park.
BELOW: a farmer
from the Southeast.

Curse of the Irish monks

The gateway to the Southeast is the town of **Kirkjubæjarklaustur ❶** (call it "Keerk-ya" and you will be understood), a green oasis in the volcanic desert formed by the eruptions of the Laki craters in 1783 – an event that devastated Iceland and is still considered to be one of the worst natural disasters in recorded history.

Kirkjubæjarklaustur was first settled by Irish monks, who fled the Vikings but left a curse that no pagan would ever live here. A Christian Norseman named Ketill the Foolish (so named by his peers for converting from the worship of Thor) lived on the site quite happily for many years. But when another Viking, Hildir Eysteinsson, decided to move in, he no sooner clapped eyes on his future farm than he dropped down dead. Perhaps, reasoned the Norsemen, Ketill had not been so foolish after all.

Religion plays a big part in the rest of Kirkjubæjarklaustur's history. In 1186, Benedictine nuns set up a convent here (*klaustur* means cloister), which was closed in the 16th-century Reformation. It can't have been a model institution, since two of the nuns were burned at the stake: one for sleeping with the devil, the other for maligning the Pope.

Iceland's edible berries include black crowberries and blueberries.

Contemporaneous with the nuns' convent at Kirkjubær, there was a monastery at Þykkvibær, a short distance away. It is said that the abbot and the monks of Þykkvibær often went up to Kirkjubær to see the mother superior and the sisters. On one such occasion both the abbot and some of the monks spent the night at Kirkjubær. The story goes that in the middle of the night the mother superior went with a light to check on the propriety of the sisters' conduct. In one cell, she came upon a monk and a nun sleeping together. The mother superior was about to reprimand the nun when the latter noticed her superior's headgear and said: "What is that you have on your head, dear mother?" Then the mother superior realised that she had taken the abbot's underpants by mistake and put them on her head instead of her bonnet. As a result, she softened her voice, saying as she retreated: "We are all sinners, sister".

During the 1783 Laki eruptions, a wall of lava looked like wiping out the settlement when the local curate, Jón Steingrímsson, herded everyone into the wooden church. There he delivered the ultimate fire-and-brimstone sermon whose effect, with great chunks of ash smashing down just outside the window, can only be imagined. When the sermon had finished, the congregation stumbled outside to find that the lava had been diverted and the church saved. The modern **Steingrímsson memorial chapel** has been built on the old church's site to commemorate this neat piece of divine intervention.

Today Kirkjubæjarklaustur is a pretty but somnolent outpost of 300 people, with the waterfall **Systrafoss** spraying down from steep cliffs as its backdrop. The 1783 lava fields, dotted with pseudo-craters, can still be seen just south of town, en route to the curious **Kirkjugólf** – the name means "church floor", since Viking settlers assumed it was part of a stone floor built by the curse-

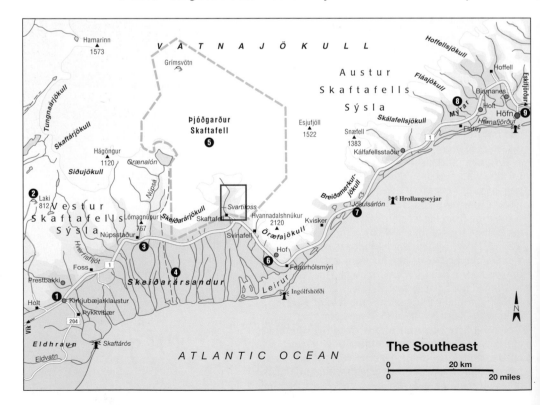

happy Irish monks. It is, however, a natural formation, with the tops of hexagonal basalt colums fitting together as perfectly as tiles.

Most people stay in Kirkjubæjarklaustur as a jumping-off point to the infamous **Laki craters ❷**, responsible for the 1783 eruptions. Over a period of 10 months, 30 billion tons of lava and three times as much sulphuric acid belched forth from the so-called "Skaftá fires". Not only were whole communities wiped out by the flow, but Laki sent up a cloud of noxious gas that began the "Haze Famine" and killed a fifth of Iceland's already much-diminished population and half its livestock – a toll so dramatic that plans were made to evacuate the island completely. Today Laki is extinct, but the craters at its base are still steaming. There are some fantastic views to be had from the peak.

The Ring Road east of Kirkjubæjarklaustur runs to the attractive farm of **Foss**, named for the thin waterfall flowing from the cliffs on the property, followed by the basalt columns of **Dverghamrar**. A sunken plain of moss-covered lava – once again created by Laki – must be crossed before finding the farm of **Núpsstaður ❸**, at the base of the imposing 770-metre (2,500-ft) cliff called **Lómagnúpur** ("loon peak"). Núpsstaður has one of Iceland's most charming 17th-century churches and a still-working antique harmonium.

At this point begins **Skeiðarársandur ❹**, the biggest of the southern *sandurs* – great wastelands of black sand and glacial debris carried out by volcanic eruptions from underneath Vatnajökull. Before the Ring Road was built, the only way across here was on horseback, accompanied by one of the farmers from Núpsstaður who had spent their lives learning to navigate the treacherous terrain. Today, cyclists dread this stretch of road most in Iceland: it is completely monotonous, and regular sandstorms make any open-air activity a misery.

Laki can be reached only by four-wheel-drive vehicles. Tours run there daily in summer from Kirkjubæjarklaustur.

BELOW: the 18th-century chapel at Núpsstaður.

Long bridges and flood barriers have been built to counteract any further glacial flows created by eruptions of **Grímsvötn** – although located under Vatnajökull, the most active and potentially lethal of Iceland's many volcanic craters. The last eruption under the ice began at the end of September 1996. More than two months later, on the morning of November 5th, the long-awaited glacial burst began. Large parts of Skeiðarársandur disappeared under black and muddy floodwater, electric cables across the sands were destroyed, as was the main road itself. The bridges over the rivers Sæluhúsakvísl and Gígja were swept away, and the 906-metre (2,980-ft) long bridge over the River Skeiðará, was badly damaged. South of the road the flood carried immense amounts of sediment to the sea and the beach stretched 800 metres (2,600 ft) further out into the ocean than it had before the flood. Two days later, when the burst came to an end, a million tons of ice had broken away from the margin of Skeiðarárjökull glacier, which dominates the view on the north side of the road. Since the glacial burst, the bridges and road have been renewed and restored.

Road-building in the Southeast has been adapted to take account of frequent flooding. The basis of the road is the ubiquitous volcanic rubble; a paved surface is laid on top. If the road is swept away, much of the raw material is on hand for quick rebuilding.

The great outdoors

Approached from the west, **Skaftafell National Park ❺** is announced by views over its rugged peaks and the three glaciers that have worked their way between them: from the left, **Morsárjökull**, **Skaftafellsjökull** and **Svínafellsjökull**. The twin glaciers of **Kvíárjökull** and **Fjallsjökull** can be seen further on. Finally, seen from the park, these are all dwarfed by **Öræfajökull** to the east, whose peak, **Hvannadalshnúkur**, is 2,120 metres (6,700 ft) high. All are fingers of the icecap **Vatnajökull** – which, like other icecaps in Iceland, is believed to have been formed not during the Ice Age but in another cold period 2,500 years ago.

BELOW: Jumping over a crevass on Vatnajökull.

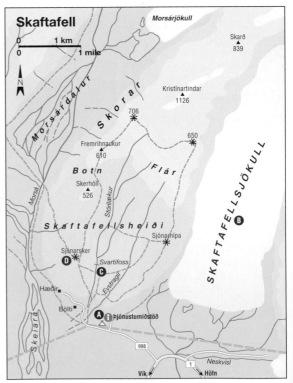

The National Park was established in 1967 and expanded in 1984 to take up some 1,600 sq. km (580 sq. miles). Settlers first came here in the Saga Age, and there are still two farms in the park, one of which now operates as a guesthouse. The park service operates an **information centre Ⓐ** next to a parking area and large camping ground. On summer weekends, this becomes a cross between a particularly raucous Reykjavík pub and a refugee camp, so anyone interested in communing with nature should come on a weekday. There is also a supermarket and snack bar, which overflows with card-playing backpackers in rainy weather.

All walks into the park depart from this point. The easiest is to the snout of the glacier **Skaftafellsjökull Ⓑ**, less than half an hour away. Covered in volcanic refuse, the ice is actually a shiny grey, like graphite. You can climb onto the edge of the glacier, but be careful. It's slippery – and a fall would dunk you straight into a near-freezing meltwater stream that soon disappears underground.

The most photographed attraction in Skaftafell is **Svartifoss** waterfall **Ⓒ**, a short walk along the road up to the Bölti farm/guesthouse west of the camping ground. Svartifoss is surrounded on both sides by basalt columns, giving it a grand organ-pipe effect. The path continues on to the peak of **Sjónarsker Ⓓ**, with a view disk, and then further into the mountains: the more energetic can make a day-trip to include views of Morsárjökull and Skaftafellsjökull which look like twin seas of ice. In the **Morsárdalur** valley, surrounded by high mountains and huge icecaps, you will also find one of the most impressive woods of the country, with birches reaching a height of 10 metres (33 ft).

The information centre can give instructions for other day trips into the park. Nature lovers can spot over 200 species of plants around Skaftafell as well as

Map
on page
216

BELOW: a couple by Fjallsárlón lagoon, east of the National Park.

VATNAJÖKULL ICECAP

Vatnajökull covers about 8,500 sq. km (3,280 sq. miles), or one twelfth of the whole country, and is 1,000 metres (3,300 ft) thick in parts. It is larger than the combined glaciated areas of the European continent, and the greatest icecap in the world, outside the countries designated as polar regions. At first sight Vatnajökull displays a general resemblance to the main polar ice sheets, but its nature is quite different. Vatnajökull is a so-called temperate glacier. Its temperature is at melting point, or very close to it, at any given depth, except in the top layers, where frost may remain until far into the summer, although that varies. The Arctic and Antarctic ice sheets, on the other hand, are polar glaciers; they are perpetually frozen all the way through. During the first centuries after settlement the glaciers of Vatnajökull were much smaller than they are now and the icecap was thinner. Towards the end of the 12th century the climate began to deteriorate and the glaciers started to expand. Vatnajökull's glaciers reached their greatest expansion during the 18th and 19th centuries. Since 1890 however, they have withdrawn and thinned, especially in the years between 1920 and 1960. Since 1960 Vatnajökull has thickened and the recession of its glaciers has slowed.

Arctic skuas are abundant in the Southeast.

Iceland's usual plethora of birds, including the largest breeding colonies of great and arctic skuas in the northern hemisphere.

The lake of ice

East of Skaftafell along the Ring Road is the farm **Svínafell**, which was the home of Flosi Þórðarson, the murderer of Njáll and his family in *Njáls Saga*, followed by **Hof ❻**, which offers picturesque farmhouse accommodation and has a small turf church. It is near here that the First Settler, Ingólfur Arnarson, lived before moving to Reykjavík – the promontory of **Ingólfshöfði** marks the site. In the farm of **Kvísker**, three self-educated, elderly brothers have each become specialists of note in different fields, a common occurrence in this area.

Immediately after a suspension bridge over the Jökulsá River is one of Iceland's most photographed sights: the iceberg-filled lake of **Jökulsárlón ❼**. The ice has calved from the glacier Breiðamerkurjökull, which runs into the lake, burying its snout underwater. The lake was formed only when the passage to the sea was blocked by land movements in the 20th century: geologists suggest it could come unblocked in the near future, draining the lake and making the Ring Road impassable. Boat cruises operate around Jökulsárlón several times daily in summer, weaving among the glistening ice formations. Sometimes the guide on the boat fishes out of the water a small piece of the astonishingly dense, clear ice so that you can have a closer look.

BELOW: perfect reflections at Jökulsárlón.

Excursions on the icecap

East of Jökulsárlón, a turn-off to the left advertises trips to **Jöklaferðir** at the top of Vatnajökull. The road itself is passable only by four-wheel-drive vehicles, but

those without such transport can meet the bus from Höfn on the so-called "Glac-ier Tour" every morning at 10am for the ride up. A small chalet has been built at the edge of the icecap, and hire of snowcats can be arranged. It's not entirely environmentally sound – so much noise and the first touches of air pollution on the pristine icecap – but such considerations are usually forgotten in the excite-ment of riding the snow. On a clear day, you can see for miles across the white sea of Vatnajökull, and trips usually include a stop at a ravine.

Map on page 214

The river valleys along this part of the Ring Road are beautiful but thinly populated, while the flatlands of **Mýrar** ❽ are excellent for birdwatching. On one farm here, **Bjarnanes**, a troll woman named Ketillaug is said to have been seen taking a kettle of gold up into the multi-coloured alluvial mountain **Ketil-laugarfjall**. There is one day of the year when humans can try and take the kettle from her, but those that attempt it are subject to hallucinations – typi-cally of the farm below catching fire – and always run back to give the alarm.

The Southeast's administrative centre, with a population of about 1,600, is **Höfn** ❾ – the name literally means "harbour" – boasting one of the few in the Southeast. The town's fortunes have improved rapidly with the completion of the Ring Road in the 1970s, turning it from a one-horse town to its present, ungainly concrete self. But what it lacks in aesthetic appeal is made up for by its beautiful setting on **Hornafjörður** fjord, almost completely cut off from the sea by spits to form a tranquil lake. There is a **Folk Museum** (open summer: daily 3–6pm and 8–9.30pm) in town with a mixture of exhibits from around the region, and plenty of fish-processing factories, but the real reason most visitors stay here is to join the summer "Glacier Tour", which includes snowcatting and a visit to Jökusárlón in a single, easy trip. ❏

James Bond fans may get a sense of déjà vu at Jökulsárlón – the opening scenes of the film A View to a Kill *were shot here.*

BELOW:
the dramatic coastline near Höfn.

AN EVER-CHANGING LANDSCAPE

From volcanoes to glaciers, Iceland is home to more of nature's wonders, both hot and cold, than any other place on earth.

In 1963, the island of Surtsey exploded out of the sea off Iceland in a great arch of flame and lava. It was only the latest natural wonder in Iceland's long, turbulent life. The Mid-Atlantic Ridge, which runs through the middle of the country from southwest to northeast, is the cause of the geothermal activity that has shaped much of Iceland's geology and unique landscape. Equally responsible are the thousands of years of glaciation, and the glacial meltwater, which together have modified the land.

The area close to the Mid-Atlantic Ridge has the greatest number of volcanoes: all around smoke and steam rise constantly. Here you will find spouting geysers, hot springs and craters – both active, like those near Mývatn, and inactive, solidified into fantastic lava shapes or filled with calm lakes. In some areas the ground is still very warm, and the Icelanders may even use a small covered pit as an oven to bake a delicious speciality – lava bread.

At the other end of the scale are glaciers, such as Vatnajökull which, when it calves, fills the nearby Jökulsárlón lake with icebergs. The glaciers are bleak and dramatic moonscapes of peaks, crevasses and a surprising range of colours from dirty black to pure icy blue. Meltwater feeds many of the powerful waterfalls that are also a feature of this dramatic, surprising land.

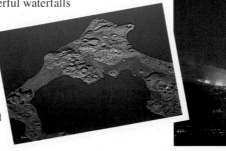

△ **MIGHTY WATERFALL**
Dettifoss is Europe's most powerful waterfall, dropping 44 thunderous metres (145 ft) into a canyon in Jökulsárgjufur National Park in the northeast.

▷ **LAVA & WATER**
Mývatn's pseudo-craters, of hugely varying sizes, formed when lava flowed over wetlands.

◁ **MOUTH OF HELL**
Molten lava glows red as it pours off Mount Hekla, one of Iceland's most active volcanoes. Its last major eruption was in 2000.

△ LIGHT SHOW

The spectacular aurora borealis, commonly known as the northern lights, are a frequent sight in the long Icelandic winter.

▽ ICE PINNACLES

Viewed from afar, some of Iceland's icecaps appear smooth and white. Up close, areas are pushed into peaks or pitted with streams.

△ COLOURFUL ROCKS

The beautiful, pastel-hued rock faces of Brennissteins-alda are a favourite walk, crossing the lava bed from Landmannalaugar.

▽ STROKKUR

Visitors are fascinated by the burst of water and steam that spouts from this geyser roughly every 10 minutes.

PRESERVING THE ENVIRONMENT

A land of some 100,000 sq. km, and only 277,000 people, with clean air and clean water, Iceland was relatively slow to see the need for conservation. But now its people know that even their beautiful environment could be harmed and are reversing soil erosion, reducing gravel mining in volcanic areas, guarding the fish that are essential to their economy and preventing pollution. Stricter conditions introduced for off-road driving are starting to work and cycling on mountain tracks is discouraged to avert erosion.

Trees are vital. Iceland was covered in trees when the first settlers arrived. "We destroyed them", one man explained, "there's a general feeling that we should give them back".

Tourism might be another threat to nature. Some 50 percent of visitors come during the short summer months. To discourage them from all going to the same lake, waterfall or volcano, others are being promoted. But most visitors care for the environment and, coming from more heavily polluted lands, have also helped to make Icelanders more aware of the threats.

SNÆFELLSNES AND THE WEST

Map on page 226

This large area between Reykjavík and the West Fjords is easy to explore and has a variety of places to visit, from sites associated with the Sagas to remote fishing villages

Icelanders, in their more lyrical moments, are apt to dub their homeland the Saga Isle. This description is particularly appropriate for the Snæfellsnes peninsula and the West, where some of the most dramatic events of the sagas took place. Names of farms, villages and towns conjure up the presence of historical characters such as the warrior-poet Egill Skallagrímsson and the chieftain and scholar Snorri Sturluson. Along these shores, constantly swept by the wind and the rain, occurred the terrifying hauntings of *Eyrbyggja Saga* and the tragic romance of *Laxdæla Saga*.

Though the West echoes with historic and literary associations, the jewel in its crown is the work of nature alone: the Snæfellsjökull icecap, at the western end of the Snæfellsnes peninsula. At 1,446 metres (4,743 ft), the glacier dominates the surrounding countryside. From as far away as Reykjavík, 100 km (60 miles) to the south across Faxaflói bay, Snæfellsjökull can be seen when the weather is clear, shimmering on the northern horizon. Snæfellsjökull, though at 11 sq. km (4 sq. miles) not one of Iceland's larger glaciers, is one of the most famous. In Jules Verne's *Journey to the Centre of the Earth*, the glacier is featured as the gateway for a subterranean route to the earth's centre. Far-fetched though the story may be, the glacier does indeed rest on top of a volcanic crater, which last erupted about 1,700 years ago to create the present three-peaked mountain.

The glacier plays a mystical role in *Under the Glacier*, a classic work by Nobel Prize-winning novelist Halldór Laxness. In recent years it has become a place of pilgrimage for New Agers in search of cosmic experiences; they congregate beneath the glacier every summer, to the bemusement of local fisherfolk.

North from Reykjavík

The glacier-bound traveller setting out from the capital can either follow the coast road to the north, or make the first leg of the journey through the new tunnel under Hvalfjörður. The tunnel itself is about 7 km (4 miles) long, and cuts distances between Reykjavík and points north by over 100 km (62 miles).

Taking Route One, the Ring Road, north out of Reykjavík, a detour east on Route 36 leads to two famous farms: **Laxness** where the writer Halldór Laxness was born; and **Mosfell**, where saga figure Egill Skallagrímsson died – supposedly after ordering his slaves to bury his treasure, and then slaughtering them to ensure secrecy. Egill had intended to take the money to Þingvellir and fling it in the chieftains' faces, but was prevented from so doing by his family.

PRECEDING PAGES: gazing into a glacier on Snæfellsjökull. **LEFT:** the harbour at Akranes. **BELOW:** Glymur waterfall frozen in winter.

The Ring Road leads along the roots of **Mount Esja**, 918 metres (3,011 ft) high before turning into **Hvalfjörður**. In the mountains at the head of the fjord, about an hour's walk above the road, is Iceland's highest waterfall, **Glymur ❶**, at 198 metres (650 ft). The modern church at **Saurbær ❷** on the northern coast of Hvalfjörður is dedicated to the memory of Iceland's greatest devotional poet, Reverend Hallgrímur Pétursson, who served this parish in the 1600s.

On the peninsula at the northern side of the fjord lies the town of **Akranes ❸** (population 5,500), offering hotels, guesthouse accommodation and restaurants. About a kilometre to the east in **Garður** is a very interesting **Folk Museum** (open summer: daily 10.30am–12 noon, 1.30–4.30pm; winter: Mon–Fri 1.30–4.30pm), with the emphasis on maritime history. In the ancient **cemetery** is a stone given to Iceland by the Irish government in 1974, to commemorate 1,100 years of settlement: an inscription in Icelandic and Gaelic remembers the role of Irish monks in the island's discovery.

Continuing north, the town of **Borgarnes ❹**, near the mouth of **Borgar-**

Whale-watching at sunrise.

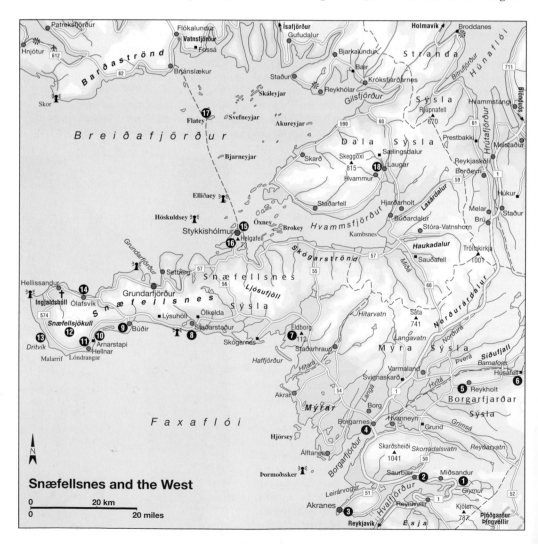

Snæfellsnes and the West

0   20 km

0   20 miles

N

Map on page 226

fjörður fjord, has grown close to the very spot, **Borg**, where Egill Skalla-grímsson lived in the 10th century. The son of one of the first Norse settlers, Egill was a paradoxical figure: a fierce and often cruel Viking warrior, he was also a great poet in the skaldic tradition of intricate word-play and metaphor. A modern sculpture by Ásmundur Sveinsson (1893–1982) at Borg commemorates Egill and his work. *Egils Saga*, which tells his story and preserves his poetry for posterity, was probably recorded by one of his descendants, Snorri Sturluson (*see panel on page 40*). In 1241 he was ambushed and murdered by his enemies on the orders of the King of Norway at his home at **Reykholt ❺** – today a tiny hamlet some 36 km (22 miles) east of Borgarnes on Route 30.

Snorri's farmstead is long gone, but a hot pool remains where the scholar and chieftain once bathed. A tunnel (now partly restored) led from the pool to the farmhouse. A modern statue of Snorri by Norwegian sculptor Gustav Vigeland stands at Reykholt, commemorating Snorri's masterly *Heimskringla (History of the Norwegian Kings)*, which saved centuries of Norwegian history from oblivion. A new church and a research centre have been built in Reykholt.

Hvalfjörður translates as "whale fjord". Until recently Iceland's only remaining whaling-station operated from here.

Lava caves and waterfalls

The green, rolling country of Borgarfjörður is at its most beautiful up beyond Reykholt. **Hraunfossar** is a multitude of tiny cascades tumbling into the Hvítá river along a 1-km (⅝-mile) stretch. A footbridge crosses the river at the churning **Barnafoss** waterfall, where the Hvítá flows through a rugged chasm. At nearby **Húsafell ❻**, summerhouses cluster in one of Iceland's largest woods. Húsafell farm is first mentioned in *Laxdæla Saga*. Its most famous occupant was Snorri Björnsson, who lived here at the end of the 18th century. Besides being a well-known sorcerer he was said to have tried his strength on the 180-kg (400-lb) boulder **Kvíahella**, which still can be seen close to the pens that he built. The area is full of geothermal water. In Húsafell alone you will find two swimming pools, three pleasant hot pools, a water slide and a steam bath. Near the farmhouse is an open-air exhibition of the sculptures of Páll Guðmundsson, who lives and works in Húsafell, using stones from river gorges in the mountains above the farm.

Hidden beneath **Hallmundarhraun** lava field lies Iceland's largest lava cave, **Surtshellir**, 1.5 km (1 mile) in length. Signposted from the road, the cave is found by following a marked trail. Good shoes and torches are essential for exploring the cave. There are guided trips from Húsafell daily in July and August. Surtshellir was already known in the Saga Age, when a band of outlaws lived in the cave. It took some time for the farmers to overcome them, and place names refer to this time in history – for example Vopnalág ("weapons hollow") and Eiríksgnípa ("Erik's pike"). Ancient traces of human habitation can still be seen in the cave today. Close to Surtshellir is another cave, **Stefánshellir**, which also makes an interesting tour. To visit the third cave in the area, called **Víðgelmir**, you have to be accompanied by a guide from the nearby farm of Fljótstunga.

To the west along paved Route 54 lies the Snæfellsnes peninsula and its mysterious glacier. The first

BELOW: statue of Snorri Sturlusson.

landmark is **Eldborg** , a crater 112 metres (367 ft) high, formed in a volcanic eruption 5–8,000 years ago. The crater, which commands magnificent views, is about 40 minutes' walk from the main road.

The **Kerlingarskarð** pass, over Route 55 which reaches 311 metres (1,020 ft) above sea level, was once a hazardous trail which claimed many lives in bad weather. Kerlingarskarð is a popular ski centre in winter.

Mineral springs and the summit of the glacier

A peculiarity of the Snæfellsnes peninsula is its mineral springs, producing naturally fizzy water – a rarity elsewhere in the country. Probably the most famous is on **Ölkelda** farm (the name, naturally enough, means "mineral spring") near **Staðarstaður** on the south side of the peninsula. Staðarstaður is believed to have been the residence of Ari the Learned (1068–1148), author of the *Book of Icelanders*, one of the most important sources on the early history of the nation.

At **Lýsuhóll**, mineral water is found in a geothermal area: it produces hot, bubbly water, which is used to heat a swimming pool. **Búðir** , once an important fishing centre, became better known for a pleasant hotel of the same name. In early 2001, however, this was destroyed in a fire. **Arnarstapi** and **Hellnar** , small fishing villages beneath the Snæfellsjökull glacier, are famed for their strange rock formations and their birdlife. Close to Hellnar is a sea cave, **Baðstofa** ("farmhouse loft"), where bizarre effects of light and colour are seen. Opposite the cave, on the beach, a small coffee-shop is run in the summer by the locals. Adjacent to Hellnar is the now-deserted farm of Laugarbakki, birthplace of Guðríður Þorbjarnardóttir, one of the heroines of the Norse discovery of Greenland around AD 1000. She emigrated to Greenland as a young girl, then

Tales of ghostly apparitions have long been attributed to the Kerlingarskarð pass, and even today stories are told of travellers who sense the presence of an "extra passenger" in the car as they cross the pass.

BELOW: natural arch at Arnarstapi.

later settled with her husband, Karlsefni, in Vínland, the Norse colony in North America, where she gave birth to her son Snorri, the first white child to be born in North America. Natural wonders at Arnarstapi include **Sönghellir** ("song cave"), with remarkable acoustics, and a huge stone arch. Sea birds nest on the cliffs in their thousands.

The focus of the peninsula, the **Snæfellsjökull glacier ⑫**, can be approached from several directions: the summit is four to five hours' walk from Arnarstapi. A ski lift goes to the top at weekends in winter. From Ólafsvík, north of the glacier, it is possible to drive part of the way and then walk on – again, a four- to five-hour hike to the summit. While the highest of the three mountain peaks is difficult to scale without special climbing gear, the walk up the glacier itself is fairly easy. In summer, however, crevasses open in the ice, so a guided walk is recommended (available from Ólafsvík).

Test your strength

Farther down the coast from Hellnar, by **Malarrif**, stand two lofty pillars of rock, **Lóndrangar**. The taller, 75 metres (248 ft) high, is called "Christian pillar", and the lower is "heathen pillar". While fishing remains the livelihood of the peninsula, some communities have now disappeared, leaving only traces of the centuries of fishing seasons: 60 boats used to row out from **Dritvík ⑬**, for example, where today there is nothing left but spectacular wilderness – including the great rock formation called **Tröllakirkja** ("church of the trolls").

Those who wish to try out their muscle-power in true Icelandic tradition should stroll along the shore from Dritvík to Djúpalón where four weighty stones present an age-old test of strength. The aim is to lift them up onto a

Map on page 226

Map on page 226

TIP

You can travel to the top of Snæfellsjökull by snow scooter or snow mobile, starting from Arnarstapi tourist centre.

LEFT: a crack in Snæfellsjökull glacier.
BELOW: the start of the descent at Snæfellsjökull in Jules Verne's *Journey to the Centre of the Earth*.

ledge of rock at about hip height. The largest, *Fullsterkur* ("full strength") is 155 kg (341 lbs), the second, *Hálfsterkur* ("strong enough"), 140 kg (308 lbs), the third, *Hálfdraettingur* ("half strength"), 49 kg (108 lbs) and the last, *Amlóði* ("weakling") 23 kg (50 lbs). *Amlóði*, unfortunately, is now broken. Lifting at least *Hálfsterkur* was a requirement for joining the crew of a boat from Dritvík.

Regional centre

Now a deserted farm and church just inland from Rif, **Ingjaldshóll** was once a major manor and regional centre. Just to the east, **Ólafsvík** ⓮ is one of the larger communities on the peninsula with a population of 1,200. It is also Iceland's oldest-established trading town, granted its charter in 1687. Ólafsvík offers a guesthouse and restaurants, a swimming pool and golf course. An old merchant's storehouse from 1844 has been restored and houses the local **museum** (open daily 1–5pm). Ólafsvík is also one of Iceland's best known whale-watching centres, with regular sightings of humpback, minke and blue whales in the cold waters off the peninsula.

    Stykkishólmur ⓯ is the principal town on the Snæfellsnes peninsula and the starting point for those who are going to the West Fjords by ferry. Nearby is **Helgafell** ⓰ ("holy mountain"), a 73-metre (240-ft) hill. According to local folklore, those who climb Helgafell for the first time will have three wishes come true, provided a few conditions are observed: you must not look back or speak on the way; you must make your wishes facing east; you must not tell anyone what they are; and only benevolent wishes are allowed. Even if your wishes are not fulfilled, Helgafell is worth climbing for the spectacular views of **Breiðafjörður** bay. Helgafell has, in fact, always been considered to have

Tradition says that Christopher Columbus spent a winter at Ingjaldshóll in 1477 when he visited Iceland as a merchant. He may well have picked up tales of Norse ventures to the Americas, helping to inspire his 1492 voyage across the Atlantic.

BELOW: seals are a common sight on the peninsula's north coast.

Map on page 226

supernatural powers. The first settler here, Þórólfur Mostraskegg, built a wooden temple to Thor at its summit. Þórólfur's son, the curiously named Þorstein Cod-Biter, claimed that on Helgafell he was able to see Valhalla, where dead Norse warriors drank with the gods.

In the 10th century, Helgafell became a Christian holy mountain with its own church built by Snorri the Priest. According to the *Eyrbyggja Saga*, a long blood-feud was sparked off when a certain family group, unmindful of Helgafell's religious significance, used it as a toilet. To cap this tradition of legends, Helgafell is supposedly also where Guðrún Ósvífursdóttir, heroine of *Laxdæla Saga*, lived out her last years as a hermit, and where she is buried. Stykkishólmur offers a hotel, guesthouse and youth accommodation. Jet-skis can be hired to skim over the harbour. The local **Folk Museum** (open Mon–Fri 3–6pm, Sat, Sun 11am–6pm) is housed in a beautifully restored timber house dating from 1828. Known simply as the **Norwegian House**, it was imported in kit form from Norway. Stykkishólmur's new church overlooks the town.

A display in the Norwegian House in Stykkishólmur.

Sub-arctic archipelago

The car/passenger ferry *Baldur* plies Breiðafjörður between Stykkishólmur and Brjánslækur in the West Fjords, calling at the island of **Flatey** ⑰. Breiðafjörður is dotted with about 2,700 islands, which once supported a large population thanks to the excellent fisheries. Flatey was the site of a 12th-century monastery and a major cultural centre until the 1800s. One of the greatest treasures of Icelandic literature, *Flateyjarbók* (the Flatey Book), was preserved here for centuries before being presented to the Danish king in the 16th century. In 1971 it returned to Iceland; it is now in the Árni Magnússon Institute, Reykjavík.

BELOW: the modern exterior of Stykkishólmur church.

Map on page 226

Just east of Stykkishólmur lies the uninhabited island of Öxney, once the home of Erik the Red, discoverer of Greenland, and his son Leifur – known as "the Lucky" – who discovered North America some time around AD 1000.

BELOW: the tiny library at Flatey.

The islanders gradually deserted their remote homes during the early part of the 20th century, and few remain. Flatey, though, is a delight, a perfectly preserved example of what an Icelandic village used to be. While the island is all but uninhabited in winter, many families spend their summers there renovating the lovely old timber houses of their ancestors. A triumph of painstaking restoration is Iceland's oldest, and smallest, library (4.75 metres by 3.43 metres, or 15 ft 6 in by 11 ft 3 in), built in 1844 to house the collection of the Flatey Progress Society.

Viking romance

North of the Snæfellsnes peninsula is **Hvammsfjörður** fjord, with the village of **Búðardalur** at its head. Route 59 runs along **Laxárdalur** (Salmon River Valley). This is saga country, and almost every place name strikes a chord for Icelanders. In the **Haukadalur** valley (Route 586) is the site of the farm **Eiríksstaðir**, the birthplace of Leifur Eiríksson, which has been excavated.

The farm **Hjarðarholt**, just outside Búðardalur, is the birthplace of Kjartan Ólafsson, whose ill-starred love for Guðrún Ósvífursdóttir from **Sælingsdalur**, 30 km (18 miles) to the north, is the central theme of *Laxdæla Saga*. Abandoned, as she believed, by Kjartan, Guðrún was persuaded to marry his friend, cousin and blood brother Bolli Þorleiksson. Guðrún incited her husband to kill Kjartan. Bolli was ambushed and killed by Kjartan's brothers in Sælingsdalur, where ruins still bear the name Bollatóttir (Bolli's ruins). Geothermal springs made Sælingsdalur an important centre in Guðrún Ósvífursdóttir's day, when there was a hot bathing pool, of which traces can still be seen, at the farm of **Laugar** ⑱. A modern swimming pool now uses the natural hot water, while a summer hotel and a small **Folk Museum** (open summer: daily 1–5pm) operate in the school. ❑

Rams' Testicles and Rotten Shark

Plenty of traditional Icelandic dishes never make their way to the tables of the restaurants of Reykjavík. However, adventurous types in search of authentic food and blessed with a cast-iron gut will relish the midwinter Þorrablot feast (around February, although many items are available all year). The feast is largely an act of homage to the old methods of preserving food.

Almost everything a sheep can provide ends up in the Þorrablot menu, most notoriously *svið* the sheep's head, burned to remove the wool and then boiled. This delight is served up at the Þorrablot feast either in halves or off the bone and pressed into a kind of aspic jelly. Accompanied by mashed turnips, it tastes better than it looks – even, surprisingly, the eyes. All cuts of the sheep's meat and innards are prepared in various ways, with pride of place going to pickled rams' testicles, pressed into a nightmarish cake. Not a dish for the faint of heart, but surprisingly digestible in small quantities.

Guts, blood, fat and a dash of meat for form's sake, nattily sown up in sheep's stomachs, create another dish appropriately called *slátur* (slaughter). *Slátur* is not confined to the midwinter feast; it is eaten regularly in Icelandic homes. The dish comes in two varieties: *lifrarpylsa*, which means "liver sausage" but isn't, and the darker, fattier *blóðmör* or blood pudding, which is like haggis without the spice.

The crowning glory of a midwinter feast, and of many functions around the year, is the ceremonious intake of rotten shark *(hákarl)* and schnapps. After being buried for three months or more, shark becomes acrid and ammoniac, like the most nostril-defying of cheeses. Rubbery and rotten, it is washed down in small lumps with ample quantitites of the Icelandic spirit Brennivin (Black Death). A few nips beforehand for courage's sake is not a bad idea! Icelanders view eating *hákarl* rather like the dark midwinter itself. It strikes an emotional chord deep within the soul, and once over, the joy of having survived makes life seem instantly brighter again.

But not every Icelandic traditional food is quite so stomach-turning. A favourite is smoked mutton – in Icelandic *hangikjöt*, which means "hung meat." Served with potatoes, white sauce and peas, *hangikjöt* is a festive dish, obligatory at least once over the Christmas and New Year holidays but eagerly eaten at any time of the year. Another dish that regularly turns up is puffin. Icelanders have no qualms about eating their national bird in a good sauce – after all, salted or smoked, puffins were one of the dietary staples of centuries past. Also well worth a try as a dessert or even for lunch is *skyr*, a rich type of curd. Competition from flavoured yoghurt and ice cream has led dairy producers to create a number of varieties of *skyr* using imported flavours. But the genuine article is still sold unflavoured, mildly sour and served with milk, or, ideally, cream stirred in. A fine topping is wild crowberries, available fresh in late summer and early autumn. ❑

RIGHT: the Þorrablot feast is a chance to sample medieval delicacies.

THE WEST FJORDS

This remote, inaccessible region has whole areas that are deserted, creating natural reserves of a beauty and fertility unknown elsewhere in Iceland

Reykjavík

Shaped like an outstretched paw, the West Fjords region is at first sight one of the least hospitable parts of Iceland. Lack of fertile lowlands has, since the days of settlement, forced the inhabitants to look to the sea rather than the land for their livelihood. Land travel has always been difficult or even dangerous in this area, which is characterised by rough and steep mountain slopes, shores that every now and then are cut off by the tides, and under constant threat from snow avalanches or earth slides. Even today this area is still at the mercy of the elements. In January 1995 an avalanche came down over the village of Súðavík, near the town of Ísafjörður, claiming 14 lives. And the same year, in October, another avalanche hit the village of Flateyri, taking 20 lives.

Since the days of settlement the inhabitants of the West Fjords have lived their lives on isolated farms, without any regular contact with the outside world, and here, at the westernmost point of Iceland, an independent, and in many ways strange, local culture has developed. Under the rough and rocky mountains the belief in monsters, ghosts and evil spirits has become deeper rooted than in any other part of the country; and no other region is home to so many sorcerers.

The mechanisation of the fishing industry in the 20th century has made life more comfortable, but government-imposed fishing quotas in recent years have led to a steady stream of emigrants from the West Fjords to Reykjavík. Meanwhile, many small farms in the area have been abandoned as unprofitable – with more and more farmers giving up as the years go by.

Travellers here face a string of serious obstacles, including some of the worst roads in the country, infrequent public transport services and abysmal weather. Yet the region offers Iceland's most dramatic fjords; soaring cliffs host literally millions of breeding sea birds; and some of the best hiking. And, once the proverbial ice is broken, its self-reliant people prove to be among the most hospitable in the land.

Of ice and trolls

Geologically speaking, the West Fjords region is the oldest part of the country, bearing the scars of intense glaciation. The area is basically a triangular plateau made up of layers of lava, most of them about 15–16 million years old. Between the layers there are, in several places, fossilised remains of luxuriant forests, which have grown between volcanic eruptions. Later, Ice-Age glaciation dug the fjords and valleys that make the area habitable today. The glacier was so powerful that it almost made an island of the West Fjords. As the crow flies the isthmus connecting the fjords Gilsfjörður and Bitrufjörður is at one point only 7 km (5 miles) wide, and just 262 metres (860 ft) above sea level.

PRECEDING PAGES: the magnificent Hornbjarg bird-cliffs in the Hornstrandir Nature Reserve. **LEFT:** an elderly couple in the West Fjords. **BELOW:** the *Fragranes* ferry.

Folklore tells another tale: trolls, it is said, decided to dig a channel at this point, competing over how many islands could be created from the excavated material. The troll in the west fared rather well and in the shallow waters of Breiðafjörður built hundreds of islands. Hindered by deeper waters, the troll in the east was less successful and in rage ripped off a huge chunk of a mountain bordering Steingrímsfjörður. Casting it into the ocean, he created the island of Grímsey, some miles offshore (not the same as Grímsey on the Arctic Circle).

A base for exploring

Most visitors start their visits at **Ísafjörður** ❶, the focal point of the West Fjords. With a population of 3,500, it is the only town of any size and has recently been connected to nearby towns by a new tunnel. The site of a 9th-century farmstead, **Eyri** is the oldest part of town, with one of Iceland's best natural harbours. On a fine summer evening, a stroll through the old town is an unforgettable walk through the past. The oldest buildings at the end of the sand-

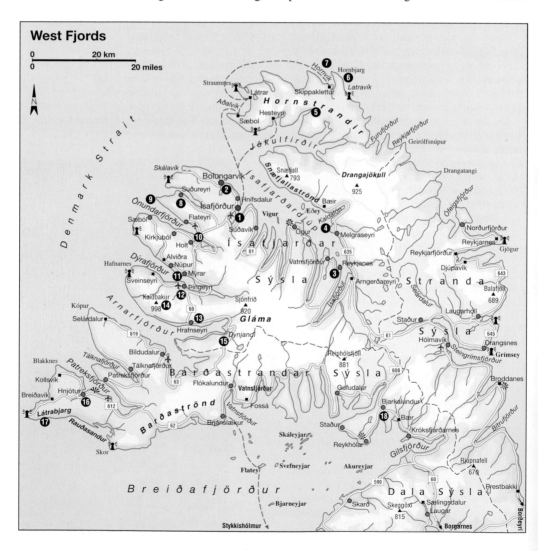

West Fjords

spit are four restored timber buildings dating from the 18th century. More by accident than design, these ancient (by Icelandic standards) houses were left standing as fish factories and warehouses sprang up around them.

Oldest of the four is **Tjöruhús**, built in 1733–42, followed by the adjoining **Krambúð**, dating from 1761 and originally a shop. The meticulously restored **Turnhús** (Tower House) was built in 1744. It once housed a salt-fish plant and now contains the **West Fjords Maritime Museum** (open May–June, Aug–15 Sept: daily 1–5pm; July: daily 10am–5pm). Exhibits trace the development of the town and its fishing industry, with all sorts of unusual nautical paraphernalia. Facing the harbour in the **Faktorshús** (Merchant's House) is Sjómannastofan, a restaurant attached to the seaman's hostel, where one can enjoy an unpretentious but genuine Icelandic fish dinner with undoubtedly the loveliest harbour view of any restaurant in the country. Ísafjörður has excellent skiing facilities in the **Seljalandsdalur** valley above town.

Around Ísafjörður

The broad fjord of Ísafjarðardjúp, on which Ísafjörður sits, almost severs the West Fjords in two. Near its mouth to the northwest of Ísafjörður, is **Bolungarvík ❷**, the second largest town in the region. Between here and **Hnífsdalur** is the steep mountainside Óshlíð, where avalanches and landslides have often occured. In Bolungarvík is Ösvör, an old fishing hut from the rowboat-era, which has been restored and turned into an interesting **Maritime Museum** (open daily). There is also a new **Natural History Museum** (open summer: daily 9am–6pm). A jeep track continues to **Skálavík** where those seeking solitude will find plenty at farmhouse accommodation in a tiny bay facing the Arctic Sea.

Map on page 238

BELOW: Ísafjörður from the air.

Cycling by the brightly-coloured houses of Ísafjörður.

Route 61, which hugs the southern shore of Isafjarðardjúp, southeast from Ísafjörður, was completed in 1975. Súðavík is the only village in these parts, developing from a Norwegian whaling-station *circa* 1900. Of the 70 houses in Súðavík 22 were completely destroyed by the 1995 avalanche.

Further along, close to the tip of the Ögurnes peninsula is **Ögur**, an impressive farmstead – built in the 19th century, it was at the time one of the largest in Iceland. At Mjóifjörður is the Djúpmannabúð roadside cafeteria, and the only petrol station along this stretch of coast. Another ancient farm site is at **Vatnsfjörður**, in its heyday a wealthy estate that produced several pastors of note. The village of **Reykjanes ❸**, at the head of Ísafjarðardjúp is one of the few places in the West Fjords with geothermal water. There is a summer hotel, swimming pool and greenhouses here.

The road continues as Route 635 along Ísafjarðardjúp's northern shore to **Kaldalón ❹**, a sheltered beauty spot. A small glacier here tumbles down from Drangajökull, the only large ice-field in the north of Iceland. At the head of the valley there are some grassy islets, then moraine brought by the descending glacier tounge. Accommodation is available at the farm Ármúli nearby.

Beyond Kaldalón, the road comes to an abrupt halt at Unaðsdalur valley, where the uninviting Snæfjallaströnd ("snow mountain coast") begins. The snow line is lower here than anywhere else in the country – even in mid-summer, some snow lies at sea level.

Islands and wilderness

Two of Ísafjarðardjúp's islands are inhabited: **Vigur** and **Æðey** ("eider island"). There are regular boat tours from Ísafjörður in the summer. A walk around

Vigur gives the visitor an opportunity to enjoy the rich birdlife in its natural environment. Thousands of eider ducks, arctic terns, puffins and other sea birds can be found on the island. There is also a small and homely coffee-shop in the mid-19th century farmer's house, as well as a mini post office, where guests can mail their cards and letters. Æðey is the biggest island in Ísafjarðardjúp and, as its name suggests, also has an impressive bird population.

Ísafjörður is also the jumping-off point for trips to the uninhabited nature reserve of **Hornstrandir ❺** to the north. The Reserve includes the whole area north of Skorarheiði from the end of Hrafnfjörður to the end of Furufjörður. Abandoned by its farming community during the first decades of the 20th century and free from the destructive grazing of sheep, plants and wildlife alike thrive on a scale unknown elsewhere in the country. Here you can wade knee-deep in meadows of wildflowers, fertilised by the guano of countless breeding sea birds, and listen at sundown for the haunting bark of the arctic fox, unpersecuted and tamer here than anywhere else in Iceland. The Nature Reserve is off limits to all motor traffic, making the only way to explore it by boat or on foot. There is no accommodation and little evidence of the once-flourishing farming community. Traces of bridle paths criss-cross the mountain passes, linking the fjords and inlets.

Map on page 238

In summer, the ferry *Fagranes* sails several times a week to the area, bringing day-trippers, hikers and descendants of the original landowners who now use the remaining old farmsteads as summer cottages. On board, take time to talk to the locals – a wealth of knowledge, of fact and folklore, has been passed down through successive generations.

Scheduled stops are at **Hornvík**, **Aðalvík** and **Hesteyri**, and by request, at other points en route. The voyage is an adventure as a day-trip, but most hikers choose to disembark and walk between Hesteyri or Aðalvík and Hornvík, usually taking 4 to 7 days. Others start at **Bær** in Ísafjarðardjúp and walk to **Jökulfirðir** and on to Hornstrandir. Twice each summer, the *Fagranes* sails to **Reykjafjörður** on the Strandir coast, opening up yet another hiking route.

At Hesteyri, abandoned houses and a church suggest a once-prosperous settlement. A trading place since 1881, Hesteyri was the base for a Norwegian whaling-station from 1894 to 1912. In the 1920s, a herring-processing factory was built in the village, where about 80 people lived. This closed in 1940 and in 1952 the last inhabitants moved away. Today there are a few summer cottages here.

Sea birds and driftwood

Not far from the Hornbjargsviti lighthouse rise the majestic bird-cliffs at **Hornbjarg ❻**, nesting ground for tens of thousands of pairs of noisy guillemots, Brunnich's guillemots, razorbills, puffins, kittiwakes and fulmars. Not for the fainthearted, **Kálfatindur** peak, the highest point along the cliffs, is a 534-metre (1,760-ft) vertical drop to the Arctic Ocean. From its lofty summit, the noise is deafening and the view simply breathtaking – some claim to have seen the distant Greenland icecap from here.

Islands have traditionally been sought-after farm sites in Iceland. On Vigur, some relics of old farming methods are preserved: beside Iceland's only windmill there is what may be the country's oldest eight-oar rowing boat, which is still in use.

BELOW: a female eider duck on her nest, surrounded by saxifrage.

In view of Kálfatindur is attractive **Hornvík Bay** ❼. It has a long sandy beach, some impressive waterfalls, a plentiful supply of driftwood and is a pleasant camping spot. In a rare bout of clear weather (for some reason, more likely in late summer), the place is nothing short of idyllic and makes an ideal base from which to explore the area. Across the bay is **Hælavíkurbjarg**, another impressive bird-cliff. Spring still draws daring Icelanders to lower themselves on ropes down the cliff-face and collect the prized guillemots' eggs.

Besides seal-hunting, coastal farmers of the West Fjords have always harvested something else from the sea: driftwood. These benefits are unevenly distributed as some farms have better driftwood-beaches than others. There has always been a lot of driftwood on Hornstrandir and it was extensively used in the past, as little timber was imported. Dealing in wood was profitable for local inhabitants, and many of them were also known as skilled craftsmen, making useful items out of driftwood, such as tubs and barrels, and selling them in the West Fjords and other parts of the country. Driftwood is still collected in Hornstrandir, now mainly used for fenceposts, which are sold all over Iceland.

Sea kayaking is a popular pursuit in this area of Iceland.

South of Ísafjörður

Route 60 winds over several high passes to link the fjords south of Ísafjörður. A tunnel has been made through the basalt rocks of Breiðadalsheiði, which at 610 metres (2,013 ft) is the highest pass in the area; it was often blocked in the past, cutting off villages for days, sometimes weeks, at a time.

The village of **Suðureyri** ❽, 17 km (10 miles) off the main road, is buried in the shadow of the steep **Súgandafjörður** fjord. The village's main claim to fame is that it lives without direct sunlight throughout the four winter months,

BELOW: camping out at Hornvík.

Map
on page
238

longer than any other village in Iceland. The sun's rays first peek over the high mountains and strike the village on 22 February each year, an occasion celebrated, as everywhere else in the West Fjords, with "sunshine coffee".

Önundarfjörður ❾, a fjord between Barði and Sauðanes headlands, is unmistakable because of its sandy beach which almost straddles the fjord in a golden arc. On a rare sunny day the shallow waters heat up and locals from nearby **Flateyri** throng to bathe in sight of the Arctic Sea. The headland, on which the 350 inhabitants of Flateyri live, was probably left there when a large part of a mountain cleaved into the sea. In 1823 Flateyri became an authorised trading place, and fish and fish-processing are still the main industries. There is said to have been a pagan temple on the hill Goðahóll above the village.

Across the fjord, the historical parsonage of **Holt** ❿ was the birthplace of the 17th-century bishop Brynjólfur Sveinsson. The attractive timber church here dates from 1869 and contains artefacts from the time of Bishop Brynjólfur.

Dýrafjörður, the next fjord south, ranks among the most scenic in Iceland – sheer mountains seem to rise straight from the shore, leaving little or no lowland for farming. The inhabitants have made do with other resources and the village of **Mýrar** ⓫ has Iceland's largest eider duck colony, with 7,000 pairs. The first settler at the nearby farm Alviðra was none other than a son of King Harald Fairhair of Norway. Today it offers accommodation to travellers.

National saints and sinners

Across the fjord, **Þingeyri** ⓬ (population 450) was the first trading post in the West Fjords. It takes its name from an ancient assembly whose sacred site was said to be enclosed by walls at either end of the mountain **Sandfell**, rising above the village. The old residents still remember the walls and in the town there are ruins of an ancient booth, used by visitors to the assembly, which are a historical monument. Don't miss the drive up Sandfell – from the top there is a beautiful view of the mountains, separating Dýrafjörður from Arnarfjörður. This mountain ridge is often called the "West Fjord Alps". In the 19th century the French wanted to establish a colony in Þingeyri to support their fishing fleet, but were turned down. In nearby **Haukadalur** valley there is a grave of French seamen. This valley is also the setting for the tragic events of the saga of Gísli Súrsson. Outlawed for a suspected vengeance killing, Gísli spent a gruelling 13 years on the run, but was eventually tracked down and slain. Gísli's farms at Hóll and Sæból (8 km/5 miles along the fjord from Þingeyri) are abandoned.

The village of **Hrafnseyri** ⓭, in Arnarfjörður fjord, was the birthplace of nationalist Jón Sigurðsson (*see panel on page 54*). There is a small **museum** (open summer: daily 1–8pm) and a **chapel** to his memory.

Further along the fjord, an indistinct route leads up Fossdalur valley to **Mount Kaldbakur** ⓮, the highest peak in the West Fjords. It is officially 998 metres (3,273 ft) high, but locals have added a cairn to credit the region with its only 1,000-metre peak. In clear weather the full-day hike is worth the effort, with views as far away as the Snæfellsnes icecap.

Traditionally the difficulty of a high pass was measured by the number of fish-skin shoes that were worn through to cross it. In the passes south of Ísafjörður a nine-skin pass was not unusual. Nowadays these routes are more of a test of the nerves of the driver and the suspension of the car.

BELOW:
the Hælavíkurbjarg bird-cliff with a view to Dalvík bay.

Dynjandi waterfall  is located at the head of the northern arm of Arnarfjörður. Also known as Fjallfoss ("mountain falls"), the 100-metre (328-ft) high cascade literally drops off the edge of the mountain, fanning out to a width of 60 metres (197 ft) at its base. Below it, a series of waterfalls cascade: Hundafoss, Strokkur, Göngumannafoss, Hrísvaðsfoss and Bæjarfoss.

Europe's most westerly point

Some kilometres beyond here the road splits. If you head west, Route 63 passes the fishing villages of **Bíldudalur** and **Tálknafjörður** (5 km/3 miles off the main road). From Bíldudalur the difficult, but impressive Route 619 passes the opening of several valleys, before it ends at the **Selárdalur** farm, where the pastor Páll Björnsson (1621–1706) lived, well known for his wisdom and his persecution of witches. He was said to have been an excellent speaker and an unusually good linguist. According to a legend, a black-sailed schooner was once seen off Selárdalur. People feared that pirates were on board. The pastor went out to the vessel, spoke to them in an eastern language and told them the area was full of witches. As a result the pirates exchanged gifts with him and sailed away. Also on Route 63 is the larger town of **Patreksfjörður**, which has a small guesthouse, although little of real interest to the visitor. Across the fjord, **Hnjótur**  has a small **Fishing and Farming Museum** (open summer: daily 10am–7pm) which is worth a stop. The museum's exhibits are neatly presented and on the walls there are original drawings showing how the old tools and equipment were used. All this is the work of Egill Ólafsson, the curator.

The real lure of the area is the bird-cliffs at **Látrabjarg** , at the westernmost point of Iceland – and thus Europe. Extending for 14 km (9 miles) and rising to

From above Dynjandi there are views down to Geirþjófsfjörður. The saga hero Gísli was slain at the head of this fjord in 977. His last hiding place is said to be visible far below the road. A silhouette of Gísli has been carved into Einhamar crag, marking where he died.

BELOW:
the picturesque cascades of Dynjandi waterfall.

444 metres (1,465 ft) at their highest point, the cliffs are home to one of Iceland's greatest concentrations of sea birds. The hundreds of thousands of puffins are happy to let visitors approach to within a few feet of their cliff-top perches.

A weekly bus service links the cliffs with **Breiðavík** 12 km (7 miles) away, which offers the nearest accommodation. This only allows a short stay, however: to reach the highest point of the cliffs involves a long, full-day hike from Breiðavík. The bird-cliffs have also been the scene of human dramas. When the British trawler *Dhoon* ran aground below the cliffs in the winter of 1947, a remarkable rescue operation by the local farmers saved all 12 crew members. Lowering themselves by ropes as if they were collecting eggs, they hauled the exhausted men up the 200-metre (650-ft) cliff-face to safety. Southeast of Látrabjarg is Iceland's most magnificent stretch of golden sand, **Rauðasandur**.

Another first settler

At the head of Patreksfjörður fjord, Route 62 crosses over to the southern coast of the West Fjords – **Barðaströnd** – a region that gets more than its share of foul weather. This entire stretch of coast has little over 500 inhabitants, largely because the shallow waters of Breiðafjörður bay do not attract the valuable cod and haddock. This was where the Viking Hrafna-Flóki made one of the first settlements in Iceland, long before Ingólfur Arnarson arrived. The *Landnámabók (Book of Settlements)* relates that the fishing was so good that Flóki neglected to make hay for his livestock, and they perished over the winter. In spring he climbed a high mountain and, looking north, saw ice-filled fjords. It was this drift ice, and not the glaciers, that prompted him to name the land "Iceland" on his eventual return to Norway. However, it is said that he came back some years later and spent the rest of his life in Iceland.

The village of **Brjánslækur**, at the entrance to Vatnsfjörður, is the terminal for the Breiðafjörður ferry, which connects twice daily with Stykkishólmur on the Snæfellsnes peninsula.

Route 60 continues south around the fjords, a long and winding drive. There is a chance of spotting the rare white-tailed sea eagle here, though only 30 or 40 pairs of this now protected species remain after centuries of hunting. The main settlement here is **Bjarkalundur ⑱**, the unofficial gateway to the West Fjords, with a hotel and camping facilities within sight of the twin peaks of Vaðalfjöll.

The Strandir coast

The rugged eastern flank of the West Fjords is one of the least visited parts of Iceland. The population of the area has been steadily declining, and now the only town of any size is **Hólmavík**, which has basic facilities. Farming is hard and good harbours few: **Djúpavík**, for example, a once-bustling herring station, is now virtually abandoned, but has a wonderfully situated summer hotel.

The village of **Norðurfjörður** is the end of the road. Beyond here, a hiking trail follows the coast to Hornstrandir. Allow between 10 and 14 days, expect all kinds of weather, take double the normal rations – and don't count on meeting another soul. ❑

Map on page 238

Sveinn Skotti was a 17th-century petty criminal and son of a mass-murderer. He was hanged on the cliff-top road to Vatnsfjörður fjord. His ghost is said to haunt the coast.

BELOW: summer colours.

IDENTIFYING ICELAND'S SEA BIRDS

One of the most unforgettable sights in Iceland is that of a huge, cliff-side sea bird colony – a common and noisy occurrence in breeding season

Sea birds can be seen and heard everywhere in Iceland – circling overhead, swimming offshore but, most often, stacked in vast, raucous colonies on steep cliffs and island coastlines. By the million they live, winter, or come to breed here – some 25 species in all, plus a few more on passage north or south. No wonder the great aim for many human visitors to Iceland is to watch these birds, sometimes by walking and climbing long distances to see the colonies without disturbing them. Watching sea birds is easiest by boat or from a nearby cliff, where the gap in between gives the birds a sense of security.

The northernmost island of Grímsey, on the Arctic Circle, is home to about 100 shepherds and fisherfolk. But great breeding colonies of birds outnumber them by their thousands – fulmars, including the rare blue fulmar, guillemots, including the Brunnich's sub-species, gannets and many others.

Even Reykjavík, with 170,000 inhabitants (over half of Iceland's population), also has its own colonies of auks, gulls such as kittiwake – easily distinguished by the cry that gives it its name – eiders and many other ducks. Near the golf course, a colony of Arctic terns use the golfers for diving practice.

Iceland's many great peninsulas, the West Fjords, Snæfellsnes and islands such as the Vestmannaeyjar offer much to discover. Pointing the binoculars at the ever-changing sea or the steadfast cliffs, you do not have to be an expert to feel the thrill of finding a species that, to you at least, is new.

◁ **A LOUD CRY**
A vivid red beak and short red legs make the arctic tern easy to spot among other birds – and its noisy cry is unmistakeable.

△ **LOOKING OUT TO SEA**
A razorbill's chunky beak, with its vertical white stripe, can be part of the mating ritual – a bird attracts a mate by using its beak to make a castanet-like rattle.

▽ ON THE WING

Many species of gull are found in huge numbers in Iceland. One of the best known is the kittiwake, with its easily recognised call.

▽ UNUSUAL GUILLEMOTS

Brunnich's guillemot is an Icelandic speciality, overlapping in many places with its more southerly cousin, the guillemot.

▽ THE NATIONAL BIRD

The tiny puffin, with its distinctive curved red, blue and yellow beak in summer, is everyone's favourite. Pairs of puffins breed and raise their young in burrows on clifftops.

△ A PRECARIOUS PERCH

Thousands of sea birds sit calmly as the waves pound against the great sea cliffs on the west of the Snæfellsnes peninsula to the north of Reykjavík.

△ THE FULMAR

Among all the gull-like birds to be seen flying over sea and cliffs, the fulmar is easily identified by its stiff-winged flight.

▷ A PAIR OF GANNETS

Big strong-flying gannets, which make spectacular steep dives for fish, come to Iceland's cliffs during the breeding season.

THE LAST OF THE GREAT AUKS

The great auk was once the king of the auk species – black and white seabirds with short, stubby necks, including guillemots, razorbills, little auks and puffins. At one time, there were great auk colonies in Iceland, North America, Greenland and the Faeroes.

But the great auk had one major disadvantage. It was flightless. Sitting stolidly on a rock, the great auk was easy prey for hunters in remote areas. The colonies grew smaller until, by the start of the 19th century, few remained except on St Kilda and on Iceland's islands. Still, they were hunted. In 1844, two hunters visiting Eldey island, southwest of the Rejkjanes peninsula, spotted a single great auk. They were swift – one stroke of the club and the great auk was gone forever.

HÚNAFLÓI AND SKAGAFJÖRÐUR

Map on page 250

This rugged region of mountains, waterfalls, cliffs and islands has been largely forgotten by tourism – few turn off the Ring Road to find the coast's remoter attractions

●Reykjavík

Jutting into the icy Arctic Ocean, the Skagi peninsula divides the northern coast of Iceland into the Húnaflói bight and Skagafjörður fjord. It is well worth taking the time to follow the narrow dirt roads, often little more than graded tracks, into a windswept wilderness of basalt cliffs crowded with nesting sea birds, black volcanic sand spits and beaches inhabited only by seals.

Rural backwater

The Ring Road runs through some rich agricultural land here, its alluvial soil weathered from some of Iceland's oldest rocks. The entry point to the area is **Brú ❶** ("bridge") – a tiny hamlet which is really little more than a petrol station. It is dominated by the huge bulk of **Tröllakirkja**, a hill that stands over 1,000 metres (3,300 ft) from the flat surrounding farmland. Brú is at the head of the narrow **Hrútafjörður** fjord formed by the extensive glacial moraines (deposits) which dominate the area. The land in this region is rich in minerals and this, coupled with the high rainfall, encourages the establishment of many rare alpine and arctic plants, particularly gentians.

LEFT: Hvítserkur arch with nesting sea birds.
BELOW: yellow lady's bedstraw.

The farmstead of **Ósar** lies 18 km (12 miles) north along Route 711 on the **Vatnsnes** promontory. From here are superb views across the **Húnafjörður bay** to Blönduós. In the foreground is the moraine-dammed inlet of **Sigríðarstaðavatn**, with the Hóp lagoon beyond. Grey seals bask on the sand spits at low tide while eider duck and terns nest among the lyme grass. A short distance along the shore are several basalt stacks eroded and awash with the ocean swell. The first, **Hvítserkur**, has a hole through its base. White guano flecks the ledges of the black rock like icing. According to folklore this 15-metre (49-ft) high stack was a troll turned to stone by the sun.

Hóp ❷ is the largest salt-water lagoon in Iceland, virtually cut in half by a narrow sand spit and almost isolated from the sea by **Þingeyrasandur**, a low-lying, black sand dune with great swards of lyme grass on its seaward side. This was used in the darker ages of Iceland's history as a seed crop to mill for flour. Over the centuries, the dune has expanded seaward as more sand has been deposited by the ocean. Tundra plants have then colonised the older dunes to provide great flashes of colour: purple thyme, yellow lady's bedstraw, white northern orchid, deep blue gentians, and parnassus grass and silverweed. Overhead, arctic skuas wheel about attacking arctic terns; below, running free across the sands, are Icelandic horses, which are particularly common in this area.

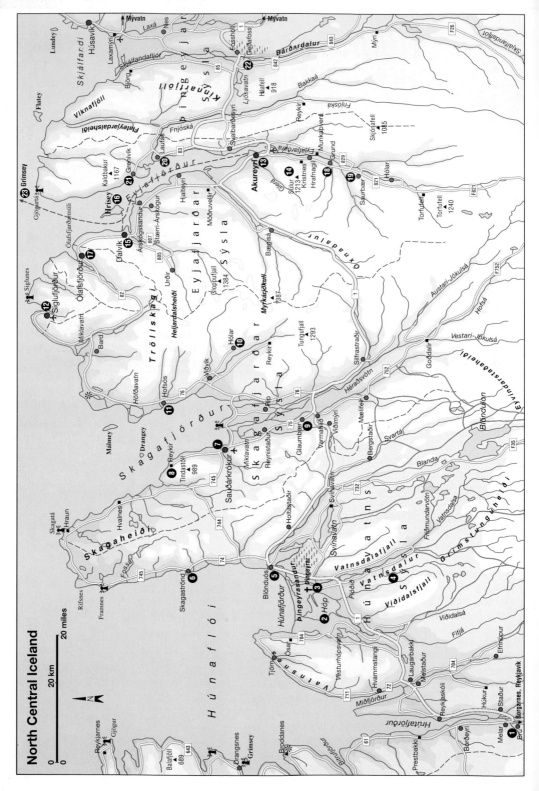

Medieval centre of learning

On the way to the dunes, the dirt track (Route 721) passes one of Iceland's greatest historical sites, **Þingeyrar ❸**. The local bishop Jón Ögmundarson built Iceland's first Benedictine monastery here in 1112. It quickly became a literary hot-spot, with monks working full-time transcribing the Bible and the sagas. The name reflects the site's original function as a þing (district assembly). All that remains today is a solitary church erected over 100 years ago.

Near to where Route 721 meets the Ring Road is **Þrístapar**, the hilly site of Iceland's last execution which occurred on 12 January 1830, when the murderers Agnes and Friðrik were beheaded. Across the road is the **Vatnsdalur valley ❹**, a geologist's dream dotted with steep mounds of ground moraine. Just as striking is evidence of the largest known landslip in Iceland that occurred here in October 1720. The side of the huge ridge, **Vatnsdalsfjall** (800 metres/2,624 ft high), collapsed and dammed the river below to create a new lake – **Flóðið**.

With a population just over 1,000 the town of **Blönduós ❺** is the best base for exploring this region. Situated where the River Blanda enters the Húnaflói, it is an important fishing community. The town's bright houses contrast with the local green fields and grey screes.

The Ring Road crosses a bridge that spans the **River Blanda** (where salmon fishing can cost up to US$1,300 a day) and there is a turn-off to the heart of Blönduós, with a large modern hospital, garage and hotel. Near to the bridge is the high school, which has a swimming pool and an open-air jacuzzi in the grounds. All smell distinctly sulphuric due to the natural hot spring water.

In the middle of the river, to the east of Blönduós, is the island of **Hrútey**, a nature reserve. It can be visited via small footbridge from the north bank. There is a circular path through the tundra scrubland and it is a good place for birdwatching. The river torrent slows as it passes into the tidal stretches of Blönduós, where rare ducks and divers congregate. From Blönduós, the Ring Road runs directly to Akureyri, passing eventually through the **Öxnadalur** valley, considered the finest scenery on the highway from Reykjavík. Alternatively, Akureyri can be reached following the rougher roads along the wild northern coast.

Remote wilderness

The **Skagi** peninsula lies to the northeast of Blönduós. The dirt highway that hugs its western edge passes through a narrow band of agricultural land overshadowed by the mountains behind. **Skagaströnd ❻**, with a population of less than 1,000, is the only settlement of any size. Established as an important trading port in the 16th century, today it is a quiet fishing centre built on a rocky outcrop joined to the peninsula by good alluvial soil. Brightly coloured wooden houses edge a sweeping bay with the snow-splashed mountain peaks of **Spákonufell** as the towering backdrop.

North of Skagaströnd sand dunes and shingle bays give way to cliffs. The ever-deteriorating road climbs upwards and across the top of the **Króksbjarg** and **Bakkar** cliffs – home to a large number of sea birds. Rows of sandstone outcrops contrast with the black basalt lava, usually hexagonal in section. Thousands

Map on page 250

TIP

One of the best views of Blönduós is from the nearby Hnjúkar hill, topped by a radio antenna. There is a steep track up to the 205-metre (672-ft) summit, which gives an uninterrupted view beyond Húnaflói to the sheer cliffs on the northwest peninsula.

BELOW: shaggy sheep rest in the rain.

of kittiwakes vie for nesting space on ledges whilst fulmars nest on the tops of the columns. Near to where the River Fossá cascades over the cliff there is a small grassy headland almost completely undermined by the sea – an excellent place from which to observe the sea birds. Beyond Bakkar is a temporary respite in the high cliffs. **Vogurviti** is an unusual outcrop of basalt rock, formed in a series of extensive hexagonal lava steps. An unmanned lighthouse looks over the small lakes, sand spits and rocky shores, the habitat for countless birds.

Moss gathers on the glacial moraine characteristic of this area.

Birds and bandits

Within the Skagafjörður fjord lie several small islands rich in birdlife. The most famous of these is **Drangey**, once a hideout for outlaws, including the saga figure of Grettir the Strong. The islands can be reached from **Sauðárkrókur ❼**, the region's administrative centre at the head of the fjord. First settled by Scotsmen from the Hebrides, today Sauðárkrókur has a population of over 2,500, making it second only to Akureyri in size on Iceland's north coast. As a result, it has many amenities including swimming pool, cinema and even a gliding club. Thermal springs supply hot water to the town's inhabitants and a number of natural baths can be visited just to the north, at **Reykir ❽**. Another mountain track (Route 744) with superb views of the area runs over **Þverárfjall** into moorlands of cottongrass. South of Sauðárkrókur, at **Glaumbær ❾**, is a finely maintained turf house **museum** (open summer: daily 9am–6pm). The several wood-fronted buildings have thick turf walls and roofs while the dark interiors are carefully laid out with furniture. Below the old turf farmhouse there is a coffee-shop, where you can get Icelandic pancakes. This is in **Áshús**, a house in the building style that supplanted the turf house in the 19th century.

BELOW: basalt rocks near Vogurviti.

The eastern flank of the fjord is lined with steep mountains barring all roads through to the interior beyond. This region can be penetrated only by back-packers: at an altitude of 1,300 metres (4,265 ft) are the remnants of an ancient icccap, consisting today of three main glaciers. Accessible by car is the ancient bishopric of **Hólar** ⑩, founded in 1106 and for over 600 years the religious centre of the North. The high-towered "cathedral", from 1763, is charming. The altarpiece, believed to be Dutch, from the early 16th century, was donated by Jón Arason, the last Catholic bishop of the area who was put to death in the Reformation. A difficult hike, from Hólar to the Urðir valley and Dalvík, crosses the snow fields of Heljardalsheiði through some of north Iceland's finest scenery.

Further north is the little fishing village **Hofsós** ⑪, with the **Icelandic Emigration Centre** (open summer: daily 11am–6pm). The Centre, on the sea-front by the harbour, houses an exhibition tracing the history of Icelanders who emigrated to America; there is also an information service, an interesting library and a souvenir shop. Another small exhibition, "Hunters and Fishers", is located in one of the oldest warehouses in Iceland, built in 1777 in the style of a log cabin.

Visitors driving north around Skagafjörður towards Siglufjörður, will find their eyes drawn to the island of **Málmey** offshore. This concave-shaped outcrop of lava is 4 km (2½ miles) long and rises at either end into sea-bird cliffs. **Siglufjörður** ⑫ is at the end of its own road, set in an exquisite fjord. Amidst a range of glaciated mountains, the town's current population of 2,000 is its lowest in recent history. A generation ago this was the centre of the herring industry. There has since been a steady decline in fishing off the north coast. An increase in tourism has helped the economy, particularly the growing popularity of winter skiing, but Siglufjörður remains a shadow of its former self. ❏

Map on page 250

The English poet W.H. Auden visited Sauðárkrókur during his travels in 1937. He was unimpressed, noting that the town "might have been built by Seventh Day Adventists who expected to go to heaven in a few months, so why bother anyway?"

BELOW: the bishopric of Hólar, once north Iceland's religious centre.

AKUREYRI AND SURROUNDINGS

Maps on pages 250/258

Akureyri is among the most pleasant of Iceland's urban centres and forms an ideal base for trips to the nearby fjords and some of the country's most photographed attractions

By Icelandic standards, Akureyri is a thriving metropolis: with a population of only 15,000, it is the country's largest town outside of the Greater Reykjavík area. Sitting squarely on the Ring Road, a hub for bus and air transport, it has grown in recent years into the undisputed centre of the North.

Despite being only 100 km (60 miles) from the Arctic Circle, it enjoys some of the warmest weather in the country. In summer, it is not unusual to see day after day of 20°C (68°F) temperatures and clear skies, bringing flowers into the streets and turning Akureyri into Iceland's version of the tropics.

Even the setting is spectacular: at the base of Eyjafjörður fjord, Akureyri has a backdrop of sheer granite mountains tipped with snow all year (in winter, an even layer of snow usually makes this Iceland's premier skiing spot). And, while Akureyri's modern architecture leaves a lot to be desired, there are enough older wooden buildings around town to give it some provincial charm.

PRECEDING PAGES: the church at Laufás looks out over Eyjafjörður fjord. **LEFT:** the steep climb to Akureyrikirkja. **BELOW:** fishing at Dalvík.

Gateway to the North

The first settler to claim the Eyjafjörður region was the Norwegian Helgi the Lean (named after a stint on the Orkneys as a child, when he was poorly fed by foster parents). Helgi had indiscriminate religious habits: in traditional pagan fashion, he tossed the high-seat pillars from his long-ship into the sea, allowing the god Thor to choose the site of his new home. But when they washed up 7 km (4 miles) south of modern-day Akureyri, Helgi named his farm Kristnes (Christ's Peninsula), just in case.

The Viking farmers who ended up around Eyja-fjörður were relatively peaceful, to judge from their low profiles in the sagas. A notable exception was Víga-Glúmur. A morose and gangly youth regarded as a buffoon by his peers, Víga-Glúmur surprised everyone on a journey to Norway by slaughtering a berserk warrior in combat. He became a worshipper of Odin and returned to Iceland to make the lives of his former tormentors a misery, becoming chieftain of the Eyjafjörður region by trickery and intimidation. However, he offended the goddess Freyja by butchering one of his in-laws in the goddess's sacred cornfield. After 40 years, Freyja had her revenge – in old age, Víga-Glúmur lost Odin's protection and had to abandon his estates. He died blind and alone.

The profit motive

The town of **Akureyri** ⑱ did not come into existence until the 16th century, when a trading post was set up as a meeting place for local farmers. In the 1770s, the

first permanent house was built, and in 1862, with a grand total of 286 inhabitants, Akureyri was made a municipality. An excellent harbour soon made this the centre of the new co-operative movement among Icelandic farmers.

By the early 20th century, grandiose wooden mansions had filled the southern part of Akureyri. The spit at the northern part of town, **Oddeyri**, became the port and warehouse area, and it remains so to this day (the name Akureyri is a blend of *Akur*, meaning field, and *eyri*, spit, after the land that projects into the fjord). Akureyri has a university and a modest local flourishing of the arts, with several theatre groups, plus a number of nightspots and cinemas.

The residents of Akureyri have a mixed reputation in the rest of Iceland. The town is seen as the bastion of middle-class values and, despite the good weather the town enjoys, its people are considered closed, traditional and even somewhat dour. Icelanders joke that you can't get to know the people of Akureyri unless you are born and raised there – being conceived in the town while your parents were on holiday doesn't count. Even being raised there may not be good enough: tales are told of Akureyri neighbours who accidentally meet in Reykjavík and have long, friendly conversations, only to act like virtual strangers once they return home. Whatever the truth of this, Icelanders have no qualms about flocking to Akureyri, especially at weekends: flights from Reykjavík are packed with holidaymakers, while people from every corner of the North drive in to their figurative "big smoke" for a taste of the action.

Exploring the town

Akureyri is compact enough to explore on foot, and the most logical place to start is the partly pedestrianised shopping mall of **Hafnarstræti**. This is the

Today Akureyri has one of the most active fishing fleets in Iceland and is home to the country's largest canning factory. It also accounts for some 30 percent of Iceland's manufacturing output.

BELOW: summer dining at the Bautinn restaurant.

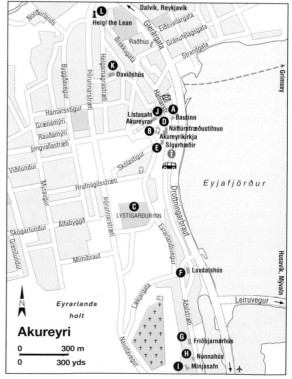

Akureyri

0 ___ 300 m
0 ___ 300 yds

Map on page 258

commercial centre of the town, if not its most attractive point: the buildings are the classic, characterless slabs typical of modern Icelandic towns, and, to top it off, loud piped music echoes through it in summer. The saving grace is an Akureyri institution, the **Bautinn restaurant** across the road from Hafnarstræti at Kaupvangsstræti. One of the most reasonably priced eating spots in Iceland, it has justly been elevated to one of Akureyri's tourist attractions – ask to eat in the glassed-in pergola, which catches the sun (when it is shining).

The fjord **waterfront** is only a short hop from the mall, usually with a few picturesque trawlers sitting in port. From here, there is a good view of the basalt **Akureyrikirkja** Ⓑ that has dominated the town since its construction in 1940. Designed by the architect Gudjón Samúelsson, the church can look distressingly unattractive in most lights. Even so, it is Akureyri's pride and joy, and worth the five-minute walk uphill for a visit. Inside, the stained-glass windows show scenes from Icelandic history and the life of Christ in a style that can only be described as cartoon-book. There is an organ with 3,200 pipes, while the centre window in the chancel was donated by England's Coventry Cathedral – it was one of the only parts that survived the bombing during World War II. Most curious is the model ship hanging from the ceiling, a tradition in Iceland, Greenland and the Faroe Islands to protect the parish's fishermen at sea.

A short climb up **Eyrarlandsvegur** leads to the **Botanical Garden** (Lystigarðurinn) Ⓒ, famed for its 2,000 species of local and foreign flowers blooming outside in Akureyri's warm microclimate. The park was set up by a local women's association in 1912, then taken over by the town in the 1950s – two of the voluntary managers are commemorated by statues. With benches and well-kept lawns, the gardens are a perfect place to relax on a sunny afternoon.

TIP

It can be extremely difficult to find a hotel room in Akureyri on summer weekends. Make a booking at least a week in advance, or try to visit on weekdays.

BELOW: view of Akureyri from the eastern side of Eyjafjörður.

TIP

On the way back into down on Eyrarlandsvegur, keep an eye out for Einar Jónsson's sculpture *The Outlaw*, depicting Fjalla-Eyvindur ("Mountain-Eyvind") and his wife Halla, who spent 20 years as outlaws, mainly in the interior of the country.

Historical tour

Starting back down in the pedestrian mall, a stroll south along Hafnarstræti follows the waterline through the oldest part of Akureyri. The town has a plethora of small museums located in this area.

First comes the **Natural History Museum** (Náttúrufræðustifnun; open summer: daily 10am–5pm; winter: Sun 1–4pm) where the main attraction is a stuffed bird put together from various odd bird species to resemble the extinct great auk. A few doors along is the **Mattías Jochumsson Memorial Museum** (Sigurhæðir; open summer: daily 2–4pm), the restored home of one of Iceland's most revered poets and dramatists. Jochumsson penned the lyrics for Iceland's national anthem, *Iceland's 1,000 Years*, in 1874.

Continuing on past the combined **Tourist Information Office** and **Bus Terminal**, Hafnarstræti runs into Akureyri's old business district. The area still has many fine mansions in the so-called Icelandic frame-house tradition – to the uninitiated, they look like Swiss chalets. The last was built in 1911, when other styles came into vogue, including the use of metal sidings pressed into a brick pattern and painted over to look like stone and mortar. Near the intersection with Lækjargata is Akureyri's oldest house, **Laxdalshús**. Built in 1795, this tiny restored wooden building (open summer: daily 11am–5pm) was occupied until 1978, mostly as home to some 30 people from three or four families.

South along the waterfront following Aðalstræti is **Friðbjarnarhús** (open summer: Sat and Sun 2–5pm), the museum of the International Organisation of Good Templars (a chapter opened in Akureyri in 1884), then the more appealing **Nonnahús** (open summer: daily 10am–5pm). This is the restored home of Reverend Jón Sveinsson, nicknamed Nonni, author of the Nonni series of

BELOW:
the pedestrian mall of Hafnarstræti.

children's books that are still well loved in Iceland and continental Europe. The house, where Nonni spent some years of his childhood, was built in 1850 and has been maintained in its original form – even the kitchen still has its old implements – making this the most interesting of Akureyri's old homes. Finally, the **Akureyri Folk Museum** (Minjasafn) **①** (open summer: daily 11am–5pm; plus in July and Aug: Tues, Thur 8–11pm) has an exhaustive collection of local memorabilia, from old farming tools to milk cartons, as well as some excellent 19th-century photographs. Outside, a small church, which was moved from Svalbard across the fjord, sits beside Iceland's first nursery.

Maps on pages 250/258

Anyone still not sated by museums can head back into town and find the **Akureyri Art Museum** (Listasafn Akureyrar) **①** (open Tues–Sun 2–6pm) and **Davíðshús** **⓴** (open 15 Jun–1 Sep: daily 3–5pm) on Bjarkarstígur, the 1944 home of poet Davíð Stefánsson left as it was when he died. A short walk away, on a rock between Glerárgata and Þórunnarstraeti, is a statue of **Helgi the Lean** **①** (*see page 257*), with an impressive view over Eyjafjörður.

Short excursions

Pleasant as strolling around Akureyri can be, the real attraction is the surrounding area. A few short trips are very close to town. Only an hour on foot or 10 minutes' drive south is **Kjarnaskógar forest**, one of Iceland's few spots with trees, and a popular picnic place. Hikers can head for the symmetrical, Fuji-like **Mount Súlur** **⓮**, visible on clear days from Akureyri. Drive west on Súluvegur (past the rubbish dump) to the small creek – look out for a wooden ladder over the barbed wire, then follow the yellow markers. You should allow several hours of hard (and not very inspiring) walking to reach the 1,213-metre

BELOW: a new paint job.

(3,980-ft) summit looking out over the **Glerá** valley. In winter, skiing fans head for the Skidastadir Lodge at **Hlíðarfjall**, offering the best slopes in the area only a 10-minute drive from town. Many non-skiers also head there for the view of the **Vindheimajökull** glacier.

Exploring the fjord

Skiers enjoying the snow around Akureyri.

Perhaps the most popular day trip from Akureyri – and one that can be driven alone or organised through the tourist office – is along the western flank of Eyjafjörður fjord. The well-paved Route 82 offers sweeping views over the rich farming land of the area, with glacier-formed mountains to the west (their peaks are often buried behind a steady line of grey cloud) and steely blue waters to the east. The district here is known as **Árskógsströnd**. As in the rest of the North, the fields are dotted in summer with hundreds of gigantic white plastic rolls containing hay for the winter – a high-tech innovation that has quickly replaced the more poetic but inefficient methods of traditional hay-gathering. Cows, sheep and geese wander at will, and it is not unusual for traffic to be stopped while a five-year-old boy leads a line of cattle over the road to pasture.

Although Route 82 can be followed directly north, a turn-off at Route 816 leads to a ruined port area, called **Gásir**, for many centuries the biggest port in northern Iceland. Many overgrown ruins of the old port can still be seen in the grass. Another short side road (Route 813) leads to the farm **Möðruvellir**, birthplace of the writer Jón Sveinsson. There is a much-photographed farmhouse at **Stærri-Árskógur**, flush against a steep mountain backdrop.

Dalvík ⑮ (population 1,500) is the dominant town on this side of the fjord. A prosperous fishing village today, Dalvík's claim to fame in Iceland is the

BELOW:
boarding the ferry at Hrísey island.

1934 earthquake measuring 6.3 on the Richter scale that brought rocks crashing down from the nearby mountainside and destroyed about half the town's homes. These days, travellers call in at Dalvík mainly to catch the ferry over to **Hrísey island** ⑯ – the second largest island off Iceland's coast, giving Eyjafjörður ("island fjord") its name. On a fine day, the 20-minute trip to Hrísey is well worthwhile – on weekends, there are usually some well-dressed folk from Akureyri making the excursion solely to dine on the island's speciality, Galloway beef, served up at the **Brekka restaurant**.

There is a small village here with a church for the 300 or so inhabitants, which during World War II was the billet for five British servicemen whose job was to check up on all trawlers entering the fjord, with only a broken machine gun to back them up. Much of Hrísey is a nature reserve and so off-limits to hikers, but there are still plenty of trails across the flat moorlands, covered in purple heather and full of birdlife.

Back on the mainland, a popular side trip from Dalvík is into **Svarfadardalur** valley, entering on Route 805 and returning along Route 807. From the end of Route 805, hikers and horseriders can head into the wilderness of **Heljardalsheiði** for camping trips in some of the finest mountain country in Iceland.

North of Dalvík, a nerve-wracking and treacherous gravel road winding along the steep coastline was made more bearable by the opening in 1991 of a 3½-km (2-mile) tunnel. A spectacular feat of engineering, this one-lane passage through the mountainside has become something of a tourist attraction in itself, although claustrophobes might prefer to risk the old road around the headland of **Olafsfjarðarmúli** – which, incidentally, is a good place to see the midnight sun in July, with views on a clear day to Grímsey island, on the Arctic Circle.

Map on page 250

Hrísey island is the only place in Iceland where Galloway cattle are raised, and it is prohibited by law to remove them to the mainland.

BELOW: the mountains of Eyjafjörður looming on Hrísey's horizon.

Ólafsfjörður is a fishing village of 1,200 people nestled amongst a ring of snow-capped, 1,200-metre (3,900-ft) high peaks. Despite the setting, it has little more of interest than fishing boats and factories.

Points south

Heading south from Akureyri, Route 821 runs along the Eyjafjarðará river valley. The pretty farm **Kristnes**, built on the site where Helgi the Lean first settled, is 7 km (4 miles) along on a hill with a strategic view of the fjord. A few minutes further south is another farm, **Grund** , with one of the most unusual churches in Iceland – with its several Romanesque spires, it looks transplanted from St Petersburg. The farmer Magnús Sigurðsson built it to his own design in 1906 to serve the whole river valley. The church broke a nearly millennium-old tradition by being built on a north-south axis instead of east-west.

A good example of a more traditional church, made of turf and stone, is at the farm of **Saurbær** , which is situated 27 km (17 miles) south of Akureyri on Route 821. The quaint interior is open to visitors. At this point, the road continues to the farm of **Torfufell** (offering farmhouse accommodation), or across the river valley to return to Akureyri on Route 829. En route is the historic farm of **Munkaþverá**. Originally known as Þverá, this was the birthplace in the 10th century of the notorious Odin-worshipping Viking Víga-Glúmur, and all around this part of the valley is the backdrop for *Víga-Glúms Saga*. In the 12th century, a Benedictine monastery was built on the site, although none of it remains. Finally, at **Ytri-Hóll**, look out for a classic turf house that is still in use: the tiny chimney poking out from the grassy roof only makes it look even more like a hobbit's house.

TIP

Horse-riding expeditions into the remote area of the Fjörður peninsula are offered by Grenivík town council, and Polar Horses at Grytubakki II farm 4 km (2½ miles) outside Grenivík.

BELOW: the church at Grund.

Eyjafjördur's eastern shore

The Ring Road runs east of Akureyri – giving some of the best views of the town – before running north and heading into the **Grýtubakkahreppur** district. Turn off at Route 83 for **Laufás** ⑳, a beautifully situated farm looking out over Eyjafjörður with a small white church and 19th-century turf farmhouse **museum** (open summer: Tues–Sun 10am–6pm). Built in the 1860s, the dirt-floored building was a vicarage and upper-crust home, and is now crowded with antiques. A famous touch is the carved woman's face and duck placed over the middle segment of the farmhouse. Just 22 km (14 miles) from the Ring Road turn-off is the picturesque but somnolent fishing town of **Grenivík** ㉑ (population 300). Only founded in 1910, Grenivík is at the edge of the rugged Fjörður peninsula, which has been uninhabited since World War II.

The Ring Road continues east towards Lake Mývatn, but first passes the small lake **Ljósavatn** ("lightwater") and a turn-off to the farm of the same name. This was the Saga Age farm of the chieftain Þorgeir Þorkelsson, Law-Speaker in the Alþingi in AD 1000, who was forced to decide whether Iceland should be pagan or Christian. As the *Kristni Saga* tells it, Þorgeir spent 24 hours under his cloak before deciding for the Christians. Riding back from Þingvellir to his home at Ljósavatn, he passed a giant waterfall and decided to toss all his carved images of pagan gods into its waters. This powerful waterfall, **Goðafoss** ㉒ ("fall of the gods"), is virtually beneath the Ring Road a few kilometres further on, and is the easiest of Iceland's major falls to visit. Most cars and buses en route to Mývatn stop here at the small petrol station/store at **Fosshóll**.

The surrounding area of the **Bárðardalur** valley is a 7,000-year-old lava flow, through which the Skjálfandafljót river has cut a path to form Goðafoss. ❑

Map on page 250

BELOW: interior of Laufás church.

Icelandic Hauntings

One in every 500 inhabitants of Iceland is a ghost. According to *Vættatal*, the spiritual *Who's Who* of Iceland by folklore historian Árni Björnsson, more than 500 ghouls, trolls, and paranormal beings haunt the island, making a substantial – or perhaps insubstantial – addition to its quarter of a million human population. This high ghost quotient is not entirely unexpected, as Iceland is the perfect home for any spook, with long periods of darkness in winter and an abundance of grotesque rock and lava formations providing perfect camouflage for monsters and ogres.

Flesh-and-blood Icelanders, it seems, enjoy excellent relations with their neighbours from the other world. In a survey on the supernatural in Western Europe, Icelanders topped the league for ghostly experiences, with 41 percent claiming contact with the dead, compared to the European average of 20 percent.

Traditionally, however, ghosts were not

harmless visitations from the dear departed. They usually took the form of an *afturganga*, a dead man turned zombie, and were capable of killing people or (worse) taking them to hell. Only the spiritual powers of a priest or the physical prowess of a strongman could exorcise such a nightmarish spook.

A very uncomfortable characteristic of the *afturganga* is his tendency to walk again before anyone knows he has died. One such was the Deacon of Dark River, who drowned on his way to pick up his girlfriend to take her to a dance. Nonetheless, he turned up, a little late, and the unsuspecting girl got on the back of his horse. As they rode through the night, she overheard him muttering:

The moon hides, as death rides,
Do you not see the white mark
On my brow, Garun, Garun.

Fortunately, this ditty held two clues to his true nature: firstly, ghosts always repeat things, and secondly they cannot say "God." The girl's name was Guðrún, and Guð is "God" in Icelandic. The terrified Guðrún managed to jump off – seconds before the ghostly rider and horse disappeared into an open grave leading straight to hell. She was never the same again, and some say she lost her mind completely.

Other forms of ghost are the *fylgja* or familiar spirit, and its close relations the *móri* or the *skotta*. These are shadowy, malevolent spirits, and when they are ill-wished onto a man, they will follow him and his descendants unto the ninth generation.

Then there are the trolls – elemental beings who, fortunately, turn into stone if they are caught outside in daylight. All of Iceland is dotted with trolls who stayed out just that little bit too long – including the great stone troll-cow, Hvítserkur, caught having a drink of sea-water just off the northwest coast.

All things considered, Icelanders probably prefer their more attractive other-worldly neighbours, the elves. Like Hollywood film-stars, they look like humans – but are richer, more glamorous and usually completely amoral. According to one legend, the elves were the children that Eve hadn't finished washing when God came to visit – they were not fit to be seen, so she had to hide them. Thus, they are also known as the Hidden People, and with good reason – only 5 percent of

Icelanders have actually met one. Nevertheless, elves are held in the highest regard, with 53 percent of the population either believing in, or not denying, their existence.

In legend, those who visit the elves and survive the experience return to the human world laden with riches but often strangely changed. In nearly all cases, the elves decide when and where they will be seen by humans. Usually it is when they need their assistance. Human women, it is said, are sometimes fetched by distraught elfen husbands to act as mid-wives to elf-mothers who are having difficulties in childbirth.

One 20th-century figure to have had an encounter with the Hidden People was trade-union leader Tryggvi Emilsson, who, as a young man, was saved from death by an elf-maiden after he had fallen down a gully. Her beauty, he said, haunted him the rest of his life. Elf-women have been known to have even more intimate physical relations with human men, and are obviously more liberated than their human counterparts, often leaving their lovers holding the baby, as it were.

It is of some consolation that these semi-supernatural offspring are usually highly talented and handsome. Elf-men, on the other hand, make conscientious and kind lovers, according to the tales told by the few women who have been lucky enough to have tried one out.

The elves of Iceland are treated with great respect. The rocks and hills in which they make their homes are diligently preserved, for great harm traditionally comes to those that tamper with these elusive neighbours. Roads skirt round well-known elf-hills. One such is the road that runs from Reykjavík to the suburb of Kópavogur, which is actually called Álfhólsvegur, or Elf-Hill Road. On the main street of the town of Grundarfjördur, a rock stands between the houses numbered 82 and 86 – the elves live at number 84.

Despite these superstitious gestures, Dr Árni Björnsson says that true believers in elves and ghosts comprise only a very small minority in Iceland. "Most of us do not actively believe in these things, but on the other hand we are reluctant to deny their exis-tence," he says. "It is really a form of scepticism. We live in a land which is highly unpredictable – what is grass and meadow today could be lava and ash tomorrow. So we have learnt not to rely too much on the factual evidence of our senses."

And of course the existence of elves is such a nice idea. "People think it would be fun if they did exist, so they pretend to believe in them. Unlike other nations, we aren't in the least ashamed of it. In fact, we are rather proud of our elves." He adds: "Iceland is a big country for such a small population. We've plenty of room for neighbours of all kinds."

Indeed, this laissez-faire attitude is ensconced in folk tradition and the sagas. The medieval bishop, Guðmundur the Good, once set off to consecrate Drangey, to drive away the multitude of ghouls, fiends and devils that haunted this island. As he went about his holy work, a voice rang out from the rocks. "Consecrate no more, Guðmundur," it cried. "The wicked need some place to be." The bishop sensibly took the point and quickly returned to shore.   ❏

LEFT: an elf-maiden rising from her grotto.
RIGHT: two rowdy trolls.

GRÍMSEY

*Situated on the Arctic Circle, the island of Grímsey is a
remote outpost, home to huge colonies of sea birds
and just under 100 islanders*

Map
on page
250

The folk on the remote, weather-beaten island of **Grímsey** ㉓ tell the tale of
a local minister who discovered that the Arctic Circle ran right through
his house. He decided that it not only bisected his bedroom, it bisected his
bed: the minister slept on one side of the Arctic Circle, his wife on the other, and
rarely did either cross the great divide.

The apocryphal story is told and retold in various forms (sometimes it's a
minister, sometimes an old magistrate), but it sums up the tongue-in-cheek attitude the Grímsey islanders have to the Arctic Circle – an imaginary line which,
to the outside world, puts Grímsey on the map. They can only regard with some
bemusement anyone who makes the pilgrimage all the way to their remote
polar outpost just to say that they've walked across a geographical abstraction.
"How did it feel?" someone might ask with good-natured concern. "Have your
feet turned blue yet?"

But, although its location on latitude 66°30' N may still be Grímsey's claim
to fame, a steady stream of travellers are finding out that the island has more
concrete attractions to offer. The sheer isolation of this tiny piece of land, with
a population of only just over 100, has its own peculiarly Icelandic appeal: the
scenery is wild and beautiful, the birdlife extraordinary, while the people remain
beguilingly eccentric. And Grímsey has one of the
strangest histories in Iceland, settled by chess-playing
Vikings and supported by a 19th-century American
millionaire. (And, frankly, it is quite fun to know that
you're standing on the Arctic Circle.)

PRECEDING PAGES:
fish-drying the
traditional way.
LEFT: the Grímsey
road sign.
BELOW: a portrait of
Willard Fiske,
Grímsey's
benefactor, in the
island's library.

Island of chess-players

Grímsey was first settled in the 10th century by a
Viking named Grímur (hence the name Grím's
island), whose descendants took the Icelandic obses-
sion with chess to new extremes. Tradition has it that
long summers and longer winters were spent devoted
to the game, with some players spending weeks confined to their beds devising new stratagems. Chess
was more important than life itself: it was not
unknown for a player to fling himself into the sea
rather than bear the shame of defeat.

Perhaps not surprisingly, Grímsey did not prosper
as a fishing port. On one occasion in the 18th century, the entire male population except for the minister was lost in a single fishing accident (perhaps they
were exhausted from playing chess). According to
folklore, the minister took responsibility for repopu-
lating the island himself.

Then, in the late 19th century, the island's eccentric
reputation was brought to the attention of a wealthy
North American named Daniel Willard Fiske – prominent journalist, Old Icelandic scholar, friend of both

EYJARBÓKASAFNID II.

Taking a boat trip off the shores of Grímsey.

the Icelandic independence hero Jón Sigurðsson and the writer Mark Twain, and, in 1857, chess champion of the US. Although Willard Fiske only glimpsed the shores of Grímsey as he passed it in a steamship, the island fired his vivid imagination and he decided to take its local population under his wing.

First Fiske sent the essentials: a gift of 11 marble chess sets to each of the farms on the island. These were followed by masses of firewood and a bequest to finance the island's first school and library. Finally, on his death in 1904, Fiske left the inhabitants of Grímsey $12,000 – at that time the most money any-one had ever given to Iceland. Today, Fiske is still revered on Grímsey as a sort of secular saint. His birthday on 11 November is celebrated with a meeting and coffee in the community hall. Fiske's portrait still hangs in the library, while a large number of male islanders sport the decidedly un-Icelandic name of Willard. Unfortunately, Grímsey hasn't kept up the love of chess. Hardly anybody plays it – these days, the favourite game is bridge.

Last stop before the Pole

Until the 1930s, the only way to reach Grímsey was on the mail ship that left Akureyri once every six months (you could return six months later, provided bad weather didn't prevent the ship from running).

Today, there is a twice-weekly ship service in summer, taking about six hours each way from Akureyri, while daily light aircraft flights take only 25 minutes to cover the 41 km (25 miles). Both allow travellers to return from the island on the same day – which, until 1991 when a new guest house opened, was just as well, since the only accommodation was on the floor of the community centre. (Camping is permitted if you site your tent discreetly.)

BELOW: the last of Willard Fiske's donated chess sets.

A NATION OF CHESS PLAYERS

Probably brought over by the first settlers in the 9th century, chess was a common pastime in Iceland through the Middle Ages, as shown by numerous old expressions from the game which have been preserved in everyday speech. When Willard Fiske visited towards the end of the 19th century, he found eager players all over the country. Fiske published Iceland's first chess magazine, providing a theoretical training ground that soon guided the game into the realms of organised sport. In 1959, Friðrik Ólafsson was the nation's first grandmaster, and fought through to finish seventh out of eight in the Candidates' series, the final play-off before the world championship match. The next generation of masters was inspired by the "Match of the Century" which took place in Reykjavík in 1972, when Bobby Fischer wrested the world championship from Boris Spassky. Among the crowds who "caught the bug" then were Helgi Ólafsson and Margeir Pétursson, then in their teens and now both international grandmasters. In their wake came two other grandmasters: Jón L. Arnason and Jóhann Hjartarson. This "fearsome foursome", the backbone of the national team, have been joined by five more grandmasters, making a total of nine.

Getting acquainted with the island is not difficult. There are 10 old farms on the island, but most of the inhabitants live in the "village" of **Sandvík** – the name for the 15 houses lined up along the harbour.

After World War II, Grímsey still didn't have electricity, there was little fresh water and the occasional case of scurvy was reported among the islanders. Modern fishing techniques have brought Iceland's new affluence here – the township may have a rather scruffy look, but the houses are modern, there are satellite dishes to pick up television, greenhouses to grow vegetables and a large indoor swimming pool. Although there is only one road on Grímsey – 3 km (2 miles) long – the island boasts 10 private cars and a dozen tractors.

The Grímsey **community centre** can be identified by the mural on its walls. Built on the site of the old school financed by Fiske, it still contains the library, original photographs of the benefactor and the only one of the 11 marble chess sets still in existence. Nobody seems to know where the rest have gone.

A short walk west of the village is the whitewashed, late-19th-century wooden **church**. Above the altar is a replica of Leonardo da Vinci's *Last Supper*, painted by a mainland artist, Arngrímur Gíslason. The nearby **parsonage**, which was built in 1909, is now run by a layman – Grímsey pays for a minister to come every three months from Akureyri (if he wants to come more often, he has to pay for the journey himself). The islanders also raise the money for rock bands to fly out from the mainland to play live from time to time.

Along the coast are the traditional fish-drying racks. There are four fish processing plants on the island, concentrating on salted fish and dried cod-heads (which are sold to Nigeria). Sheep used to wander the island until 1988, when an outbreak of the stock disease scrapie forced them all to be put down.

Map on page 250

TIP

The island is only 4 km (2½ miles) by 2 km (1¼ miles) in size, and can be circumambulated in about 5 hours.

BELOW: Sandvík, the main settlement on Grímsey.

Map on page 250

In 1973, an unexpected addition to the island's wildlife collection appeared in the form of a polar bear that had floated over from Greenland on an iceberg. It was promptly hunted down and shot and is now stuffed in Húsavík Museum on the mainland.

RIGHT: the glow of the midnight sun.
BELOW: arctic terns wheeling overhead.

Dive-bombers of the Arctic Circle

Heading back to the eastern end of the island, the road runs straight into the bitumen runway of the airport (where the Basar guesthouse, offering the island's only formal accommodation, is also to be found). The runway is carpeted by resting sea birds – before some landings or take-offs, a car is driven up and down in an attempt to shoo away these potential hazards to aircraft.

Usually that's the end of the matter. Should you be visiting in June or July, however, the scene is more like something from Alfred Hitchcock's *The Birds*. That's when the arctic terns are nesting all over the island, and anyone coming near a bird's young is fair game for a divebomb attack. The screeching call *kría! kría! kría!* (which is actually the bird's name in Icelandic) is the prelude to a possible peck on the back of the head – which is why, in this season, everyone wears a thick hat (a leather glove under a beany or beret is recommended) and carries a big stick (the Basar guesthouse will lend out plastic rods to guests for self-defence).

On the northern side of the runway is the Grímsey road sign, theoretically marking the location of the Arctic Circle. Arrows point to various world highlights (including New York: 4,445 km/2,763 miles; Sydney: 16,137 km/10,027 miles; London: 1,949 km/1,225 miles), although for some reason the North Pole doesn't get a mention.

A path leads away from the airport towards 100-metre (320-ft) cliff faces, which can be followed completely around the island. Soon the trail disappears beneath a bed of thick, matted grass, which seems to glow green against the blue of the sea. The polka-dot of yellow weeds finishes off the colourful effect (there are some 100 species of flowering plant on Grímsey).

The cliffs on the north and east sides of the island are also where the most spectacular birdlife can be found, creating a din that is little short of cacophonous. Thirty-six species of bird nest on the island, including 11 different types of sea bird. There is a large puffin community, and it is quite possible to come within a few metres of these birds (but don't walk too close to the edge of the cliffs, since underground puffin nests can be accidentally crushed). There are fulmars, kittiwakes, gulls and arctic terns, and Grímsey is the last place in Iceland where the little auk breeds (only two or three pairs are left, the rest all staying closer to the Pole).

Although it is placed on the Arctic Circle, Grímsey's summers and winters are never as extreme as one would imagine: the June midnight is bright but never blinding, and there are about four hours of vague light in December (provided the weather isn't very cloudy, that is, in which case it stays dark).

Even so, life on the island is still tough, and it says something for the islanders' spirit that they have kept their numbers at around 100 while other tiny Icelandic islands have lost their wealth and population. Schoolchildren, who spend their last three years studying on the mainland, almost always return to Grímsey. Even though not many play chess here now, the island still shows the eccentric, indomitable spirit that inspired the old benefactor Daniel Willard Fiske. ❑

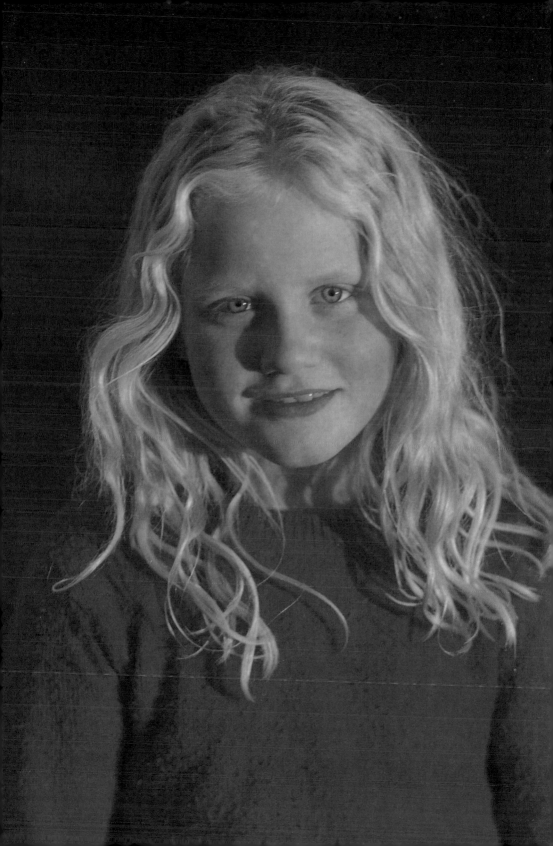

LAKE MÝVATN

*This outstandingly beautiful area has the twin attractions of the
serene lake at Mývatn, one of Iceland's major breeding grounds
for birds, and spectacular volcanic activity*

Map on page 280

itting just to the west of the Mid-Atlantic Ridge that is slowly tearing Iceland apart, the Lake Mývatn district is one of the most volcanically active
regions on earth. In the mid-1970s, earthquakes centred here were felt in the
entire north of the country, with lava erupting from nearby Mount Krafla over
several years to spectacular effect. Activity continued through the early 1980s
and today there are almost daily subterranean rumblings (although they are
mostly too small to be noticed except by scientific instruments). Nowhere else
in Iceland can you see the same combination of craters, fresh lava fields, hot
springs, geysers and bubbling mud pools.

Reykjavík

Meanwhile, the lake's natural beauty and role as a wildlife breeding ground
led to it being set aside as a national conservation area in 1974 – a status that
actually gives it more protection than a National Park. The lake is a veritable
oasis on the fringes of Iceland's bleak northern deserts, supporting, among other
things, the world's largest population of breeding ducks. As a result, Mývatn has
established itself as Iceland's number one tourist attraction outside of the
"Golden Circle" and a place that has been known to keep nature lovers occupied
for weeks. While offering plenty to explore in its own right, it also makes a
good base for trips to the Northeast and to Askja in the interior.

PRECEDING PAGES:
Route 87 from
Húsavík to Mývatn.
LEFT: Mývatn at
dusk.
BELOW: a bubbling
mud pool near
Námafjall.

In search of sulphur

Although the winters are long and cold, covering the
lake with ice for seven months of the year, Mývatn
enjoys more sunshine and receives less rain than
almost anywhere else in the country. As a result, it
has been popular with settlers from the Saga Age
onwards: in 1908, archaeologists dug up a Norse longhouse whose wall was over 40 metres (130 ft) in
length, and may have contained a temple of Thor.

Dating their ancestry back to those days are the
Reykjahlíð family, whose farm covers the whole surrounding area – at some 6,000 sq. km (2,300 sq.
miles) in size, it is the biggest farm in Iceland and
more than twice the size of Luxembourg. The family's days of glory were in the 14th century, when sulphur was mined from Námaskarð on their land and
sent to Europe to be made into gunpowder. This
remote corner of Iceland helped keep the world's wars
rolling until the 19th century, when other sulphur
sources were found.

Farming in the area also prospered despite the devastating eruption of the Leirhnjúkur crater (10 km/
6 miles northeast of Reykjahlíð). The "Mývatn-fires"
lasted for five years, from 1724 to 1729, wiped out
three farms and wrecked Reykjahlíð's buildings – but
created some of the bizarre lava formations which
now make the area so fascinating.

Birdwatching in the bright sunshine.

BELOW: a lone bather among the pseudo-craters to the south of Lake Mývatn.

Today the farm is still working, although the owners have invested in the tourist business and allow visitors access to almost every part of the property. Travellers started arriving in numbers to see Mývatn and its surroundings in the early 20th century, and the family built the first hotel, the **Hotel Reykjahlíð**, in the 1940s – it has since housed everyone from Prince Harald of Norway to a steady stream of backpackers. In 1968, a diatomite plant was opened at Bjarnarflag near Mývatn, and a small village, also known as **Reykjahlíð ❶**, sprang up around the hotel northeast of the lake to become the service centre of the area.

With hotels, camping grounds, supermarkets and snack bars, Reykjahlíð is a functional base for travellers. It does boast the local **church** – although it was rebuilt in 1972, it is on the site of the original church that was in the path of the lava flow in 1729 and seemed certain to be destroyed. Miraculously, the lava parted literally at the church door and flowed on either side of the wooden building, an event that the devout ascribed to divine intervention. In the school building at Reykjahlíð, beside the swimming pool, is a **Visitors' Centre** run by the Icelandic Nature Conservation Agency. It has information on routes around the area and its natural history, with some excellent lava exhibits.

Circuit around the lake

A road – most of which amounts to no more than a dirt track – circles Lake Mývatn, connecting the various points of interest. The lake itself is 37 sq. km (14 sq. miles) in area, making it the fourth-largest in Iceland, but unusually shallow – the average depth is only 2 metres (7 ft), with the deepest point only 4½ metres (15 ft). This shallowness allows the sun's rays to reach the bottom to create a thriving growth of algae and plankton. There are 50 islets.

Lake Mývatn

The name Mývatn actually means "midge lake" and, for long stretches of the summer, clouds of these tiny flying insects can make any visit a misery. Billions usually emerge in June and August to dive into eyes, noses and ears with relentless energy. They are often joined by biting blackflies, so make sure you bring some insect repellent. (Head nets are, not surprisingly, sold in most shops.) It is cold comfort to learn that the midges are crucial to the lake's ecosystem: their corpses fertilise the lakeside and the larvae are a staple for birds and fish.

The surfeit of midges as fodder has also made the River Laxá, which flows through Mývatn, the source of Iceland's biggest salmon (they spawn in the lower part of the lake). Mývatn offers the best trout fishing in the country.

The fields of fire

Heading north from Reykjahlíð, Route 87 crosses the lava flow from the 1720s that dominates the topography of the village and the northern landscape of the lake. Called **Eldhraun** ("fire lava"), this barren landscape gives a glimpse of the desert that Route 87 runs into – so devoid of life that NASA sent its Apollo 11 crew for training missions here in the late 1960s. Keep an eye out on the left-hand side for a giant bubble of dried lava, where the surface layer has been cracked like a huge egg.

Turning left onto Route 848, the landscape becomes much greener and quickly enters the marshes of the **Conservation Area**. This is the main breeding ground for the lake's birds, and during the nesting season (15 May to 20 July) its shoreline is off-limits. Fifteen species of duck have been recorded on the lake, and up to 100,000 birds can be gathered here at once. Among other species, almost the entire European population of Barrow's goldeneye birds

Map on page 280

In winter local farmers still cut holes through the ice to lower their hooks – part of a ritual that dates back to the Middle Ages, when fish were the only winter food and could mean the difference between life and death.

BELOW:
the Hverfjall crater overshadowing Reykjahlíð.

breed here. The view overlooking the bird-dotted lake from **Neslandatangi peninsula** ❷, which almost cuts the lake in two, is particularly serene at dusk.

South of the conservation area, the 529-metre (1,735-ft) peak of **Vindbelgjarfjall** ❸, seen to the right, can be climbed in a couple of hours for views of the lake. Beyond that, another smaller lake, **Sandvatn**, is probably the best place in the area to see gyrfalcons.

South of here, the road now runs into the Ring Road. On the southern shore of the lake is Mývatn's secondary service centre of **Skútustaðir** ❹, with a petrol station, church and snack shop.

From here, there is an easy hour-long path around the **Skútustaðagígar pseudo-craters**. These were formed when water was trapped beneath flowing lava, boiled and burst up through the surface, creating what looks like volcanic cones. Some were formed so recently that their sides are still charred.

Picnic promontory

One of the most sheltered and relaxing spots on the lakeside is **Höfði** ❺, a forested promontory that has been turned into a reserve, with a small admission fee. There is a vaguely fairy-tale atmosphere to the place, with paths running through flower-covered lava outcrops and forests of birch trees. Large rocks by the lakeside rocks also provide ideal picnic hide-aways.

A turn-off to the right leads to **Dimmuborgir** ❻ ("black castles"), a vast, 2,000-year-old field of contorted volcanic pillars, some extending as high as 20 metres (65 ft). There is a viewing platform over the expanse, and visitors can wander about among the haunting arches, caves and natural tunnels. The most famous formation is **Kirkjan** (the Church), a cave that looks like the interior of

TIP

Birdwatching devotees swear that the bridge on the Ring Road over the Laxá river is Iceland's premier location, bar none, for spotting birds.

BELOW: the bizarre lava formations at Dimmubórgir.

a Gothic cathedral, and a 3-metre (16-ft) hole that provides an amusing opportunity to take a photograph.

Map on page 280

Further along the same road is the looming crater of **Hverfell** ❼, formed in an eruption 2,500 years ago and these days likened to a giant football stadium. A steep path runs up the side of the crater which is made entirely of loose volcanic rubble, or tephra. Hverfell's rim provides one of the most sweeping views of the Mývatn area. Inside the 1,000-metre (3,280-ft) wide crater, hikers have written messages in huge letters of light-coloured stone.

En route back to Reykjahlíð, by the left side of the road is **Grjótagjá** ❽, an underground hot spring made by a buckle in the earth (the site is unmarked but a space for it has been cleared beside it). The green waters feel tepid to the touch but below the surface can be scalding, so swimming is forbidden.

Volcanologists' paradise

The Ring Road running east of Reykjahlíð immediately leads to a completely different landscape, a desolate, sandy plain of mixed orange and brown hues known as **Bjarnarflag** ❾. On the left is Mývatn's diatomite plant, processing the microscopic fossils called diatoms that are taken from the lake's floor; on the right is a brick factory, putting the local excess of tephra to practical use. These are the only survivors of a long string of entrepreneurial failures here in the 20th century, including attempts to mine sulphur and harness geothermal energy. Easily visible is a huge spraying vent of steam from a bore hole dug 2 km (1¼ miles) down into the earth, the result of a test for a proposed geothermal plant.

One of the specialities of Icelandic cuisine, the sweet, sticky bread called *hverabraud*, is baked in the ground here (metal lids can be spotted in between

BELOW: studying the moss.

The continuous volcanic activity can make for rough and tortuous roads.

the brick factory and the highway). The finished product can be bought at the supermarket. A less appetising local dish is fermented duck eggs; these tend to be foul-smelling and only for the more adventurous.

An overwhelming stench of sulphur greets travellers as the road climbs over the ridge of **Námafjall**, whose series of cracks – the largest appeared as recently as 1975 – betray its location plumb on the Mid-Atlantic Ridge. The Námafjall geothermal field has been drilled, revealing temperatures over 290°C (554°F) at a depth of 1¾ km (1 mile). Steam and mud craters formed in this field during the Mývatn-fires of 1724, and new fissures spread south into the area in April 1728. At the pass is a parking area with views over the lake, and, stretching out on the other side is the famous boiling mud pit of **Hverarönd** ⑩ – perhaps one of Iceland's most infernal and fascinating sights. Walkways run across the multi-coloured clay of the area, through dozens of bubbling pits and steaming vents. The surface here is particularly thin, and at some places likely to crumble, so to avoid being boiled alive in a mud pot, keep well within the marked paths.

Man-made disaster

BELOW: the hissing and steaming mud pools of Hverarönd.

A rough dirt road leads 7 km (4 miles) north to the **Krafla area** ⑪, named after one of the mountains at the centre of the region, and heart of the most recent volcanic activity. Pipes from the Krafla geothermal power plant form a metal doorway to the area, which is strangely appropriate: the construction of the plant in 1973, with its many bore holes into the earth's crust, is considered by some scientists to be responsible for triggering the eruptions that began here in 1975 – the first since the 1700s. Between 3 and 8 km (2–5 miles) beneath the Krafla field lies a magma reservoir which is the source of the

volcanic activities in the area. Magma builds up in the reservoir, causing the earth to rise, until it is released as rock intrusions or in the form of volcanic eruptions, resulting in the earth's surface sinking again.

Map on page 280

The activity in the early 1970s, known as the "Krafla-fires" began with a dramatic spurt of molten lava that lit up Reykjahlíð by night. Some 15 eruptions followed in the next decade, but luckily the lava all flowed away from the small village and no major damage was done. Even so, the earth's thin crust has regularly risen and fallen several centimetres at a time as magma moves through underground chambers – during the Krafla-fires 21 cycles of land rising and sinking occured. Volcanologists are expecting Krafla to blow again any time.

A stern warning sign (volcanic hazard zone – do not enter) at the first parking area here was put up in the 1980s to keep tourists away, but had the opposite effect: hundreds gathered here to see what would happen. The warning sign has now been removed, and during the summer there is still a stream of visitors who go out to the black, partly warm lava field of the Krafla caldera that was spat up from the earth during the 1970s and 1980s, and the crater of **Leirhnjúkur** (formed during the explosions of the 1720s). If you can forget the disconcerting possibility of being blown to kingdom come, this whole lifeless, primeval area gives as good a glimpse of the freshly formed earth as anyone is likely to get.

The name of the crater Víti means "hell". Víti was the initial source of the 1725 volcanic eruptions.

Further on, a second parking area sits at the base of **Víti**, a colourful explosion crater, about 320 metres (1,050 ft) wide, which is now thought to be inactive. This is close to Mount Krafla itself, which, far from being a classic volcanic cone, is the rim of a larger caldera that has been worn and exploded almost beyond recognition. ❑

BELOW: Víti crater near Mount Krafla.

Map
on page
290

●Reykjavík

THE NORTHEAST

*In this remote and little-visited region you can see sea birds
and whales in their natural, unspoilt environment, and visit the
unexpectedly lush Jökulsárgljúfur National Park*

Bypassed by the Ring Road and its stream of regular traffic, the Northeast is one of Iceland's most isolated areas. Only the growing fame of the Jökulsárgljúfur National Park usually brings travellers here, with very few continuing on to explore the rugged coastline – largely because of poor transport services, bad roads and few good hotels.

Yet the coastal route has a number of attractions for those with their own transport and an interest in finding out what lies off the beaten track. Dozens of atmospheric fishing towns cling precariously to this shore just south of the Arctic Circle. Exploring these quiet, conservative outposts and the craggy cliffs and wilderness areas around them reveals the harsh seafaring world that is in many ways Iceland's backbone.

PRECEDING PAGES:
the Ásbyrgi canyon
in Jökulsárgljúfur
National Park
BELOW: the view
from Húsavík
across Skjálfandi
bay.

Gateway to the Northeast

The transport artery of the region, following the whole coastline, is Route 85. Approaching from either Akureyri or Lake Mývatn, this road runs through the Aðaldalur valley right down to the shoreline of Skjálfandi ("shivering fjord"), an expanse of sand dotted by small lakes with an impressive wall of mountains as a backdrop.

Rows of picturesque fish-drying racks by the roadside fittingly announce the main town in the region, **Húsavík ❶** (population 2,500). The name "house bay" was given by the Swedish Viking Garðar Svavarsson, who journeyed to Iceland in AD 850 after his mother had seen it in a dream.

Long before the official First Settler, Ingólfur Arnarson, set foot on the island, Garðar spent a winter at Húsavík – and, when he left, an unfortunate fellow named Náttafari was left behind with two slaves. The trio settled down permanently across the bay from Húsavík (the site can be seen from town), but have been disqualified from being considered Iceland's first settlers because their presence was involuntary.

Húsavík today is a tidy and agreeable town set above the first-rate harbour that provides for its existence: nearly everyone who lives here is involved with fishing or fish-processing. The view of the colourful trawlers, murky black waters and snow-spattered granite mountains across the bay is particularly impressive. Near the docks is the headquarters of the Þingeyjarsysla Co-operative Society, which was established in 1882, the first of its kind in Iceland and a landmark in Húsavík's growth.

Dominating the town is an unusual cross-shaped **church**, with a 26-metre (85-ft) spire and modern sculptures in the garden. The church, built in 1907, was designed by the Icelandic architect Rögnvaldur Ólafsson and made from Norwegian timber. It is counted among Iceland's most attractive churches and seats about 450 people. When it was built there were only 500 people living in the parish. The impressive altarpiece, depicting Lazarus raised from the dead, was painted in 1931 by Sveinn Þórarinsson from the nearby farm of Víkingavatn. The local **museum** (Safnahúsið) (open summer: 10am–12 noon, 1–5pm; tel: 464 1860) is the best in the Northeast: prize exhibits include a replica of the 1584 Guðbrandur's Bible (the first translation of the Old and New Testaments into Icelandic, still considered the most ambitious publishing project ever undertaken in Iceland); and the polar bear that floated from Greenland to Grímsey island in 1973 only to be greeted by a bullet in the skull and then stuffed. Húsavík is an excellent place for whale-watching with a huge variety of whales off the coast, including humpback, minke, sei and fin whales, killer whales, dolphins and porpoises. Two companies operate four boats that go on whale-watching trips with a 99 percent success rate.

Arctic vista

For a panoramic view over the whole Húsavík area, drive a kilometre north of town to the unmarked yellow gate on the right, then continue as far as your car can take you (only a four-wheel drive should attempt the full distance on this dangerously slippery road). There is a viewfinder at the top, from which you can spot two small islands in the bay: **Flatey** had over 100 inhabitants 50 years ago but has now been abandoned, while **Lundey** is crowded only with puffins.

From this point, the roads become dustier and road signs fewer. Lying north along Route 85 is the squat peninsula of **Tjörnes ❷**, whose 60-metre (200-ft) cliff faces are renowned among geologists for their

BELOW: the Húsavík church.

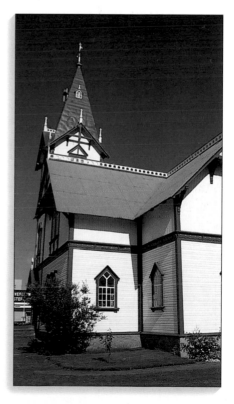

ancient fossils and easily visible geological strata. Non-geologists can get an idea of what is going on at a well-known but difficult-to-find site by the seashore, turning off on a dirt road to the left at the **Ytri-Tunga** farmhouse (the farm is unmarked but the road is before the **Hallbjarnarstaðir** farm, and crosses an electric fence). At Hallbjarnarstaðir there is a small **mineral-and-fossil museum** (open summer: 9am–8pm; tel: 464 1968). This was once the home of the farmer Kári Sigurjónsson, who helped scientists to research shells. The exhibition tells the story of the prehistoric fossils from the Tjörnes layers in the cliffs below.

Emergency hut at Peistareykir, southeast of Húsavík.

The road reaches the coast, then steeply descends the alarming cliff face at **Hallbjarnarstaðakambur Crest**, a dip on either side of the river where the layers of geological deposits are obvious to the naked eye and fossils of molluscs can be picked from the earth. At the shore, look out for a large greenish slab of rock, not native to Iceland, thought to have arrived from Greenland on sea-ice.

East of Tjörnes, the plain of **Kelduhverfi** is made up of sandy glacial wash (similar to the larger *sandur* in the South), and is at the northern point where the two halves of Iceland are splitting apart. Volcanic activity in the 1970s here was related to the eruptions at Krafla near Lake Mývatn, with fissures appearing that are still visible. The whole area is at the mouth of the **Öxarfjörður** fjord. To the north of the highway is **Lake Víkingavatn ❸**, and two farms of the same name; the newer offers farmhouse accommodation, while the older has been occupied by descendants of the same family since the 1700s.

Giant hoof print

The great attraction of the Northeast, and one that has become increasingly popular in recent years, is the **Jökulsárgljúfur National Park ❹** (the full

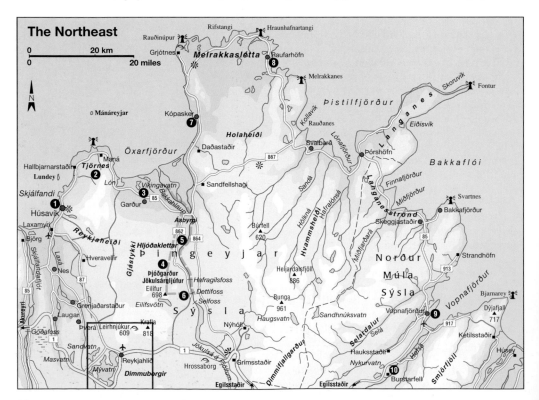

The Northeast

name, meaning "glacial river canyon", is difficult for non-Icelanders to pronounce but can be referred to as Jökulsá Canyon – pronounced *yer-kool-sar*). Once private property within the huge Ás estate, the park was formed in 1973 and extended later to cover approximately 150 sq. km (58 sq. miles).

One of the park's gems is the great horeseshoe-shaped canyon of **Ásbyrgi**, located almost immediately at the turn-off from Route 85. It's not hard to see why the first Viking settlers decided that the canyon had been formed by Sleipnir, the god Odin's flying horse, crashing a giant hoof into the earth. A 100-metre (330-ft) cliff-face makes a smooth, 1 km- (⅝-mile) wide ring around a profuse carpet of greenery, while a smaller outcropping of cliffs (suitably called Eyjan or "island") rises in the middle.

Geologists believe that the canyon was formed relatively recently by a gigantic *hlaup* or glacial flow from an eruption under the faraway icecap of Vatnajökull. The best view is from the furthest part of the canyon, which can be reached after a 100-metre (330-ft) walk west from the parking area. Turning east from the car park leads to a natural spring for drinking water, while taking the trail straight ahead ends up at a small lake full of ducks – their quacks echo around the natural amphitheatre.

Camping is permitted in the canyon near its entrance, where a park ranger keeps an **information office** and sells small brochures giving detailed descriptions of some of the main hiking routes in the park. From here, a path also leads to the top of the cliffs, climbing the canyon at its easiest point (although a rope is provided to help in the ascent). Once up, walkers can follow the cliffs, with excellent views over the whole canyon, or even take the trail as far south as Dettifoss – two days' walk away.

Map on page 290

 TIP

If you are planning to camp in the National Park, stock up at the Ásbyrgi petrol station and supermarket at the Ásbyrgi farm outside the park. This is the only place selling supplies within about 25 km (15 miles).

BELOW: trrekking to the Jökulsá canyon.

No matter whether you walk for an hour or a day, this is one of the most pleasant hikes in Iceland, and if you get tired, just lie on the heather and eat some of the wild berries that grow abundantly in the canyon's summery climate.

Geologists have evidence of at least two catastrophic floods in Jökulsá since the end of the Ice Age. The amount of water in these floods has been estimated up to 400,000 cubic metres (over 14 million cubic ft) per second – over three times the maximum flow of the Amazon.

Towards Dettifoss

The rest of the park follows the powerful **Jökulsá á Fjöllum**, Iceland's second-longest river. Two roads run down the length of the park, one on either side of the river: the western road runs across some classic highland heather to **Vesturdalur** ("west valley") walking trails and the mysterious natural columns of **Hljóðaklettar ❺** (echoing rocks), which form a sort of ghostly stone forest that can be explored for hours. Further on, the road heads to **Hólmatungur**, a lush stretch along the river canyon, before crossing a suddenly barren desert landscape to Dettifoss.

Unfortunately, the western road is deeply corrugated and, while two-wheel drives can make the journey, they need to crawl along at a gruelling 15 kph (10 mph). The eastern road is better, but after Dettifoss it becomes a jeep track.

Either way, it's worth the effort: **Dettifoss ❻** is Europe's largest waterfall, and the effort needed to reach it only seems to add to the excitement. There is nothing contained or artificial about Dettifoss, no wooden boardwalks or viewing balconies installed to detract from Nature. Clouds of spray can first be seen several kilometres away; from the car parks, visitors scramble over square blocks of grey lava, hearing the thunderous drumming before getting a glimpse of the falls. Some 500 cubic metres of water spill over its ledges every second: although it is just 44 metres (145 ft) tall, the sheer hypnotic volume of the flow makes this arguably Iceland's most awesome sight.

BELOW: a waterfall in Jökulsárgljúfur National Park.
RIGHT: the canyon of Hólmatungur.

For those who want to see more falls, **Hafragilsfoss** is 2 km (1½ miles) downstream, and **Selfoss** about the same distance upstream. A four-wheel-drive road heads from Dettifoss south to Lake Mývatn, but other cars will have to track back to Route 28.

Map on page 290

Cod coast

Heading north from the entrance of the National Park leads to Iceland's least visited area. Tourist officials say that even the uninhabited centre of Iceland attracts more travellers than the Northeast coast.

The first village, **Kópasker** ❼, with a population of 184 souls almost all involved in the fishing of shrimp, can seem like a ghost town on most days. Like the other villages of the area, Kópasker thrived on the herring boom until the late 1960s when herring migration patterns changed.

Beyond Kópasker is the flat, exposed peninsula of **Melrakkaslétta** ("fox plain"), where winds howl straight from the North Pole in winter and, on a bad day, summer can seem almost as dismal. The cliffs at **Rauðinúpur** are the only place in the world where it is possible to watch gannets nesting on land from below and the side rather than just from above. The northernmost part of mainland Iceland (and, incidentally, the spot where the saga character Þorgeir Hávarsson was finally brought down after he had slaughtered 14 attackers), **Hraunhafnartangi**, is marked by a lighthouse – the Arctic Circle lies just 2.5km (1½ miles) offshore.

Even so, the remoteness of the barren plain, which can support very little agriculture, is perversely appealing. The coastline is covered with driftwood from as far away as Siberia and supports a good deal of birdlife.

BELOW: Dettifoss, swathed in spray.

Map
on page
290

Just south of the Arctic Circle, this area is never truly dark between May and early August.

BELOW: a remote stretch of road entering the Raufarhafnarhreppur district.

Although **Raufarhöfn** ❽ made the transition from herring to cod fishing in the 1970s, it has never recaptured the great days when thousands of seasonal workers came to its factories. Today there are many more buildings and jetties than the population of 450 can use, and Raufarhöfn is losing more young people to the cities. Trying to keep people in this economically important area, the Icelandic government recently built an airstrip (during long winters, the town had been completely cut off except by sea). Even so, the isolation of this town – which over long periods has not even had a local doctor – is extreme.

Lying south of Raufarhöfn is the **Langanes** peninsula, whose marshy, cliff-bound expanses are the last word in Icelandic remoteness – it can really only be visited with a four-wheel drive or on foot. At the peninsula's tip is a monument to some shipwrecked English sailors who managed to climb the 100-metre (330-ft cliffs) only to die subsequently of exposure.

Heading south, the villages of **Þórshöfn** and **Bakkafjörður** fit the nondescript pattern of the Northeastern landscape, but **Vopnafjörður** ❾ (population 850) is in a surprisingly picturesque setting. The snow-capped mountains behind the town seem to trail down into huge rocks broken into the sea, complemented by the granite range across the fjord. Here the weather is better and the atmosphere more optimistic – the feeling is closer to the East Fjords than the Northeast. Vopnafjörður had its 15 minutes of fame in 1988, when local girl Linda Pétursdóttir became Miss World. From Vopnafjörður, the highway runs away from the coast, passing **Burstarfell** ❿, an excellent **Folk Museum** (open summer: daily 10am–7pm) in a 19th-century farmhouse. The road now climbs into the northeastern desert, passing a viewing platform over **Lake Nykurvatn**, before rejoining the Ring Road in some of Iceland's most barren landscape. ❏

The Most Useful Servant

One of the incidental advantages of Iceland's almost total isolation over the centuries is that the Icelandic horse, the stocky breed introduced by the first Nordic settlers, has survived almost unchanged for over 1,000 years. Today, it is protected by strict regulations which forbid the import of horses into Iceland, and which state that an Icelandic horse sent out of the country can never return to Iceland, for fear of importing diseases to which the local breed would have no immunity.

"Elegant" is not an adjective which springs to mind to describe the Icelandic horse. These chunky, thick-set, muscular animals bear little resemblance to their leggier European relatives, though they can put on a fine turn of speed. They have adapted to the cool climate by growing a thick, shaggy overcoat for winter, which is shed in the spring. In summer, their coats can be groomed to shining smoothness.

In spite of their relatively small stature (13 hands on average), Icelandic horses are famed for their strength and stamina. They have played a vital role in Iceland's history, for centuries a roadless, bridgeless land. Known affectionately as þarfasti þjónninn ("most useful servant"), the horse was the sole form of overland transport in Iceland until the 19th century. In many remote regions, the horse's supremacy has continued, and even today has a vital role to play during the autumn round-up when sheep are herded from remote mountains.

Surefooted, intelligent, affectionate, home-loving and sometimes headstrong, the horse is also known for its five gaits. In addition to the conventional walk, trot and gallop, it has two additional steps in its repertoire: the *tölt* or running walk, and the *skeið* or pace. Some can't manage the *skeið*; these are known as four-gaiters. The *tölt*, almost unknown in other breeds of horse, is a smooth run, which (unlike the trot) does not shake the rider about in the saddle and is understandably very popular for overland travel, particularly for those who are not used to horseback travel.

Horse-riding is now Iceland's number-one leisure activity. Riding clubs flourish all over the country, and various competitions, races, shows and meets are held throughout the summer months. Iceland's equine population numbers in the region of 50,000. Horse breeding and trading, on a fairly modest scale compared to many other countries, is becoming an important business.

Fifteen national organisations in Europe and North America are affiliated to the International Iceland-horse federation (FEIF), and international Iceland-horse championships are held annually. Iceland always sends a team of horses and riders to the world championships, and invariably that team carries off many of the prizes – although, frustratingly, the top local-bred Icelandic horses can never be sent to the international contests. Since horses taken overseas are not re-admitted, no devoted rider would think of taking their best horse to compete in Europe only to leave it behind. ❏

RIGHT: the shaggy-haired Icelandic horse.

THE EAST FJORDS

This region of Iceland, often overlooked by tourists, offers peace and tranquillity – from the long, thin lake Lögurinn, surrounded by forest, to remote farms and small fishing villages

Map on page 300

For travellers arriving from mainland Europe and the Faroe Islands by ferry, the jagged, snow-capped profile of the East Fjords provides the first glimpse of Iceland. It's a breathtaking sight as the boat edges into Seyðisfjörður fjord towards the town's ornate wooden buildings strung out along the seaboard. But not many stay to see what else this region has to offer. Iceland's eastern coast has a reputation of a place to be passed through quickly en route to somewhere else.

This is a pity, and not just because the East enjoys the sunniest weather in the country. The rugged coastline and dry interior here are full of wilderness areas rarely visited by foreigners, although they are well known among Icelanders. And along the way are remote farms and fishing villages that, unusually for Iceland, have still hung on to a degree of old-world charm.

Hub of the East

Whether arriving by ferry, car or bus, travellers use as an orientation point the East's most important urban crossroad, **Egilsstaðir ❶** (population around 1,500). The first houses were built here less than 50 years ago, and Egilsstaðir still has an unfortunate prefabricated feel: like many smaller towns in this part of Iceland, its social and economic life seems to hinge around the Esso petrol station. Flanking the station are the camping ground, tourist information office and a huge supermarket – a place that can turn into an elbows-only feeding frenzy on days when the ferry arrives in nearby Seyðisfjörður.

Still, Egilsstaðir also has a number of hotels, among them a brand new one with all modern facilities, which makes a convenient base. Its sister-settlement, the tiny village of **Fellabær ❷** (population 50) lies across a long bridge – at 301 metres (990 ft) this was the longest bridge in Iceland for many years – and enjoys a picturesque setting. Try for lakeside accommodation in huts on the Skipalækur farm, although they are often booked up months in advance.

The port of **Seyðisfjörður ❸**, where the ferry from mainland Europe docks, lies directly east along the mostly paved highway Route 93. The journey is worth making even for those not taking the boat: in complete contrast to Egilsstaðir, Seyðisfjörður is full of Scandinavian character, a town that approximates to one's mental image, so rarely fulfilled, of an Icelandic fishing town. Set on the fjord of the same name and surrounded by sheer mountains, it was founded in the 1830s and soon became the largest and wealthiest town in the East of Iceland – resulting in the construction of many wooden homes in an elegant Norwegian style.

PRECEDING PAGES: a house at the fishing village of Reyðarfjörður.
LEFT: Seyðisfjörður from the ferry.
BELOW: a wooden cross on the way to Borgarfjörður-Eystri.

Turf-covered house in Borgarfjörður-Eystri

Most of Seyðisfjörður's 800 or so inhabitants are involved in fishing in some way, and the arrival every autumn of herring schools in the shallow waters of the nearby fjords is still a cause for mass mobilisation, bringing everyone from schoolchildren to the aged out to the fish factories. (The autumn herring catch is from different stock to the summer catch, which between the 1930s and the 1960s turned Iceland's northeastern outposts into Klondike-style boom towns, before overfishing wiped out the population.) In summer, the frequent ferry traffic keeps much of Seyðisfjörður busy, and on Wednesday evenings and Thursday mornings an arts and crafts market is held to coincide with arrivals and departures. Classical music and light jazz concerts are held in Seyðisfjörður church every Wednesday in summer. There is a fine view of the town and fjord from the highway, which winds up past small waterfalls into the **Fjarðarheiði** mountains. The best spot for taking photos is a columnar basalt monument to the first postman of the region, who regularly made this journey on horseback when it was decidedly more dangerous than it is today.

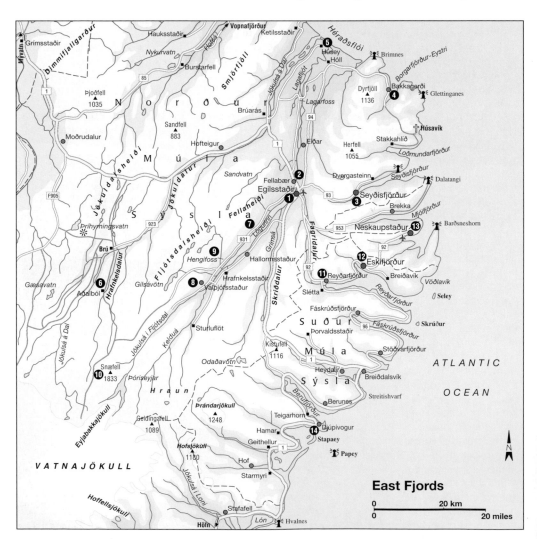

East Fjords

| 0 | 20 km |
| 0 | 20 miles |

Map
on page
300

Haunted highway

Another spectacular excursion from Egilsstaðir is to Borgarfjörður-Eystri, following Route 94 north. The highway passes the Edda Hotel at **Eiðar** before entering an expanse of marshland bordered to the north by the Jökulsá á Dal river. The whole area is crowded with birdlife.

Over a high pass, **Dyrfjöll**, one of Iceland's most dramatic mountain ranges, comes into view. Watch out on the left for the bridge of a fishing trawler sitting in a field – it was dragged there on truck-back by a local, Fitzcarraldo, who wanted to piece together a boat in Borgarfjörður. He gave up half way, leaving a surreal vision for passers-by. This is an unnerving stretch of highway, with dramatic drops down into the sea and graphic evidence of recent landslides. A wooden cross records that the road was once said to be haunted. Fatal accidents were so common here in the Middle Ages that they were attributed to a ghost named Naddi, supposed to live in a scree called Naddagil. In the early 1300s, a priest was dragged out here to perform an exorcism, and just to make sure, locals erected a cross in 1306. The cross has been replaced innumerable times, but each bears the Latin inscription, *Effigiem Christi: qui transis pronus honora* – "You who are hurrying past should honour the image of Christ."

The town of **Borgarfjörður-Eystri ❹** (East Borgarfjörður, to distinguish it from the bigger Borgarfjörður in western Iceland) is also known as **Bakkagerði**. It is ringed by dramatic mountains: the ochre range to the east, past the black sand beach, is made from an acidic form of lava called rhyolite. This black rock, along with pieces of jasper and agate, is polished into everything from paperweights to gravestones at the **Álfasteinn stone and mineral works** (open Mon–Fri 8am–5pm), at the north end of the village.

BELOW: Dyrfjöll near Borgarfjörður-Eystri.

BELOW:
an abandoned
farm by the side
of a fjord.

Ask at the shop for the key to the local **church**, with an altarpiece painted by the renowned artist Jóhannes Kjarval, who was born in Borgarfjörður and made the area famous in his paintings. He was said by one critic to have "taught the Icelanders to experience the beauty of their own landscape". A monument to the artist can be seen by the main road, just outside the village. Across the street from the church is a colourful turf house that is still inhabited and, towards the beach, a stone hillock called **Álfaborg** ("elf hill"), held to be inhabited by the hidden people (*see also* Icelandic Hauntings, *pages 266–7*).

Eastern isolation

A second road north of Egilsstaðir (Route 925, via the Ring Road) leads to **Húsey 5**, a farm that has earned a measure of fame for its remoteness and serenity – representing, as one traveller put it, "the real Iceland." Lying in the flatlands just south of the Jökulsá á Dal river, in the shadow of the Dyrfjöll mountains, Húsey's gaily painted corrugated-iron buildings date from the 1930s. The farm is still operational and until recently was one of the few in Iceland to still engage in the controversial practice of sealing. Walks can be made across the heather to the black sand beach nearby, where the Iceland's two species of raptor – gyrfalcons and merlins – can often be seen hovering overhead; horseback trips can also be made into the surrounding wilderness. Húsey's utter peacefulness is seductive, and many visitors stay much longer than planned. The old-style guesthouse accommodation offered is simple but comfortable, and lying in bed at night listening to the howling wind, one gets a vivid idea of just how isolated pioneering Icelandic farmers have been through the centuries.

Inland from Húsey, the Ring Road follows the **Jökulsá á Dal** river valley before hitting the central deserts en route to Lake Mývatn. The bridge across the river was held to be haunted by a monster who would occasionally dine on unsuspecting travellers. There has been a bridge here since 1564. In 1994 a new bridge was built about 1 km (½ mile) south of the old one. It is the highest in the country, 40 metres (130 ft) above the river. Farmhouse accommodation is available at a space-age concrete building at **Brúarás**. Further west, look out for the rise of Goðanes overlooking the river south of the highway: this was supposedly once a temple of Thor, and sacrifices were held nearby. Today there are ruins below the hill, of indeterminate age.

The rough Route 923, which turns south off the Ring Road along the Jökulsá á Brú, heads for the farm of **Aðalból** ❻ and country related to the much-beloved *Hrafnkels Saga*. The story tells of Hrafnkell Hallfreðarson, an unsavoury chieftain who lived at Aðalból and worshipped Freyr, the Norse god of war. Hrafnkell swore to Freyr that he would kill anyone who rode his favourite horse, Freyfaxi, and when one of his shepherds innocently did so, felt obliged to hunt him down and chop open the poor fellow's skull. A blood feud resulted in Hrafnkell being outlawed at the Alþingi and ambushed by the victim's cousin, Sámur – who, rather than killing Hrafnkell, maimed him horribly by stringing him up with a rope through the Achilles tendon and seizing his lands. The horse that had caused all the trouble was flung into a pond and drowned.

At this stage, Hrafnkell decided that Freyr was little practical use as a deity and abandoned his worship. Appearing to turn over a new leaf, he slowly rebuilt his fortune at a nearby farm. Of course, Hrafnkell was only biding his time: six years later, he took his revenge, descending on Sámur with a band of warriors and driving him from the East. According to the Saga, Hrafnkell then lived happily ever after. Some ruins from Viking times have been found at the farm Aðalból, but fans of the sagas will mostly have to use their imaginations.

The great Icelandic forest

South of Egilsstaðir stretches the pencil-shaped lake of **Lögurinn** ❼. Over 100 metres (330 ft) deep, the lake is said to be home to the Lagarfljót serpent. Sightings of this strange creature have been recorded since the 14th century. It appears on the lake, according to written documents and eyewitnesses, in different forms – as a snake, dragon, seal, horse or even in the shape of a house.

Lögurinn is also famed as the site of the country's largest wooded area, **Hallormsstaðarskógur**. Nearly all of the woods were protected from grazing animals between 1905 and 1927. The wood is now 740 sq. km (285 sq. miles), the total fenced-in area being 1,850 hectares (around 4,500 acres). In 1903 a nursery, called Mörkin, was established to grow different kinds of native and foreign trees. Since then it has distributed some 12 million plants. An arboretum was formally opened in 1993, with a total of 54 tree species – 31 coniferous and 23 broadleaved. The reafforestation programme here (using tough plants from Alaska and Siberia among others) has created optimism that

Map on page 300

TIP

If you wish to explore the woods of Lögurinn, there is a network of footpaths, and both individual trees and groups are labelled. A small descriptive booklet is also available.

BELOW: camping by the banks of Lögurinn.

A farmer in the East Fjords outside her painted house.

other parts of Iceland might return to their pre-Viking state of being "covered by woods from mountain to shore".

On the lake, **Hallormsstaður** is a popular spot for Icelandic vacationers (there is a camping ground and an Edda hotel). A little further towards the end of the Fljótsdalur valley is the farm Hrafnkelsstaðir, where Hrafnkell, the hero of *Hrafnkels Saga*, went after he had been maimed. At the southern end of the lake, **Valþjófsstaður** ❽ farm is where the beautiful carved wooden church door, dating back to AD 1200 and on display in the National Museum in Reykjavík, was found. The box-like modern church now on the site sports a shiny new replica. Nearby **Skriðuklaustur** was the site of a monastery from 1493 until the Reformation (1550). In 1939 the author Gunnar Gunnarsson, who was well known for his novels in Denmark and Germany, settled at Skriðuklaustur and built a large, quirkily designed house, which he later presented to the Icelandic state. North of Lögurinn, a steep hour-long walk leads to the "hanging falls" of **Hengifoss** ❾, 120 metres (393 ft) high.

Hiking country

A rough four-wheel-drive road runs south of Lögurinn to **Mount Snæfell** ❿, the 1,833-metre (6,013-ft) peak that dominates the valley. Further on are the **Kverkfjöll** mountains at the northern edge of the icecap. Special buses run from Egilsstaðir to the hut at the base of Snæfell in the summer. The mountain is in fact an ancient primary volcano, surrounded by colourful rhyolite. If you are in good shape you can hike up to the peak from the hut, which stands about 800m (2,600 ft) above sea-level. The hike to the top takes about 4–6 hours.The warden at the hut will provide all the necessary information.

BELOW: a bike ride at dusk near Valþjófsstaður.

For those who want to spend more time exploring the area, a popular long-distance walk is between Snæfell and Lónsöræfi – taking up to 7 days, depending on how long is spent at each stop. This is a spectacular hike in an uninhabited wilderness. Colorful rhyolite rocks can be found in many places, while impressive canyons and ravines cut through the land from time to time. There are plenty of flowers in early summer, and reindeer herds can sometimes be seen along the way. It is essential to have a good, up-to-date hiking map and to contact the local tourist information centre (in Egilsstaðir), to obtain all the necessary information on the route, especially concerning the state of rivers and streams, and not least, the expected weather in the area. Do not attempt the walk alone – much of it is remote and can be misty and icy.

Starting from Snæfell hut it is best to organise a lift in a four-wheel-drive towards Vatnajökull glacier. From here is is possible to walk over the **Eyjabakkajökull** glacier, a tongue of Vatnajökull (you will need crampons) towards the hut at **Geldingafell**. From there the next hut to head for is at **Kollumúli**. The hut here is run by the local Travellers' Association and situated by the tranquil lake **Kollumúlavatn**. It is a good idea to spend two nights here and use a whole day for exploring the surroundings, perhaps hiking down into the **Víðidalur** valley. The next stage of the walk is down to **Nes**, where you may also need a day to explore the magnificent scenery. The last day's hike takes you to the crest of **Illikambur**, where you can catch a ride on the daily bus to Höfn.

Following the fjords

The Ring Road runs directly south of Egilsstaðir, although many prefer to take the slower but better-paved and more scenic route hugging the coast. The start

Map on page 300

BELOW: a lone trawler plies an eastern fjord.

of the coast road runs through a steep river valley lined by pencil waterfalls at regular intervals – each would be a marvel in other countries but in Iceland is just part of the backdrop. **Reyðarfjörður** is the first of many quiet fishing villages along this part of the coast, magnificently situated at the base of the steepest fjord in the East. The town's old streets give it an unusually authentic, human feel: small plants are neatly lined up in the windows of corrugated-iron buildings and, on a fine day, old fishermen promenade along the split-level streets.

From Reyðarfjörður Route 92 runs north along the coast to **Eskifjörður** (population 1,100), noted for its **Maritime Museum** (open summer: daily 2–5pm) with exhibits on fishing and whaling dating back to the 18th century. Among the many interesting items in the museum is a model of the whaling-station that was in nearby Hellisfjörður between 1904 and 1913. At this time there were five whaling-stations in the East Fjords. The museum is housed in the oldest building in Eskifjörður. Built in 1816 as a shop, it was later used as a warehouse, fish-processing house and storage space for fishing-tackle.

Further along Route 92, **Neskaupstaður** , with a population of 1,700, is the largest town in East Iceland, despite its remote position at the end of the narrow, winding highway. In the summer boat trips go from Neskaupstaður to the site of the former whaling-station in the deserted **Hellisfjörður**. On the trip you visit the highest sea-cliff in Iceland, along with some inlets for birdwatching.

Heading south along the fjords from Reyðarfjörður, the road is squeezed between the choppy North Atlantic and steep mountains – their twisted peaks are usually shrouded in a haunting mist, making this look like troll country. The small villages of **Fáskrúðsfjörður**, **Stöðvarfjörður**, **Breiðdalsvík** and **Djúpivogur** all pass in quick succession, but it is worth making a stop in

Map on page 300

Stöðvarfjörður to visit the interesting stone collection of Petra Sveinsdóttir, which is signposted from the main road towards the end of the village. About 5 km (3 miles) northwest of Djúpivogur lies the farm **Teigarhorn**, known for the most beautiful and varied zeolites in the world. The cliffs at the coast, where the zeolites are found, are now a nature reserve, but you can walk down to the farm and have a look at the farmer's private collection, which is on display in a small cottage below the farmhouse.

The uninhabited island of **Papey** is visible out to sea from Djúpivogur, named after Irish monks, who are said to have lived on the island before the settlement. The island was then inhabited by farmers, and an old house, built at the beginning of the 20th century, is still there, along with the smallest and oldest wooden church in the country, believed to date from 1807.

A short distance southwest of Djúpivogur is the farm of **Stafafell**, which offers accommodation to travellers and has become a popular base for hikers making day trips into the surrounding river valleys. It has a small church with some interesting artefacts. Nearby is the large and peaceful **Lón** lagoon.

The surrounding area of **Lónsöræfi** is renowned for its wild and dramatic landscape, where deep valleys and chasms have been carved among the mountains by the glacial river Jökulsá. There are plenty of fine hiking trails throughout the area. Using Stafafell as a base, there is a relatively easy day hike, taking about four to six hours. It starts by taking the path up the mountain above the farm, and from there through the Selárdalur valley down to the colourful Hvannagil gorge. The trail carries on along the stream at the bottom of the gorge, towards the river Jökulsá, and ends on a track, passing a few summer-cottages, before returning to Stafafell. ❑

BELOW: the church at Stafafell.

THE INTERIOR

The huge central area of Iceland is crossed by a number of routes through the country's wildest, most extreme scenery

During the Age of Settlement few Viking colonists braved the desolation of the interior. Only outlaws, banished from their society and the fertile coast, took refuge in its chilly expanses. By the 13th century, some paths had been created through the Central Highlands for short cuts from north to south. Today, 800 years later, the vast region of the interior is still almost totally uninhabited.

Despite this – or rather, because of it – the interior is Iceland's premier attraction for adventurous travellers. Nowhere else in Europe is so remote from civilisation, or offers such a range of scenery, the most dramatic Iceland has to offer: broad icecaps which split their sides into great glacial tongues; volcanoes of every size with extensive fields of block lava and pumice; freezing deserts and endless outwash plains of black sand. There are two main routes that go right across the interior: the Kjölur and the Sprengisandur. Other routes offer further opportunities for exploring this unique area.

Challenge of the wild

There are serious logistical problems to be overcome before visiting the interior. Roads are reduced to mere tracks, most passable only in four-wheel-drive vehicles. Many of the interior routes are open only in the middle of summer and even then snowfalls and blizzards can still occur. There are years when some tracks never open due to the severe weather.

The weather is unpredictable and camping is the only real form of accommodation. There are exceptions in the form of a few huts operated by the Icelandic Touring Club (Ferðafélag Íslands). Located in key areas, like the Sprengisandur and Kjölur, facilities are very basic but useful in emergencies.

Modes of transport through the interior vary from the latest high-tech 4x4 or beaten-up Land-Rover, to mountain bikes and walking. Whichever way you choose, extreme care is required in preparation. You must take everything you will need with you, including all food and water, and in some cases fuel, and to be aware of how to deal with the punishing terrain and weather conditions (*see also pages 333, 344–5, 365*). Because of the dangers, many travellers opt to embark with one of the adventure-tour operators based in Reykjavík. These use short wheelbase, four-wheel-drive coaches for tours ranging from day excursions to longer-term camping trips. For the latter, the vehicles are heavily modified, often to include a kitchen and a full complement of picnic tables and chairs. A popular alternative form of adventure tour is traversing the interior on horseback. ❑

PRECEDING PAGES: a winter drive through Landmannalaugar in central Iceland.
LEFT: a stream flowing from under lava at Herðubreið in summer.

Map on page 314

THE KJÖLUR ROUTE

Close to Reykjavík and comparatively short and straightforward to drive, this route through the Central Highlands is the most popular venture into the interior for travellers

The Kjölur route, based on an ancient byway used in Saga times, is one of the main routes across the interior, passing between the Langjökull and Hofsjökull icecaps. A four-wheel drive is advisable but other vehicles are seen on the main track which begins at the majestic **Gullfoss** waterfall in the Southwest (*see page 190*) and runs northwards to the **Blöndudalur** valley. The first part of the journey, to the hot springs of Hveravellir, is on a road of gravel, stones and rock, with the occasional small river to be forded. Beyond Hveravellir, the route deteriorates as the track becomes muddy with several extended river crossings. In comparison with other routes across the interior, the Kjölur is relatively busy during the summer and could be tackled in a day.

Into the interior

Leaving Gullfoss, the grassland on the plain above the falls soon changes to lichen-dotted stones. There is a steady drop in temperature as the landscape looks increasingly bleak and uninviting. On the skyline the only relief is the snow-sprinkled mass of **Mount Bláfell** (1,204 metres/3,950 ft).

Before Bláfell there is a ford across the **River Sandá** and a track branching off to the left. This detour from the main route, taking several hours as a round

BELOW: In a four-wheel-drive across the interior.

trip, goes to the large glacial lake **Hagavatn ❶** and the icecap of **Langjökull**. As the track winds and bumps its way towards the edge of the ice, it crosses a once volcanically active fissure several miles in length. All that remains today is a high ridge of black rock with a narrow break that allows access through to the edge of the glaciers. The final approaches to the icecap are very steep due to huge deposits of glacial moraine, and vehicles should be left below. Water gushes out from the top of the moraine where lake Hagavatn has formed. Standing on the edge of the moraine, buffeted by the cold wind, there is a view of the lake, edged in ice, and, way below, the sweeping plains of black sand that are blown southward and enrich the agricultural land beyond Gullfoss.

Back on the main Kjölur route you head towards a second, even larger glacial lake, **Hvítárvatn ❷**. Skirting around the bulk of Mount Bláfell to the east, the track descends to the **River Hvítá**, plunging through four or five tributary streams and small rivers. A spectacular view opens up across desolate dark tundra towards the distant blue glaciers of Langjökull icecap and Hvítárvatn lake.

On the horizon lies another icecap, **Hofsjökull**: the conflicting winds from the two icecaps create swirling dust clouds in between. From the bridge over the Hvítá, there is a clear view to the lake. Small icebergs can usually be seen in the water, and on the far shore towers the outlet glacier from which they originated. A good base for a more extended exploration of the area is the Touring Club hut at **Hvítárnes**. Beyond here, the brown dusty plain gives way to expanses of gravel and then great black stretches of volcanic clinker, with mountains and glaciers always on the horizon.

Travellers wading through one of the many glacial streams.

The track soon crosses the southern stony slopes of the small mountain, **Innri-Skúti**. As well as affording a panoramic view over the **Jökulfall** river valley to the Hofsjökull icecap and Kerlingarfjöll mountains,

BELOW: huts and tents at Kerlingarfjöll.

the slopes are particularly rich in tundra plants. Most are no more than tiny specks which eke out an existence sheltered between the rocks. Small pink cushions of moss campion compete with white mountain avens and other alpines for space. In common with other tundra life, such plants have to cope with long, severe winters, followed by short, relatively warm summers. This ensures that any growth is very stunted. Woolly willows grow barely centimetres above the ground; as soon as they grow above this height, they become bent over by the constant wind.

The track detour to **Kerlingarfjöll ❸** is well signposted as it dips down into the Jökulfall river valley. The river can become a raging torrent when it rains, making it difficult to cross. Nearby is a small airstrip. These are dotted throughout the interior for emergency use but this one also allows access to the summer ski school of **Árskarð**. The Kerlingarfjöll region is an excellent climbing area with superb views of Hofsjökull, many deep ravines and well-vegetated slopes. The mountain peaks, rising to 1,400 metres (4,600 ft), are made of rhyolite, making a stark contrast to the dark plains of Kjölur. In a succession of small gorges, sulphur and boiling water vent to the surface – which looks particularly eerie when there is a mild drizzle in the air and great clouds of steam rise out of the myriad small fissures in the ground.

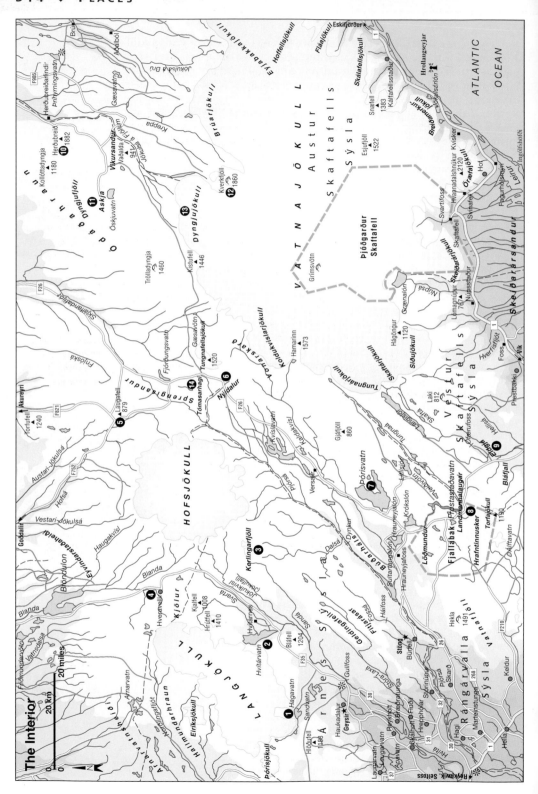

The Interior

Map on page 314

Boiling pools have splashed mineral-laden waters across rocks, colouring them green, red and yellow. These mountains can be a very cold place to camp and there are occasional snowfalls even in August. At the end of the track, near to the ski school, is a touring hut which operates a small café in season. It makes a delightful refuge, even if only for a brief coffee!

Returning to the main Kjölur route, you will see the table-mountain **Kjalfell** (1,008 metres/3,307 ft). To the northeast of it, on a low lava ridge, is **Beinahóll** ("hill of bones"). In 1780 four men from Reynistaður farm in Skagafjörður perished here in bad weather with a flock of sheep. Because of this incident most travellers over Kjölur for the hundred years afterwards passed on the west of Kjalfell, instead of using the main track to the east of the mountain.

A warm oasis

Hveravellir ❹, 100 km (60 miles) from Gullfoss, is an oasis within the cold desert. The hot springs here are very different from those at Kerlingarfjöll. Deep pools of brilliant, near-boiling blue water, are lined with white silica; all around are small mud pools of black, brown and red minerals. Hissing jets of steam emerge from tall rocky cones, while a number of springs cascade water which runs gently down the slopes. The deposits of silica and sulphur cover the ground like great sheets of glass with fine traces of yellow.

Hveravellir is close to being classified as the interior's only settlement due to the presence of a touring hut, campsite and weather station. Some of the blue pools are as near as the natural world comes to a jacuzzi. With the air temperature near freezing, bathing is possible in one of the outlet pools located by the car park. Among the peculiar hot springs in the area are **Bláhver** and **Öskurshólshver**, the latter being so noisy in earlier times, that it reminded 18th-century travellers in Hveravellir of a screaming lion. Another is **Eyvindarhver**, named after the 18th-century outlaw Fjalla-Eyvindur, who is said to have boiled his meat in the spring. Ruins of the outlaw's shelter can be found on the edge of the lava, near the spring. Born in 1714, Eyvindur became a thief. In his early thirties he went into self-imposed exile in the mountains, for over 20 years. He met and married Halla Jónsdóttir. They settled in the beginning at Hveravellir, where they lived rather comfortably, gradually joined by a gang of thieves. On one occasion, though, Halla was captured and taken away. One night, as the kidnappers camped in Borgarfjörður in West Iceland, the exhausted guards fell asleep. Next morning Halla was gone. The swiftest horse was also missing and so were the provisions. Clear footprints of two horses led to the mountains – Eyvindur had come in the night to free his wife.

North from Hveravellir runs 70 km (43 miles) of rough track until the hard road at the Blöndudalur valley. The winding **River Seyðisá** has several fording places which frequently change: great care is needed when crossing. The shallower parts attract water birds, such as phalaropes, which churn up the bottom by walking in circles to dislodge small animals for food. Much of the water comes from the two icecaps and on a clear day the views are magnificent. ❑

The Icelandic playwright Jóhann Sigurjónsson (1880–1919), a resident of Copenhagen, wrote a very successful play about the lives of the outlaw Eyvindur and his wife Halla, who lived at Hveravellir. In 1917 the play was turned into a film.

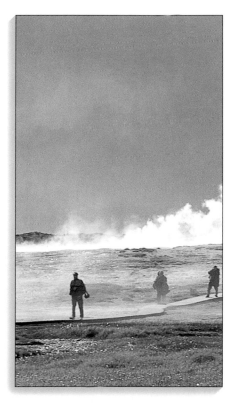

BELOW: crossing steaming ground on a walkway at Hveravellir.

Map on page 314

SPRENGISANDUR AND LANDMANNALAUGAR

The Sprengisandur is the cold desert that is crossed by a rough, barren route ending at the hot springs and colourful mountains of Landmannalaugar

Reykjavik

The route through the Sprengisandur area can be reached in several ways from the north of Iceland. Although it is easier to reach than the Kjölur route, a four-wheel drive is still necessary. There are three main ways to reach the start of the route proper, all of which converge at or near Laugafell at the edge of the Sprengisandur. After making the crossing through the interior the main route reaches the beautiful and remote area around Landmannalaugar, where it is well worth taking the time to go hiking, before continuing down to the south coast.

Reaching the Sprengisandur

The most easterly way into the interior takes Route 842 then F26 through the Bárðardalur valley via Goðafoss. A scraped road soon degrades into a rough track, which climbs past the beautiful waterfall of **Aldeyjarfoss** with its tall basalt columns. On clear days there are spectacular views across the Ódáðahraun towards Askja. The shield volcano of Trölladyngja, part of the Gæsavatnaleið route, is clear on the horizon to the south.

BELOW: Aldeyjarfoss with its fast-flowing, milky glacial water.

A more central route on the F821 goes from the end of the Eyjafjörður valley. Passing the abandoned farm of Nýibær, where there used to be a weather station, the road continues to Laugafell. The third, most westerly route to the Sprengisandur is via Route F752 through the Vesturdalur valley which starts in Skagafjörður. The jeep track begins by the farm of Þorljótsstaðir which was abandoned in 1944. The track crosses **Orravatnsrústir**, wet grasslands covered with cottongrass and sedge, around the two lakes of **Reyðarvatn** and **Orravatn**. The area is extremely marshy, with large hillocks covered with low-growing bushes. In the centre of the area is a small hill, **Orrahaugar**, where there is a refuge hut. Shortly before this route joins Route F821 near Laugafell it crosses the river **Austari Jökulsá**, a huge glacial river fed by several streams and rivers from the Hofsjökull glacier. The river used to be a great obstacle to those travelling this route, but there is now a bridge at **Austurbugur**.

A cold desert

At **Laugafell** ❺, on a ridge leading northwest from the mountain of the same name (890 metres/2,900 ft) there are several warm springs, which reach 40–50°C (104–120°F), and a warm bathing pool. Various kinds of grass flourish around the springs. Close to the tourist hut, which was built in 1948, there is a small trough, most likely man-made, containing warm water. According to an old story a woman named Þórunn, daughter of Jón Arason, Iceland's last Catholic bishop, brought her family to stay here in the 15th century during the Black Death, and made the pool with her own hands. Near Laugafell the gravel expanse of the **Sprengisandur** truly begins with magnificent vistas eastwards to **Vatnajökull** and the smaller icecap of **Tungnafellsjökull** and westwards to Hofsjökull. A number of river crossings later, the blue tongues of glaciers come into view. A track forking to the east leads off the gravel plain to **Gæsavötn**, a small yellow-green oasis and crystal-clear lake amid the dark dramatic landscape. Beyond lie the Gæsavatnaleið and Askja routes.

At **Nýidalur** ❻, close to the geographical centre of Iceland, stand several huts – invariably a welcome sight. There is a small campsite on the only patch of green in the area, but even in the middle of summer high winds and near-freezing temperatures make camping a desperate option. The better choice is to stay in the huts which offer both warmth and hospitality. Wardened during the summer months, they have occasionally been cut off for a few hours by snow and bad weather. But, whatever the climate outside, the atmosphere inside these huts is always congenial, with travellers habitually swapping tales and sharing food. The next stop on the route is shortly after the mountain of **Kistualda** (790 metres/2,600 ft) which offers panoramic views. There is a petrol station and a cosy little coffee-shop at **Versalir** where one can get delicious home-made Icelandic waffles.

The dusty track south to **Þórisvatn** ❼ (Iceland's second largest lake) continues the landscape of glaciers and black gravel plains. Just beyond the lake and on the main track is the tiny settlement of **Hrauneyjafoss**, where there is a petrol station, a coffee-shop

BELOW: hills reflected in a lake near Landmannalaugar.

A motorcyclist at a crossroads on the Sprengisandur.

and a small guest-house. With the development of new hydroelectric schemes several lakes, not shown on all maps, can be seen close to the fork in the main track southeastwards to Landmannalaugar.

After a relative absence of vehicles, there is a steady increase in traffic south of Hrauneyjafoss en route to Landmannalaugar. The greatest change here is in the colour of the scenery. Instead of the dark Sprengisandur gravel, gaudy green mosses now coat the ancient rhyolitic rocks. The hills are bright yellow, green and red, dotted with deep blue lakes, creamy brown outwash plains and snow patches lying on grey Rhacometrium mosses. Shortly before Landmannalaugar a side road to the east leads to the edge of **Ljótipollur** (the "ugly puddle"), a picturesque explosion crater which has colourful sides and some greenish water at the bottom.

Exploring Landmannalaugar

Hot springs form the nucleus of **Landmannalaugar** ❽, and steam rises from every corner of the valley. Volcanic activity in the last 10,000 years has been restricted to a few northeast to southwest fissures. The youngest, the **Veiðivötn** fissure, created lava formations and other craters, including Ljótipollur, extending about 30 km (21 miles) to the north.

This is a popular centre for tourists and there are several camping areas but in midsummer the main site near to the hot pools, used for swimming, tends to become crowded. Landmannalaugar lies near the outskirts of the **Torfajökull** volcanic district. Warm and cold springs at the foot of the lava flows make it a true "paradise in the desert". **Laugahraun**, the lava above the tourist hut, was deposited in a relatively recent eruption, probably at the end of the 15th century.

BELOW: natural patterns in the Fjallabak Nature Reserve.

The streams of geothermal and spring water, coming from under the lava-wall, mix to make streams and pools of an ideal temperature for bathing. There are trout in most of the lakes around Landmannalaugar, including Ljótipollur and Frostastaðavatn. Arctic char have also been added to some lakes in the area.

Landmannalaugar is a part of the **Fjallabak Nature Reserve** and forms a good base for the many walks in the area. With the cold climate and frequent sandstorms, vegetation is scarce, although least willow grows on the dry sands and lava, and cotton grass in the marshes.

The bedrock of Fjallabak dates back about 8–10 million years. The volcanoes in the area have been most active in the last 2 million years, during the last Ice Age. The varying and delicate colours of the mountain peaks that predominate in Fjallabak are due to their composition of rhyolitic rock. Interglacial rhyolite lava can be found in **Brandsgil**, which is only about an hour's walk from the hut at Landmannalaugar. Other popular hikes are to the summit of **Bláhnúkur** (940 metres/3,100 ft), formed by sub-glacial rhyolites (erupted under ice or water), and to the fumaroles of **Brennisteinsalda** – these walks take between one and two hours each. Sub-glacial activity has also produced some hyalo-clastite ("móberg") mountains such as **Loðmundur** and **Mógilshöfðar**.

Slightly longer walks in the area include a five or six hour hike to the summit of **Háalda** (1,090 metres/3,600 ft) and a walk around Frostastaðavatn taking two to three hours. The major trek in this area is down to Þórsmörk in the Southwest, which takes four or five days if you are reasonably fit. It is best attempted only between mid-July and early September. The scenery encompasses lava flows, rhyolite hills and spectacular views over glaciers. Along the way there are overnight huts at Hrafntinnusker, Álftavatn and Emstrur.

Map on page 314

TIP

If you want to try your hand at fishing while in Landmannalaugar, permits are available from the warden in the tourist hut.

LEFT:
a rainbow over Landmannalaugar.
BELOW:
patterns formed by lichens at Landmannalaugar.

Map on page 314

Returning to the coast

Travellers are faced with several routes from Landmannalaugar. It is possible to take a track southwestwards on Routes 26 or 32 to join up eventually with the Ring Road near the south coast. Perhaps the most dramatic, however, is southeast to **Bláfjall** and eventually the coast. Although improved, the track here still provides adventure in the form of numerous river crossings, many of which require long periods of wading down the rivers to check their depth. Again only four-wheel drives should attempt these crossings due to the depth of the water and the possibility of quicksand.

Before Bláfjall there is a track off to the gorge and waterfall of **Eldgjá ❾** (the "Fire Fissure"). Eldgjá is the most extensive explosion fissure in the world. It is a 40-km (25-mile) long volcanic rift, reaching from the Mýrdalsjökull glacier to the mountain **Gjátindur** (950 metres/3,100 ft). The most impressive part is the northern end, where it measures 600 metres (2,000 ft) wide and 200 metres (660 ft) deep. A part of it is supposed to have been formed in a violent basalt eruption around AD 934. There are indications that the fissure is related to the volcano Katla, which is under the ice of Mýrdalsjökull glacier.

Cascading into the rift is the famous waterfall of **Ófærufoss**. It used to have a much-photographed natural arch of basaltic rock which formed a footpath over the lower cascades. The arch, which featured in the Icelandic film *In the Shadow of the Raven*, has since collapsed due to heavy snow and flooding. The hilly region around Bláfjall is a popular walking area. Ancient lava flows are carpeted with mosses and lichens, while innumerable streams and small waterfalls pour out of rocky fissures only to disappear again under broken lava and cushions of moss. ❑

Characteristic reddish volcanic rock at Eldgjá.

BELOW:
camping out in Landmannalaugar.

Flowers among the Lava

Most unfairly, Iceland is often called "barren". True enough, it's hardly a riot of flowers, fields and forests from coast to coast – in fact, well over half the country's area is wasteland. Visitors arriving at Keflavík Airport often think they could be on the moon when they look out on the treeless lava fields and the dark mountain slopes beyond. This impression is, however, misleading. While Iceland has next to no trees (a waggish visitor once remarked, "if you're lost in an Icelandic forest, stand up"), there is plenty of compensation. Mosses, lichens and flowering plants flourish all over the country. And even in the barest highlands sections, an occasional bloom takes root.

Birch, Iceland's most widespread tree, generally takes the form of a relatively low-growing shrub, often in dense copses and thickets. In the rare locations where it can grow straight and tall, the birch may reach 10–12 metres (30–35 ft). Afforestation efforts have introduced many foreign tree species, particularly evergreens. Some have flourished in their new environment, so mixed glades and woods are seen in many parts of the country today. Iceland's largest forest is at Hallormsstaður, in the east.

Botanists believe that half of Iceland's plant species are survivors of the Ice Age, while around 20 percent have been introduced, deliberately or by chance, since humankind's arrival in the 9th century.

The local vegetation has been characterised as oceanic sub-arctic in character. About one-third of the plant species are of the arctic-alpine type. Many species of sedges and rushes are found in marshes and bogs; cottongrass (common and Schewchzer's), which flourishes in wetlands all over the country, was formerly used to provide wicks for fish-oil lamps which were the main form of lighting.

In addition to its 470 vascular plants (30 of them rare enough to be protected by law), Iceland has no fewer than 500 different mosses and liverworts. Mosses are generally the first plants to take root on lava fields, preparing the ground for later colonisation by grasses, ferns and later trees. One of the most interesting species among Iceland's flora is the misnamed *Bryoxiphium norvegicum*, sword moss. Though named "norvegicum," sword moss has never been found in Norway, and was first identified at Lake Kleifarvatn in 1928. Found in the US, Mexico and parts of Asia, it is unknown elsewhere in Europe.

About 450 lichens and 250 fungi are known in Iceland. Very few of Iceland's mushroom species are harmful to eat (though some do not taste very nice), and none is deadly poisonous, so mushroom-picking is a popular autumn pastime. Courses in mushroom identification are held from time to time, generally culminating in field trips to gather mushrooms under expert supervision.

Berry-bearing plants such as the crowberry, blueberry and bog whortleberry are common on heathlands, and after a good summer they give abundant berries for jam-making. Families often travel out in the autumn into the country in search of the biggest, juiciest berries. ❑

RIGHT: a splash of colour in a lava field.

Map on page 314

●Reykjavík

THE ASKJA ROUTE

The route to the huge Askja caldera takes you through a landscape of contrasts, from jagged black volcanic plains and mountains to yellow pumice, with vistas over Vatnajökull icecap

This track through the interior is more difficult than the Sprengisandur and Kjölur routes, and four-wheel drives are sorely put to the test. Most tracks are marked by yellow poles or cairns of stones and, with reference to good maps, navigation is fairly straightforward.

The track that leads off Route One (the Ring Road) to the east of Lake Mývatn is marked by several makeshift signs warning against two-wheel drive vehicles attempting to go any further. The track travels for some 64 km (39 miles), following close to the glacial river **Jökulsá á Fjöllum**, before reaching the mountain of Herðubreið. To begin with, the view west across the Ódáðahraun plain is quite intimidating. A flat expanse of black gravel and pebbles (called *grjot* in Icelandic), which is made up from the country's largest lava flow, stretches almost to the horizon.

The going is hard due to the severe corrugations in the track. A small range of black hills has to be negotiated, giving from the summit a spectacular view of the Jökulsá – a vast braided glacial river. Patches of black sand become more frequent with pockets of stabilising lyme grass. In this desert, few plants survive. The ancient and twisted frames of dwarf willow are testimony to the harshness of the environment. Among the dark gravel lie balls of primordial-looking grey

BELOW: reindeer crossing barren ground in the interior.

lichens. Under stones protected from the wind sit small brown moths, barely moving, the only visible sign of animal life.

The track twists and turns eventually towards the edge of the River **Lindaá**, a tributary of the Jökulsá. This is the first major river crossing and along the river banks are great carpets of the pink-flowered arctic river beauty, contrasting against the black sand.

A black landscape

The track undulates considerably for the next 20 km (12 miles) as it climbs and descends an extensive lava field. The bare rock is covered at times with patches of sand and pumice. The mountain of **Herðubreið** ❿ gradually comes to dominate the view as it rises some 1,060 metres (3,500 ft) above the surrounding plain. On a cloudy day the upper reaches of Herðubreið are often hidden from view, which only adds to the mountain's gloomy splendour.

For centuries Herðubreið was held to be impossible to climb. The first attempt was made by the English traveller Richard F. Burton in 1872. Accompanied by a local farmer from the Mývatn-area, Burton had to turn around, because of rockfalls, shortly before they reached the top. First to get to the top of the mountain were the German geologist Hans Reck and the Icelander Sigurður Sumarliðason in 1908. Those who intend to climb the mountain should contact the warden in the hut at **Herðubreiðarlindir**, in order to get thorough information about the best route.

Herðubreiðarlindir is a wonderful oasis in the middle of black sands and lava fields. It is rich in vegetation and water springs, which appear from under the lava. In the lava, ruins of an ingeniously fashioned shelter made by the 18th-century outlaw Fjalla-Eyvindur can be found. He spent one winter here, which was, according to him, the worst time of his long exile, since he had no warm water and was forced to live on raw horse-meat all winter long. The Jökulsá á Fjöllum nearby becomes a violent glacial torrent, creamy brown with rock flour and running between banks of dark lava.

At both Herðubreið and Askja there are basic tourist huts as well as campsites. The latter are very primitive and expensive, with wardens present for only six weeks in the middle of summer – tents have to be pegged into the pumice and the only flattened area doubles as an airstrip.

The journey from Herðubreið to Askja is another 35 km (21 miles), much of which is across the yellow pumice fields of **Vikursandur**. The soft honey-combed segments of pumice, originally produced by the eruption of Víti in 1875, have been blown by the wind into small yellow dunes, contrasting with the dark block lava beneath. Storms in this area can make travelling very hazardous.

To the north of Askja lies the centre of the vast **Ódáðahraun** ("ill deeds lava field") which, at over 3,000 sq. km (1,080 sq. miles), is the world's largest. This vast area remained unexplored for centuries and was thus seen as mysterious, giving rise to tales of extensive outlaw settlements. Organized travel and exploration did not begin until the early 19th century.

Herðubreið aptly means "broad-shouldered": it is a great flat-topped block of sheer-sided palagonite rock thrusting up out of a skirt of vast scree slopes.

BELOW: the snowy summit and steep, ridged sides of Herðubreið.

A forbidding caldera

Mount Askja **⓫** is not the neat cone that it appears on the horizon. Seen from closer up, it is a 45 sq. km (16 sq. mile) caldera of black lava, cream pumice screes and white snow. Low cloud often clings around the summit, which is located amid the sprawling **Dyngjufjöll** massif. A narrow track winds around the base of Askja, through the **Öskjuop** pass to a small parking area. A walk leads through the outer walls of Askja into the huge crater, where the great jagged **Vikraborgir** lava field was created as recently as 1961. A deep inner crater is partially flooded with steaming water and marks the site of the 1875 eruption.

Reindeer are relatively common in the interior, though often hard to spot

Öskjuvatn, a lake several kilometres across, is the deepest in Iceland at 217 metres (715 ft). The water of the lake has collected in a deep depression that developed following a tremendous volcanic explosion in the Askja caldera in 1875. This eruption was the first in the Dyngjufjöll mountains that was subjected to scientific research. At the beginning of 1875 powerful and consistent earthquake shocks were felt in the surrounding area. At the same time an increasing volcanic cloud was seen over the mountains. Four men from the Mývatn district then took it upon themselves to venture in the middle of the winter south to Dyngjufjöll, where they discovered craters in the southeastern corner of Askja. They found three slag cones, two of them active, little or no new lava, but the ground had subsided a good deal, and deep cracks had developed in the vicinity of the craters. After the men returned, the eruptions continued and came to a climax at Easter. Then there was an enormous volcanic explosion that spread a thick layer of grey pumice over a great part of the eastern countryside, devasting many farmsteads and damaging others. This explosion has been traced to the Víti crater, but others in the area were probably also active at the same time.

BELOW: Víti crater lake in the foreground, and Öskjuvatn behind.

Map on page 314

First to arrive at Askja after the eruption was an Englishman, W.L.Watts, accompanied by two guides. The same spring Watts had trekked across the Vatnajökull icecap, reaching Askja on 14 July. He discovered a deep depression with a circumference of about 8 km (5 miles), and down in it gaping fissures and seething hot springs, spewing steam and water high into the air. A black column of smoke was rising out of the Víti crater, scattering clay dust in all directions. Because of the tremendous volume of smoke, it was difficult for Watts and his guides to get a clear viewof the crater. Throughout the summer of 1875 there were considerable outburts in Askja, causing volcanic dust or ash to fall in the nearest rural districts.

Several travellers, most of them Englishmen, visited Askja during the following decades. In the early 20th century, German scientists began making expeditions into the area. One of the first was the Knebel expedition of 1907, which came to a tragic end. Two members of the expedition, Walter von Knebel and Max Rudloff, disappeared, and were probably drowned in the lake, for their companion, Spetmann, who was collecting samples in a different part of the mountains, found no trace of his friends. The next year, 1908, Knebel's fiancée, Ina von Grumbkow went to Askja, accompanied by the geologist Hans Reck. Their attempts to throw light upon the disappearance of Knebel and Rudloff proved fruitless.

The last eruption of Askja began at the end of October 1961 and lasted for a little more than three months. The lava flowed from five craters, now named Vikraborgir, covering a great part of Öskjuop, the entrance to the caldera.

Onward from Askja

From the route between Herðubreiðarlindir and Askja there is a signposted side track to the magnificent **Kverkfjöll** ⑫ ("Nook Mountains") at the northern edge of Vatnajökull. Close to the centre of the range is the second highest volcano in Iceland, rising to 1,860 metres (6,102 ft). It is split from north to south by a steep and rugged glacier named **Kverkjökull**, which has burrowed out a deep valley, leading to an almost entirely ice-filled caldera. Kverkfjöll has erupted several times in recorded history, although it is less notable for its volcanic activity than for its geothermal nature. A valley named **Hveradalur** ("hot spring valley") cuts southwestwards into the mountains at a height of 1,600 metres (5,250 ft). The traveller who hikes into the valley will be rewarded with the entire spectrum of yellow, red and green nuances that characterise *solfatara* areas. Vapours rise everywhere from fumaroles and bubbling mud pits, and in the northeast where the valley is at its narrowest, it is almost blocked off by vapours from the largest vent. The valley is more than half-way surrounded by a brilliant white névé glacier, and at its southwest end there is an oval lake with greenish-blue ice walls. On a clear day, there is a magnificent view over the wasteland of Ódáðahraun and to the mountains rising up above the high plateau. Beautiful ice caves have also been discovered in the area. A tourist hut can be found north of Kverkfjöll, and another one high in the mountains. ❏

The 1875 eruption of Mount Askja was a major cause of the emigration of thousands of Icelanders to North America.

BELOW: view to Dyngjujökull from Kverkjökull.

Map on page 314

● Reykjavík

THE GÆSAVATNALEIÐ ROUTE

Although this is one of the hardest routes in the interior, and only for the more adventurous and well-equipped, the rewards are spectacular in the form of solitude and wild landscapes

Running southwest from Askja there is a hazardous track, connecting the Askja route with the more westerly one that runs through the Sprengisandur. Known as the Gæsavatnaleið route, it passes very close to Vatnajökull, the largest icecap in Iceland. This 120-km (72-mile) track from Askja to Tómasarhagi was immortalised in Desmond Bagley's thriller *Running Blind*. The way that the book's hero Alan Stewart drove in his Land-Rover has changed little since then except for the bridging of the River Tungnaá at the end. It may be difficult, but at least you're unlikely to have a hail of bullets at your back, as Stewart had.

Since this route is particularly hard going in places, it is essential to have a tough four-wheel-drive vehicle with an experienced driver. It should take about four or five hours from start to finish. Spring meltwater brings a flood from the Vatnajökull icecap and, with it, black volcanic sand. This outwash plain runs for many kilometres towards Askja and offers the first major obstacle on the track. Late on warm summer days and after heavy rain meltwater comes roaring out of Dyngjujökull creating wide rivers that flow all over the sands east of Urðarháls, an old glaciated volcano. These rivers are called Síðdegisflæður ("Evening morasses") and can be dangerous for all motor vehicles – avoid them

BELOW: a plane flies over the deep crevasses of the Vatnajökull icecap.

at times when water levels are likely to be high. Marked at intervals with yellow poles, the track reaches the icecap at the forbidding black glacier of **Dyngjujökull ⓭**. Close inspection reveals that the ice is covered in black volcanic ash. Up above is the tuff mountain **Kistufell** (1,450 metres/4,750 ft). In September 1950 the Icelandic aircraft "Geysir" crash-landed on Bárðarbunga in Vatnajökull. The famous and successful rescue operation had its headquarters on Kistufell.

A bleak stretch of road

Navigation becomes more treacherous as the route crosses the difficult boulder-strewn sides of **Trölladyngja**, the greatest shield volcano in Iceland, measuring 10 km (6 miles) in diameter and rising to about 600 m (2,000 ft) above the surrounding area. Lava flows from Trölladyngja are thought to have run all the way down to the Bárðardalur valley, which comes out on the north coast, just to the east of Akureyri. The weather here can be cold and wretched, and blizzards are commonplace in summer. Yet the solitude of this wilderness is awe-inspiring.

After hours of slow driving across block lava spewed out by a succession of volcanic craters, the track emerges above a ridge of cairns high on the edge of the Mid-Atlantic Ridge that runs through Iceland. Below lies the Sprengisandur, the vast gravel plain sandwiched between the icecaps of Hofsjökull and Vatnajökull. This is also where the meltwater from the icecaps collects in a succession of rivers, many of which are bisected by the track.

The Gæsavatnaleið route ends at the small oasis of **Tómasarhagi ⓮**, with a junction of braided rivers, beneath the glacier **Tungnafellsjökull** which reaches 1,540 metres (5,050 ft). ❑

Tómasarhagi oasis was first found by the clergyman Tómas Sæmundsson in 1835. According to his description, there was considerably more vegetation there at that time that there is today.

BELOW: glacial streams flowing through black volcanic deposits. **FOLLOWING PAGE:** spectacular Gullfoss waterfall.

INSIGHT GUIDES
Travel Tips

Insight FlexiMaps

Maps in Insight Guides are tailored to complement the text. But when you're on the road you sometimes need the big picture that only a large-scale map can provide. This new range of durable Insight Fleximaps has been designed to meet just that need.

Detailed, clear cartography
makes the comprehensive route and city maps easy to follow, highlights all the major tourist sites and provides valuable motoring information plus a full index.

Informative and easy to use
with additional text and photographs covering a destination's top 10 essential sites, plus useful addresses, facts about the destination and handy tips on getting around.

Laminated finish
allows you to mark your route on the map using a non-permanent marker pen, and wipe it off. It makes the maps more durable and easier to fold than traditional maps.

The world's most popular destinations
are covered by the 125 titles in the series – and new destinations are being added all the time. They include Alaska, Amsterdam, Bangkok, Barbados, Beijing, Brussels, Dallas/Fort Worth, Florence, Hong Kong, Ireland, Madrid, New York, Orlando, Peru, Prague, Rio, Rome, San Francisco, Sydney, Thailand, Turkey, Venice, and Vienna.

INSIGHT GUIDES
The world's largest collection of visual travel guides

CONTENTS

Getting Acquainted

The Place

Area: 103,000 sq. km (39,750 sq. miles). Europe's second largest island.
Capital: Reykjavík.
Largest Geographical Feature: Vatnajökull, a plateau icecap, is 8,300 sq. km (3,200 sq. miles) in area, equivalent to all of continental Europe's glaciers combined.
Population: 283,000, of which 175,000 reside in the greater Reykjavík area.
Language: Icelandic, a very pure descendant of Old Norse.
Religion: 90 percent of Icelanders belong to the Lutheran Church, with the remaining 10 percent divided up among various denominations. About 1 percent of is Roman Catholic.
Time Zone: Iceland is on Greenwich Mean Time (GMT) throughout the year. In winter: same time as London, 5 hours ahead of New York. In summer: 1 hour behind London, 4 hours ahead of New York.
Currency: The Icelandic króna (ISK); in April 2002 the exchange rate was approximately ISK136 to the pound sterling and 94 to the US dollar.
Weights and Measures: Metric.
Electricity: 220 volts alternating at 50 cycles. Visitors from the US will need to use a transformer. Two-pin plugs are the norm, so take a universal adapter.
International Dialling Code: To call Iceland from overseas, dial +354 then the seven-digit phone number without area code.

Climate

Influenced by the warm Gulf Stream and prevailing southwesterly winds,

Weather Information

The Icelandic Meteorological Office provides recorded weather bulletins in English; tel: 902 0600, then choose 44 on a touch tone phone (this service is not available from all phones). For a weather forecast on the internet (in English), go to www.vedur.is

Iceland's temperate oceanic climate is surprisingly mild for the latitude (63–66°N). Reykjavík's average January temperature is similar to that of Hamburg, -0.5°C (31°F), though the July average is a cool 11°C (52°F). Because the Gulf Stream influences the south and west of the country, there are marked regional differences in climate. This is due also to the prevailing winds and the position of mountain ranges.

The north, east and interior experience colder winter temperatures but warmer summers, and markedly less precipitation. The south side of Vatnajökull can see up to 10 times the annual 400 mm (16 inches) of rain of those areas north of the glacier. This is quite evident in the vegetation cover on lava flows. In the northeast, lava dating back thousands of years is still bare, while in the south of the country a

The People of Iceland

With just 283,000 inhabitants, Iceland ranks among the least densely populated nations in the world. Around 175,000 people live in Reykjavík and the surrounding area; the remainder are scattered around the country in smaller towns (the largest, Akureyri, has only 15,000 inhabitants), villages and farms. The principal farming districts are the lowland plains of the south and west, the valleys of the north and the area around Egilsstaðir in the east. The steep-sided mountains of the fjord country offer little level land for farming, but have excellent sheltered harbours supporting

200-year-old flow is covered with thick spongy moss.

Whatever the weather, you are likely to experience Iceland's most ubiquitous natural element – wind. The Icelandic language allows for at least eight different degrees of wind, from *logn* (calm) to *rok* (strong gale), and you can expect to encounter most of them during your stay. Finding shelter is not generally a problem in the settled lowlands but for the hiker or cyclist, a storm in the central highland deserts or glacial outwash plains may mean hours, even days, of unimaginable misery. The soil whipped up by such winds can blot out the sun, covering the land in a brown haze.

Government

Since proclaiming full independence from Denmark in 1944, Iceland has been an independent republic with parliamentary rule. The Icelandic parliament has 63 members, elected for a term of four years on a system of proportional representation. The voting age is 18. The country is divided into 8 constituencies, with 27 district commissioner offices. In addition there are 124 municipalities (*sveitarfélög*), a number that has been declining in the recent past due to mergers between two or

many of Iceland's fishing villages. Icelanders are the least Nordic of the Scandinavian peoples. According to research there is a stronger Celtic element than was once believed, but the exact percentage has yet to be established. Immigration is strictly controlled and foreigners are encouraged to integrate. Migration from the country districts and villages to Reykjavík continues at a rate of 3–5 percent. Life expectancy in Iceland is among the highest in the world, attributed to a low infant-mortality rate, a fish-based diet and excellent health care.

more municipalities. Since 1944, no political party has attained an absolute majority in parliament and with few exceptions all of Iceland's governments have been coalitions of the larger and sometimes smaller parties.

At the fore of the political spectrum is the Independence Party (Sjálfstæðisflokkur), with a fusion of conservative and liberal ideals, and the Progressive Party (Framsóknarflokkur), rooted in the co-operative movement and farming communities. These are the largest parties, and have 26 and 12 elected MPs respectively. The socialist Alliance (Samfylkingin) and the Left Green Movement (Vinstri grænir) have 17 and six elected MPs respectively, while the Liberal Party (Frjálslyndi flokkurinn), catering mainly to Iceland's fishing community, has two elected MPs. The next Alþingi elections are in 2003.

Iceland's head of state is a democratically elected president, serving a four-year term of office. Unless opposed, a president is normally re-elected for another term. Dr Ólafur Ragnar Grímsson was elected President of the Republic in 1996 and was automatically re-elected in 2000.

Economy

Iceland's economy is heavily dependent on fish, its principal export. Although employing only 11 percent of the workforce, fish and fish products make up nearly three quarters of export earnings of goods. A national fleet of some 1,000 vessels, ranging from small boats to the most modern of stern trawlers, brings in the annual catch of around 2 million tonnes. Cod is the most valuable catch for export followed by redfish, capelin and shrimp. Other species include haddock, saithe and lobster.

In a country lacking natural resources, diversification of exports is difficult. Iceland does, however, have huge tapped and untapped potential for hydro-electric power generation. A number of viable schemes have been developed and

Public Holidays

- **January** New Year's Day/Nýársdagurinn (1st).
- **March/April** Maundy Thursday, Good Friday, Easter Monday; First Day of Summer/Sumardagurinn fyrsti (third or fourth Thursday in April).
- **May** Labour Day (1st); Ascension (sixth Thursday after Easter); Whitsun (eighth Monday after Easter).
- **June** Independence Day (17th).
- **August** Verslunnarmannahelgi (first Monday).
- **December** Christmas Day (25th), Boxing Day (26th). Christmas Eve and New Year's Eve are half-day holidays.

the government aims to attract power-intensive industry from abroad. Two such industries, a large aluminium plant and ferro-silicon works, were built in the 1970s, just outside Reykjavík. Another large aluminium smelter was fully constructed in 1998 and still others are in the pipeline.

Other significant exports are equipment for the fishing industry, diatomite, and in recent years, software for various industries. Although unable to compete on the export market, Iceland is self-sufficient in meat and dairy produce. Woollen goods, skins and leather garments are the principal contribution to exports from the farming sector. Icelandic salmon and lamb have also been introduced onto foreign markets with promising results.

Planning the Trip

When to Visit

Summer

Summer in Iceland is a brief affair. By June the lowlands are snow-free and the land bursts into colour. Between mid-May and the end of July there is almost perpetual daylight. July signals the opening of the highland routes and travellers take to their vehicles in a frenzy of activity. By mid-August the nights are cooler, the long hours of daylight tail off and the tourist season draws to a rapid close.

Mid-June to mid-August, the high tourist season, sees the warmest, though not necessarily the best, weather. Most people visit at this time and accommodation can be hard to find. However, if you travel off the beaten track, you will still find plenty of open space.

The first half of June and last two weeks in August see less tourist traffic and often have fine weather, though nights can be chilly. Most campsites, summer hotels, tours and excursions only operate from June to the end of August. This may, however, soon change, as the growing number of tourists may stretch the season by as much as a month at either end.

For birds and flowers the first half of summer is undoubtedly better, but if you want to get into the highlands don't travel before mid-July. You can catch the midnight sun in June in the north of Iceland but the northern lights do not start to appear until the cooler and darker nights of late August.

Autumn

The first of September signals the end of summer and many tourist operations start winding down. The weather starts to get cooler at that time, the days become shorter, and many of those who work in the travel business during the summer go back to school. The Edda chain of hotels are boarding schools during the winter, so they have to return to their normal operations.

However, farms and other hotels will welcome business and if you have brought a tent, camping presents no problems. Many of the highland routes are passable with care throughout September – the added dimension of autumn colours and a dusting of snow on the mountain ranges making this one of the most beautiful months.

Winter

Reykjavík is increasingly gaining popularity as a winter break destination, and a number of tour operators offer bargain packages out of season. Hotels, most museums and some excursions operate all year in Reykjavík. If you are prepared to take a chance with the weather, Iceland in winter has its own rewards for independent travellers. Some bus routes and all flights operate all year round but schedules can be severely disrupted by weather. If you plan to hire a vehicle in winter, a four-wheel drive is a must; car rental firms and hotels have special winter rates.

Some tour operators offer winter activity holidays with travel by jeep, snowmobile or on cross-country skis *(see Tour Operators, page 335).*

Entry Regulations

The normal entry stamp in your passport is valid for a stay of up to three months. You may be asked to produce evidence of funds to support yourself and an air or ferry ticket out of the country. Icelandair offices abroad are not allowed to sell one-way tickets to non-residents unless in conjunction with a return ferry ticket. If you wish to extend your stay after arrival, this can be done at the main police station in Reykjavík, at Hverfisgata 115, or at police stations around the country.

Tourist Offices Abroad

USA: tel: 212-885 9700, fax: 212-885 9710. Mailing address is PO Box 4649, Grand Central Station, New York 10163-4649

There is no tourist office in the UK; for information on the internet, visit www.icetourist.is

If you intend to work in Iceland, you will need a pre-arranged job and a residence and work permit which your prospective employer applies for before you enter the country. Residents of the European Economic Area (EEA states) may stay in Iceland for up to three months without having an air or ferry ticket out of the country and may also look for work.

Residents of the following countries may enter Iceland using their personal identity card: Austria, Belgium, France, Germany, Italy, Liechtenstein, Luxembourg, The Netherlands and Switzerland.

Angling gear that has been used outside Iceland, including boots and waders, must be disinfected by a vet before being taken into the country. You may be asked to produce a certificate stating that this has been done. Your equipment can be disinfected on arrival at your own expense.

It is forbidden to introduce any animal into Iceland without permission from the Ministry of Agriculture. A lengthy period of quarantine is invariably required for all animals. The British Foot and Mouth Disease crisis of 2001 resulted in strict regulations, especially for travellers from the UK. At the time of publication things were returning to normal.

Customs

Visitors aged 20 and over are allowed to bring in 1 litre of spirits up to 47 percent alcohol content and 1 litre of wine up to 21 percent alcohol content. Six litres of foreign beer or 8 litres of domestic beer may be brought in instead of either

the wine or spirit allowance.

Visitors aged 18 and over may bring in 200 cigarettes or 250 grams of tobacco. As alcohol is expensive, it is worth bringing your full allowance. If you do not use it yourself, it will make a very welcome gift.

You may bring in 3kg of food up to the value of ISK4,000 free of duty, but the import of uncooked eggs, raw milk products and uncooked meat, including salami, bacon and uncooked ham, is prohibited.

Money Matters

The monetary unit is the Icelandic króna (plural krónur), divided into 100 aurar. Notes are in denominations of ISK5,000, 2,000, 1,000 and 500. Coins are in denominations of ISK100, 50, 10, 5 and 1. In April 2002 the exchange rate was ISK140 to the pound sterling, ISK98 to the US dollar.

You can bring in unlimited foreign currency in the form of travellers' cheques or bank notes and up to ISK14,000 in Icelandic currency. It is generally not worth purchasing large amounts of Icelandic króna abroad as a poorer rate of exchange is given. Similarly you should change back all unused króna before leaving Iceland (this can be done at the airport departure lounge) and you may need to produce receipts of exchange transactions from foreign currency or travellers' cheques to króna.

Exchange Facilities

The simplest way to obtain Icelandic króna is to find an ATM cash

Banking Hours

Banks are open Mon–Fri 9.15am–4pm, but country branches may have limited opening hours. All banks have a few branches with extended opening hours, particularly in shopping malls such as Kringlan. All offer foreign exchange services.

Lost Credit Cards

In case of loss you can cancel your credit cards as follows:
Visa, Álfabakki 16, Reykjavík, tel: 525 2000. Emergency (24 hours): 525 2200. Toll-free number: 800 5252.
MasterCard/EuroCard, Ármúli 28, Reykjavík, tel: 550 1500 (24 hours). Lost or stolen cards: 00 (45) 3673 7373.
American Express, emergency number (toll-free): 800 8111.
Diners Club, Engjateigur 9, Reykjavík, tel: 588 0050. Emergency number (in Denmark): 0045-3673 7373.

machine – plentiful in Reykjavík and other Icelandic towns. Banks will change foreign currency or travellers' cheques – US dollars, sterling, euros and Scandinavian currencies are all easily exchanged. Many hotels, local shops, even roadside restaurants and taxi drivers will accept pounds and US dollars.

Hotels usually exchange travellers' cheques and banknotes for guests, at a rate slightly below the bank rate, depending on the availability of cash in the till.

Outside normal banking hours 24-hour exchange facilities are available at Keflavík Airport:
Landsbankinn on the second level, for departing and arriving passengers; amounts in excess of ISK10,000 are not accepted before 9am and after 5pm weekdays, nor on weekends.
Change Group on the lower level, past customs control. The Change Group also operates an exchange bureau in Reykjavík, at the **Tourist Information Centre** on Bankastræti (open 15 May–15 Sept daily 8.30am–7pm; rest of the year Mon–Sat 9am–5pm).

Credit Cards

Credit cards are used everywhere in Iceland, with the most ubiquitous being Visa and MasterCard/EuroCard. American Express, JCB and Diners are far less common.

Cash advances are available on Visa and MasterCard/EuroCard from all banks, savings banks and automatic cash machines displaying the respective logos. Holders of JCB cards can obtain cash advances from the MasterCard/EuroCard offices at Ármúli 28, Reykjavík. For Diners Club holders this service is available in Reykjavík at Póstgíro, Ármúli 6. At the time of printing, American Express did not have an agent in Iceland.

Debit Cards

Visa, Delta, Maestro/EDC and Electron debit cards are widely accepted. Cash may be obtained against these cards in all banks and automatic cash machines displaying the relevant logos.

VAT refunds

Foreigners making purchases in excess of ISK4,000 are entitled to a partial VAT refund when they leave Iceland. For full details, *see Tax Free Shopping on page 366.*

Health and Insurance

Iceland is a very healthy country. Nonetheless, all visitors should have adequate medical insurance, though an agreement exists between Iceland and the member states of the European Economic Area for limited health insurance coverage of its residents. Travellers from those countries should obtain the necessary E111 forms before leaving home. No vaccinations are required for visitors, unless you are arriving from an infected area. Tap water is perfectly safe to drink.

What to Bring

Iceland is expensive; the 24.5 percent VAT on most goods means that many items are double the price you would pay elsewhere. Bring everything you are likely to need for your stay in the way of clothing, medicine, camera film and other equipment. If you plan to backpack around the country it is worth bringing in your duty-free food allowance (3kg/6.6lb, up to

ISK4,000 in value) in the form of dried foods. Freeze-dried products are very costly and virtually unavailable outside specialist shops in Reykjavík.

Iceland's freak wind gusts have been known to wreak havoc at campgrounds – a summerweight tent will not survive these winds. If you bring your own tent, make sure you are able to repair bent poles, broken guy ropes and holes in canvas. Bring heavy-duty tent pegs; lightweight aluminium pegs may not be enough.

What to Wear

In summer, light woollens or a fleece, and a wind- and rain-proof jacket or coat are essential, along with something for warmer days (wearing layers works best in Iceland's changeable summer weather). If you plan to travel around the country, go walking or head into the uninhabited interior, you must dress accordingly. Your best investment for Iceland will be a quality rain/wind jacket and leggings together with a thick sweater (or a fleece, which will still insulate when wet), scarf, hat and gloves. For footwear, bring a thick-soled pair of walking shoes or trainers. Even if you don't plan to do any serious hiking, a pair of lightweight hiking boots is a good idea – many of Iceland's most visited sights are reached on foot via uneven paths.

Bring swimwear – even the most confirmed non-swimmers will enjoy Iceland's geothermal bathing pools.

Icelanders are very clothes-conscious, reflected in the range of styles in Reykjavík's fashion shops. If you plan to eat out at one of the city's better restaurants, you should dress up. Although most pubs are casual, at clubs it's a jacket and tie for men and no jeans or trainers for either men or women. Most bouncers are relentless in their determination to keep to the rules.

For travel in Iceland between October and May conditions can be severe. Although prolonged cold spells are rare, thanks to the warming effects of the Gulf Stream, temperatures as low as -20°C (-6°F) can occur and, with the wind chill factor, it can feel very much colder than that. So, any visitor planning to travel outside the Reykjavík area in winter must be well kitted out, for example with thermals, a down jacket and a windproof shell jacket and hat.

Photography

Crystal-clear air and long hours of daylight create ideal conditions for photography, and enthusiasts may go through more film than they plan to. Note that you should always use a UV/skylight filter when photographing outdoors. All photographic equipment, film and processing is very expensive (think of a number and double it), so bring your own or purchase it at the Duty Free Shop at the Keflavík airport. If you do have to buy film in Iceland, bear in mind that outside Reykjavík slide film, in particular, may be hard to obtain.

Getting There

BY AIR

All international flights arrive at Keflavík airport, 50km (31 miles) from Reykjavík. After every flight arrival a bus transports passengers to the Hotel Loftleiðir at the domestic airport – about 1.5 km (1 mile) from the centre of Reykjavík; the journey takes about 45 minutes and costs ISK900 (pounds sterling and US dollars accepted); from the Hotel Loftleiðir, minibuses continue to various hotels in Reykjavík.

Icelandair operates regular scheduled flights from Europe and North America to Iceland. Standard prices are around £350 from London (return), although it is usually possible to obtain much cheaper tickets – even in summer it's not difficult to find a return flight from London for less than £200 if booked in advance. Icelandair fares dropped when the low-cost airline Go began operating very reasonably

priced (summer-only) flights from London Stansted to Reykjavík in 2000. However, these have been temporarily suspended; they are expected to resume in the spring of 2003 once the airline's fleet of aircraft has been increased. Contact Go on 0845 607 6543 for information, or visit their website – www.go-fly.com.

Icelandair maintains regular scheduled flights to Iceland year round from London (Heathrow), Glasgow, Paris, Frankfurt, Copenhagen, Oslo, Stockholm, the Faroe Islands, Amsterdam, Boston, New York, Orlando, Baltimore, Minneapolis and Halifax in Canada. From May to September there are flights from Barcelona, Berlin, Hamburg (transfer in Copenhagen), Zürich and Milan.

Flight schedules change regularly; contact the offices below for more information.

Icelandair:
Iceland: Reservations, tel: 50 50 100. Ticket Offices, Hotel Esja, Kringlan (Mall), tel: 50 50 100. www.icelandair.is
UK: 172 Tottenham Court Road, 3rd floor, London W1P 9LG, tel: 020 7874 1000, fax: 020 7387 5711. www.icelandair.co.uk
US: 5950 Symphony Woods Road, Suite 410, Columbia, MD 21044, tel: 1-800-223 5500, fax: 410-715 1600. www.icelandair.com

Stopovers
Icelandair offers a free stopover in Iceland for people travelling between Europe and North America. Maximum stay is 72 hours.

BY SEA

Smyril Line, which is based in the Faroe Islands, offers a weekly car ferry service from mid-May to early September, linking the port of Seyðisfjörður in eastern Iceland with Tórshavn (Faroe Islands), Lerwick (Shetland Islands, UK), Bergen (Norway) and Hanstholm (Denmark). From the UK the service links with P&O sailings between Aberdeen and

Lerwick (14 hours). From Lerwick to Iceland the ferry takes around 32 hours – departing at 2am on Wednesday, stopping at the Faroes between 3 and 6pm on the same day, before arriving at Seyðisfjörður at 9am on Thursday. If you are travelling from Denmark, you should allow plenty of time, as the return journey takes seven days, of which two nights must be spent in the Faroes. Details are available through Smyril Line and P&O offices:
Faroe Islands: J Broncksgøta 37, P.O. Box 370, FO-110 Tórshavn, tel: 298-345 900, fax: 298-345 950. www.smyril-line.fo
Shetland (UK): P&O Scottish Ferries, Holmsgarth Terminal, Lerwick, ZE1 0PR, tel: 01595-695252; fax: 01595 695496. www.poscottishferries.co.uk
Iceland: Norræna Travel, Laugavegur 3, 101 Reykjavík, tel: 562 6362, fax: 552 9450.

If you are planning to bring your car on the ferry, *see "Bringing Your Vehicle" on page 344.*

Tour Operators

A wide range of travel packages are offered by tour operators in Iceland and abroad. Itineraries range from short coach-based sightseeing tours to longer camping tours and activity holidays – including horse-riding, whale-watching, hiking, river rafting, snowmobiling and mountain biking. Those who prefer a roof over their heads but do not mind roughing it a little could try sleeping-bag accommodation holidays. Winter packages offer cross-country skiing, snowmobiling and jeep touring.

Outside main towns with tourist offices, it is worth asking at your hotel for details of local tours. Some operators offer a special service for schools and universities. Local Tourist Offices usually offer sightseeing tours ranging from a morning to several days.

For more detailed information contact the Icelandic Tourist Board or Tourist Information Offices.

Tour Operators in Iceland

Arinbjörn Jóhannsson, Brekkulækur Farm, 431 Hvammstangi, tel: 451 2938, fax: 451 2998, e-mail: brekka@nett.is, website: www.geysir.com/Brekkulaekur. A company offering unique holidays in northwest Iceland. Especially notable are a 10-day Icelandic-style Christmas/New Year celebration and a spring hiking tour in May to observe nature's awakening. Also does horse-riding *(see page 336)*

Austurleið sbs, Kirkjubæjarklaustur, tel: 545 1717, fax: 545 1718, website: www.austurleid.is. Offers a variety of trips to places including Þórsmörk, Landmannalaugar, Skaftafell, Vatnajökull glacier and Jökulsárlón lagoon; bus tours and tailor-made excursions with rural accommodation.

Eldá Travel Service, Bjargi, 660 Reykjahlíð, tel: 464 4220, fax: 464 4321, e-mail: info@elda.is, website: www.elda.is. Based next to Lake Mývatn, Eldá offers a wide variety of tours in the northeast including the "Grand Mývatn Tour", tours to Gjástykki and Dettifoss, and whale-watching. Many run daily during the summer months.

Gudmundur Jónasson Travel, Borgartún 34, Reykjavík, tel: 511 1515, fax: 511 1511, e-mail: gjtravel@gjtravel.is, website: www.gjtravel.is. A diverse variety of tours including horse-riding and river rafting.

Iceland Excursions Allrahanda, Tunahöfði 17, 110 Reykjavík, tel. 540-1313, fax 540-1310, e-mail: allrahanda@allrahanda.is, website: www.allrahanda.is. Day tours from Reykjavík to the southwest of the country, including whale-watching, the Blue Lagoon and glacier tours.

Destination Iceland, Vatnsmírrarvegur 10, 101 Reykjavík, tel: 591-1020, fax: 591-1050, e-mail travel@dice.is, website: www.dice.is. Hotel tours, hiking, camping, ski-trekking excursions, special interest tours, as well as tours tailored to individual group interests.

Iceland Travel Ltd, Lágmúli 4, 128 Reykjavík, tel: 585 4300, fax: 585 4390, e-mail: it@icelandtravel.is, website: www.icelandtravel.is. Well established agency, with a full range of tours to all parts of Iceland – including a variety of adventure tours.

Icelandic Farm Holidays, Síðumúli 13, Reykjavík, tel: 570-2700, fax: 570-2799, e-mail: ifh@farmholidays.is, website: www.farmholidays.is. A variety of tours, including farm holidays and farmhouse accommodation.

Nonni Travel, Brekkugata 5, Akureyri, tel: 461 1841, fax: 461 1843, e-mail: nonni@nonnitravel.is, website www.nonnitravel.is. Offers trips around Akureyri and nearby areas including Mývatn, and Grímsey, by boat or air.

Reykjavík Excursions, Vesturvör 6, 200 Kópavogur, tel: 580-5400, fax: 564-4776, e-mail: main@re.is, website: www.re.is. Organises day trips and sightseeing tours in and around Reykjavík.

Samvinn Travel, Sætún 1, Reykjavík, tel: 569 1010, fax: 569-1095, e-mail; iceland@samvinn.is, website: www.samvinn.is Hotel, sleeping-bag accommodation and camping tours.

Snæland Grímsson, Langholtsvegur 115, 104 Reykjavík, tel: 588 8660, fax: 588 8661, e-mail: snaeland@mmedia.is, website: www.iceland.de/snaeland/home.htm IHiking tours, group tours, day excursions, winter excursions, jeep safaris and more.

Sælubúið Travel Service, Hvolsvöllur, tel: 487 8781, fax: 487 8782, e-mail: njala@islandia.is, website: www.islandia.is/njala. Offers guided two-day tours through the sites of Njáls Saga, one of the best-known Icelandic Sagas, in the south of the country.

Westman Island Tours (Ferðaþjónusta Vestmannaeyjar), Brekastíg 11, Vestmannaeyjar, tel: 481 1909, fax: 481 1927, e-mail: gmtours@eyjar.is, website: http://eyjar.is/~gmtours/. Offers tours around Vestmannaeyar by boat and bus.

Adventure Tours

A number of tour operators specialise in adventure tourism, such as river rafting, glacier tours, kayaking, winter excursions and mountain climbing. Many larger tour operators may also offer such trips as part of their regular programme.

Activity Tours, Vegamót, 560 Varmahlíð, tel. 453 8383, fax: 453 8384, e-mail: hestaact@isholf.is, website: www.rafting.is. White-water rafting in the Skagafjörður region of north Iceland. Three rivers, graded according to difficulty.

Add Ice Travel, Tangarhöfði 7, 112 Reykjavík, tel: 577 5500, fax: 577 5511, e-mail: addice@addice.is, website: www.addice.is. Individual/ group tours, expeditions. Snowmobile and jeep safaris, glacier tours including popular seafood buffet on a glacier, helicopter tours, river rafting etc.

Terra Nova, Stangarhylur 3a, 110 Reykjavík, tel: 567-8545, fax: 587-0036, e-mail: info@terranova.is, website: www.terranova.is. Organises adventure tours for both individuals and groups.

Blue Biking, Stokkjarhvammur 60, 220 Hafnarfjörður, Iceland, tel: 565 2089, e-mail: bluebiking@simnet.is. Made-to-measure bicycle tours, designed to suit your needs. All the necessary equipment is provided.

Glacier Tours, Alfaheidi 1E, 200 Kopavogur, tel/fax: 564 6452, e-mail: vatnajokull@vatnajokull.com, website: www.vatnajokull.com. Snowmobiling onto the Vatnajökull ice-cap, seafood buffet on the glacier for groups, and sailings on Jökulsárlón glacial lagoon. Protective gear provided.

Icelandic Superjeep Safari, Fosshals 17–25, 110 Reykjavík, tel: 552-4200, fax: 552-4202, e-mail: info@jeepsafari.is, website: www.jeepsafari.is. Jeep tours combined with hiking, snow scooting, ice climbing and more. Designed for fit people of all ages; small groups and relaxed ambience. Their pride and joy is a Hummer jeep, which seats nine people. There is no minimum number for group tours.

Icelandic Mountain Guides
(Íslenskir Fjallaleiðsögumenn),
Vagnhofdi 7b, 110 Reykjavík, tel:
587 9999, fax: 587 9996, e-mail:
guide@simnet.is, website:
www.solver.is/guide. An association
of mountain and trekking guides
with years of experience, which
offers tours with a difference. Also
custom tours for individuals and
groups.
Mountaineers of Iceland,
Langholtsvegur 115, 104 Reykjavík,
tel: 581 3800, fax: 581 3810.
Offers super-jeep tours off the
beaten track.
Öræfaferðir, Hofsnes-Öræfi, 785
Fagurhólsmýri, tel: 478 1682,
fax: 478 1682. Located in south
Iceland, specialising in glacier and
coastal tours. Bird watching, ascent
onto Hvanndalshnúkur, Iceland's
highest mountain, ski
mountaineering expedition, ice
climbing and more.

Horse-Riding Tours

The Icelandic horse is a delightful
creature: small, sturdy, sure-footed
and good-natured. It also has five
different gaits, including the *tölt*, a
fast, smooth trot. Since the 1980s
the Icelandic horse has been
gaining in popularity throughout the
world and many foreign Icelandic-
horse lovers come to Iceland
especially to be able to ride the
horse in its natural environment.
Besides, experiencing Iceland on
horseback is utterly exhilarating. A
number of tour operators specialise
in horse-riding tours of long or short
duration.
Arinbjörn Jóhannsson, Brekkulækur
Farm, 531 Hvammstangi, tel: 451
2938, fax: 451 2998, e-mail:
brekka@nett.is, website:
www.geysir.com/Brekkulaekur.
Based in the northwest of Iceland. A
variety of longer and shorter horse-
riding tours, including winter
excursions to observe the northern
lights and starry night sky.
Eldhestar (Volcano Horses), Vellir,
Ölfus, P.O. Box 90, 810 Hveragerði,
tel: 483 4884, fax: 486 5577, e-
mail: info@eldhestar.is, website:
www.eldhestar.is. Offers short and

long riding tours, riding camps,
lessons, and special holidays
including tours to the National
Equestrian Meets.
Íshestar (Icelandic Riding Tours),
Sörlaskeið 26, 220 Hafnarfjörður,
tel: 555 7000, fax: 555 7001, e-
mail: info@ishestar.is, website:
www.ishestar.is. Íshestar organises
diverse riding tours of various
lengths, including visits to the
annual sheep round-up, driving
herds of horses, and historical
trekking routes across the beautiful
Icelandic interior.
Polar Horses, Grýtubakki 2, 601
Akureyri, tel: 463 3179, fax: 463
3144, e-mail: polarhorses@nett.is,
website: www.nett.is/polar. A
family-run outfit offering tours with
such intriguing names as "Elves
and Trolls Tour" and "Polar
Special". Also organises tours to
the National Equestrian Meet and
farm holidays with daily riding tours
incorporated.
For more on horse-riding, *see page
364*.

Hiking Tours

Two local outdoor organisations –
the Icelandic Touring Association
(Ferðafélag Íslands) and Útivist –
offer guided backpacking tours and
day walks. For more on hiking, *see
page 364*.
    The former are graded according
to level of difficulty and
accommodation is usually in
mountain huts. The tours and walks
both generally depart from the BSÍ
bus terminal in Reykjavík.
    Both organisations are practically
national institutions and are
extremely popular with Icelanders,
and consequently these tours
provide an excellent way to meet
the natives. The downside is that
the tours are guided in Icelandic,
though the majority of guides do
speak English as well.
Iceland Touring Association
(Ferðafélag Íslands)
Mörkinni 6, 108 Reykjavík, tel: 568
2533, fax: 568 2535, email:
fi@fi.is, website:
www.fi.is/eindex.htm. Founded in
1927, offers various hiking and

cross-country skiing tours with
mountain hut accommodation. Also
operates bus tours.
Útivist, Laugavegur 178, 105
Reykjavík, tel: 562 1000, fax: 562
1001, e-mail: utivist@utivist.is,
website: www.utivist.is. Hiking tours
to Þórsmörk and other south
Iceland locations, with camping and
mountain hut accommodation.

Sightseeing Air Tours

Flugfélag Vestmannaeyja,
Vestmanneyjar airport,
Vestmannaeyjar, tel: 481 3255,
fax: 481 2652. Aerial sightseeing
around Vestmannaeyjar.
Jórvík HF, Flugsk 31D. PO Box
5308, 125 Reykjavík, tel: 894
0369, fax: 533 1509. Various
sightseeing flights from Reykjavík
airport and Skaftafell.
Mýflug Air Service, Reykjahlíð
airport, tel: 464 4400, fax 464-
4401. Offers sightseeing flights
around Lake Mývatn from the
airfield behind the campsite. On a
clear day the 20-minute flight over
the lake is stunning. They also fly
over Krafla, the Jökulsá Canyon,
and the central highlands to Askja
and Kverkfjöll. A minimum of four
persons is usually needed to go
ahead with the flight.

Tour Operators Abroad

UK
Arctic Experience Ltd, 29 Nork
Way, Banstead, Surrey, tel: 01737
218800, fax: 01737 362341, e-
mail: sales@arctic-experience.co.uk,
web: www.arctic-experience.co.uk.
A comprehensive travel and
information service for Iceland.
Hotel tours, camping and sleeping-
bag accommodation tours, activity
holidays including mountain biking,
hiking, river rafting and
snowmobiling, fly drive and
independent travel arrangements,
bus and air passes. Also offers
winter activity holidays and a book
and map service. Special
arrangements made for school and
university groups.
Dick Phillips, Whitehall House,

Nenthead, Alston, Cumbria, tel: 01498 81440. Iceland specialist with backpacking and coach tours and independent arrangements. Information and book and map service. Special arrangements made for school and university groups.
Sherpa Expeditions, 131a Heston Road, Hounslow, Middlesex TW5 0RF, tel: 020 8577 2717, fax: 020 8572 9788, e-mail: sales@sherpa-walking-holidays.co.uk, website: www.sherpa-walking-holidays.co.uk

North America
Icelandair Holidays, 5950 Symphony Woods Road, Suite 410, Columbia, MD 21044, USA, tel: 1-800-223 5500 ext. 4; e-mail: america@icelandair.is, website: www.icelandair.com. Icelandair's in-house travel agency. Offers a broad range of escorted and unescorted programmes for groups and individuals year round, including fly-drive packages and stopovers.
Distant Journeys, PO Box 1211, Camden, Maine, 04843, USA, tel: 888-845 5781; fax: 207-236 0972, e-mail: djourney@midcoast.com, website: www.distantjourneys.com. Hiking and walking tours.

Practical Tips

Media

Newspapers and Magazines
With 100 percent adult literacy and more books published per capita than anywhere else in the world, it hardly comes as a surprise that Icelanders read a lot. Nor that they have several national and daily papers, weekly regional press and countless glossy magazines covering every conceivable subject.

Morgunblaðið, the longest-established daily, has excellent coverage of foreign affairs, reflecting an isolated nation's desire to keep pace with the world. *DV*, the other major daily, has a more popular appeal but is still based on serious news coverage. *Fréttablaðið*, published from Mon–Fri, is free and relatively lightweight in both content and size.

The English-language glossy *Iceland Review* is published quarterly and is available from newsagents or by subscription from: Edda, Suðurlandsbraut 12, Reykjavík, tel. 522-2000, e-mail: icenews@icenews.is. They also publish the quarterly Iceland Business. Most major English-language magazines are available from large news outlets across Reykjavík.

Pick up a copy of the free listings magazine *What's On in Reykjavík* at the tourist office.

Television
That a nation of 283,000 should have no fewer than six television channels is also astounding, with a number of locally produced programmes. Channel 1 is state-run, Skjár 1 is independently run, Omega is a Christian station and the others are pay-TV, by

subscription; these feature a fair number of foreign films, serials and documentaries that are usually undubbed, save for children's programmes. Satellite TV is available by subscription in Iceland, giving direct access to some 14 television stations, including CNN and the BBC.

News in English
The BBC World Service broadcasts on FM 90.9. From 1 June–31 Aug there is a daily news broadcast in English from the Icelandic National Broadcasting Service (FM 92.4/93.5) at 7.30am. A recording of the same broadcast may be heard at other times; tel: 515 3690.

Postal Services

Post offices *(Íslandspóstur)* are found in all major towns and villages and some country districts. The postal system is efficient with letters taking 3 to 5 days to reach Europe or North America. Air-mail letters or postcards to Europe cost ISK50; to other areas they are ISK75. You can buy stamps from post offices though it is often worth checking at shops that sell postcards, as some also stock stamps. The Central Post Office, Posthússtræti 5, Reykjavík has a philatelic section, but stamp collections are also sold at souvenir shops. Icelandic stamps often show birds and natural phenomena and many are inexpensive, perhaps making an unusual and affordable gift to take home.

Poste Restante is available at post offices throughout the country – mark letters clearly with the surname in capitals or underlined.

Post offices are generally open Mon–Fri 9am–4.30pm. The post office on Grensásvegur (near Laugardalur) in Reykjavík is open Mon–Fri from 9am–8pm, Sat 10am–2pm.

Telecommunications

The Icelandic word for telephone is *Sími*. Public telephone kiosks are something of a rarity in Iceland so making a telephone call demands ingenuity and perseverance. Restaurants, roadside service stations and hotels often have coin-box telephones, taking 10, 50 and, usually, 100 króna coins. Most call boxes will also accept phonecards – available from post offices. Calls made between 7pm and 8am are charged at a reduced rate. Try to avoid calling from your hotel room – hotels often charge three times the official rate.

Direct dialling is available to most countries – to call internationally from Iceland, first dial 00 followed by the country code. Country codes and international dialling procedure in English are listed in the telephone directory. Alternatively, you can dial 114 to enquire about the correct country code and 115 for the international operator.

All Icelandic telephone numbers have seven digits, with no area codes. The international code for calling Iceland from abroad is 354.

Fax services are available from post offices around the country and many hotels also offer this service to guests and sometimes to non-residents. The main tourist information office in Reykjavík also has good phone and fax facilities which are available to visitors.

Embassies

UK: Laufasvegur 31, tel: 550 5100.
US: Laufasvegur 21, tel: 562 9100.
Canada: Túngata 14, tel: 533 5550, fax: 533 5551.

Gay Travellers

For information and advice contact:
The Gay and Lesbian Association/ Samtökin '78, Lindargata 49, 101 Reykjavík, tel: 552 8539. Open Mon–Fri 11am–noon; telephone helpline on Mon and Thur 8–11pm. During opening hours, including Mon and Thur evenings there is a library and a coffee bar for those who want to drop by. Samtökin '78 also have a website: www.gayiceland.com.

Travellers with Disabilities

Wheelchair access is available at most of the major hotels. The rough terrain and the lack of developed facilities mean wheelchair access to Iceland's natural wonders is rare. There are paved paths at Geysir, Gulfoss and Þingvellir National Park. For information on vehicles for hire suitable for disabled persons, contact one of the tour operators or tourist information offices. Highland buses for wheelchair users are available on request.

The Icelandic Hotel and Restaurant Association publishes a leaflet entitled Hotels and Guesthouses, which lists establishments that are accessible to the disabled. Larger department stores, as well as the Kringlan Mall, are accessible to wheelchair users. The ferries Baldur and Herjólfur also have good facilities for the disabled. All airlines flying to and from the country can accommodate disabled passengers.

Sjálfsbjörg, the Association of the Disabled in the Capital Area, has published an English-language booklet entitled Accessible Reykjavík, which lists establishments and institutions accessible to the disabled.

For information or assistance in planning a trip contact
Sjálfsbjörg, Hátún 10, 105 Reykjavík, tel: 552 9133, fax: 562

Main Tourist Offices

Reykjavík: Tourist Information Centre, Bankastræti 2, 101 Reykjavík, tel: 562 3045. 15 May–15 Sept: daily 8.30am–7pm; 16 Sept–14 May: Mon–Sat 9am–5pm.
Akureyri: Tourist Information Centre, Hafnarstræti 82, 600 Akureyri, tel: 462 7733. June, July and August: Mon–Fri 8am–8.30pm, Sat, Sun 8am–5pm; Sept–May: Mon–Fri 8am–5pm (Fri until 6.30pm).

3773. Their website is at www.obi.is/English/Members/Sjal fsbjorg_Nat_disabled.htm

Student Travellers

Student discounts are rarely, if ever, advertised. It is worth asking at museums. Icelandair offers a standby youth fare, which may help students planning on spending longer than the standard one and three month apex tickets allow.

Business Travellers

Iceland may be isolated but it has never been insular. From its early days of settlement the nation has relied on trade for survival. Iceland continues to trade avidly and there is as much enthusiasm for imports as there is energy in establishing markets abroad for its many excellent products. To establish business contacts, the following addresses may be useful:
Federation of Icelandic Trade, Kringlan 7, Reykjavík, tel: 588 8910, fax: 568 8441, e-mail: fis@centrum.is.
Iceland Chamber of Commerce, Kringlan 7, Reykjavík, tel: 510 7100, fax: 568 6564, e-mail: mottaka@chamber.is.
Ministry of Trade, Arnarhvoll, Reykjavík, tel: 560 9070, fax: 562 1289, e-mail: postur@ivr.stjr.is.
Trade Council of Iceland, Hallveigarstígur 1, Reykjavík, tel: 511 4000, fax 511 4040, e-mail: tradecouncil@icetrade.is, website: www.icetrade.is.

Doing business in Iceland is generally informal and always on a first-name basis. Smart dress is really only essential if you plan to eat out at one of the better restaurants or visit one of Reykjavík's less casual nightspots. In business, most Icelanders dress "smart casual".

If you are invited to a business associate's family home, a gift of flowers would be most appropriate, or a bottle of whisky. But a word of warning – some Icelanders drink but others never touch a drop.

Religious Services

Just over 90 percent of Icelanders belong to the Lutheran Church, about 1 percent are Roman Catholics and various denominations account for the remaining 9 or so percent of the population.

Reykjavík has a number of churches which hold regular services on Sundays and in the week. Churches in central Reykjavík include: **Hallgrímskirkja**, Skólavörduhæd, tel: 510 1000; **Dómkirkjan** (the cathedral), Kirkjustræti 16, tel: 551 2113; **Catholic Church**, Túngata, tel: 552 5697 (celebrates Holy Mass in English on Sundays at 8pm); **Fríkirkjan** (Free Church), Fríkirkjuvegur 5, tel: 551 4579.

Outside Reykjavík there are Lutheran churches in all towns and villages and on many farms as well, though services may not be held every Sunday in rural districts. Apart from main **Akureyrikirkja**, Akureyri also has a Catholic church at Eyrlandsvegur 26.

Medical Treatment

For medical help call **The National Hospital** (Landsspítali-Háskólasjúkrahús) on 525 1000, weekdays from 8am–4pm. A doctor is on call after those hours, and at weekends. In case of serious illness or accidents, the emergency ward at the **Reykjavík City Hospital** (Sjúkrahús Reykjavíkur) is open around the clock, tel: 525 1700.

For non-emergency medical treatment outside normal hours the **Medical Centre** (Læknavaktin), Smáratorg 1 (in Kópavogur), is open 5pm–8am weekdays and 24 hours on weekends and public holidays. Call 554 1770 for help or advice. A nominal charge is made.

A children's doctor is on call at the **Domus Medica Medical Centre**, Egilsgata 3, Reykjavík, tel: 563 1010, evenings until 10pm, Sat and Sun 11am–3pm.

Emergency **dental care** is available, tel: 575 0505 for information about dentists on duty.

Most **pharmacies** *(apótek)* are open normal business hours (9am–6pm); Háaleitis Apótek is open from 8am–2am daily in the Austurver mini-mall (near the Kringlan mall) at Háaleitisbraut 68, Reykjavík, tel: 581 2101. Some other pharmacies also have extended opening hours; call 551 8888 for information.

Left Luggage

Hotels, guesthouses and hostels will often store luggage free of charge for guests. The BSÍ Bus Terminal at Vatnsmýrarvegur 10, Reykjavík, has left-luggage facilities, open Mon–Fri 7.30am–8pm, Sat and Sun 7.30am–noon.

Lost and Found

The lost and found office in Reykjavík is at Borgartún 33, tel: 569 9018, open weekdays 10am–noon and 2–4 pm.

Security and Crime

Iceland is one of the world's safest countries. Violent crime is virtually non-existent, bar the odd domestic dispute and drunken brawl. The latter is most likely on Friday and Saturday nights, when the city's youth takes to the streets of central Reykjavík on a (mostly good-humoured) drunken spree.

Though Icelanders are relaxed when it comes to security, for the visitor all normal precautions apply. Petty theft does occur, particularly in swimming-pool changing rooms (always leave valuables at the pay desk) and in bars and nightclubs. In the event of theft or loss, contact the nearest police station, where you will be required to fill in a statement. A copy is invariably required to claim on insurance.

Emergencies

For police, ambulance, the fire brigade or other distress situations, call 112.

Etiquette

Shyness towards visitors may be mistaken for coldness, but Icelanders are by nature hospitable and innately curious about foreigners and their ways. Family ties are strong yet they are great socialisers and many a tale is told around the coffee table. In such a small, closeknit society Icelanders invariably find that they are all related, albeit distantly, to one another and are quick to establish connections when introduced, by delving into their family trees.

If you are invited to an Icelander's home, it will most likely be for coffee, often accompanied by copious quantities of cakes and biscuits. The younger generation may be more likely to invite you for dinner; in this case a small gift – wine or flowers, for instance – is appropriate though not essential. It is customary to shake hands, when greeting and leaving, and Icelanders always remove shoes before entering their home.

Smoking is prohibited in public buildings and the gracious visitor to a private home should always ask for permission before lighting up.

Iceland uses the old system of patronymics, once common throughout Scandinavia. It raises eyebrows when an Icelandic family checks into a hotel abroad – mother, father, son and daughter will all have different last names. Very few Icelanders have surnames. Instead a child takes his father's first name, to which is added son or dóttir (son or daughter) as the case may be. Thus, if a father named Magnús has a son, Jón, and a daughter, Kristín, their full names will be Jón Magnússon and Kristín Magnúsdóttir. And as Icelandic women never change their names on marriage, their mother too will have a different name. A child may also take the mother's name by law, though this is less common. If the identity of the father is not established the child may take the mother's or grandfather's name.

Icelanders always use first names and visitors will be expected to follow suit. The concept of titles, except for ministers of religion, is unknown. The exception to this is on formal letters when Herra (or Hr.) Magnús Jónsson or Frú Kristín Jensdóttir would be a correct form of address on the envelope.

In the telephone directory, all entries are listed under first names. If the prospect of sifting through pages and pages of Jón Jónsson is daunting, many entries also give the person's profession (in Icelandic) as well as the address.

Getting Around

For the independent traveller, a first visit to Iceland can seem a daunting prospect. Getting to Iceland, both by air and ferry can be a major expense, although for travellers from the UK flights have become significantly cheaper in recent years, and domestic air travel is relatively inexpensive. When you get there, however, car hire is expensive – four-wheel drive is even more costly but a necessity for the highland routes.

Many independent travellers opt for a travel package. Tour operators offer a wide range of options from a simple fly-drive or flight and bus or air pass deal to a week in Reykjavík or a full-board hotel, farmhouse or camping tour. It is often cheaper to take a package of some sort.

Arrival and Departure

Almost all travellers arrive in Iceland at Keflavík Airport.
Some Greenland flights land at Reykjavík Airport and the odd international flight lands at Akureyri, in the north of Iceland, or Egilsstaðir, in the east. Arriving by sea you will dock either at Seydisfjörður, in the east of the country, or Reykjavík.

The "Fly Bus" transfer coach meets all incoming flights and takes about 45 minutes to cover the 50km (31 miles) by road from Kelflavík to the Hotel Loftleidir at Reykjavík Airport (about 2km/1½ miles from the city centre). From here an onward transfer service is provided to the major hotels, or you can ring for a taxi on one of the free phones. Bus No. 7 to the centre of town operates at 20-

minute intervals in the day and hourly in the evening.

For returning to the airport, the Fly Bus leaves Hotel Loftleidir two hours and fifteen minutes before flights leave Keflavík. Arrange pick up at the reception desk; buses are provided from other major hotels to connect with the Fly Bus. Many people flying out of Iceland combine the journey to Keflavík with a visit to the Blue Lagoon. Most tours to the Reykjanes peninsula let you get off at the airport for afternoon flights.

Maps

Visitors can obtain a useful (and free) tourist map of the country and city plan of Reykjavík, which is adequate for general planning purposes and orientation but not for actual touring from tourist information centres, airports, bus terminals and accommodation throughout Reykjavík and the rest of the country.

More detailed maps can be bought from most tourist offices and all larger bookshops in Iceland, as well as at many fuel stations. For general touring purposes the Insight Fleximap (1:898,000) has a laminated finish ideal for withstanding Iceland's wind and rain. The 1:500,000 touring map Ferðakort is excellent, as is the Kortabók Road Atlas. Greater detail is on the nine sectional maps in the Landmælingar 1:250,000 series but for most visitors the cost precludes the purchase of a full set. Large-scale 1:100,000, 1:50,000 and 1:25,000 maps of areas of particular interest to visitors, such as Þórsmörk/ Landmannalaugar, Mývatn, Skaftafell, Hekla, Vestmannaeyjar and Hornstrandir, are also available. But a word of warning – the accuracy of such maps, especially when marking footpaths and cliff faces, falls far short of maps in other countries. A general map series on the same scales also covers all areas of the country but some sheets are still under preparation or out of print. Highly recommended is the excellent geological map

Domestic Air Routes and Prices

Stand-by reductions are available on certain flights. For the best price, book at least two days in advance. It is worth checking before paying for a full-price ticket. Full price one-way fares are expensive and better rates can be obtained by booking through tour operators abroad.

Air Iceland (Flugfélag Íslands) serves nine locations throughout the country. The cheapest adult fares from Reykjavík are as follows (inclusive of airport tax):

Akureyri: one way ISK5,195, return ISK10,390. 6 daily flights.

Egilsstaðir: one way ISK 5,995, return ISK11,990. 2 daily flights.

Ísafjörður: one way ISK5,195, return 10,390. 2 daily flights.

Vestmannaeyjar: one way ISK4,665, return ISK9,330. 3 daily flights.

Grímsey: one way ISK6,965, return ISK13,930. 1 daily flight.

Vopnafjörður: one way ISK7,765, return ISK15,530. 1 daily flight.

Þórshöfn: one way ISK7,765, return ISK15,530. 1 daily flight.

Íslandsflug services Bíldudalur, Gjögur and Sauðárkrókur from Reykjavík: . Regular adult fares are ISK6,465 one way, 12,930 return; if you book and pay two days in advance the fare is ISK9,930 return.

1:500,000, with a key in English and Icelandic.

By Air

There are two main domestic carriers in Iceland: Air Iceland (Flugfélag Íslands) and Íslandsflug. Between them they serve all major towns and some minor ones throughout the country. In winter, when many roads are blocked by snow, flying is simply the only way to get around. Needless to say, flight schedules can be disrupted by weather, even in summer. Icelandic pilots are reputed to be among the most experienced in the world because of the variety and frequency of extreme conditions that they fly in. Reservations are advisable on all routes, especially in the summer months:

Air Iceland (Flugfélag Íslands): Reykjavík Airport, tel: 570 3030, fax: 570 3001, website: www.airiceland.is.

Íslandsflug: Reykjavík Airport, tel: 570 8030, fax: 570 8031, e-mail: islandsflug@islandsflug.is, website: www.islandsflug.is.

By Bus

Bus travel in Iceland is efficient but not cheap. It can in fact work out more expensive than flying on most of the longer routes. From Reykjavík

long-distance buses depart from the **BSÍ Bus Terminal** at Vatnsmýrarvegur 10. In summer, buses depart daily for destinations around Route 1 (the Ring Road) and elsewhere. On some routes, brief stops are made at tourist attractions en route.

Because of road conditions and distances, some destinations, such as Egilsstaðir in the east, require an overnight stop in Akureyri or Höfn. On other routes, for example to the West Fjords, services are less frequent. BSÍ also operates scheduled bus tours in summer, some with a guide but mostly unguided, to places of interest, including Þingvellir, Gullfoss and Geysir, Þórsmörk, Landmannalaugar and Eldgjá (all daily) and across the central highlands over the Kjölur (daily) and Sprengisandur routes (twice a week).

Full details of routes and schedules are available in the BSÍ Iceland Summer booklet, published each year, available from tourist offices and tour operators.

Coaches may also be hired through the following: **BSÍ Travel**, Vatnsmýrarvegur 10, 101 Reykjavík, tel: 562 3320, fax: 552 9973. **Gudmundur Jónasson Travel**, Borgartún 34, 105 Reykjavík, tel: 511 1515, fax: 511 1511. **United Bus Central**

(Hópferdamidstödin), Hestháls 10, 110 Reykjavík, tel: 587 6000, fax: 567 4969, e-mail: hopferd@hopferd.is, website: www.hopferd.is.

Bus Passes

BSÍ offers two bus passes that are well worth considering. The **Omnibus Pass** gives unlimited travel on most routes for a period of one (ISK19,400), two (ISK28,200), three (ISK36,100) or four (ISK40,100) weeks. The Circle Pass (ISK17,700; ISK26,200 if the West Fjords are included) allows one full circuit around the Ring Road following the same direction. The **Full Circle Pass** is unlimited in time and on both passes you can stop off as often as you like. Both passes offer discounts on other services – tours, accommodation, bike hire and ferries.

Combined bus and air travel tickets – **Air/Bus Rover** tickets – permit a round trip including some of the highland bus routes and offer a small discount. You can purchase them abroad through many of the tour operators. To travel from

Main Bus Routes

Below are the scheduled main BSÍ bus routes, summer frequency, journey times and approximate cost:

Reykjavík-Akureyri: daily (6 hours) ISK4,900.

Akureyri-Mývatn-Egilsstaðir: daily in summer, otherwise Mon, Wed, Fri (4 hours 30 mins) ISK4,200.

Egilsstaðir-Höfn: 4 times weekly in summer only (4 hours) ISK4,390.

Höfn-Reykjavík: daily in summer, otherwise Tue, Fri, Sun (8 hours) ISK6,070.

Reykjavík-Hólmavík: 3 times weekly in summer only (6 hours) ISK3,500. From there it is possible to transfer to Ísafjörður (4 hours) by another coach company.

Reykjavík-Stykkishólmur: daily (2 hours 30 mins) ISK2,600.

Reykjavík to Akureyri by plane and return by bus will cost around US$160 ($175 if you return via the interior route).

Hitchhiking

If you have unlimited time and patience and are prepared to carry a tent and plenty of food and walk where necessary, then hitchhiking will get you round the Ring Road and on some of the more travelled minor roads. However, bear in mind that the sparse traffic on Icelandic roads often consists of visitors and locals on holiday, with little space to spare in their vehicles. There is hardly any long-distance commercial traffic, and you may find that most rides are from locals on a trip to the nearest shop.

Hitchhiking is reasonably safe, and though quite reserved, most Icelanders do speak some English. Once the ice is broken they may go out of their way to help and provide fascinating snippets of information about their country. If you plan to hitch on the highland routes be prepared for a long wait – on some routes you may only see one or two vehicles a day.

Cycling

For the mountain-bike enthusiast, Iceland might seem an obvious choice. There are miles of rugged mountain tracks empty of traffic, and even the main roads can hardly be called busy. However, there are snags: accommodation and shops are far apart and virtually non-existent in the highlands, so carrying a heavy load is unavoidable; high winds, sandstorms and driving rain can make the cyclist's life a misery; if you damage your bike, you may have to resort to a bus to get you to a repair shop. It is fair to say that most Icelanders regard foreign cyclists as clinically insane.

But Iceland is growing in popularity for cyclists, and a number of tour operators offer biking holidays with support vehicle back-up.

Airlines will carry your bike free, providing it forms part of your 20 kg (45 lb) luggage allowance. When booking, make sure you specify that you are taking a bike and preferably pack it in a box. Around Iceland you can transport your bike on the buses, if there is space available, but you may be asked to remove pedals and wheels. Iceland does not have many specialist cycle shops, but for repairs most villages have a verkstæði (workshop).

Useful Addresses

Icelandic Mountain Bike Association, P.O. Box 5193, 125 Reykjavík, tel/fax: 562 0099, e-mail: ifhk@mmedia.is, website: www.mmedia.is/ifhk.
Bike shops in Reykjavík:
● GÁP, Faxafen 7, tel: 520 0200.
● Nanoq, Kringlan 4–10, tel. 575 5156.
● Örninn, Skeifunni 11, tel: 588 9890.
Repairs in Reykjavík:
● Nanoq, Kringlan 4–10, tel. 575 5156.
● Hjólið, Eiðistorg 13,

Scheduled Ferry Services and Prices

Þorlákshöfn-Heimaey
(Vestmannaeyjar): daily 8.15am from Heimaey, noon from Þorlákshöfn. Extra service in summer on Thurs, Fri and Sun: 3.30pm from Heimaey, 7pm from Þorlákshöfn. The journey takes 2 hours 45 mins each way. There are bus connections to Reykjavík for each sailing through BSÍ, tel: 562 3320. Price: one way, ferry only ISK1,500 for adults, ISK750 for children (12–15 years; under 12s go free) and seniors, ISK1,500 per vehicle up to 5m (15ft). Reservations are essential for vehicles, at least 30 minutes prior to departure. Information from Herjolfur, tel: 483 3414.
Árskógssandur-Hrísey: Sævar sails daily every 2 hours each way between 9am and 9pm. The journey takes 15 minutes. Price: ISK500 one way. A special bus service is available from Akureyri. For information and bookings

contact Sævar at Hafnarstræti 82, Akureyri, tel: 462 7733, or Nonni Travel, Brekkugata 3, Akureyri, tel: 461 1841.
Dalvík-Grímsey: Mon and Thurs, leaving Dalvík at 11am, arriving in Grímsey 3 hours 30 mins later and departing from there at 5.30pm. There is a special bus service from Akureyri, leaving at 10am and picking up passengers when the ferry docks on its return. Price: one way, ferry only ISK3,500; with bus ISK4,200. Same contact details as for Hrísey ferry (above).
Stykkishólmur-Flatey-Brjánslækur: twice daily in June, July and August from Stykkishólmur at 9am and 4pm, returning from Brjánslækur at 12.30 and 7.30pm respectively. Once daily in other months, departing from Stykkishólmur at 10am (1pm on Sun, Mon and Thurs). The journey takes 3

hours, and all sailings call at Flatey Island. If you wish you can stop over in Flatey and catch a later sailing. Price: ISK1,500 one way, ISK750 for children 12–15. Cars up to 5 m (15 ft) long pay ISK1,500 one way. Reservations must be made for cars. For details, tel: 438 1450. Connecting buses run from Brjánslækur to various places in the West Fjords in summer only. For information and bookings contact Iceland Excursions Allrahanda, Funahöfði 17, Reykjavík, tel: 540 1313.
Ísafjarðardjúp-Jökulfirðir-Hornstrandir: from Ísafjörður there are regular scheduled ferry services to various locations in this part of the West Fjords in the summer. They vary in departure days and length, and each leg of the journey has a different price: call Vestuferðir on 456 5111 for schedules and prices.

Seltjarnarnes, tel: 561 0304.
● Reiðhjólaverkstæðið, Borgarhjol, Hverfisgata 50, tel: 551 5653.
Mountain bike hire:
● BSÍ Travel, at the main bus terminal, tel: 562 3320.
● Borgarhjól, Hverfisgata 50, tel: 551 5653, e-mail: citybike@mmedia.is, website: www.mmedia.is/citybike.

Many places around Iceland hire out normal bikes; make enquiries at hotels and campsites. Both Akureyri Bus Station and Lake Mývatn by Hotel Reynihlíð also have a reasonable selection.

By Ferry

Iceland has a number of small offshore islands dotted around its highly indented coastline. Many are inhabited because in past centuries they offered easy defence against enemies as well as good fishing. Sea birds too were an important supplement to the diet and their droppings fertilised the grassy islands, making them ideal for farming. Scheduled ferry services link many of these islands with towns on the mainland; services are less frequent from September to May *(see panel on previous page)*.

Reykjavík Transport

Reykjavík's city centre is tiny in comparison to its sprawling suburbs. You can easily wander around on foot through the narrow streets clustered around the harbour and lake and cover most points of interest in a morning.

By Bus

Many hotels and guesthouses, as well as the main youth hostel and camping site, are all outside the centre, so it makes sense to use the excellent public bus system run by the Reykjavík bus company SVR. Most services operate 6am–midnight Mon–Sat with a reduced service on Sunday. At peak times buses run at 20-minute intervals and at 30-minute or one-hour intervals in the evenings and at weekends. Bus stops are marked

Reykjavik Tourist Card

The Reykjavík Tourist Card is valid for free and unlimited travel on city buses, and free admission to swimming pools and municipal museums. It is available for 1, 2 or 3 days and costs ISK1,000, 1,500 and 2,000 respectively. The cards may be purchased at the Tourist Information Centre in Bankastræti, at the Reykjavík City Hall, hotels and guesthouses, bus terminals, museums and swimming pools.

"SVR" and a flat fare is charged with no change given. If you need to change buses, ask for a transfer ticket *(Skiptimidi)*, which is valid for 45 minutes. If you plan to use the buses a lot, it is worth buying either a Reykjavík Card *(see above)* or pre-paid tickets, which give a small discount, available along with a route map from the two terminals at Lækjargata and Hlemmur. For bus information tel: 551 2700.

By Taxi

Hailing taxis on the street is a hit and miss affair. It is easier to go to one of the taxi ranks around town or ring the taxi firms directly:
Hreyfill, tel: 588 5522.
BSR, tel: 561 0000.
Bæjarleiðir, tel: 553 3500.
The majority of taxis seat four passengers but some larger vehicles seating up to seven people are available on request. If you have unusually large or long items of luggage ring **Sendibílastöðin**, tel: 552 5050, and ask for a minibus *"Sendibíll"*. These are often less expensive than a taxi but are only licensed to carry one or two passengers plus the luggage.

Tipping taxi drivers is not customary in Iceland. All taxis are metered and if you require a receipt ask for a *Nóta*. Most drivers speak some English. The busiest time for taxis is after midnight on Friday and Saturday nights, when it can be virtually impossible to find one.

Driving

Rules of the Road

Iceland drives on the right. It is mandatory to drive with headlights on at all times; the use of seat belts, both front and rear, is also mandatory. Drink driving is a serious offence – just one can of lager takes you over the legal limit. Priority, unless otherwise indicated, is given to traffic from the right – when in doubt, give way.

Speed limits are 50kph (30mph) in urban areas and 30kph (20mph) in residential areas. On gravel roads outside urban areas the limit is 80kph (50mph), and 90kph (60mph) on paved roads.

From November–May, snow tyres or studded tyres are mandatory; all rental cars will be fitted with them.

By law, driving off marked roads and tracks is prohibited. The high latitude and cool climate means the growing season is very short: four months in the lowlands but only two months in the highlands. As a result, damaged vegetation takes years, sometimes decades, to recover. Particularly at risk are marshlands and mossy areas where deep ruts caused by vehicles leave huge scars. The very fine, loose soil is vulnerable to erosion and damage is likely to accelerate the process.

Driving Conditions

Though road conditions in general fall below the standard of their European and North American counterparts, Route 1, also known as the Ring Road, which goes around the island, together with minor roads in settled districts, present no major problem to the normal two-wheel drive car in summer. Most of Route 1 is now paved, as are many of the minor country roads, particularly in the south and west of Iceland. A tunnel under the Hvalfjörður fjord, near Reykjavík, was opened in 1998 and has markedly improved communications in the southwest of the country. The price for passing through is somewhat steep: ISK1,000 one way for a normal family car.

Unpaved sections of road can become pot-holed and rutted, unpleasantly dusty in dry weather and muddy when it rains, but are still perfectly passable. Where the surface is loose gravel, it is vital for vehicles to slow down for oncoming traffic. In fact, you should always drive on gravel surfaces with great caution; there have been a number of fatal accidents involving tourists in the past few years.

For travelling around the coast, a two-wheel drive is perfectly adequate. Anyone contemplating a trip to the interior is entering a different league. Four-wheel drives are essential, and even then you should travel in teams of two or more cars (note that insurance companies will not cover hire cars taken into the interior).

For the jeep enthusiast Iceland is a playground of unbounded delights, its many rugged mountain tracks and unbridged rivers a challenge for even the most experienced. Travel through the uninhabited highlands also requires extreme caution and year after year unwary visitors (and Icelanders) undergo the unpleasant and sometimes fatal experience of their vehicle overturning in a seemingly innocuous river or the less serious but still frequent occurrence of getting stuck in sand. Fording rivers requires the utmost care.

Highland routes generally open the first week in July and close at the end of August, but this varies from year to year and route to route. A map is published every summer showing which highland routes are open and is constantly updated throughout the season. It is forbidden to attempt these routes before they are opened. The Ministry of Tourism publishes a brochure on travels in the Iceland Highlands which is available free in many travel agencies and tourist information centres. Details of road

conditions, updated every few minutes for all routes in Iceland, can be found on the internet at www.vegagerdin.ls/vefur2.nsf/pages/english.html.

For more information about mountain roads and the best routes to travel in the highlands, tel: 563 1500.

Bringing your Vehicle

Given the high cost of hiring vehicles in Iceland, it may seem an obvious choice for Europeans to bring their own vehicle. However, remember that road conditions are not good, and unless you drive only at low speed, your suspension may suffer. Flying stones from passing vehicles are likely to damage your paintwork, whatever speed you drive. The constant vibrations from rutted and potholed roads may also damage your vehicle, not to mention the copious quantities of dust that will enter every nook and cranny. Nevertheless many visitors do bring their own car, year after year, without suffering major damage. *See page 334 for details on catching car ferries to Iceland.*

On arrival in Iceland your vehicle may be inspected to ensure that it is roadworthy. You will need to produce the following documentation: a passport, driving licence, car registration document and a green card or other proof of auto insurance while in Iceland. A temporary importation permit will then be issued for the duration of your stay, which may not exceed three months. Other conditions for temporary import of vehicles are that the vehicle must be imported by the owner only or anyone having legal possession of it (eg through hiring) the vehicle must be brought to the country when the owner arrives, or within one month of arrival the vehicle must be used by him, his spouse or a hired chauffeur the vehicle must not be lent, sold or hired and the vehicle must be re-exported within the stipulated time period.

Fuel may only be imported in the vehicle's fuel tank. If your vehicle

uses diesel, it will be subject to a special tax on arrival in Iceland. This is because diesel fuel is very much cheaper than petrol and normally this tax is built into the purchase price of the vehicle. The amount will depend on the make of vehicle and intended length of stay. Full details can be obtained from Icelandic embassies abroad.

Use of mudguards is compulsory to minimise stones being thrown onto oncoming vehicles on gravel roads. It is advisable to buy a grille for the front of the car to protect headlights from damage. Before leaving home try to make sure your vehicle is completely dust-proof and ensure that any luggage stored on the roof is adequately protected against both dust and water.

Hiring a Vehicle

You can hire anything from a small car to a 40-seater coach in Iceland, depending on your needs and group size, but prices are high (less so outside the peak tourist season). Four-wheel drive vehicle hire is very expensive. It is often better to arrange vehicle hire with one of the tour operators abroad who offer a package that includes flights and car hire.

When arranging your rental, check what the rates include. The majority of rates advertised are for up to 100 km (65 miles). Prices double for unlimited mileage, if that is available. Many hire companies do not even offer unlimited mileage, nor do they include the hefty 24.5 percent VAT or the highly recommended fully comprehensive insurance in their daily rental price. Rental charges do include basic third-party insurance but not a collision damage waiver, which is always payable locally.

If you wish to hire locally, the following companies offer a full range of vehicles:

ALP Car Rental, at BSÍ Bus Terminal, Vatnsmýrarvegur 10, Reykjavík, tel: 562 6060, fax: 562 6061, e-mail: alp@alp.is.

Atak Car Rental, Smiðjuvegur 1,

Kópavogur, tel: 554-6040, fax: 554-6081, e-mail: atak@islandia.is, website: www.atakcar.com.
Avis, Dugguvogur 10, Reykjavík, tel: 533 1090, fax: 533 1091; or at Keflavík Airport tel: 562 4423, fax: 562 3590, e-mail: avis@avis.is.
Budget Rent-a-Car, Malarhöfði 2, Reykjavík, tel: 567 8300, fax: 567 8302, website: www.budget.is.
Hertz/Icelandair, Reykjavík Airport, 101 Reykjavík, tel: 505 0600, fax: 505 0650, e-mail: herz@herz.is.
SH Car Rental, Nybylavegur 32, Kópavogur, tel: 554 5477, fax: 554 5519, e-mail: sh@simnet.is, website: www.rentacar.is.
Many hire companies offer one-way rentals, allowing you to drive from Reykjavík to Akureyri, for example, and then return by air. Provided you stick to roads designated for the category of vehicle, assistance will be provided in the event of breakdown. Hire nothing but a four-wheel drive for a tour across the highlands. It is worthwhile going over your intended route with the rental company to check what roads are allowed for your type of vehicle.

Petrol

Petrol is quite expensive in Iceland, and is roughly the same price everywhere across the island:

approximately ISK105 per litre. Regular, super and unleaded petrol and diesel fuel are available in towns, villages and even in remote country districts, but not always at frequent intervals.

Before leaving a town or village it is always a good idea to check how far it is to the next petrol station. In uninhabited areas there is no petrol available and you will need to take spare fuel tanks with you. Remember that petrol consumption is particularly heavy on the rough interior routes. Petrol stations also stock basic spare parts and most have toilets and either a cafeteria or a restaurant available.

Petrol stations usually open daily at 7.30, 8 or 9am and close any time from 7.30–11.30pm. On Sundays they generally open between 10am–1pm. Shell petrol stations marked "Select" are open 24 hours. After-hours petrol can be bought at station pumps – these are labelled *Sjálfsali* (self-service) and they usually accept both cash and credit/debit cards.

Driving in Reykjavík

Reykjavík is still small enough for drivers not to experience serious traffic jams, though the city centre – particularly Miklabraut – can often

get congested during rush hour. Negotiating the inner city by car can also be tricky since there are a lot of narrow and one-way streets. The best compromise is to park in one of the numerous car parks on the fringe of the inner city, and then walk into the centre.

Most car parks close during the night; their hours are clearly stated on the ticket machine upon entering. Note that you must pay at the vending machine before returning to your car. Prices are generally ISK80–150 per hour.

Payment at parking meters and in metered parking lots is mandatory from 10am–6pm on weekdays and 10am–2pm on Saturdays. Parking meters cost ISK80–150 for an hour. Parking fines are a hefty ISK1500 if paid within 14 days, ISK2,250 if paid after that.

Crossing Rivers by Four-wheel Drive

Many rivers, particularly if glacial, can vary enormously in flow. Heavy rainfall or a warm sunny day can treble their flow in hours. Generally, in warm weather, the flow is highest in late afternoon and lowest in early morning.

If the river looks deeper than knee height, stop before crossing and look for the best place to ford, checking the flow in several places. With sediment-laden glacial rivers it is difficult to judge the depth. Narrow crossings are the deepest, wider crossings will be shallower, especially on straight stretches. On bends, the deepest water is usually on the outside. Where there is an

obvious fording place, where the water enters a calm phase forming a pool, the water will be shallower on the downstream side.

Watch out for large boulders, swept down into the fording place by strong flow, or sand – both should be avoided. If it is necessary, and safe to do so, wade first, using a safety rope. If in doubt, do not cross. Wait for another vehicle, get a second opinion, and help each other through. Keep in first gear, in low ratio if available, and drive slowly and steadily without stopping. If there is a strong current, try to cross by heading downstream to avoid fighting against the current.

Where to Stay

Making Bookings

Although accommodation in Iceland is expensive, facilities are generally good and the overall standard is high. The growth in tourism heralds an increasing number of hotels. Most accommodation outside Reykjavík and other towns is only open in the summer months, from June–September. Especially in July and August reservations are essential for all but dormitory sleeping-bag accommodation and campsites. Even youth hostels are often full at this time. All accommodation, except campsites, can be booked through tour operators abroad, and better rates can often be obtained this way. Hotels accept credit cards but payment for guesthouses, farms, hostels and campsites is usually cash only.

There are several useful publications listing accommodation. For an overview, try:

● *Accommodation in Iceland*, available from Áning Publications, Breiðvangi 3, 220 Hafnarfjörður, tel: 555 2405, fax: 555 2419.

● *Hotels and Guesthouses in Iceland*, available from Association of the Travel Industry, Hafnarstræti 20, 101 Reykjavík, tel: 511 8000, fax: 511 8008, website: www.saf.is, e-mail: info@saf.is. Other more specific publications are mentioned below under the relevant sections.

Hotels

International-style hotels with a full range of facilities are mainly found in the Reykjavík and Akureyri areas. Elsewhere they are few and far between. Top prices are over ISK18,000 for a twin room in a luxury hotel, en-suite shower or bath and breakfast included. Most international-style hotels have good facilities for disabled people. Eleven top-quality hotels have formed the Foss Hotel chain and have hotels in various locations around the country. Prices for a double room with en-suite bath/shower and breakfast range from ISK10,500–13,000. They also offer a special discount scheme called Scan+, which lowers rates after four nights. They do not generally have facilities for the disabled.

Tourist-class hotels offer fewer facilities but most have rooms with private shower/bath and a restaurant. They are to be found in Reykjavík and in towns around the country and are open all year round. Prices are usually somewhat less than those of the international-style hotels and facilities for the disabled tend to be lacking.

In summer Iceland's country boarding schools open as "summer hotels", most operating under the **Hotel Edda** chain. They offer comfortable accommodation, generally in rooms with basin but not private shower/toilet. Prices start from ISK5,600 for a twin with basin and ISK9,500 with en-suite bath. Breakfast costs ISK800. Most summer hotels have their own restaurant.

Guesthouses

These are usually small, often family run, and offer basic bed-and-breakfast accommodation. Prices vary, depending on the range of facilities and location, but start as low as ISK5,000 with breakfast for a twin room. Guesthouses are a good bet for those travelling on a budget; they are less expensive than hotels but often the facilities are of a high standard, and they are invariably clean. In most cases, however, the rooms do not have private baths, nor special facilities for the disabled. In the peak season book well in advance.

Private Homes

Because of the shortage of hotel space in the height of the summer, some families offer bed-and-breakfast accommodation in their own homes, mostly in the Reykjavík area. Bookings can be made through local tour operators. Private lodgings in Reykjavík can be booked via the Tourist Information Office, Bankastræti 2, tel: 562 3045. Prices for private homes are similar to those given for guesthouses.

Farm Guesthouses

Over-dependent on sheep-farming, many farmers have been encouraged to move into other areas of economic activity, such as tourism. Farms around the country offer a variety of services to visitors from bed-and-breakfast and sleeping-bag accommodation to self-catering holiday cottages (or summer houses as they are known locally), rented on a weekly basis. Excursions on horseback, fishing and other activities can be arranged. Not all are working farms.

Farm guesthouses are listed in the Icelandic Farm Holidays booklet, available through tourist offices across the country, tour operators, which also handle bookings, or direct from **Icelandic Farm Holidays**, Síðumúli 13, tel: 570 2700, fax: 570 2799, e-mail: ifh@farmholidays.is, website: www.farmholidays.is.

Prices start at around ISK1,500 per person for sleeping-bag accommodation, ISK2,200–3,500 per person in a twin (an extra ISK750–800 with breakfast). There is an extra fee of ISK1,050 for a single. Cottages cost ISK20,000–43,000 per week in summer, depending on the facilities and number of people they sleep; they cost less in winter.

Travelling via farmhouses is highly recommended for anyone interested in really getting to know Iceland. Many of the farms are in unique, sometimes remote locations, and staying on a working farm gives an insight into the

Holiday villas beyond indulgence.

BALEARICS ~ CARIBBEAN ~ FRANCE ~ GREECE ~ ITALY ~ MAURITIUS
MOROCCO ~ PORTUGAL ~ SCOTLAND ~ SPAIN

If you enjoy the really good things in life, we offer the highest quality holiday villas with the utmost privacy, style and true luxury. You'll find each with maid service and most have swimming pools.

For 18 years, we've gone to great lengths to select the very best villas at all of our locations around the world.

Contact us for a brochure on the destination of your choice and experience what most only dream of.

INTERNATIONAL
CHAPTERS

INSIGHT GUIDES

The classic series that puts you in the picture

Alaska
Amazon Wildlife
American Southwest
Amsterdam
Argentina
Arizona & Grand Canyon
Asia, East
Asia, Southeast
Australia
Austria
Bahamas
Bali
Baltic States
Bangkok
Barbados
Barcelona
Beijing
Belgium
Belize
Berlin
Bermuda
Boston
Brazil
Brittany
Brussels
Buenos Aires
Burgundy
Burma (Myanmar)
Cairo
California
California, Southern
Canada
Caribbean
Channel Islands
Chicago
Chile
China
Continental Europe
Corsica
Costa Rica
Crete
Cuba
Cyprus
Czech & Slovak Republics
Delhi, Jaipur & Agra
Denmark
Dominican Rep. & Haiti

Dublin
East African Wildlife
Eastern Europe
Ecuador
Edinburgh
Egypt
England
Finland
Florence
Florida
France
France, Southwest
French Riviera
Gambia & Senegal
Germany
Glasgow
Gran Canaria
Great Britain
Great Railway Journeys
  of Europe
Greece
Greek Islands
Guatemala, Belize
  & Yucatán
Hawaii
Hong Kong
Hungary
Iceland
India
India, South
Indonesia
Ireland
Israel
Istanbul
Italy
Italy, Northern
Italy, Southern
Jamaica
Japan
Jerusalem
Jordan
Kenya
Korea
Laos & Cambodia
Lisbon
London
Los Angeles

Madeira
Madrid
Malaysia
Mallorca & Ibiza
Malta
Mauritius, Réunion
  & Seychelles
Melbourne
Mexico
Miami
Montreal
Morocco
Moscow
Namibia
Nepal
Netherlands
New England
New Orleans
New York City
New York State
New Zealand
Nile
Normandy
Norway
Oman & The UAE
Oxford
Pacific Northwest
Pakistan
Paris
Peru
Philadelphia
Philippines
Poland
Portugal
Prague
Provence
Puerto Rico
Rajasthan
Rio de Janeiro

Rome
Russia
St Petersburg
San Francisco
Sardinia
Scandinavia
Scotland
Seattle
Sicily
Singapore
South Africa
South America
Spain
Spain, Northern
Spain, Southern
Sri Lanka
Sweden
Switzerland
Sydney
Syria & Lebanon
Taiwan
Tenerife
Texas
Thailand
Tokyo
Trinidad & Tobago
Tunisia
Turkey
Tuscany
Umbria
USA: On The Road
USA: Western States
US National Parks: West
Venezuela
Venice
Vienna
Vietnam
Wales

INSIGHT GUIDES

_**The world's largest collection of
visual travel guides & maps**_

country's ancient rural lifestyle.

Booklets of 10 pre-paid nights at farms can be bought either in Reykjavík or from tour operators, giving some discount. If you opt for sleeping-bag accommodation you may get your own room, although not all farms provide this service. Many farms offer kitchen facilities for cooking, and almost all will cook guests' meals. Prices for meals vary from farm to farm.

Each farm has its own character and range of services, so careful perusal of the Icelandic Farm Holidays booklet is recommended. Reservations at the individual farms can be made by telephone, or you can simply drop in at any farm where the IFH sign is displayed.

Holiday Chalets

Holiday chalets are not easy to come by for travellers to Iceland. One company, however, rents out six chalets, near Hella, south Iceland, some 95km (60 miles) from Reykjavík. The chalets sleep 3–7 people and are fully equipped. Each chalet has a sauna and outdoor hot tub. Many of Iceland's main attractions are nearby, including Landmannalaugar, Þórsmörk, Gullfoss and Geysir. The chalets cost ISK5,000, 7,900 or 9,500 per day, depending on the size. Contact Rangarfluðir, tel: 354 487 5070, e-mail: allah@binet.is, website: www.rang.is/ferda/rangarfludir.

Youth Hostels

There are 24 youth hostels around Iceland, situated in towns, villages and farming districts. Offering dormitory sleeping-bag accommodation with cooking facilities, many hostels also provide meals. Some prohibit sleeping bags, providing a duvet or blankets, but you will need to hire or use your own sheet lining. Hostels are open to people of all ages and in Iceland you do not have to be a member of the IYHF (International Youth Hostels Federation) though prices are slightly lower for members.

In July and August it is advisable to pre-book hostels through tour operators or directly with:
Icelandic Youth Hostels Association, Sundlaugavegur 34, P.O. Box 1045, 121 Reykjavík, tel: 553 8110, fax: 588 9201, e-mail: info@hostel.is, www.hostel.is. The Association also provides a booklet listing hostels and the facilities they offer. Sleeping-bag accommodation costs ISK1,400–1,700 per person a night at the hostels, or ISK1,100–1,400 for Association members. Breakfast costs ISK600–800.

Mountain Huts

Marked on maps by a triangle, you find mountain huts in uninhabited areas. Mountain huts are owned and maintained by:
Ferdafélag Íslands (The Touring Club of Iceland), Mörkinni 6, 108 Reykjavík, tel: 568 2533, fax: 568 2535, e-mail: fi@fi.is, website: www.fi.is.
Útivist, Hallveigarstíg 1, 101 Reykjavík, tel: 561 4330, fax: 561 4606, e-mail: utivist@utivist.is, website: www.utivist.is

Some huts are accessible by road but others are intended solely for hikers. Some are small, sleeping six to eight persons and have no facilities – others sleep over 100 and offer cooking facilities and flushing toilets. It is always wise to pre-book the huts, as some are kept locked with no resident warden. For these a key is obtained from the Touring Club's office. All huts are uncatered, so please bring your own supplies. Non-members are charged a fee of about ISK1,300.

Sheep Round-up Huts

These are basic huts, owned by farming communities and used during the annual sheep round-up in September. Often marked on maps as *Kofi*, many will be kept locked at other times of the year and are not intended for use by tourists.

Emergency Huts

Located on mountain passes, remote stretches of road and

Sleeping Bags

Anyone interested in saving money should bring their sleeping bag with them. As well as being essential for mountain huts and some hostels, many farmhouses and guesthouses offer "sleeping bag accommodation" at a reduced rate.

along uninhabited coasts, these orange-painted huts are stocked with food, stove, blankets and a radio. They are, by law, only for emergency use.

Campgrounds

Camping is allowed in most places in Iceland, though on private or farming land it is subject to the owner's permission. Within national parks and conservation areas, it is only allowed at designated areas.

Official campsites are found in most towns and villages, at national parks, nature conservation areas, places of natural beauty and some farms and community centres. The standard varies. Expect to pay ISK350–650 per person per night for a layer of pumice and an earth closet to soft turf and hot showers. A leaflet listing campgrounds is published by the Iceland Tourist Board.

Hire equipment from **Sportleigan**, Laugavegur 25, Reykjavík, tel: 551 9800, fax: 561 3082.

Accommodation Listings

The following listings include a range of accommodation of all types and in most price ranges.

REYKJAVÍK

City Hotel
Ránargata 4a
Tel: 511 1155
Fax: 552 9040
E-mail: cityhotel@islandia.is
On a quiet street in the city's west end, very close to the town centre.

Modern facilities and small but comfortable rooms. **$$$**

Fosshótel Lind
Rauðarárstígur 18
Tel: 562 3350
Fax: 562 3351
A modern chain hotel on the outskirts of the old centre, close to Hlemmur bus terminal. There are very good facilities for disabled travellers and non-smoking rooms are available. **$$$**

Grand Hótel Reykjavík
Sigtún 38
Tel: 568 9000
Fax: 568 0675
E-mail: info@grand.is
Comfortable hotel with full facilities, located close to the Laugardalur swimming pool. Spacious rooms and excellent service. **$$$$**

Guesthouse 101
Laugavegur 101
Tel: 562 6101
Fax: 562 6105
E-mail: guesthouse101@islandia.is
This is one of the few guesthouses offering good facilities for the disabled. On the main shopping street just a short distance from the Hlemmur bus terminal. **$$**

Guesthouse Adam
Skolavordustigur 22
Tel: 896 0242
Fax: 551-1506
E-mail: adam@adam.is
Good location close to the Hallgrimskirkja; open all year. Breakfast is ISK800 extra. **$$**

Guesthouse Aurora
Freyjugata 24
Tel: 552 5515
Fax: 551 4894
On a quiet tree-lined street near Hallgrímskirkja church, about a 10-minute walk from the centre. One of the best places at this price. **$$**

Guesthouse Baldursbrá
Laufásvegur 41
Tel: 552 6646
Fax: 562 6647
E-mail: heijfls@centrum.is
One of the best guesthouses in the city, run by a German-Icelandic couple. The service is friendly and hospitable and there is a hot tub in the back yard. **$$**

Guesthouse Hólaberg
Hólaberg 80

Tel: 567 0980
Fax: 557 3620
A very good bet for those on a budget. Located in the Breiðholt suburb with good bus connections to the city centre. Free pick-up from Reykjavík air or bus terminals. Good walking and biking paths nearby. Bike rental and free use of bike if staying more than four nights. Breakfast costs ISK600 extra. **$**

Guesthouse Svala
Skólavörðustígur 30
Tel: 562 3544
Fax: 562 3650
This guesthouse is housed in a stately old residence in the heart of the city. Several unique shops on the same street sell everything from designer gear to quirky toys. **$$**

Hótel Borg
Pósthússtræti 11
Tel: 551 1440
Fax: 551 1420
E-mail: hotel.borg@centrum.is
website: www.hotelborg.is
The city's first hotel, right in the old town centre. Beautifully renovated in Art Deco style, with a very popular restaurant. **$$$$**

Hótel Cabin
Borgartún 32
Tel: 511 6030
Fax: 511 6031
E-mail: keyhotel@centrum.is
A budget hotel, modern, with small but comfortable rooms, about a 20-minute walk from the town centre. Has good views of the ocean and mountains beyond. **$$$**

Hótel Holt
Bergstaðastræti 37
Tel: 552 5700
Fax: 562 3025
E-mail: holt@holt.is
Website: www.holt.is
Luxury hotel in central Reykjavík, decorated throughout with Icelandic works of art. It also has one of the finest ranges of whiskies in the country. **$$$$**

Hótel Klöpp
Klapparstraeti 26
Tel: 511 6062
Fax: 511 6070
E-mail: info@grand.is
Website: www.centerhotels.is
Pleasant new hotel right in the middle of town. The nearby Hótel

Skjaldebreið (Laugavegur 16) is run by the same company. **$$$$**

Radisson SAS Hótel Ísland
Ármúli 9
Tel: 568 8999
Fax: 568 9957
E-mail: Info.Island.Rek@Radissonsas.com
A modern, comfortable hotel with the largest nightclub in Iceland on the premises. The location is not very picturesque but is close to a number of attractions, such as the Laugardalur geothermal pool. **$$$$**

Hótel Leifur Eiríksson
Skólavörðusígur 45
Tel: 562 0800
Fax: 562 0804
Attractive and comfortable hotel, centrally located opposite Hallgrímskirkja church. **$$$**

Price Guide

Prices are for a double room per night in high season. Rates can be 30 percent lower Sept–April.
$$$$ Over ISK15,000
$$$ ISK10,000–15,000
$$ ISK6,000–10,000
$ Under ISK6,000

Hótel Loftleiðir
Reykjavíkflugvöllur
Tel: 505 0900
Fax: 505 0905
Website: www.icehotel.is
Owned by Icelandair and located at Reykjavík airport. Modern and comfortable with an excellent restaurant. Situated close to the Öskjuhlíð nature reserve and the Perlan, with a panoramic view of the city and surroundings, but a bracing 25-minute walk to the centre of town. **$$$**

Hótel Óðinsvé
Óðinstorg 11
Tel: 511 6200
Fax: 511 6201
E-mail: odinsve@hotelodinsve.is
Website: www.hotelodinsve.is
A charming hotel on a quiet street in the heart of the city. Tasteful decor. A restaurant on the premises was recently rated one of the 100 best new restaurants in the world by Condé Nast. **$$$$**

Hótel Reykjavík
Rauðarárstígur 37
Tel: 562 6250
Fax: 562 6350
E-mail: reception@hotelreykjavik.is
Website: www.hotelreykjavik.is
A modern hotel with a friendly
atmosphere to the east of the
centre. There are ample private
parking spaces for guests; those
not in their own vehicles will find
the Hlemmur bus terminal only a
short distance away. **$$$$**

Radisson SAS Hótel Saga
Hagatorg
Tel: 525 9900
Fax: 525 9929
E-mail:
Info.Saga.Rek@Radissonsas.com
A top-class hotel not far from the
city centre and next door to the
University Theatre, home of the
Iceland Symphony Orchestra. The
Saga has excellent conference
facilities and one of the best
restaurants in the country on the
top floor, with a wonderful view over
Reykjavík and beyond. **$$$$**

Salvation Army Guesthouse
Kirkjustræti 2
Tel: 561 3203
Fax: 561 3315
The cheapest guesthouse in
Reykjavík. There are no frills but the
place is neat and clean and the
central location is excellent. There
are facilities for cooking on the
ground floor. **$**

Youth Hostel
Sundlaugavegur 34
Tel: 553 8110.
Fax: 588 9201.
Well-run hostel with good facilities.
Situated on the fringe of

Camping in Reykjavík

Reykjavík Campsite
Laugardalur, Sundlaugavegur
Tel: 568 6944
Located behind the youth hostel
at the edge of Laugardalur valley,
next to the city's largest
swimming facility. The campsite
offers cooking and laundry
facilities. Things get busy in the
summer and pre-booking is
advisable for larger groups. **$**

Self-catering Apartments in Reykjavík

Hótel Barón
Barónsstígur 2–4.
Tel: 562 3204.
website: www.baron.is
Self-catering apartments for rent
close to the main shopping street
and the Hlemmur bus terminal.
Sizes and prices vary but start at
ISK12.950 per night. Apartments
with two bedrooms are
ISK13,950.

Room with a View
Laugavegur 18, 6th floor.
Tel: 552 7262.
Fax: 515 2505.
E-mail: arnike@mm.is.
website: www.roomwithaview.is
Luxurious furnished apartments,

Laugardalur, next to the open-air
swimming pool. Good bus
connections nearby. **$**

GREATER REYKJAVÍK

Hraunbyrgi Hostel
Hjallabraut 51, by Víðistaðatún
park, Hafnarfjörður
Tel: 565 0900
Fax: 555 1211
A quieter alternative to the busy
hostel and campsite in Reykjavík.
The trip to the capital takes about
30 minutes by bus. **$**

THE REYKJANES
PENINSULA

Hótel Blue Lagoon
P.O. Box 13, 240 Grindavík
Tel: 426 8650/7050
Fax: 426 8651
E-mail: hotelbluelagoon@simnet.is
Located at the Blue Lagoon, mainly
serving transit passengers en route
to or from the nearby airport. **$$$**

Hótel Flug
Hafnargata 57, Keflavík
Tel: 421 5222
Fax: 421 5223
Upmarket hotel, mainly for airport
passengers, with restaurant and
bar. All rooms are en-suite.
$$$–$$$$

which sleep up to seven people. In
accordance with the name, most
of the rooms have a balcony and a
great view. Sizes and prices vary,
starting from ISK11,000 per night
for an apartment sleeping four.

Home Away from Home
Skálholtsstígur 2a
Tel: 520 6122.
Fax: 562 9165.
E-mail: apartment@thewinner.is.
Modern furnished apartments,
centrally located near the Tjörn
lake. Prices start at ISK12,900
per night for a studio apartment
(20 sq m); larger apartments (40
sq. m), sleeping four, cost
ISK16,900.

Hótel Keflavík
Vatnsnesvegi 12–14, Keflavík
Tel: 420 7000
Fax: 420 7002
Comfortable hotel near the airport
with various services on-site and
restaurants nearby. The hotel runs a
much cheaper guesthouse (**$$**)
across the street at No.9. **$$$–$$$$**

Strönd Youth Hostel
Njarðvíkurbraut 48–50, Njarðvík
Tel and fax: 421 6211
This hostel is across the small bay
in Reykjanesbær, the old workers'
quarters for the nearby fish factory.
A local bus connects the hostel with
the main part of town. **$**

THE SOUTHWEST

Guesthouse Árhús
Rangarbakkar, 850 Hella
Tel: 487 5577
Fax: 487 5477
Open year-round, with 21 cottages
and camping on the banks of the
Ytri-Ranga river in the village of
Hella. **$**

Guesthouse Ásgarður
860 Hvollsvöllur
Tel: 487 8367
Fax: 487 8387
e-mail: asgard@isholf.is
Rooms, chalets, sleeping bag
accommodation and a campsite.
$–$$

Guesthouse Norður-Vík
Suðurvegur 5
Myrdal, 870 Vík
Tel: 487 1106
E-mail: nordur-vik@simnet.is
Just outside Vík, this is a basic
hostel and guesthouse. **$**

Guesthouse Syðra-Langholt
845 Flúðir
Tel/fax: 486 6674
Based in a farm south of Flúðir and
open all year. **$**

Hótel Edda
Skógar, 861 Hvolsvöllur
Tel: 487 4900
Fax: 487 4614
One of 16 Edda hotels in Iceland.
Close to the Skógafoss waterfall.
Sleeping-bag accommodation is
available. Open in summer only. **$$$**

Hótel Geysir
Haukadal, 801 Selfoss
Tel: 486 8915
Fax: 486 8715
Small hotel and self-catering
accommodation a stone's throw
from the famous geysers. **$$**

Hótel Hvolsvöllur
Hlíðarvegur 7, 860 Hvolsvöllur
Tel: 487 8187
Fax: 487 8391
e-mail: hotelhvol@simnet.is
Comfortable small hotel close to
the Saga Centre. **$$–$$$**

Hótel Örk
810 Hveragerdi
Tel: 483 4700
Fax: 483 4775
One of the Key group of hotels, with
comfortable rooms and a pool.
swimming **$$–$$$**

Hótel Vík
Klettsvegur, 870 Vík
Tel: 487 1480
Fax: 487 1302
An all-year hotel offering good
facilities, with sleeping bag
accommodation available. **$$**

Þórsmörk Hut
Ferðafélag Íslands, Mörkinni 6, 108
Reykjavík
Tel: 568 2533
Fax: 568 2535
E-mail: fi@fi.is
A noisy and busy hut and crowded
campsite in summer, although
empty in winter. Sleeps 75 people
in bunks. Makes a good base for
walks in the Þórsmörk valley. **$**

VESTMANNAEYJAR

Guesthouse Heimir
Heiðarvegur 1
Tel: 481 2929/3329
Fax: 481 2912
Guesthouse/sleeping-bag
accommodation. **$**

Guesthouse Hvíld
Höfðavegur 16
Tel: 481 1230
A very good-value budget
guesthouse. **$**

Hótel Brædraborg
Sólhlíð 17
Tel: 481 3636
Fax: 481 3638
The largest hotel in the islands.
Rooms with en-suite or shared
facilities. **$$**

Hotel Þórshamar
Vestmannabraut 28
Tel: 481 2900
Fax: 481 1696
A fairly upmarket hotel, with the
lower-priced Guesthouse Sunnuhöll
attached. **$$–$$$**

THE SOUTHEAST

Guesthouse Hrollaugsstaðir
Suðursveit, 781 Höfn
Tel: 478 1057
Fax: 478 1905
Located between Jökulsárlón
(25km) and Hofn (55km).
Sleeping-bag accommodation
available. **$–$$**

Hótel Kirkjubæjarklaustur
880 Kirkjubæjarklaustur
Tel: 487 4900
Fax: 487 4614
Open all-year, a comfortable hotel in
the small village of
Kirkjubæjarklaustur. **$$$**

Fosshótel Vatnajökull
Lindarbakki, 781 Höfn
Tel: 478 2555
Fax: 478 2444
All facilities in a wonderfully
convenient location for the south
Vatnajökull area, 10km from the
town of Hofn. **$$$**

Nýibær Youth Hostel
Hafnarbraut 8, 780 Höfn
Tel: 478 1736
Fax: 478 1965
E-mail: nyibaer@simnet.is

An old house on two floors near
Hofn harbour. Rooms with bunks. **$**

Smyrlabjörg Hostel
Suðursveit, 781 Hornafjörður
Tel: 478 1074
Fax: 478 2043
Old farmhouse hostel and
guesthouse near Höfn. Rooms with
washbasins. **$**

SNÆFELLSNES AND THE WEST

Fosshótel Bifröst
Bifröst 311 Borgarfjordur
Tel: 433 3090
Fax: 562 4001
Located just off Route 1, 32km
north of Borgarnes. A busy and
pleasant summer-only hotel. **$$$**

Price Guide

Prices are for a double room per
night in high season: Rates can
be 30 percent lower Sept–April.

$$$$ Over ISK15,000
$$$ ISK10,000–15,000
$$ ISK6,000–10,000
$ Under ISK6,000

Fosshótel Stykkishólmur
Borgarbraut 12, 340 Stykkishólmur
Tel: 430 2100
Fax: 430 2101
Well-appointed hotel with
tremendous views over the pretty
town of Stykkishólmur. **$$$**

Guesthouse Snjófell
Arnarstapi
356 Snæfellsbær
Tel: 435 6783
Fax: 435 6795
E-mail: snjofell@snjofell.is
Website: www.snjofell.is
A value-for-money guesthouse,
located near some stunning
scenery. Good cooking facilities for
guests. Tours onto Snæfellsjökull
glacier leave from here. **$**

Hamar Youth Hostel
310 Borgarnes
Tel: 437 1663
Fax: 437 1041
Set in a beautiful farmhouse at the
golf club a short distance northeast
of Borgarnes, the hostel has views

over nearby Borgarfjörður and the Skarðsheiði mountains. **$**

Hótel Reykholt
320 Reykholt
Tel: 435 1260
Fax: 435 1206
A former boarding school converted into a hotel with its own restaurant. **$**

Sjónarhóll Hostel
Höfðagata 1, 340 Stykkishólmur
Tel: 438 1095
Fax: 438 1417
Large but comfortable hostel in the old town, overlooking the harbour. **$**

THE WEST FJORDS

Gistiheimilid
Borgarbraut 4, Hólmavík
Tel: 451 3136
Fax: 451 3413
Guesthouse with self-catering and sleeping-bag accommodation available. Wonderful views. **$**

Guesthouse Áslaugar
Austurvegi 7, 400 Ísafjörður
Tel: 456 3868
Fax: 456 4075
E-mail: gistias@snerpa.is
A guesthouse/homestay in the middle of the old town, next to the indoor swimming pool. Also has sleeping-bag accommodation. **$**

Guesthouse Breiðavík
Breiðavík, 451 Patreksfjördur
Tel: 456 1575
Fax: 456 1189
Guesthouse in a former boarding school, with a magnificent setting. Walks to the Látrabjarg cliffs and Hvalláturold. **$**

Hótel Djúpavík
Djúpavík, 522 Árneshreppur
Tel: 451 4037
Fax: 451 4035
In the remote village of Djúpavík, this former hostel for women workers (Djúpavík was once a fish-processing centre) has been renovated and is now a comfortable hotel. **$$**

Hótel Flókalundur
Flókalundur, Vatnsfjördur
Tel: 456 2011
Fax: 456 2050
Close to Brjánslækur (ferry to Stykkishólmur), with a good restaurant and rooms with facilities.

Also runs a small guesthouse nearby. Sea kayak rental and guided kayak trips available. Free campsite. **$$$**

Hótel Ísafjörður
Silfurtorg 2, 400 Ísafjörður
Tel: 456 4111
Fax: 456 4767
E-mail: info@hotelisafjordur.is
A rather characterless hotel in the middle of town. Also runs a cheaper summer hotel, Torfnes, in the boarding school at the western end of town. **$$–$$$**

Hótel Edda
Núpur, Þingeyri
Tel: 456 8222
Fax: 456 8236
Old-style summer hotel, run in the old boarding school. **$$**

HÚNAFLÓI AND SKAGAFJÖRÐUR

Geitaskarð Farm
Langadal, 541 Blönduós
Tel: 452 4341
Fax: 452 4301
Farm-stay just outside Blönduós, near the Ring Road. **$–$$**

Hólar i Hjaltadalur
Hólar i Hjaltadalur, 551 Sauðárkrókur
Tel: 453 6303
Fax: 453 6301
Cabins and rooms are available during the summer months at the agricultural college. Swimming pool and camping. **$–$$**

Hótel Lækur
Lækjargata 10, 580 Siglufjörður
Tel: 467 1514
Fax: 467 1911
E-mail: bkh@isholf.is
Offers singles and doubles with shared bathrooms. Also sleeping-bag accommodation. **$$**

Ósar Youth Hostel
Vatnsnesi, 531 Hvammstangi
Tel/fax: 451 2678
Farmhouse hostel in a peaceful spot by the sea; good for birdlife. **$**

Sunnuberg Guesthouse
Suðurbraut 12, 565 Hofsós
Tel: 453 7434/7310
Fax: 453 7935
Offers basic rooms, some of which are en-suite. **$–$$**

AKUREYRI AND SURROUNDINGS

Akureyri Youth Hostel
Stórholt 1
603 Akureyri
Tel: 462 3657
Fax: 462 5037
Busy hostel, a fair distance from the centre of town. It's advisable to book ahead in summer. **$**

Guesthouse Brekka
Brekkugata 5, 630 Hrísey
Tel: 466 1751
Fax: 466 3051
E mail: brekkahriscy@isl.is
Comfortable but small guesthouse with restaurant. **$–$$**

Guesthouse Gula Villan
Þingvallastræti 14, 600 Akureyri
Tel: 461 2860
Fax: 461 3040
Comfortable guesthouse next to the excellent swimming pool; also has sleeping bag accommodation. **$–$$**

Guesthouse Dalvík
Storhólsvegur 6, 620 Dalvík
Tel: 466 3088
Fax: 466 1661
This summer-opening guesthouse has its own restaurant. **$$**

Guesthouse Sólgarðar
Brekkugata 6, 600 Akureyri
Tel/fax: 461 1133.
Small but comfortable guesthouse in the town centre, which also has sleeping bag accommodation. **$–$$**

Hótel Bjørk
Hafnarstræti 67, 600 Akureyri
Tel: 461 3030
Fax: 461 3033
Located in a quiet spot just outside the town centre, with good views out to the fjord. **$$$**

Hótel KEA
Hafnarstræti 83–85, 600 Akureyri
Tel: 460 2000
Fax: 460 2060
E-mail: kea@hotelkea.is
Website: www.hotelkea.is
A very reliable hotel in the centre of town. Shares restaurant and reception with the Hótel Harpa. **$$$$**

Syðri-Hagi Farm
Árskógsströnd, 621 Dalvík
Tel: 466 1961
Fax: 466 1903

Farm accommodation near the ferry to Hrísey. Wonderful views over the fjord. **$–$$**

GRÍMSEY

Guesthouse Básar
Tel: 467 3103
Next to the airstrip, with standard rooms and sleeping-bag accommodation. **$**

LAKE MYVATN

Guesthouse Birkihraun
Vikurnes, 660 Reykjahlíð
Tel: 464 4285
Fax: 464 4380
Basic guesthouse, handily situated near the swimming pool. **$–$$**
Guesthouse Stöng
Mývatnssveit, 660 Reykjahlíð
Tel: 464 4252
Fax: 464 4352
This is a simple farm-style guesthouse. **$–$$**
Hlíð Travellers Centre
Hraunbrun, Kytrur, 660 Reykjahlíð
Tel: 464 4103
Fax: 464 4305
A busy centre offering camping, self-catering huts and sleeping-bag facilities. **$–$$**
Hótel Reynihlíð
Reynihlíð, 660 Reykjahlíð
Tel: 464 4170
Fax: 464 4371
This established hotel forms the hub of most activities in the area. Also has sleeping bag accommodation. Book ahead – it gets very busy in high season. **$$$**
Skútustaðir Farm
Mývatnssveit, 660 Reykjahlíð
Tel: 464 4212,
Fax: 464 4322
Slightly away from the crowds. **$$**

THE NORTHEAST

Fosshóll Farm Hostel
Bárðardal, 645 Fosshóll
Tel: 464 3108
Fax: 464 3318

In a beautiful setting right next to the Goðafoss falls between Akureyri and Mývatn. Also has camping facilities. **$**
Guesthouse Árból
Ásgarðsvegur 2, 640 Húsavík
Tel: 464 2220
Fax: 464 1463
A comfortable old guesthouse in the middle of town. **$$**
Hóll Farm
671 Kopasker
Tel: 465 2270
Fax: 465 2353
Ideally located for visiting Jökulsárgljúfur National Park. **$–$$**
Fosshótel Húsavík
Ketilsbraut 22, Húsavík
Tel: 464 1220
Fax: 464 2161
Open all year, this friendly hotel has a good restaurant and is centrally located. **$$$**

Price Guide

Prices are for a double room per night in high season: Rates can be 30 percent lower Sept–April.
$$$$ Over ISK15,000
$$$ ISK10,000–15,000
$$ ISK6,000–10,000
$ Under ISK6,000

Fosshótel Laugar
650 Laugar
Tel: 464 6300
Fax: 562 4001
An old boarding school, well located for exploring the area between Mývatn and Akureyri. Summer only. **$$–$$$**
Víkingavatn Farm
Kelduhverfi, 671 Kópasker
Tel: 465 2293
Fax: 465 2293
This farm offers a selection of rooms plus sleeping-bag accommodation. **$–$$**
Þinghúsið Hraunbæ
V. Laxa i Aðaldal, 641 Húsavík.
Tel: 464 3695
Fax: 464 3595
Renovated old community house, which makes a good base.
$–$$

THE EAST FJORDS

Berunes Youth Hostel
Berunes 1, 765 Djúpivogur
Tel/fax: 478 8988
A very comfortable but small hostel in a renovated old farmhouse. **$**
Egilsstadir Guesthouse
Kennitala 700
Tel: 471 1114
Fax: 471 1266
Clean, pleasant accommodation situated on the shores of Lake Lagarfljót. **$**
Fosshótel Valaskjalf
Skógarlóndum, 700 Egilsstaðir
Tel: 471 1000
Fax: 471 1001
In the middle of town, with restaurant/bar and solarium.
$$$
Guesthouse Borg
720 Borgarfjörður-Eystri
Tel: 472 9870
An old building which has been recently renovated; excellent walks are possible nearby. **$**
Guesthouse Reyðarfjörður
Búðargata 4, 730 Reyðarfjörður
Tel and fax: 474 1447
An old and basic guesthouse-cum-hostel in the middle of town. **$**
Hafaldan Hostel
Ranargata 9, 710 Seyðisfjörður
Tel: 472 1410
Fax: 472 1610
One of the best hostels in Iceland, with lots of character. **$**
Hótel Bláfell
Solvellir 14, 760 Breiðdalsvík
Tel: 475 6770
Fax: 475 6668
A well-priced and comfortable hotel, which also offers sleeping-bag accommodation – cheaper than the price of a standard room.
$–$$
Hótel Framtíð
Vogaland 4, 765 Djúpivogur
Tel: 478 8887
Fax: 478 8187
A well-located and comfortable hotel, with sleeping-bag accommodation also available. Camping is also available nearby. The hotel organises boat trips to the offshore island of Papey and also arranges bike hire and sea-angling trips. **$–$$**

Hótel Svartiskógur
Hallgeirsstöðum, 700 Egilsstaðir
Tel: 471 1030
Fax: 471 1016
This is a new country hotel – phone ahead for directions as it can be difficult to find. **$–$$**

Húsum Farm
Ferðaþjónustan Húsum, 701 Egilsstaðir
Tel: 471 2003
Fax: 471 2004
A small farm guesthouse with great character and excellent, friendly service. **$**

Snæfell Hut
Ferðafélag Fljótsdalshéraðs (Fljótsdalur touring club) 701 Egilsstaðir
Tel: 853 9098 (summer),
471 1433 (winter)
A comfortable mountain hut and adjacent campsite with a full-time warden in summer, hot showers and WC. A good base for walks in the Snæfell area. The same organisation runs the Geldingafell and Egilssel huts on the Vatnajökull east traverse route. **$**

Stafafell Hostel
Lón, 781 Höfn
Tel: 478 1717
Fax: 478 1785

Booking in Advance

It's advisable for visitors to reserve accommodation, especially during the peak summer months of July and August. You should be able to find dormitory sleeping-bag accommodation and space to bed down at campsites, but even youth hostels are usually full during the peak summer period. You should be able to book all accommodation, except that at campsites, through tour operators in your home country; this often works out cheaper than reserving in Iceland after you've arrived there. Hotels usually accept payment by credit card but payment at guesthouses, farms, hostels and campsites is generally cash only.

The Stafafell is a farmhouse that is over 100 years old, which has been restored to a basic hostel. It makes an excellent base for treks to Lónsöræfi and Geithellnadalur. Camping also available. **$**

THE INTERIOR

Guesthouse Hrauneyjar
Sprengisandi, 851 Hella
Tel: 487 5078
E-mail: eyrraros@islandia.is
Website: www.islandia.is/~eyrraros
On the Sprengisandur route, with basic rooms. Attached service station and campsite. **$**

Guesthouse Versalir
Sprengisandi, 851 Hella
Tel: 852 2161/487 5078
Fax: 487 5278
Offers basic rooms and cabins on the Sprengisandur route. A petrol pump and restaurant are also available here. **$**

Herðubreiðarlindir Hut
Touring Club of Akureyri
PO Box 48, 602 Akureyri
Tel: 462 2720
Fax: 462 7240
An old but comfortable hut, accommodating 30 people. **$**

Hólaskjól Hut
Skaftárhreppur (community office),
Kirkjubæjarklaustur
Tel: 487 4840
Fax: 487 4842
Mountain hut near Eldgjá on Fjallabaksleið. Basic but comfortable and not usually busy. Great walking and cycling nearby. **$**

Hveravellir Hut
Ferðafélag Íslands, Mörkinni 6
108 Reykjavík
Tel: 568 2533
Fax: 568 2535
E-mail: fi@fi.is
A very busy hut, which is used by tour groups passing over the Kjölur route. Club members have priority over non-members. **$**

Kverkfjöll Hut
Ferðafélag Fljótsdalshéraðs,
700 Egilsstaðir
Tel: 853 9098 (summer),
471 1433 (winter)
A comfortable mountain hut with a full-time warden in summer, hot

showers and WC. Ideal base for walks in the Kverkfjöll area. **$**

Landmannalaugar Hut
Ferðafélag Íslands, Mörkinni 6,
108 Reykjavík
Tel: 568 2533
Fax: 568 2535
E-mail: fi@fi.is
A crowded hut in summer, with bunkbeds, plus a busy campsite. A good starting point for the many treks in the area. Ties in with other huts on the Laugavegur trail. Club members have priority. **$**

Laugafell Hut
Touring Club of Akureyri
PO Box 48
602 Akureyri
Tel: 462 2720
Fax: 462 7240
Heated hut north of Hofsjökull ice field. Accommodates 15. **$**

Nýidalur Huts
Ferðafélag Íslands
Mörkinni 6
108 Reykjavík
Tel: 568 2533
Fax: 568 2535.
E-mail: fi@fi.is
A good base for walks and cycling in a desolate location on the Sprengisandur route. Camping available. Accommodates 120 people in two huts. **$**

Sveinstindur Hut
Útivist, Hallveigarstíg 1
101 Reykjavik
Tel: 561 4330
Fax: 561 4606
E-mail: utivist@utivist.is
Website: www.utivist.is
Small, basic but new hut in a traditional design. Situated east of Landmannalaugar, this makes an excellent base for walks off the beaten track. **$**

Eating Out

What to Eat

Traditional Icelandic food is based on fish and lamb, the two ingredients most readily available in the country. Throughout the centuries they have been boiled fresh, and smoked, salted, pickled or dried to store for the winter months. Many of these traditional foods have survived to this day and are as popular as they have been for centuries. Nothing is wasted, and you will find cod's cheeks and roe alongside salmon and prawns on the fish counter. Blood pudding, singed sheep's head and pickled rams' testicles can be tried at Þorrablót, a traditional feast that takes place each February. For the really adventurous, how about rotted shark or sheep's head jelly? Many of these specialities will not feature on the restaurant menu but can be bought at supermarkets.

Seabirds, particularly puffin and guillemot, were an important supplement to the diet in days of old but are now rather a delicacy.

For the more conventional palate, try Icelandic smoked lamb, often served in the home with pickled red cabbage and sugar-browned potatoes. Lamb in any form is delicious in Iceland.

Haddock and halibut are often boiled or grilled and served with a prawn sauce or simply with butter. Salmon and trout are served fresh or smoked – traditionally using dung. Thin slices of smoked fish are served with hot spring-baked rye bread. Try herring, smoked, pickled or the tinned variety in mustard or garlic sauce.

Icelandic dairy produce is excellent. *Skyr*, a skimmed-milk curd preparation, is whipped with milk and eaten with generous lashings of cream. High in calcium and low in calories (without the cream) there is nothing quite like it outside Iceland. *Súrmjólk*, soured milk, is eaten at breakfast and with brown sugar. (If you want normal milk, pick out the *nýmjólk* from the plethora of choices, or *léttmjólk*, which is fat-reduced.) *Mysingur*, a sweet spread made from whey, is popular with children. At the bakery, try rye bread and the excellent *flatkökur* (rye pancakes).

Where to Eat

Dining out in Iceland has undergone tremendous changes in the past twenty years or so. The number of restaurants has multiplied and along with that the choice of cuisine. A diverse variety of ethnic food barely heard of in 1990 is now readily available in Reykjavík. Also, a vast number of Icelandic chefs have sought training abroad and returned home to experiment with different ways of cooking traditional Icelandic ingredients. It has also become fashionable for restaurants to invite guest chefs to the country to concoct both their native and regional specialties for Icelandic gourmet aficionados.

Icelandic restaurants tend to be of a high standard. And while in the past dining out in Iceland was invariably expensive, it need no longer be so. Many restaurants offer good-value special tourist menus or lunch or dinner buffets. There is usually an unlimited supply of fresh bread and butter, as well a a jug of cold tap water.

One thing should be stated, however: wine prices in Icelandic restaurants are sky-high. The bottle that is expensive enough at the state liquor store will invariably be around three times higher in price at a restaurant. Even house wines, generally costing around ISK500 per glass, will quickly push the price of the meal up, up, up.

Almost all restaurants accept Visa and MasterCard and many will take American Express and Diners cards. All restaurants displaying the sign Tourist Menu offer a set menu during the summer months with a soup or starter followed by a fish or meat main course and coffee, for a fixed price. Prices are lower at lunch, ranging from ISK750–1500 per person with anywhere from ISK1,500–2,500 for the evening meal. Children under 6 usually eat free and 6–12 year olds pay half price.

Most restaurants are open for lunch 11.30am–2.30pm and evening meals 6–10.30pm or 11pm. In Reykjavík it is advisable to book ahead for evening meals at weekends.

Restaurant Listings

REYKJAVÍK

Amigos
Laekjargata 8
Tel: 511 1333
Lively Mexican restaurant with good tacos and enchiladas. **$$**

Á næstu grösum
Laugavegur 20b
Tel: 552 8410
Delicious, wholesome vegetarian food, an airy, relaxed atmosphere and good value for money make this a very popular place. Lunches tend to be busy between noon and 2pm. The entrance is on Klapparstígúr. **$**

Apótek
Austurstræti 16
Tel: 575 7900
Trendy bar, cafe and restaurant. One of the places to be seen in the capital. **$$$**

Argentína Steak House
Barónsstígur 11
Tel: 551 9555
Excellent steaks are grilled over an open fire. The atmosphere is warm and inviting. Stays open late. **$$$**

Austur Indíafjelagið
Hverfisgata 56
Tel: 552 1630
What happens when you mix Icelandic ingredients with Indian-style cooking? Here, at least, the result is delectable. The service is among the best in Reykjavík – friendly, professional and tactful. **$$**

Gallery Restaurant
Hótel Holt, Bergstaðastræti 37
Tel: 552 5700

Top-quality restaurant with exquisite art work decorating the walls. Formal atmosphere and excellent service. **$$$**

Grænn Kostur
Skólavörðustígur 8
Tel: 552 2028
A small vegetarian restaurant serving excellent, imaginative and wholesome food at reasonable prices. Offers meals for those suffering from candida. It may be a bit tricky to find: the entrance is through a car park at the corner of Bergstaðastræti. Closes at 9pm. **$**

Price Guide

The price guide is for the average price of dinner per person, without wine:

$$$ Over ISK2,500
$$ ISK1,500–2,500
$ Under ISK1,500

Hornið
Hafnarstræti 15
Tel: 551 3340
This was the first Italian restaurant to open in Iceland and it has been popular ever since. The atmosphere is relaxed and charming and the seafood and pizzas are excellent. It is almost always packed in the evenings so a reservation is recommended. **$$**

Hótel Borg
Pósthússtræti 11
Tel: 551 1247
Gorgeous restaurant decorated in Art Deco style and a curious mixture of classic and trendy. Big windows facing Austurvöllur square and the Alþing. Delicious, good-quality continental cuisine. **$$$**

Hótel Loftleiðir Floral
Reykjavík Airport
Tel: 505 0925
Serves international cuisine à la carte, with the emphasis on fish and lamb. The atmosphere is pleasant and the service friendly and professional. **$$**

Hótel Óðinsvé
Þórsgata 1
Tel: 511 6677
Run by a celebrity chef, this restaurant was recently named one

of the top 100 new restaurants in the world by Condé Nast Traveller. Book early. **$$$**

Hotel Saga Grill
Hagatorg
Tel: 525 9900
This exclusive restaurant, situated on the top floor of the hotel with a fine view of the city, is favoured by business people. The emphasis is on lamb and fresh fish. **$$$**

Humahusið
Amtmannsstígur 1
Tel: 561 3303
Quality restaurant located in a cosy 19th-century wooden building close to the main tourist office. Specialises in lobster. **$$$**

Indókína
Laugavegur 19
Tel: 552 2369
An ethnic restaurant serving Chinese and Vietnamese food. The decor is no-frills but the price is right. They also do take-away. **$**

Kaffivagninn
Grandagarður 10
Tel: 551 5932
Unpretentious place on the quay where fishermen congregate for coffee and home-cooked fare. Good for anyone keen to mingle with hardy Icelandic seamen and watch fishing boats outside the window. Closes at 7pm. **$**

La Primavera
Austurstræti 9
Tel: 561 8555
Italian restaurant with a chic and airy decor. Gourmet food and they import their own Italian wines. **$$**

Lækjarbrekka
Bankastræti 2
Tel: 551 4430
In a restored wooden building in the town centre. Serves Icelandic fish and lamb specialities, and there is a tourist menu. The decor is quaint and there is a cosy lounge upstairs. **$$–$$$**

Litli ljóti Andarunginn
Laekjargata 6B
Tel: 552 9815
Good value Icelandic buffet (evenings until late); also serves lunch and light meals. **$**

Múlakaffi
Hallarmúli
Tel: 553 7737/6737

One of the best deals in the city, home-cooked meals at highly reasonable prices. Frequented by both blue- and white-collar workers, particularly at lunchtime. **$**

Nings
Suðurlandsbraut 6
Tel: 588 9899
For lovers of Chinese food, this is the place to go. The location is somewhat off the beaten path and there is a fast-food feel to the place; the food, however, is absolutely delicious. **$**

Perlan – The Pearl
Öskjuhlíð
Tel: 562 0200
An unmistakable landmark, built on top of the geothermal hot-water storage tanks on Öskjuhlíð hill. A revolving restaurant that makes a revolution every two hours. Award-winning chef. **$$$**

Restaurant Salatbarinn
Pósthústræti 13
Tel: 562 7830
Located next to the Hotel Borg, this restaurant serves tasty vegetarian buffet food at a relatively affordable price. **$**

Sticks 'n Sushi
Aðalstræti 12
Tel: 511 4440
Simple, stylish interior and excellent Icelandic seafood, prepared and served Japanese-style. Classy and cool. **$$–$$$**

Við Tjörnina
Templarasund 3
Tel: 551 8666
One of the city's top seafood restaurants. Unique types of delicious fish are creatively prepared and served. **$$**

Viðeyjarstofa
Viðey Island
Tel: 568 1045
Fine Icelandic cuisine in a unique historic setting on this island off the coast of Reykjavík. The ferry leaves from Sundahöfn; details of the times and frequency of trips may be had from the restaurant. **$$$**

Þrír frakkar hjá Úlfari
Baldursgata 14
Tel: 552 3939
Anyone who would name their restaurant "Three overcoats/ Frenchmen" ("Frakkar" is a pun

and means both) has to be worth a try, and this place certainly is. Fish and whalemeat are specialities. Small and intimate. Great food. **$$**

AROUND ICELAND

Below is a small selection of eating places around Iceland. In many towns it is worth trying the local hotel or guesthouse, as most have restaurants attached – in some towns this may be the only eating place available. Good-value meals can often be found at the many petrol stations and roadside snack bars. The Pizza 67 chain is scattered in towns all over the country and offers other options as well as pizza. *See also Pubs, Bars and Cafés, page 357.*

Reykjanes Peninsula
Glóðin
Hafnargata 62, Keflavík
Tel: 421 1777
The local upmarket restaurant, serving a variety of main dishes, pasta and salads. **$$–$$$**
Hótel Keflavík
Vatnsnesvegi 12, Keflavík
Tel: 420 7000
Café, restaurant and take-away, attached to the east side of this large hotel. **$$–$$$**
Tilveran
Linnetsstig 1, 220 Hafnarfjörður
Tel: 565 5250
A quiet but good-value restaurant serving very tasty meat and fish dishes. **$$**
Vitinn
Hafnargata 4, Sandgerði
Tel: 423 7755
Next to the harbour, serves meals, beer and coffee to the fishermen and harbour workers. **$–$$**

The Southwest
Við fjöruborðið
Eyrarbraut 3
825 Stokkseyri
Tel: 483 1550
E-mail: info@fjorubordid.is
Website: www.fjorubordid.is
A highly popular restaurant by the sea, famed for its lobster. Worth

the drive from Reykjavik. **$$–$$$**
Víkurskáli
By the main road, Vík
Tel: 487 1230
Roadside restaurant and service station. **$–$$**

The Southeast
Ósinn
Shell petrol station, Höfn
Tel: 478 2200
Standard fare at moderate prices. **$$**

Snæfellsnes and the West
Guesthouse Snjófell
Arnarstapi
355 Ólafsvík
Tel: 435 6783
Fax: 435 6795
E-mail: snjofell@snjofell.is
Website: www.snjofell.is
A wood-panelled restaurant serving unpretentious food. **$–$$**
Knudsen
Aðalgata (near the old church), Stykkisholmur
Tel: 438 1600
Local restaurant and pub with plain decor, serving filling main dishes, including pizzas and burgers. **$–$$**

The West Fjords
Hótel Flókalundur
Vatnsfjörður
Tel: 456 2011
The only restaurant in the area, often serving excellent food. Closed in winter. **$$–$$$**
Hótel Ísafjörður
Silfurtorg, Ísafjörður
Tel: 456 4111
Excellent, if slightly pricey, hotel restaurant. **$$–$$$**
Nýja Bakaríið/Pizza 67
Aðalstræti 62, Patreksfjörður
Tel: 456 1301
Renovated into a pub-cum-pizza restaurant. Great pizza. **$–$$**

The West Fjörds
Café Riis
Hafnarbraut 39, Holmavík
Tel: 451 3567
Fax: 451 3557
Renovated old wooden house in the town centre. It is advisable to check the opening hours before setting out. **$$–$$$**

Húnaflói and Skagafjörður
Hótel Mælifell
Kaupvangstorg 1, Sauðárkrókur.
Tel: 453 5265
A small hotel restaurant serving up filling meals. **$$**

Akureyri and Surroundings
Bautinn
Hafnarstræti 92, Akureyri
Tel: 462 1818
An Akureyri institution serving a huge choice from salads to meat, fish and vegetarian meals. **$$–$$$**
Brekka Restaurant
Brekkugata 5, Hrísey Island
Tel: 466 1751
Set in beautiful surroundings, the only restaurant in Iceland serving Galloway steaks. **$$–$$$**

Price Guide

The price guide is for the average price of dinner per person, without wine:
$$$ Over ISK2,500
$$ ISK1,500–2,500
$ Under ISK1,500

Fiðlarinn
Skipagata 14, Akureyri
Tel: 462 7100
Excellent views over the fjord and delicious meals. **$$–$$$**
Greifinn
Glerárgata 20, Akureyri
Tel: 460 1600
Very popular restaurant in a good location, serving a wide choice from Italian to game dishes. **$$–$$$**
Kaffi Menning
Hafnarbraut 14, Dalvík
Tel: 466 1213
A quirky little café and restaurant; regular live music. **$–$$**

Lake Mývatn
Gamli Bærinn
Reykjahlíð
Tel: 464 4170
This restaurant often gets busy and serves good-value meals including vegetarian options. **$–$$**
Skútustaðir Restaurant
Skútustaðir Farm
Tel: 464 4212
Great food at good prices. **$–$$**

The Northeast
Hafnarbar-inn
Eyrarvegi 3, Þórshöfn
Tel: 468 1338
A very popular café, pub and
restaurant. **$–$$**

The East Fjords
Ormurinn
Kaupvangi 2, Egilsstaðir
Tel: 471 2321
Relatively upmarket restaurant and
café in the middle of town. **$–$$**
Pizza 67
Lyngasi 5, Egilsstaðir
Tel: 471 2424
True to the name, this is mainly a
pizza place, but it does offer other
types of food as well. There is
sometimes live music. **$$**

Cafés

There is an established coffee
culture, with a number of cafés
specialising in gourmet coffees.
Most places offer free refills,
American-style.

Most cafés in Iceland are
licensed and also function as bars
after 6pm. Most stay open until the
small hours at weekends. Because
of this dual role we have listed
these establishments together with
pubs and bars.

Nightlife

Since the early 1990s Reykjavik
at night has been transformed
from a sleepy provincial city to
one of the hottest venues in
Europe, with as lively a nightlife
as you will find anywhere. Many
locales which masquerade as
perfectly civilised cafés during
the day transform into rip-roaring
bar rooms in the evening. But
most places don't even start
getting lively until 11pm. If you
are intent on serious drinking
come prepared – a half litre of
draught beer costs around
ISK550–650 in most places.

In most cafés and night spots,
the clientele is young and dress
is casual. For upmarket Reykjavik
establishments you have to
dress smartly, as for night clubs.

Drinking

Iceland has strict rules about
buying and drinking alcohol.
You have to be at least 20 years
old to buy alcohol and you may
be asked to show proof of your
age. Visitors wanting a regular
tipple should bring in their full
duty-free allowance, because all
alcoholic drinks are expensive
in Iceland.

Wines, spirits and beers over
2.25 percent alcohol are only sold
at state-controlled outlets, ÁTVR
shops. Light beer can be bought in
general supermarkets.

Iceland's local home-produced
drink is Brennivin, a caraway-seed-
flavoured spirit, drunk icy cold. It is
generally referred to as "Black
Death", to give you an idea of its
strength.

Pubs, Bars and Cafés

Opening hours were extended in
2000, with pub/club owners
permitted to keep their places open
pretty much as long as they liked.
This was partly to help alleviate the
congestion on the streets that took
place when the legal closing hour
was 3am. These days Reykjavík's
nightlife doesn't get into full swing
until after 1am. Most pubs and bars
are open Sun–Thur 6pm–1am and
Fri–Sat from 6pm–5am, or even
later.

In Reykjavík
Café Paris, Austurstræti 14
(opposite the main post office),
tel: 551 1020.
A cosmopolitan café offering light
meals at reasonable prices. This
chic watering hole wouldn't be out
of place in any major European city.
The Dubliner, Hafnarstræti 4, tel:
511 3233. This was the first Irish
pub in Iceland and it remains very
popular. The atmosphere is always
fun, with live Irish music performed
on a regular basis.
Gaukar á Stöng, Tryggvagata 22,
tel: 551 1556. One of the
mainstays of the Reykjavík late-
night scene; open until 7am at
weekends, with live music.
Hús Málarans, Bankastræti 7,
tel: 562 3232. This high-ceiling café
in the heart of the city is great for
people-watching, by virtue of its
huge windows.
Kaffibarinn, Bergstaðastræti 1,
tel: 551 1588. Extremely trendy,
small and very crowded. Favoured
hang-out of actors, pop musicians
and other media types – possibly
because it is owned by Blur front
man, Damon Albarn. Warning: the
clientele is hand-picked from the
queue outside.
Kaffibrennslan, Pósthússtræti 9,
tel: 561 3600. Trendy café by day
and pub by night. Prides itself on
101 types of beer. Good light meals
at reasonable prices.
Kaffi List, Laugavegur 20a, tel: 562
5059. Popular Spanish-style pub.
Gets very crowded at weekends.
Kaffi Reykjavík, Vesturgata 2,
tel: 562 5540. Located in an

historical building near to the harbour, this place is everything you could wish for at once: café, pub, cocktail lounge, singles bar. Features live music every evening.
Kaffitár, Bankastræti 8, tel: 511 4540. Non-licensed, non-smoking, and possibly the best coffee in town. The staff routinely win prizes in cappucino-making competitions. Closes at 6pm.
Kaffi Thomsen, Hafnarstræti 17, tel: 561 5757. This addition to the pub scene became trendy seemingly overnight. A DJ sees to the entertainment at weekends.
Kofi Tómasar Frænda, Laugavegur 2, tel: 551 1855. Cosy and friendly and often a welcome retreat from the push-and-shove atmosphere of nearby night spots.
Leikhúskjallarinn, Hverfisgata 19, tel: 551 9636. Located in the basement of the National Theatre, this nightclub features live music on weekends. Dress smartly.
Rex, Austurstræti 9, tel: 511 9111. Very hip, trendy and crowded; designed by British style guru Sir Terence Conran.
Súfistinn, Laugavegur 18, Reykjavík, tel: 552 3740. Located in the Mál og menning bookshop, this "book cafe" has excellent coffee and wondeful – if pricey – cakes.
Vídalín, Aðalstræti 10, tel: 562 9898. Bistro bar located in the oldest house in Reykjavík.

Akureyri

Kaffi Akureyri, Strandgata 7, tel: 461 3999. Pleasant café/bar in the centre of town.
Við Pollinn, Strandgata 49, tel: 461 2757. Lively bar in an old building by the harbour.

Elsewhere in Iceland

Álafoss föt bezt, Alafossvegi 22, Mosfellsbær, tel: 566 8585. A combination of rural bar/café, often staging plays, exhibitions or live music. In the old wool factory just outside the centre of town.
Gjáin, Austurvegur 2, Selfoss, tel: 482 2555. Local pub, often with live music.

Hafnarbjörninn, Hafnargata 6, Grindavík, tel: 436 8466. The local pub in Grindavík, with drinks and light meals.
Hreiðrið Café, Brakarbraut 3, Borgarnes, tel: 437 2017. Pub/café with live music at weekends.
Kaffi Flug, Hafnargata 57, Keflavík, tel: 421 5222. A small café in the mall by the largest hotel in Keflavík.
Kaffi Lefolii, Gunnarshús, Eyrarbakki, tel: 483 1113. A small café in a restored house.
Nönnakot, Mjosund 2, 220 Hafnarfjörður, tel: 565 2808. A charming old café, serving coffee and cakes the traditional way.
Radhuskaffi, Tjamargotu 11. Have a drink at the café in the city hall, and you can enjoy glorious views across the lake out towards the mountains.
Strikið, Hafnargata 37, Keflavík, tel: 421 2012. A pub but mainly a disco on the main street.
Súfistinn, Strandgata 9, Hafnarfjörður, tel: 565 3740. One of the best cafés in Iceland, with a wide selection of coffees roasted and ground on the premises.

Gay and Lesbian Venues in Reykjavík

Spotlight, Hafnarstraeti 17. Gay and lesbian nightclub in the heart of Reykjavík, open Thurs–Sun.
MSC bar, Ingólfsstrati. Men only bar opposite the Sólon Islandus café. Ring the bell to get in.
22, Laugavegur 22, tel: 551 3628. This has long been the city's unofficial gay bar and a popular spot with punters of all persuasions for its great atmosphere. The dance floor is tiny and the ventilation is terrible, but it is usually packed.

Culture

Sources of Information

That a country with a population of 283,000 has three professional theatre companies, a thriving film industry, a national ballet, opera and symphony orchestra and hosts an international arts festival every other year is itself remarkable. Add to this the two-dozen or so museums and galleries in Reykjavík and over 50 others throughout the rest of the country, internationally acclaimed opera singers, a jazz band that has made it into the UK charts, world-famous rock bands and a world-class female pop star – can anywhere else match Iceland for variety and intensity of cultural activity in such a small community?

Any tourist information office should have copious amounts of information about the cultural events taking place at any given time. The two tourist brochures *What's On in Reykjavík* and *Reykjavík This Month* have extensive cultural listings. Over and above that they are invaluable sources of information for travellers, with maps, bus schedules, descriptions of walking tours and more. These are available just about anywhere tourists go and are free of charge.

Museums and Galleries

Many museums and galleries in Reykjavík are closed on Mondays and during the winter. Some will open at special times for groups, by arrangement. Entrance fees, where charged, are usually modest –

ISK200–400 with reductions or free entry for children and sometimes students. Many also have "free" days – usually Monday or Wednesday. A Reykjavík Card *(see page 343)* gives free entry to most museums in the city.

The majority of country museums are either folk or maritime museums. Folk museums are often housed in turf farm buildings and contain furnishings and farm and household implements used in the past. Many maritime museums have on show well-preserved examples of boats and fishing equipment and photographs that document the hardships of life in these remote communities.

Museum and Gallery Listings

Museums that are described in the Places section of the book are listed below with a cross-reference. Minority-interest museums not in the text are described below.

Reykjavík

Árbær Open-Air Museum, page 167
Árni Magnusson Institute, page 163
Ásgrímur Jónsson Collection, page 164
ASI Art Gallery, Freyjugata 41, tel: 511 5353. Paintings primarily by Icelandic artists. Open Tues–Sun 2–6pm.
Ásmundur Sveinsson Sculpture Gallery, page 166
Culture House, page 156
Einar Jónsson Museum, page 164
Gerðuberg Cultural Centre, Gerðuberg 3–5, tel: 575 7700. Holds regular exhibitions. Also houses a library and café. Open Mon–Fri 11–7pm, Sat/Sun 1–4.30pm.
Kjarvalsstaðir Municipal Gallery, page 164
Kópavogur Art Museum, (Gerðarsafn), Hamraborg 4, Kópavogur, tel: 554-4501. Has a permanent exhibition on display and hosts regular exhibits and concerts. Open Tues–Sun noon–6pm; entrance fee. Bus no. 140 from Hlemmur terminal.

Living Art Museum, page 164
Medical History Museum, Seltjarnarnes, tel: 561 1016. This was the seat of the country's first surgeon-general. Exhibition of medical instruments from the 18th century onwards. Open summer: Tues, Thur, Sat and Sun 1–5pm; winter: by arrangement; entrance fee. Bus no. 3 from Lækjartorg or Hlemmur, westbound.
National Gallery, page 162
National Museum, page 163
Natural History Museum, page 164
Numismatic Museum, Einholt 4, tel: 569 9964. Collection of coins and bank notes. Open Mon–Fri 9am–5pm; other times by arrangement.
Phallological Museum, Laugavegur 24, Reykjavík, tel: 561 6663. A weird collection of animal penises. Open summer (1 May–31 Aug) Tues–Sat 2–5pm; winter Tues and Sat 2–5pm.
Reykjavík Art Museum, page 158
Reykjavík Energy Museum, Rafstödvarvegur, Elliðaárdalur, Reykjavík, tel: 567 9009, the history of harnessing geothermal power. Open in summer Tues–Sat 1–5pm, Sun 1–5pm; winter Sun only 3–5pm.
Reykjavík Photographic Museum, Tryggvagata 15, Reykjavík, tel: 563 1790. A collection of old photographs of Reykjavík and surrounding area. Open Mon–Fri 10am–4pm.
Sigurjón Ólafsson Museum, page 166

Cinema

Icelanders are avid cinema-goers and Reykjavík has an amazing number of screens considering its small size. Most films are from the US though a certain number of Icelandic and European films are also shown. All films are advertised in the daily press and shown with the original soundtrack, sub-titled in Icelandic. There is a large film festival in Reykjavík every two years, as well as the occasional smaller festival of alternative or artistic films. Check *Around Reykjavík* or *What's*

Telecommunications Museum, Sudurgata, Reykjavík, tel: 550 6410. History of communications in Iceland. Open Tues, Thurs and Sun 1–5pm.

The Reykjanes Peninsula

Hafnarborg Arts Centre, page 174
Hafnarfjörður Folk Museum, Vesturgata 6, Hafnarfjörður. Next to the Maritime Museum. Open June–Sept: 1–5pm daily; Oct–May: Sat/Sun 1–5pm; entrance fee.
Hafnarfjörður Maritime Museum, page 174

The Southwest

Eyrarbakki Maritime Museum, page 184
Saga Centre, Hvolsvöllur, page 193
Skógar Folk Museum, page 194
Stokkseyri Maritime Museum, page 183
Stöng excavations, Þjórsárdalur, pages 191–2

Vestmannaeyjar

Heimaey Aquarium and Natural History Museum, page 204
Heimaey Folk Museum, page 203

The Southeast

Höfn Folk Museum, page 219.

Snæfellsnes and the West

Garður Folk Museum, page 226
Laugar Folk Museum, page 232
Ólafsvík Museum, page 230
Stykkishólmur Folk Museum, page 231

On for details. Essential viewing for anyone interested in Iceland's natural history is the Volcano Show, Hellusund 6a (opposite Hótel Holt), tel: 551 3230. A two-hour film programme documents volcanic eruptions in recent years in Iceland. There are daily showings in summer in English (11am, 3pm, 8pm) and other languages, including German at 6pm. Other towns throughout Iceland have cinemas and smaller villages show films once or twice a week.

Cultural Festivals

Contact the Tourist Information Centre in Reykjavík *(see page 338)* for details on the following events:
Dark Music Days: Every other year in January. A festival organised by the Composers' Society, with emphasis on new Icelandic music.
Reykjavík Jazz Festival: An annual event in late summer or early autumn, with acclaimed international jazz performers.
Reykjavík Arts Festival: First held in 1970, this takes place every other year for three weeks in June. It features music, theatre, visual arts, opera and ballet, and attracts national and international artists.
Festival of Church Arts: Held biannually in Reykjavík, around Pentecost and in Akureyri in early summer. The main emphasis is on music, though visual art, dance and theatre also feature.
International Film Festival: Held every other October. A range of mainstream and experimental works – a must for film buffs.
Reykjavík Cathedral Music Days: An annual November festival featuring organ and choral music, with a guest composer or organist.
Reykjavík Cultural Night: Held on a Saturday in late August. The city centre turns into a cultural mecca, with every venue utilised. Musical events are staged in shops, poetry readings in cafés, street theatre flourishes and self-appointed performers set up wherever they can. The night culminates with a fireworks display; pubs and cafés are open extra late and are packed until the small hours.

The West Fjords
Bolungarvík Maritime Museum, page 239
Bolungarvík Natural History Museum, page 239
Hnjótur Fish and Farming Museum, page 244

Jón Sigurðsson Museum, Hrafnseyri, page 243
West Fjords Maritime Museum, Ísafjörður, page 239

Húnaflói and Skagafjörður
Glaumbær Museum, page 252
Icelandic Emigration Centre, Hofsós, page 253
Reykjaskóli Folk Museum, Hrutafjördur, tel: 451 0040. This museum shows the reconstructed interior of a 19th-century farmhouse, an old shark-fishing boat and household and farm implements from past days. Open July–Aug 10am–noon and 1–6pm; at other times visits are by arrangement only.

Akureyri and Surroundings
Akureyri Art Museum, page 261
Akureyri Folk Museum, page 261
Davíðshús, Akureyri, page 261
Friðbjarnarhús, Akureyri, page 260
Laufás Museum, page 265
Mattías Jochumsson Memorial Museum, Akureyri, page 260
Natural History Museum, Akureyri, page 260
Nonnahús, Akureyri, page 260

Lake Mývatn
Reykjahlíð Visitors' Centre, page 280

The Northeast
Burstafell Folk Museum, page 294
Húsavík Museum, page 289
Grenjaðarstaður Folk Museum, Aðaldalur, tel: 464 3545. Visitors can check out a 19th-century turf farm museum and an interesting gravestone in the nearby church with runic inscriptions. Open June–Aug daily 10am–6pm.
Mineral Museum, Hallbjarnarstaðir, page 290

The East Fjords
Eskifjörður Maritime Museum, page 306

Music

Icelanders are a nation of music lovers, as witnessed by the vast number of concert recitals given over the course of a year and by the numerous choirs active in the country over the winter months.

The Iceland Symphony Orchestra, which has recently been gaining widespread international acclaim, holds concerts during the winter only. Not to worry: a vibrant music scene kicks in at the beginning of the summer, both in and outside of Reykjavík. Below is a listing of the main musical events and venues, year-round. Please note that cafés and pubs often have live music – check the listings at the back of *Morgunblaðið* or *What's On in Reykjavík* for more details.

Venues in Reykjavík
Iceland Symphony Orchestra, University Concert Hall, Hagatorg (opposite Hótel Saga), tel: 562 2255. Weekly concerts in winter, featuring international guest artists.
Iðnó, Vonastræti 3, tel: 530 3030. This renovated theatre hosts various types of concerts during the summer, anything from jazz to piano and theatre music recitals.
Jazz at Jómfrún, Lækjargata 4, tel: 551 0100. This restaurant serves excellent Danish-style open sandwiches and has jazz recitals on Saturdays from 4–6pm during the summer.
Kaffileikhúsið (The Café Theatre), Vesturgata 3 (rear), tel: 551 9055. This charming old building is a unique venue for performances of various kinds. There is a summer concert series: jazz music, classical and jazz vocalists and more.
Nordic House, Hringbraut (by the university campus), tel: 551 7030. Hosts concert recitals year-round.
Sigurjón Ólafsson Museum, Laugarnestangi, tel: 553 2906. A yearly concert series with recitals every Tuesday evening in summer.
Summer Nights at the Organ, Hallgrímskirkja church. A group of music lovers have formed an association that plans Sunday concerts all year in Hallgrímskirkja church. In summer these feature organ music.

Venues outside Reykjavík
Contact the Tourist Information Centre in Reykjavík for information

on dates and bookings for the following events:

Bright Summer Nights, Hveragerði. A three-day concert series, held early each summer, featuring both Icelandic and foreign works.

Kirkjubæjarklaustur Chamber Music Festival, Kirkjubæjarklaustur. This yearly festival takes place for one weekend each August, in beautiful surroundings. Both national and international musicians are featured.

North Iceland Concert Series, various churches in northern Iceland. This takes place mostly in and around Akureyri and often features church music.

Reykholt Festival, Reykholt. A three-day concert festival held every summer, with the emphasis firmly on premiering contemporary Icelandic works.

Skálholt Festival, Skálholt Church. The church at this ancient bishopric in the southwest hosts a yearly concert series on weekends in July and August. The focus tends to be on baroque music and musicians are from around the world. Admission to all events is free.

Stykkishólmur Concert Series, Stykkishólmur church. A series of six concerts that are held in this modern church over the summer.

Theatre, Ballet and Opera

For information on current productions contact the Tourist Information Centre in Reykjavík, check the back pages of daily *Morgunblaðið*, or *What's On in Reykjavík*.

Iceland offers up exceptional theatre with actors and directors of international calibre. All productions at the main professional theatres are in Icelandic, but often they are stagings of famous works with which tourists will be familiar.

Opera and dance, of course, transcend the language barrier. The Icelandic Opera is a world-class professional company, featuring top performers. The Icelandic Dance Company has in the past few years

focused exclusively on modern dance. It is made up of both Icelandic and international dancers and has toured extensively abroad.

Venues in Reykjavík

City Theatre (Reykjavík Theatre Co.), Listabraut 8, tel: 568 8000. Icelandic Opera, Ingólfsstræti, tel: 551 1475.

Kaffileikhúsið, Vesturgata 3 (rear), tel: 551 9055. Regular and diverse theatre in a café setting. Dinner can usually be had before the show.

Light Nights, Iðnó, Vonarstræti 3 (by the lake in the city centre), tel: 551 9181. A unique theatrical presentation in English of scenes from Iceland's history and literature. Performing mid-June to the end of August; check local press or the tourist office for days. A synopsis of the show is available at the door in several languages.

The Icelandic Dance Company, the City Theatre *(see page 360)*. National Theatre, Hverfisgata 19, tel: 551 1200.

Venues outside Reykjavík

Venues for cultural events outside the capital include:

Akureyri Theatre Company, Hafnarstræti 57, Akureyri, tel: 462 1400. Open Sept–June.

Hafnarfjarðarleikhúsið, Vesturgata 11, Hafnarfjörður, tel: 555 0553.

Festivals

Diary of Events

February

Þorrablót: Although there is no fixed day for Þorrablót, most communities celebrate it in February. Essentially an occasion to eat, drink and be merry, Þorrablot has its roots in a long-forgotten pagan ritual. A feast of Icelandic delicacies, including the dreaded rotten shark *(hákarl)* and singed sheep's heads, is washed down with Brennivin and plenty of song and dance. If you are in Iceland in February it is well worth enquiring if there is a Þorrablót scheduled. Many are private affairs but those in the smaller villages are open to all, though must usually be booked in advance.

Sunshine Coffee: For many of the remote fishing villages situated in the steepsided West Fjords, real winter starts when the sun ceases to rise above the mountains and even in fine weather the village is in perpetual shadow. It is often absent for several months but when its first rays hit the village again, everyone celebrates with sunshine coffee.

March

Bolludagur, Sprengidagur and Öskudagur: The Monday before Shrove Tuesday everyone bakes *bollur*, a kind of pastry eclair filled with cream, hence Bolludagur. Shrove Tuesday is called Sprengidagur (Explosion Day) and traditionally a hearty meal of salted lamb and split peas is served. On Ash Wednesday, or Öskudagur, children collect money for sweets and delight in pinning small cloth bags – in the old days, they used to contain ashes – to the backs of unwary strangers.

April
First Day of Summer: In a country where winter seems to drag on interminably, celebrating the first day of summer in April (usually the third Thursday in the month) seems a little premature. Even so, there are big festivities in Reykjavík.

June
Sjómannadagur (Seafarer's Day): The first Sunday in June is the greatest celebration of the year in many fishing villages. Often a holiday for the whole village and always for seamen, there are rowing and swimming races and a chance for the young and not so young to test their skill and strength in contests from tugs of war to sea rescue. A fun-filled and lighthearted occasion with lots going on.

Independence Day: Iceland's national day is celebrated on 17 June, the day in 1944 when the country declared full independence from Denmark and also the birthday of Jón Sigurðsson who contributed more than any other Icelander to the struggle. The greatest celebrations are in Reykjavík, with parades, street theatre and music, side shows and dancing, but throughout the country the day is a festive occasion.

August
Verslunarmannahelgi: The first weekend in August is a long weekend throughout Iceland and everything is shut on the Monday. Icelanders by the thousands take to their cars and head out of town to camp in the wilds or join in one of the organised events that are held throughout the country. These range from teetotalling family festivities to loud rock festivals. Most visitors will probably want to avoid popular destinations for Icelanders at this time. On the same weekend, Heimaey in the Vestmannaeyjar (Westmann Islands), celebrates its own Þjóðhátíð festival commemorating the day in 1874 when Iceland got its constitution. Bad weather prevented the islanders from reaching the mainland so they celebrated independently and have done so ever since. The occasion draws Icelanders from all corners of the country to a huge outdoor camp for a weekend of music, song and dance and a fair amount of drinking.

September
Réttir: During the month of September farmers set off on horseback to gather up their sheep that have grazed freely in the highlands over the summer. When the sheep are brought down to the lowlands they are herded into pens and sorted. The end of this major event in the farming calendar is celebrated with singing, dancing and general festivities. If you are in Iceland around this time it is well worth checking out where Réttir is scheduled to take place. The Tourist Information Centre in Reykjavík will be able to assist.

December
Christmas and New Year's Eve: see pages 170–171.

Sport

Spectator Sports

Most Icelanders are avid sports fans and handball, football and basketball are all popular. Football is a summer sport, while handball and basketball, being indoor sports, are played year round. In all three sports Iceland has excellent players under contract to well-known teams abroad. Most international matches take place in Reykjavík and international and national games are advertised in the press. For information contact: **Iceland Sports Association/Íþróttasamband Íslands**, Íþróttamiðstöðin, Laugardalur, Reykjavík, tel: 514 4000.

Boxing is banned in Iceland, but Glíma, a form of wrestling from settlement times, is still practised. Contact Glímusamband Íslands at Iceland Sports Association. Possibly Iceland's best-known spectator event is chess and the country has produced several grand masters in recent years. International chess tournaments are regularly held in Iceland. Riding clubs hold races and other events throughout the summer. The Reykjavík Marathon takes place in August each year and includes the marathon, half marathon and a 7½-km (4½-mile) fun run. For information and registration contact the **Athletics Federation of Iceland**, Laugardalur Sports Centre, tel: 514 4000.

Skiing

Facilities and conditions for skiing in Iceland fall far short of the Alps or North America. Snow cover is most consistent in the north. In the south, foul weather, even lack of snow, often closes the slopes for days on end.

Downhill Skiing

On a clear, calm weekend the whole of Reykjavík seems to head out of town and there can often be long queues for the lifts. Skiing is one of Iceland's bargains – a day ticket costs around ISK1,000 and children pay half price. The best facilities are in Reykjavík and Akureyri but other towns also have skiing areas and shorter drag lifts.

Reykjavík

Bláfjöll, one of the main skiing areas, is about half an hour's drive from Reykjavík. Scheduled buses depart from the BSÍ bus terminal in Reykjavík several times a day. The track to the ski slopes is open to private four-wheel-drive vehicles. The lifts are open 10am–6pm daily and until 10pm on Tues, Wed and Thur, when the slopes are floodlit. There is one chairlift and several drag lifts and boot and ski hire is available. There is no overnight accommodation but a cafeteria serves snacks and drinks. For up-to-date information (recorded message in Icelandic) on conditions and opening times, tel: 570 7711.

Akureyri

There is more reliable snow and similar facilities at Hlíðarfjall, just above Akureyri, which has one chair lift and three drag lifts. Buses leave the city bus terminal three times a day and the slopes are open 1–6.45pm, until 8.45pm on Tues, Wed and Thur, and 10am–5pm at weekends. There is a café and sleeping-bag accommodation. For information, tel: 562 7733.

Cross-country Skiing

Both Bláfjöll and Hlíðarfjall have marked cross-country ski trails but most people will probably want to head off on their own. This is safe in the farmed lowlands; venturing into uninhabited areas is only for the properly equipped and fit. Some tour operators offer cross-country skiing excursions *(see Tour Operators, page 335, for details)*.

Summer Skiing

The Kerlingarfjöll Mountains, just off the Kjölur route through the central highlands, offer summer skiing. The season starts as soon as the track opens and goes on as long as the snow lasts (mid-June to late-Aug). There are drag lifts, a campsite and sleeping-bag accommodation available. Buses to Kerlingarfjöll are operated through BSÍ *(see Tour Operators, page 335)*, who have up-to-date information on departures.

Angling

Unlike many other countries, Iceland has clean water, and salmon runs have not been disturbed by sea fishing. Excellent fishing is therefore available but at a very high price. Permits per day cost ISK6,300–24,000, and sometimes even more. The other snag is that most rivers have to be booked months if not years in advance. For further advice and permit information contact:
Angling Club of Reykjavík, Háaleitisbraut 68, Reykjavík, tel: 568 6050, e-mail: svfr@svfr.is, website: www.svfr.is.
National Angling Association, Bolholt 6, Reykjavík, tel: 553 1510, fax: 568-4363, e-mail: info@angling.is, website: www.angling.is.
Trout fishing can often be arranged on-the-spot and at a reasonable price. Many of the farms in the Icelandic Farm Holidays booklet *(see Tour Operators, page 335)* offer trout fishing. An open voucher system is available for some of the farms in this network.

Sea angling can be arranged from many fishing villages and coastal farms and can be combined with a boat trip to offshore islands, or whale-watching excursions. This is usually best arranged directly with hotels and farms.

Iceland's waters are disease-free, so all equipment coming into the country, including waders and boots, must be disinfected *(see Entry Regulations, page 332)*.

Golf

Golf is thriving in Iceland with over 50 courses, most of which have just nine holes. However, there are 18-hole courses at: Reykjavík, Hafnarfjörður, Garðabær, Hella, Keflavík, Vestmannaeyjar and Akureyri. For further information contact: **Golfsamband Íslands**, Engjavegur 6, Reykjavík, tel: 514 4050.
The major golfing event in Iceland is the Arctic Open, which takes place in June each year and is open to professional and amateur golfers alike. Hosts to the event are the **Akureyri Golf Club**, PO Box 896, 602 Akureyri, tel: 462 2974. A complete package including flights, accommodation and entrance fees can be booked through tour operators abroad.

Swimming

If Iceland has a favourite national sport, it has to be swimming. The country's vast geothermal resources account for the selection of great pools throughout the country: just about any place with a population over 500 will have one. These range from the ultra-modern pools in the Reykjavík area to the more primitive examples, such as the mineral-water pool at Lýsuhóll on the Snæfellsnes peninsula, complete with algae-covered bottom.

In Reykjavík, just about everyone will have their own favourite pool. The Laugardalur swimming pool is perennially popular, though many locals complain that it is too big, favouring the smaller-scale Vesturbæjarlaug in the west end of the city, or the small but modern facilities on Seltjarnarnes. Those with small children might prefer the recreation-centre-like facilities of Árbæjarlaug pool, with its hot pots, spouting fountains, water slides and reclining jacuzzi seats.

Outdoor Activities

Hiking

For walking off the beaten track and variety of scenery Iceland is unsurpassed. Hiking in Iceland is very popular with Icelanders and foreigners alike and both facilities and varieties of hiking trails have improved tremendously since the early 1990s.

The most popular marked long-distance trail runs from Landmannalaugar south to the coast at Skógar and takes four to five days. Known to the locals as "Laugavegur", which is also the name of Reykjavík's main shopping street, the route is scenically quite stunning but well trodden, though venturing off the track you are unlikely to encounter another soul. There are huts along the way, owned by Ferðafélag Íslands and Útivist, from whom a key can be obtained in Reykjavík to gain entry, but it is advisable to take a tent as well in case the huts are full.

In the Jökulsárgljúfur National Park a two-day walk follows the length of the spectacular gorge from Ásbyrgi to Dettifoss, with camp sites en route. Within the two other national parks of Þingvellir and Skaftafell and protected areas such as Mývatn, there are marked paths suitable for day hikes.

Another area that is attracting growing numbers of backpackers is Hornstrandir, in the extreme northwest. A series of indistinct and mostly unmarked trails link the fjords and bays of this rugged, uninhabited area. Hornstrandir is linked to Ísafjörður by a scheduled boat service.

The East Fjords district from Borgarfjörður Eystri southwards, and Lónsöraefi in the southeast both offer challenging and varied wilderness hiking.

For some the ultimate challenge is to traverse Iceland's interior, following one of the highland tracks that run north to south. In clear weather the views are stunning, but much of the route is over bare sand and stone desert with little variation in terrain or scenery. Far more interesting hiking is often to be found in the areas immediately bordering the settled districts. The Kjölur and Sprengisandur routes are tough but highly rewarding to part hike. Take a map, compass and overstock on food just in case – routes are largely unmarked and it may take you longer than expected.

Hiking Maps

National parks and some nature conservation areas produce leaflets, including maps and hiking times. These are often more accurate and up-to-date than the general map series *(see Maps, page 340)*. Maps of Hornstrandir, Landmannalaugar and Þórsmörk areas mark paths but should be used with caution – the Hornstrandir map, for example, does not mark cliff faces. Always use these maps combined with the general map series.

Safety for Hikers

All safety rules apply, doubly so when hiking in uninhabited areas or crossing rivers; fatal accidents are not uncommon among foreign travellers. Wherever possible seek the advice of local people at farms, mountain huts and national park wardens' offices and leave details of your intended route. Remember to inform people when you have arrived back safely.

Venturing off the beaten track is only for properly equipped hikers with considerable wilderness experience. Many of the BSÍ and other highland bus services will take hikers into remote areas and if pre-arranged, will pick up again further along the route, several days later. Obtain all you need for a trip beforehand, including sufficient food. Water is not always available, particularly in the cold desert region of the Ódáðahraun. Even if you find water, you may have to filter it to remove the fine particles of rock in the glacial rivers. In case of problems, rescue is often difficult. Wardened huts and most vehicles have radio communications and can summon aid in an emergency.

When crossing rivers on foot face upstream and link arms with other members of the party to steady yourself, forming a wedge shape. Glacial rivers can flood after heavy rainfall or on a warm summer day. They can be very dangerous and if in doubt it is always best to wait until the flood subsides, often in only 12 hours.

Along uninhabited stretches of coastline, at regular intervals, are emergency huts for shipwrecked seamen. These huts are equipped with radios and are not for hikers' use except in a real emergency.

Horse Riding

The sturdy Icelandic horse is a pure and unique breed, descended from stock brought over by the first settlers from Norway in the 9th century. No horses have been imported for 800 years so the breed has remained pure. It has adapted to the demands of harsh weather and rough terrain and is ideally suited to local conditions.

The Icelandic horse still plays a vital role in the autumn round-up, when farmers throughout the

Whale-watching

Whale-watching has been growing steadily in popularity in Iceland in recent years, and a vast number of whale-watching tours are now offered across the country. Some tour operators even promise that you will get your money back if you don't spot a whale.

The most commonly sighted whale is the minke, with killer whales, sperm whales, finbacks and humpbacks less often seen. The larger whales can usually be seen in the north, around Húsavík and in the Breidafjörður bay, while dolphins most often appear off the south coast.

The best time for whale sightings is late spring and summer and you do not always have to be on a boat to see them: sometimes just a close look out to sea will reveal a whale's back breaking the surface.

The following agents operate specialist whale-watching tours, while many others groups offer boat tours with the possibility of whale sightings:

Bátsferðir ehf, Nökkvi, Arnarstapi, Snæfellsnes Peninsula, tel: 435-6795.

Hauganes Whale-Watching, Nonni Travel, Brekkugata 5, 602 Akureyri, tel: 461 1841, fax: 461 1843.

Húni II, Skerseyrarvegur 2, Hafnarfjörður, tel: 555 6310, fax: 555 2758. huni@islandia.is.

H.I. Tourist Service, Ferðaþjónusta Suðurnesja, PO Box 92, 232 Keflavík, tel: 421 7777, fax: 421 3361.

Norður Sigling Whale-Watching, PO Box 122, 640 Húsavík, tel: 464 2350, fax: 464 2351.

Ólafsvík Whale-Watching, Ólafsvík Guesthouse, Ólafsbraut 19, Ólafsvík, Snæfellsnes Peninsula, tel: 436 1300, fax: 436 1302.

Saeferðir, Aðalgata 2, 340 Stykkishólmur, tel: 438 1459, fax: 438 1050.

Sjóferðir ehf, Town Hall, 620 Dalvík, tel: 466 3355, fax: 466 1661.

country set off for the highlands on horseback to gather their sheep. Mostly, however, horses are used for recreation and riding is a popular sport among Icelanders. Farms all over the country offer visitors anything from a one-hour ride to a seven-day trek. The majority of these can be booked in advance through tour operators abroad (see Tour Operators and Horse Riding Tours, pages 334–6).

Prices start at ISK2,500 for an hour's ride. On long treks food and lodging is included; price per day is ISK9,000–14,000. Information on stables can be obtained from the Tourist Information Office, Reykjavík, or from: **Icelandic Farm Holidays**, Síðumúli 13, Reykjavík, tel: 570-2700, fax: 570-2799, e-mail: ifh@farmholidays.is, website: www.farmholidays.is

Snowcatting

Snowcatting (skidooing), is an exhilarating sport that has to be experienced. An essential means of communication on remote farms in winter, snowcats are increasingly used for recreation.

In summer, trips run daily from Höfn to the Vatnajökull icecap, from where you can join a one- or two-hour guided excursion by snowcat.

A full-day trip is also possible but must be booked in advance through **Jöklaferðir** Glacier Tours, 780 Hornafjörður, tel: 478 1000, fax: 478 1901, website: www.vatnajokull.com, e-mail: vatnajokull@vatnajokull.com. Check out their website for a full list of tours and prices.

If you have a four-wheel-drive jeep, you can take the track up to the glacier (off from the Ring Road at Smyrlabjarg) – an experience in itself.

For excursions onto other glaciers around Iceland, contact:

Geysir Snowmobile Expeditions, Dugguvogur 10, Reykjavík, tel: 568 8888, fax: 581 3102. Offer skidoo trips on Mýrdalsjökull glacier.

Ferðaþjónustan Snjófell, Arnarstapi, 355 Ólafsvík, tel: 435 6783, fax: 435 6795, e-mail: snjofell@snjofell.is, website: www.snjofell.is. Excursions onto Snæfellsjökull glacier.

Ice Climbing

In summer guided day-walks on the glaciers can be arranged from Skaftafell National Park, through the park warden's office. For more ambitious expeditions contact the following organisations:

Iceland Alpine Club/Íslenski Alpaklúbburinn, Mörkinni 6, Reykjavík, tel: 581 1700.

Öræfaferðir, Hofsnes-Öraefi, 785 Fagurhólsmýri, tel/fax: 478 1682.

River Rafting

River rafting has gained steadily in popularity as a sport since 1990 and there are now a number of tour operators offering such trips. (See Adventure Tours, page 335 for details.)

Shopping

In the past Iceland tended to attract tourists for whom shopping was not on the travel agenda, mostly because the main attraction was the landscape, but also because prices were considered ridiculously high. At best foreign visitors might purchase some woollen goods. But things are changing. Today Reykjavík is actively promoted as an up-market and accessible shopping option, and special shopping trips to Reykjavík arranged for foreign residents have proved popular.

Icelandic taxes remain extremely high – although note that most shops offer a sales-tax rebate *(see below)*, which reduces the price by 15 percent. However, Reykjavík is being marketed at those who believe in paying for style and quality. Geographically, the capital is also very shopper friendly, with the stores concentrated into a relatively small area.

What to Buy

Woollen Goods
The Icelandic sheep is an almost pure breed descended from the animals brought over by the first settlers. Its fleece is of an exceptional quality and produces a wool that is durable and naturally water resistant, yet soft and warm. It is this wool that is used to make the handknitted sweaters with traditional patterns around the yoke.

A simple cottage industry has grown to create one of the country's major agricultural exports, and though the traditional sweaters are still handknitted, the bulk of woollen goods are now machine-made. For a handknitted sweater expect to pay

ISK7,000–10,000; however, if you buy the wool, circular needles and pattern (available in several foreign languages) you can knit yourself one for under ISK4,500.

Sheepskin goods
These are expensive but the quality is excellent. Hats, slippers and gloves sell for approximately ISK2,500–5,000.

Tax-free Shopping

All non-residents (other than Icelandic citizens) are entitled to a VAT refund on goods purchased in Iceland if their value exceeds ISK4,000 in one shop.

You pay the full amount, vat included, in the shop. Ask for your vat-refund and the shop assistant will fill out a special "Global Refund Cheque", which you then take to the tax refund desk at the airport. Although the Global Refund is by far the most common system in Iceland, there are other refund systems which may have other rebate procedures – ask at the shop where you buy the goods. The refund (less about 5 percent handling charge) will amount to approximately 15 percent of the purchase price.

As you leave Iceland, show the customs officers the goods you have purchased and ask for your refund cheque to be stamped. Woollen goods do not need to be shown. Global Refund cheques can be cashed in at your departure point from Iceland or at any Global Refund centre world-wide. You can also mail cheques which have been stamped by customs to the Global Refund office and they will credit any account you specify. If you are leaving Iceland from Keflavík Airport and your refund amount is less than ISK4,000 you need only show your goods at the airport bank where you cash your cheque.

For more information on refunds see the *Shopping in Iceland* brochure that is available in most shops, free of charge.

How to Pay

Most shops accept payment by credit card or travellers' cheques. Some offer discounts for cash and it is always worth asking.

Books
There are many fine books on Iceland intended for the visitor and almost all are available in English. Many can be bought abroad through tour operators who also run a book and map service *(see Tour Operators, page 335)*. Books published outside Iceland will be cheaper to buy abroad.

Fine Art Cards
There are some very attractive yet inexpensive cards depicting the works of some of Iceland's finest painters such as Johannes Kjarval and Ásgrímur Jónsson. These are available at the National Gallery in Reykjavík and at bookshops.

Slides
If bad weather was a feature of your holiday, excellent slides can be bought to supplement your own. There are also good slides of volcanic eruptions sold in souvenir and bookshops.

Ceramics
If the rather garish lava ceramics are not to your taste, shop around. Pottery in Iceland tends to be artistic rather than functional, so expect to pay accordingly. There are some fine potters producing unusual pieces. Often they will sell their own work in their studio, or will be members of an artisans' co-operative *(see the Commercial Galleries panel on page 367 for details)*.

Food
If you can protect your luggage against the smell, pack some dried fish. It weighs nothing, keeps for ever and may amuse your friends. Eat it with lashings of butter. Smoked trout and salmon also keep quite well. If you like skyr, take some home – you can make your

own culture in the same way as yoghurt and it freezes well. A wide range of Icelandic foods is sold at the duty free shop at Keflavík Airport for departing passengers.

Music

Two CDs of Icelandic folk songs in particular can be recommended: Íslensk alþýðulög – Icelandic Folk Songs and Vikivaki – Songs from the Saga Island. There are also fine classical recordings by the Iceland Symphony Orchestra, particularly of works by late composer Jón Leifs (try to listen before buying – his music is intense and not for everyone), as well as by other Icelandic classical musicians. Look out for CDs by Björk, especially her jazzy recording Gling Gló.

Where to Shop

There are two main shopping areas in Reykjavík: in the centre of the city, most of the tourist shops are in and around Hafnarstræti and Austurstræti, though Laugavegur, leading out of the centre, is home to the majority of the fashion shops.

The other main shopping area,

which houses most of the usual European high-street chain stores, is the Kringlan mall; this is located outside the city centre but can be easily reached by bus. The woollen goods and souvenir shop Íslandia is located in the Kringlan mall, as is the Nýkaup supermarket, which offers the most extensive selection of food products in Iceland. Kringlan is also home to a wide variety of attractive boutiques.

Recommended Shops in Reykjavík

Try the following for a wide variety of gifts, woollen goods, ceramics, crafts and jewellery:
Íslandia, Kringlan shopping mall.
Rammagerðin, Hafnarstræti 19.
Ullarhúsið, Aðalstræti 4.
Thorvaldsen's Basar, Austurstræti 4. (All proceeds go to charity.)
Víkurprjón, Hafnarstræti 1–3.
There are also a number of good gift and craft shops situated on Skólavörðustígur, near Hallgrímskirkja church.

For books try:
Eymundsson, Austurstræti 18.
Mál og Menning, Laugavegur 18.
For photographic equipment:

Woollens

For handknitted sweaters it is worth trying some of the farms in the Icelandic Farm Holidays network. Sweaters on sale here are usually cheaper than those in the shops and they will be fully homemade and handknitted.

Hans Petersen, Bankastræti 4, Laugavegur 82, and Kringlan mall.

Opening Hours

Shopping hours vary in Iceland – some smaller shops in the centre of Reykjavik may open only for a few hours on Saturdays, for example, or not open at all. By contrast some shops stay open late every day of the week, particularly book and record shops. Most shops are open Mon–Thur 9am–6pm, Fri 9am–7pm and Sat 10am–4pm.

Shops in the Kringlan mall are open Mon–Wed 10am–6.30pm, Thur 10am–9pm, Fri 10am–7pm and Sat 10am–6pm. Some shops are open from 1–5pm on Sundays, particularly in winter.

Shops in the two main supermarket chains, Hagkaup and Nóatún, stay open until 8pm and 9pm, respectively. The 10–11 and 11–11 supermarket chains stay open until 11pm, as their names imply. Many corner shops, selling sweets and basic groceries, stay open until 10pm or later. In the country, some supermarkets in the Kaupfélag (Co-op) chain, notably those attached to petrol stations, may stay open until 8 or 10pm. In the evenings basic groceries, snacks and confectionery are sold at a Sjoppa (kiosk).

Commercial Galleries in Reykjavik

The following galleries mostly feature sales exhibitions.
Galleri Fold, Laugavegur 118d (entrance from Rauðarárstígur), tel: 551 0400. Diverse selection of paintings and crafts. Mon–Fri 10am–6pm, Sat 10am–4pm, Sun 2pm–5pm (closed Sun in July and Aug). Also in Kringlan mall, tel: 568 0400. Open in mall hours.
Galleri Jens, Kringlan Mall, tel: 568 6730. Jewellery designed and crafted by Icelandic artists, the unique styling drawn from the Icelandic landscape. Open in mall hours.
Kirsuberjatréð, Vesturgata 4, tel: 562 8990. Unique and beautiful crafts made from such unconventional materials as fish skin and pig's bladders. Mon–Fri noon–6pm, Sat 11am–5pm.

Kogga, Vesturgata 5, tel: 552 6036. Ceramics by one of the country's foremost potters. Mon–Fri 9am–6pm, Sat 10am–2pm.
Listvinahús, Skólavörðustígur 41–43, tel: 551 2850. Ceramics, unique in texture and colour; nice designs, woollens. Mon–Fri 9am–6pm, weekends 10am–4pm.
Snegla, Grettisgata 7, Reykjavík; tel: 562 0426. Run by a collective; lovely crafts, paintings and objets d'art. Mon–Fri noon–6pm, Sat 11am–3pm.
Textilkjallarinn, Barónstígur 59, tel: 551 3584. Hand-printed and painted textiles. Bedcovers, sheets, scarves and more, made of cotton, satin silk and wool. Mon–Fri noon–6pm, Sat. 10am–noon, or by arrangement.

Children

Facilities for Children

In Iceland, children are greeted with enthusiasm and welcomed at hotels, restaurants and homes. Many restaurants provide baby chairs and children's portions. Tourist Menus give free meals to children of five and under and a 50 percent discount to those aged 6–12. Hotels, if notified in advance, will provide a cot but families with a baby would be advised to bring their own carry cot. Children aged four and under will often stay free if not occupying a separate bed, but where an extra bed required a reduction for the child is usually given. The Iceland Farm Holidays network offers free accommodation to under fours and half price to those aged between 4 and 11.

Places to Take Kids around Reykjavík

There are a number of places of special interest to kids in the Reykjavík area. Some cost money, others do not; a case in point is the **Tjörn** in central Reykjavík, which on weekends normally attracts hoards of children and their families to feed the ducks and geese.

The Family Park and Farmyard Animal Zoo, Laugardalur Valley, tel: 553 7700. Open summer: daily 10am–6pm; winter: 10am–5pm, closed Wed. This is a great spot for a family outing. When the kids tire of looking at the seals, foxes, reindeer, horses, cows, pigs and all the other animals, they can head over to the Family Park. There they can try their hand at operating little electric automobiles, pull themselves across a man-made

lake on a raft, climb in a Viking-ship replica and much more. There is a large grill, which can be used free of charge for barbecuing hot dogs or whatever else. And the seals are fed twice a day: at 11am and 4pm. Price: children ISK200, adults ISK300, free for under fives.

Harbour Area, Reykjavík Harbourfront. During the summer there are little trampolines and other play equipment. There are also several large tubs with fish, crabs, starfish and so on. Those who dare can hold a crab or starfish. All free.

Natural History Museum, Hlemmur 5, tel: 562 9822. Open summer: Tues, Thur, Sat/Sun 1–5pm; winter: same days 1.30–4pm.

Swimming Pools; just about any and all will do. The best ones for kids are the Árbær pool, Fylkisvegur, tel: 567 3933, with its outdoor/indoor pool, hot pots, water slides for big and little kids, whirlpool, sauna and solarium, and the Laugardalur pool, Laugardalur valley, tel: 553 4039, which has a very large children's pool and big, big water slide.

Language

About Icelandic

Icelandic is one of the Nordic family of languages and most closely resembles Norwegian and Faroese. Remarkably, the Icelandic spoken today has not changed greatly from the language of the early Norse settlers. In fact modern Icelanders can read, without difficulty, the sagas written in the 13th century.

The *Landnámabók (Book of Settlements)*, compiled probably in the 12th and 13th centuries, tells of a number of settlers from the British Isles, some of whom may actually have been themselves descendants of Norwegians. The exact numbers will never be known but of significance is the virtual absence of words of Celtic origin in the language. These are limited to a few place names, such as Papey and Dímon and personal names such as Kjartan and Njáll.

For the foreigner, Icelandic is daunting. The good news is that most Icelanders, particularly the young, speak English fluently, as well as Danish, Norwegian or Swedish. German and French are less widely spoken, but also taught at school. Icelanders are by nature quite reticent with foreigners. It may take a while to draw them into conversation but it will be worth it. If you can pick up a few phrases of Icelandic, it will be appreciated.

Pronunciation Tips

Stress, in Icelandic, falls naturally on the first syllable of a word. The following examples of pronunciation are for guidance only – many Icelandic sounds simply do not exist in English.

Vowels and Consonants

a as in *hard*
á as in *how*
e as in *get*
é as in *yet*
i or y as in *thin*
í or ý as in *been*
o as in *ought*
ó as in *gold*
ö as in *first*
u as in *hook*
ú as in *fool*

ae as in *fight*
au between the sounds in *fate* and *oil*, as in the French *feuille*
ey/ei as in *day*

Ð/ð is th as in *the*
Þ/þ is th as in *thing*
fn is pn as in *open*
g when followed by i (except at the start of a word) is y as in *yet*
hv is kf as in *thankful*
j is y as in *yet*
ll is tl as in *bottle*
r is always lightly rolled
rl is rtl as in *heartless*
rn is tn as in *button*
tn and fn when at the end of words are almost silent.

Geography

The following lists show common elements in place names, English translation and an example.

Á	river
Hvítá	white river
Borg	rocky crag
Dimmuborgir	dark crags
Breiður	broad
Breiðafjörður	broad fjord
Brekka	slope
Brekkulækur	slope stream
Dalur	valley
Fljótsdalur	river valley
Drangur	column
Drangavík	rock bay
Eldur	fire
Eldfell	fire mountain
Eyja	island
Flatey	flat island
Eyri	sand spit
Þingeyri	assembly sand spit
Fell	mountain
Snæfell	snow mountain

Fjall	mountain
Bláfjöll	blue mountains
Fjörður	fjord
Hafnarfjörður	harbour fjord
Fljót	large river
Markarfljót	wood river
Foss	waterfall
Gulfoss	gold falls
Gígur	crater
Lakagígar	cow stomach craters
Gil	ravine
Jökulgil	glacier ravine
Gjá	fissure
Grjótagjá	rock fissure
Heiði	heath
Hellishciði	cave heath
Hellir	cave
Sönghellir	song caves
Hlíð	hillside
Reykjahlíð	steamy hillside
Hóll	hill/hillock
Vatnsdalshólar	lake valley hills
Holt	hill
Brattholt	steep hill
Hraun	lava
Ódáðahraun	ill deeds lava
Höfði	cape
Höfdabrekka	cape slope
Höfn	harbour
Þórshöfn	Thor's harbour
Jökull	glacier
Vatnajökull	lake glacier
Kvísl	river
Jökulgilskvísl	glacier ravine river
Lækur	stream
Varmilækur	warm stream
Laug	hot spring
Laugarvatn	hot spring lake
Lind	spring
Hvannalindir	angelica springs
Lón	lagoon
Jökulsárlón	glacier river lagoon
Mýri	marsh
Mýrdalsjökull	marsh valley glacier
Nes	peninsula
Snæfellnes	snow mountain peninsula
Reykur	steam
Reykjanes	steam peninsula
Sandur	sand
Mýrdalssandur	marsh valley sand
Skarð	pass

Kerlingarskarð	troll wife's pass
Skógur	wood
Skógafoss	wood falls
Staður	place
Egilsstadir	Egil's place
Strönd	coast/beach
Hornstrandir	horn peak coast
Tindur	peak
Tindfjöll	peak mountains
Tjörn	pond
Störu-tjarnir	big ponds
Vatn	lake
Hvítárvatn	white river lake
Vík	small bay
Reykjavík	smoky bay
Vogur	inlet
Kópavogur	seal pup inlet
Völlur	plain
Þingvellir	assembly plains

At the Restaurant

Most restaurant staff speak some English or other Scandinavian languages. The words and phrases below will help you order from simpler menus.

Ég ætla að fá...	I would like...
Áttu til...?	Have you got any...?
Meira...	More...
Ekki meira takk	No more thank you
Mjög gott	Very good
Ég er	I am
grænmetisæta	vegetarian
Matseðill	Menu
Forréttir	Starters
Fiskréttir	Fish dishes
Fiskur	Fish
Kjötréttir	Meat dishes
Kjöt	Meat
Eftirréttir	Desserts
Drykkir	Drinks
Lambakjöt	Lamb
Nautakjöt	Beef
Svínakjöt	Pork
Kjúklingur	Chicken
Hangikjöt	Smoked lamb
Ýsa	Haddock
Lúda	Halibut
Rækjur	Prawns
Lax	Salmon

Numbers

Núll	zero
Einn	one
Tveir	two
Þrír	three
Fjórir	four
Fimm	five
Sex	six
Sjö	seven
Átta	eight
Níu	nine
Tíu	ten
Ellefu	eleven
Tólf	twelve
Þrettán	thirteen
Fjórtán	fourteen
Fimmtán	fifteen
Sextán	sixteen
Sautján	seventeen
Átján	eighteen
Nítján	nineteen
Tuttugu	twenty
Tuttugu og einn	twenty one
Þrjátíu	thirty
Fjörutíu	forty
Fimmtíu	fifty
Sextíu	sixty
Sjötíu	seventy
Áttatíu	eighty
Níutíu	ninety
Hundrað	one hundred
Tvö hundrað	two hundred
Þúsund	one thousand
Milljón	one million

Silungur/Bleikja	Trout
Grænmeti	Vegetables
Kartöflur	Potatoes
Franskar	Chips
Blómkál	Cauliflower
Grænar baunir	Peas
Rauðkál	Red cabbage
Sveppir	Mushrooms
Gulrætur	Carrots
Rófur	Turnips
Salat	Salad
Sósa	Sauce
Súpa	Soup
Ís	Ice-cream
Kaka/Terta	Cake
Brauð	Bread
Smjör	Butter
Te	Tea
Kaffi	Coffee
Mjólk	Milk

Sykur	Sugar
Appelsínusafi	Orange juice
Bjór	Beer
Pilsner	Low-alcohol beer
Hvítvín	White wine
Rauðvín	Red wine
Vatn	Water

Useful Words and Phrases

The Icelandic language does not have an equivalent to "please". The phrase *Gerðu svo vel* is employed to invite a person into a house, to the table or to begin eating. It also translates to "here you are" when giving something to somebody. On a public notice "please" is *vinsamlegast*. For example, "please take your shoes off", a common request when entering a home or changing room is *vinsamlegast farið úr skónum*. When leaving the table or saying goodbye after a meal or drinks it is customary to thank the host by saying *Takk fyrir mig*.

Hello/good morning	Góðan dag
Good evening	Gott kvöld
Goodnight	Góða nótt
What is your name?	Hvað heitir þú?
My name is...	Ég heiti
How are you?	Hvað segirdu gott?
Fine, and you?	Allt fínt, en þú?
Fine	Allt fínt
Alright	Allt í lagi
Goodbye	Bless
Yes	Já
No	Nei
Thanks	Takk
Thank you very much	Takk fyrir
Yes please	Já takk
No thank you	Nei takk
May I have...	Má eg fá...
When?	Hvenær?
Today	Í dag
Tomorrow	Á morgun
Yesterday	Í gær
In the morning	Fyrir hádegi
In the afternoon	Eftir hádegi
Cheers!	Skál!
How much does this cost?	Hvað kostar þetta?
Come!	Komdu!

Excuse me	Afsakið
Sorry	Fyrirgefðu
I do not understand	Ég skil ekki

Signs

Toilet	Snyrting
Gents	Karlar
Ladies	Konur
Open	Opið
Closed	Lokað
Danger	Hætta
Forbidden	Bannað
Campsite	Tjaldstæði
Entry	Inngangur/Inn
Exit	Útgangur/Út
Parking	Bílastæði
Schedule	Áætlun
Airport	Flugvöllur
Blind summit (road sign)	Blindhæd
Jeep track	Jeppavegur
Police	Lögreglan
Hospital	Sjúkrahús
Health Centre	Heilsugæslustöð
Doctor	Læknir
Dentist	Tannlæknir
Bank	Banki
Post Office	Póstur og Sími
Chemist	Apótek
Co-op store	Kaupfélag
Swimming pool	Sundlaug
Mechanic/garage	Verkstæði

Further Reading

A Guide to the Birds of Iceland by Þorsteinn Einarsson, Örn og Örlygur, Reykjavík, 1991. A practical guide to identifying nearly all species of Icelandic birds.
A Guide to the Flowering Plants and Ferns of Iceland by Hörður Kristinsson, Örn & Örlygur, Reykjavík, 1987.
Icelandic Whales Past and Present by Sigurður Ægisson, Jón Ásgeir and Jón Baldur Hlíðberg, Forlagið, Reykjavík, 1997. A book describing all the whale species around Iceland and where they are likely to be found.
The Visitor's Key to Iceland by Steindór Steindórsson, Icelandic Publishing House, 1996. Now in its fifth printing, this invaluable guide to the country includes detailed maps and a description and history of just about every landmark there is.
The Xenophobes Guide to the Icelanders by Richard Sale, Ravette

The Sagas

Many of Iceland's Sagas have been translated into English and other languages; particularly readable are Egils Saga, Laxdæla Saga and Njáls Saga, which are all published under the Penguin Classics label.
   The Sagas of the Icelanders, translated by Robert Kellogg and (appropriately) published by Viking in 2000 to commemorate 1,000 years since Leifur Eriksson made his voyage to the New World. The book includes 12 Sagas, notably the Vinland Sagas. A complete translation of the Sagas in English is also published as a set – for information contact Mál og Menning bookshop, PO Box 392, 121 Reykjavík, tel: 515 2500. fax: 515 2505, e-mail: erlent@mm.is, website www.mm.is.

Books, London, 1994. A pocket-sized spoof on the Icelanders and their peculiarities.

Literature in Translation

Angels of the Universe by Einar Már Guðmundsson, Mare's Nest, London, 1995. This acclaimed novel won the Nordic Council's Literary Award in 1995. It tells the story of mental disintegration and features a host of colourful characters whose world is at odds with social convention.
The Atom Station by Halldór Laxness, Second Chance Press, New York, 1982. A wonderful dark comedy with a political slant by Iceland's late nobel laureate.
Independent People by Halldór Laxness, Vintage (Random House), USA, 1997. A classic story of a man's struggle for independence, symbolic of the Icelandic nation. The novel won the Nobel Prize.
Treasures of Icelandic Verse by various authors, Mál og Menning, Reykjavík, 1996. An anthology of various Icelandic poems, with both the original and the translation.
Troll's Cathedral by Ólafur Gunnarsson, Mare's Nest, London, 1996. The story of a family beset by violence.

Other Insight Guides

Apa Publications has more travel guides in print than any other guide-book publisher, with over 200 **Insight Guides**, more than 100 **Pocket Guides** and over 200 **Compact Guides**.

Insight Guides

Insight Guides provide the reader with the full cultural background to a destination, accompanied by high-quality colour photography. Titles to Northern European destinations include **Denmark, Norway, Sweden and Finland**.

Pocket Guides

Insight Pocket Guides are written by host authors, who show you the best of the places they know well.

The books are designed in a series of day trips and excursions, and are particularly useful for people with only a short time in which to make the most of a destination. Each title comes complete with a pull-out map that can be used independently of the guide. The series includes guides to **Oslo/Bergen, Denmark** and **St Petersburg**.

Compact Guides

Insight Compact Guides are handy quick-reference books, which are packed with essential information for the visitor. The text, which is arranged around a series of routes, is cross-referenced to maps and colour pictures, making these guides ideal for on-the-spot consultation. Titles in the series include **Denmark, Finland, Iceland** and **Norway**.

ART & PHOTO CREDITS

Picture Spreads

Cartographic Editor **Zoë Goodwin**
Production **Linton Donaldson**
Design Consultants **Carlotta
Junger, Graham Mitchener**
Picture Research
Hilary Genin, Monica Allende

Index

*Numbers in italics refer
to photographs*

A
B
D
E
F
G
H
I
J
a
b
c
d
e
g
h
i
j
k
l

☀ INSIGHT GUIDES

The world's largest collection of visual travel guides

A range of guides and maps to meet every travel need

Insight Guides
This classic series gives you the complete picture of a destination through expert, well written and informative text and stunning photography. Each book is an ideal background information and travel planner, serves as an on-the-spot companion – and is a superb visual souvenir of a trip. Nearly 200 titles.

Insight Pocket Guides
focus on the best choices for places to see and things to do, picked by our local correspondents. They are ideal for visitors new to a destination. To help readers follow the routes easily, the books contain full-size pull-out maps. 120 titles.

Insight Maps
are designed to complement the guides. They provide full mapping of major cities, regions and countries, and their laminated finish makes them easy to fold and gives them durability. 60 titles.

Insight Compact Guides
are convenient, comprehensive reference books, modestly priced. The text, photographs and maps are all carefully cross-referenced, making the books ideal for on-the-spot use when in a destination. 120 titles.

Different travellers have different needs. Since 1970, Insight Guides has been meeting these needs with a range of practical and stimulating guidebooks and maps